RUSSIAN NATIONAL INTERESTS AND
THE CURRENT CRISIS IN RUSSIA

To the staff of main reading halls of the Library of Congress - an extremely helpful and friendly bunch of professionals

Russian National Interests and the Current Crisis in Russia

HENRY TROFIMENKO

Ashgate

Aldershot • Brookfield USA • Singapore • Sydney

Published by
Ashgate Publishing Limited
Gower House
Croft Road
Aldershot
Hampshire GU11 3HR
England

Ashgate Publishing Company
Old Post Road
Brookfield
Vermont 05036
USA

British Library Cataloguing in Publication Data
Trofimenko, Henry
  Russian national interests and the current crisis in Russia
  1.Russia (Federation) - Politics and government - 1991 -
  2.Russia (Federation) - Economic conditions - 1991-
  I.Title
  320.9'47

Library of Congress Cataloging-in-Publication Data
Trofimenko, G. A. (Genrikh Aleksandrovich)
  Russian national interests and the current crisis in Russia /
  Henry Trofimenko.
      p.   cm.
  ISBN 1-84014-405-X
  1. Russia (Federation)--Foreign relations. 2. Nationalism--Russia
(Federation) 3. National security--Russia (Federation) I. Title.
DK510.764.T76 1998
327.47--dc21   98-8637
                                                          CIP

ISBN 1 84014 405 X

Printed and bound in Great Britain by MPG Books Ltd, Bodmin, Cornwall

Contents

Preface and Acknowledgments

This study was prepared with the help of a grant from the United States Institute of Peace during the period 1993/98.

The main difficulty in researching the topic "Russian national interests" was identifying the real national interests of Russia, as they are understood and formulated by a small sector of the current Russian elite, when it thinks about this problem, and then separating national interests from the well intentioned declarations of various Russian officials, which are designed essentially for foreign consumption.

Another difficulty is the volatile nature of Russian politics at the present time. It is the politics of a state in transition and there are very few more or less stable variables to guide the researcher. I shall address this issue in the Introduction.

I want to express my sincere gratitude to the management of the United States Institute of Peace and personally to its President Dr. Richard Solomon, Vice President Dr. Charles Nelson, Director of the Grant Program Dr. David Smock, Director of Education and Training Program Hrach Gregorian and Grant Administrator April Hall for all the help they gave me in the process of my work.

I also want to express my heartfelt thanks to the member of the Board of the USIP, my old friend, Dr. William Kintner, who recently passed away. His pertinent advice and guidance, based on his tremendous experience, were very valuable for my research.

Dr. Joseph Churba - the President of the International Security Council in Washington, D.C. - the institution that sheltered me for a year, was very generous with his time, often engaging me in a debate that broadened my horizons whilst trying to understand complex international situations. The Senior Vice President of the ISC, William Mazzocco, and Administrative assistant Mary Frye, were always ready to give me much needed aid and to cheer me up during certain gloomy moments.

I am also indebted to my good friends - Mrs. Janet Willen of New York, Dr. Jim Moncure and Mrs. Jane Moncure of Seven Lakes West in North Carolina, who invariably encouraged and supported me in my work.

My deep gratitude goes to the Ashgate Publishing House and its consulting editor, John Irwin, who made the appearance of this book possible. Two wonderful ladies from Ashgate Mrs. Valerie Saunders and Miss Kirstin Howgate became my guardian angels during the preparations of this book for printing and my appreciation of their help is boundless. My sincere heartfelt thanks go to Dr. Christopher Williams, Reader in Russian studies at the University of Central Lancashire, who opened a green light to my manuscript. Dr. Williams gave me a lot of constructive advice about how to improve my earlier draft and was very helpful in making my English more readable.

Finally my thanks go to my son Sergey, who rendered me a lot of technical assistance, and to my dear wife Tamara, who created for me excellent conditions for work and rest, and who was very instrumental in obtaining some out of print Russian books as well as obscure memoranda from various offices in Russia.

I should add that the opinions, findings, and conclusions, expressed in this book, are those of the author and do not necessarily reflect the views of the Russian government, the United States Institute of Peace, the International Security Council in Washington, D.C., or the Institute for the US and Canada Studies in Moscow, where the author is presently employed.

August 1998,
Moscow, Russia.

Introduction

My choice of the subject of Russian national interests for this study was not accidental. For a long time, I have considered the fate of the new Russia. The course of present reforms in Russia illustrate that the pivotal problem for the new Russia's domestic and foreign policy is the necessity for a clear definition of the final goals of our social and economic reforms and of political and military strategy from the point of view of Russia's interests as a whole, from the position of its people's objective aspirations. The key question is: "Where is Russia going?". This question has occupied the thoughts and minds of the cultural strata of Russian society, and has been the subject of great debate among grand dukes and Tsars, communist commissars and now - to somewhat lesser extent - this issue is a matter of concern for the so-called democrats. Such non-stop public philosophical musings about Russia's future and the destiny of its people is probably a particular feature of a Russian mind.

Naturally, in every country there are occasional public debates on the means and directions of its development, but only in a very few cases are these issues the subject of heated debate, this is the case in Russia. This is reflected in Russian literature dating from the first chroniclers of Russian history - the Orthodox monks of Kievan Rus - and ending with such world famous authors as Peter Chaadayev, Alexander Herzen, Nikolay Gogol, Leo Tolstoy, Fyodor Dostoyevsky, Vladimir Solov'yov, Nikolay Berdyaev, Alexander Solzhenitsyn and a great martyr of the Soviet society Andrei Sakharov.

The answer to the question—where is a particular country going—boils down to a proper definition of its national interests. In today's Russia they are not well defined, if at all. But with every political turn, with every major measure undertaken - be it diplomatic activity on some foreign policy issue, the problem of export-import balancing, or the working out of the basic tenets of Russian national security policy - the inevitable first question that is being asked is: "what is Russian national interest in this field?". The Russian media also points to the lack of coherent national security and economic policies, the inadequacy of the present Russian military doctrine and the wavering nature of Russian foreign policy, as shown by the absence of a clear cut understanding of the Russian national interests on the part of the Russian leadership. Of course, the problem lies not only in the need for a more or less coherent, even if not altogether comprehensive, definition of the basic national interests of Russia. Closely linked to this problem is the choice of priorities in pursuing various interests and the assessment of available resources - human, financial, industrial etc. - needed to realize them.

A much more important problem is the understanding of a new Russian identity. It is banal to simply state that with the collapse of the Soviet Union, Russia's geopolitical situation has drastically changed. Russia is only one of the fifteen independent republics that sprang into existence on the territory of the former USSR (some lesser ethnic entities, such as Abkhazia, Chechnya, the Dniester republic and several others are also claiming independence). The adjective "geopolitical" is the most frequently used word in present political writings in Russia. But while over-emphasizing the notion of geopolitics in their political pronouncements and writings, and persistently blabbing about "changed geopolitical situation", most Russian leaders and politicians cannot forget the image of Russia as the continuation of the USSR superpower - not simply as a legal inheritor, but as a still mighty and influential player on the world arena - just as the former Union was, albeit slightly curtailed territorially.

Such notions or "Manilov's projects" to use Gogol's expression (or pipe-dreams in English) are constantly being built in the new, tremendously weakened, impoverished, destitute Russia. These notions stem from the hope that Moscow can continue to behave internationally in the same assertive, forceful way, as it did in the old days. The media and the *camarilla*, surrounding the president, constantly report Russia's tremendous successes in many sectors of the international arena, and often present capitulations as victories in order to flatter Yeltsin.

When President Yeltsin, a little while ago, publicly pounded the table with his fist before the television cameras, threatening his Western partners/adversaries with unspecified dire consequences if they proceeded with NATO expansion, he probably sincerely believed that such threats would have some diplomatic effect, even though his Russian listeners knew that his gesture was simply an empty bluff.

The hard facts speak for themselves. Russia used to be a superpower, but all the indicators of such a status are now gone. The only option left for present Russian leaders is to verbally cling to such a status and to point to the existence of a tremendous arsenal of nuclear missiles equal to that of the United States. According to most criteria, Russia nowadays is just a medium country of the world, and by some economic indicators, it lags behind many developing countries.

Real Russian Gross Domestic Product (GDP) now equals only 12% of the GDP of the former Soviet Union.[1] This fact explains not only the economic, but also military and political, weakness of the new Russia. Russia's national interests must first and foremost be considered against the backdrop of the present economic and social crisis. A country, such as Russia, that only manages to pay wages to its workers employed in the overwhelmingly state-run economy, and to state employees, scholars, teachers, doctors etc., by borrowing money from the foreign financial institutions and governments, has limited freedom of action in the world arena. This too makes it necessary to analyze the national interests of Russia.

A thorough objective assessment of Russia's opportunities in the international arena, and of the main and secondary factors influencing its efforts, is absolutely necessary for the optimal conduct of government policies. This was the main reason why the author decided to undertake this study.

The general approach regarding the study of the national interests of Russia, and detailed examination of the notion of a national interest, is outlined in the first chapter of this book. The following two chapters deal with the most basic national interests of Russia, including its survival as a federated state and the ensuring of national security against different kinds of existing and potential threats and challenges. In the following three chapters, Russian interests in different parts of the world are discussed. The author concentrates on the three main areas of the globe with which Russia actively interacts politically and economically: Europe, Asia-Pacific and the Middle East. The last region is redefined for the purpose of this study by the author. In view of the epoch-making developments in the Central Asian part of the former Soviet Union, this study proceeds from the notion of greater Middle East, including not only the countries traditionally constituting the area, but also former Soviet republics of Central Asia, because with every passing year they develop ever stronger and ramified links with traditional Middle Eastern states. The last chapter is devoted to an analysis of the national interests of Russia with regard to the United States - the main power of the modern world that became a winner in the almost half a century long Cold War between the two nuclear superpowers of the 20th century - the United States and the Soviet Union.

While working on this study the author, as the study neared completion, constantly felt that his research was incomplete. Initially I attributed this to the very notion of national interests of a country in turmoil, to the difficulty of defining national goals in a divided society and of a fractured elite, or to the failure to smoothly align a more or less scholastic, semi-abstract definition of the gamut of national interests of Russia, with the directions of its actual policies that were supposed to implement those interests.

But finally it dawned on the author that his worries stem from a different problem, a problem of a fundamental nature, which makes the definition of national interests of Russia extremely difficult, namely that for the first time in a thousand years long history of Russia, the people, who are presently standing at the wheel of the ship of state, are not *gosudarstvenniki* (statesmen). They can be called helmsmen, rulers, top government officials, leaders etc., but they cannot be defined as statesmen in the true sense of the word because they do not so much care about the interests of the state, its integrity and stability, instead they are more concerned with their own and their kin's personal enrichment.

Now, in August 1998, when I am putting finishing touches to this introduction, the country is facing collapse, due to the absolutely incompetent governance during the previous 6 years. But the President, instead of resigning in shame together with his team, is again forcing upon the parliament and the country Viktor Chernomyrdin for the post of the prime minister - the man who actually brought the country to the edge of a precipice, if not already over it - because Chernomyrdin has been very instrumental in previous years in creating in Russia an economic environment very propitious for speedy enrichment of crooks and embezzlers on top!

A very reliable source told the author that Andrei Gromyko, who occupied the office of the Foreign Minister of the USSR during all the Cold War period, once remarked in a private conversation that: "Stalin, all the negative features of his character considered, was a *gosudarstvennik*, he too was the gatherer of lands as all the former Russian rulers were". Russia definitely does not now need to gather anew all the lands that it lost during the collapse of the USSR (although the majority of the population in most of the republics of the former Soviet Union (FSU), with the exception of the Baltic states, dream about the restoration of the Union). But Russia does need to preserve its integrity and most of all it needs rulers, who care about the interests of the state as a whole not just about their own personal interests or those of their clan, which is the case nowadays.

In his recently published memoirs Alexander Korzhakov - former bodyguard and a buddy of Boris Yeltsin (he was also the head of the presidential bodyguard service) writes that Yeltsin

had everything allowing him to competently carry out the reforms, to stave off corruption, to improve lives of millions of Russians. But Boris Nikolaevich was amazingly quickly crushed by all that usually goes with the unlimited power: flattery, material wealth, total absence of control... All the changes, promised to the people, in essence came down to endless reshuffles at the high echelons of government. After a recurrent series of retirements and new appointments the people, who were coming to power, were even less inclined to pursue the interests of the state. They were lobbying the interests of anyone: commercial structures, foreign investors, gangsters, personal contacts. And even Yeltsin himself, while adopting decisions, proceeded on the basis of the needs of his family clan, not those of the state.[2]

The current "revolution" in Russia, which is supposedly continuing, was started as a revolution from the top and to a great extent it remains so, despite all the lip service to participation by the masses. Actually with every passing year popular support for the "revolution" or reform substantially declines. The people of Russia for the time being are still a silent and to a great extent obedient majority, as in the old days under "socialism". However, socialism itself is publicly denounced and rejected by the ruling class, as well as, allegedly, by a large proportion of the population, though the accuracy of the latter claim has not been convincingly proved. But the "socialism" that appears to have been rejected was of the Soviet variety, which in practice never had much to do with the Great Socialist Idea: the idea of happy people, *equal* in pursuit of their well being and *free from exploitation* of man by man, joining in a communitarian brotherhood for the building of a prosperous global society on the basis of those two lofty principles.

True, the large majority of people in the Soviet Union for a long time believed that they were making great personal sacrifices in the pursuit of the Great Socialist Idea. However, Russian "socialism" was from the beginning a *de facto* mixture of state capitalism with feudalism. It rejected the inherent truth of theoretical Socialism, the truth of a collectivist society based on real equality of free people, irrespective of their origin, race, gender, position in a state hierarchy, or the level of wealth accumulated by their parents and other ancestors. Karl Marx and Friedrich Engels, and quite a few of their predecessors - noble idealists, or social utopians as they are usually called - were trying to expose the truth of capitalism - a society based on private ownership of property and the free market which consists of materially unequal individuals who strive not to unite in brotherly love but to outstrip each other in the pursuit of personal gain. Whether a True Socialist Idea is realizable at all in this world is another matter. What Soviet communists finally built appeared to be not just a reconstruction of a class society, it was worse - a caste society with rigid barriers between social groupings, while society as a whole was finally transformed into a gigantic prison camp, the Gulag archipelago[3] from which even its rulers could not escape, while they were gradually losing the competence, skill and stamina necessary to manage it.

However, after the death of Stalin, the descendants of the revolutionaries, who in 1917 "expropriated the expropriators", "nationalized" the plundered property and used it for their own benefit for 70 years and more, then reluctantly came to the conclusion that it was no longer possible to go on squeezing anything tangible for themselves from such "nationalized" ("people's") property. The best and the brightest among the political servants to the ruling class reached this conclusion as early as the end of the 1950s. Even mediocrities, like Khrushchev, realized that economically the system had ceased to work efficiently. He therefore started to advocate change in the economic management of Russia without changing its political system and to experiment with economic reform. Even the alleged perpetrator of economic stagnation - General Secretary of the Communist Party of the Soviet Union (CPSU) Leonid Brezhnev - was actually not averse to privatizing shoe-shine sheds, cafeterias and repair shops. Finally the boldest of the reformers - Mikhail Gorbachev - decided to go further and introduce more radical "socialist economic reform" than that of Khrushchev who had earlier failed. Gorbachev understood much clearer than Khrushchev before him that reform was impossible without some shake up of the entrenched top party elite, because the latter had become totally unmanageable, lazy, corrupt and a hindrance to his plans.

On the other hand, younger people in the top echelons of the elite, who welcomed change, initially went along with Gorbachev but soon realized that he was nothing more than a self-adoring chatterbox, devoid of any qualifications of a leader necessary for radical transformation. And they too abandoned him. Hence Gorbachev - the greatest dictator in the history of mankind by his own definition - decided to grab even more dictatorial powers for himself in order to stay on top. He undercut the CPSU, shook up the party elite, and tried to rejuvenate the system of popularly elected councils - the *soviets*, putting himself at the head of the new main *soviet* - the reformed Supreme *Soviet*, whose composition was custom-designed to personally follow his orders. But, as he belatedly realized, that was a great mistake, because the soviets, which allegedly took power in Russia in 1917, in fact *never had any real power* in the Soviet Union, as long as the Communist party elite ruled.

The official aim of *perestroika* - the restructuring of the society - that was initiated to solve the main economic problem of Russian-style socialism, namely the depletion of available economic resources, became a serious issue for the Russian leadership: how to continue to feed the masses of overexploited people, thus sustaining them as a viable non-violent work force,[4] without curtailing the "supply" allocated to the all-devouring super-monster that Soviet "socialism" created: the insatiable military-industrial complex (hereafter simply MIC). Gorbachev and all his post-Stalin predecessors, devoutly served the MIC.

As with Khrushchev before him, Gorbachev miserably failed with his hare-brained project of a socialist *perestroika*, while greatly, albeit unwittingly, undermining the police state he presided over and disposing of the Communist Party - his own power base and the main instrument for managing the country. This led to the collapse of the USSR.

Gorbachev, even less than Khrushchev, realized that many problems within Soviet society stemmed from the oversized development of the MIC, which became increasingly superfluous for the task of ensuring Russian security, as she possessed several thousand strategic nuclear warheads and the means for their delivery to any point on the globe.

The Russian ruling *nomenklatura* threw Gorbachev out, the same way it had previously disposed of the reformer Khrushchev.[5] But while rejecting Gorbachev, the *nomenklatura*, that gradually grasped the consequences of stalling reform, did not reject the idea of improving the economic management of their collective state property *without changing the basic property relations* in a modernized class society, which they had started to build.

Under the guise of "privatization", the Russian ruling elite carried out a reform of the management of "socialized" property without sharing property rights, by and large, in any meaningful way, with the other strata of Russian society.

The aim of the reform was to give the managers of large state industrial and agricultural enterprises more leeway in managing them and the chance to make profits, while the state, that is the top elite's, collective control over that property, remained intact. In other words, the ruling group, the old communist elite, finally accepted the usefulness of allowing socialist enterprises to operate on the basis of self-sufficiency and limited independence from the government's daily control, as advocated for the past 40 years by the Soviet proponents of a "socialist economic reform", starting from well-known theories of Soviet economist Yevsey Lieberman and ending with Mikhail Gorbachev and Yegor Gaidar.

The new leader of Russia - of a truncated USSR - Boris Yeltsin, in a mockery of common sense, proclaimed the end of the "*all-powerfulness* (?!) *of soviets*". This "great democrat" dismissed the Russian Supreme Soviet with a barrage of tank gun salvoes and re-established a regime of a *de facto* single supreme ruler - a presidential regime along imperial Russian lines.

So what new social system did the new leadership of new Russia embrace? It is not exactly socialism, as the Russian people have known it. Neither it is real capitalism, because the latter is not the system the present Russian leadership consciously aspires to. The New Russian Constitution defines Russia as a "democratic federal state based upon the rule of law with a republican form of government" whilst the liberal mass media in Russia refers to the new regime as "*nomenklatura* capitalism".

What is the pivotal axis of this new Russia, what is its credo? Does Russia now consider its *raison d'être* to be the fulfillment of its destiny as a God ordained country - a newly born essentially Christian nation, as shown by the mass transformation of crass atheists into allegedly devoted

Christian neophytes? Hardly so. Everybody in Russia knows that any demonstration of devotion to Christian values on the part of the powers that be is absolutely facile, having nothing to do with real spirituality. The number of churchgoers in Russia has increased dramatically, but the norms of morality, of which the Church is supposed to be the teacher and the guardian, are universally ignored or trampled upon. Heinous crime with its total contempt for human life is on the rise and is not being combated.

Even the Russian Orthodox Church itself is governed not by "born again" pastors but by the same old KGB stooges, who used to obey every whim of its patron organization, and who even under the conditions of *perestroika* and *glasnost* (openness) did not have the courage to acknowledge the colossal destruction of their own Church and the slaughter of several thousands of its priests and disciples by the Communist authorities.

So the problem remains: what are you, Russia, and where are you going? It is probable that those who are now ruling Russia, do not know the answer to this question, or better still even care to ask. The present regime does not give a damn about such philosophical questions. Its *raison d'être* is a redistribution of power and wealth within almost the same circle of the ruling class. This is the background against which current economic "reform" in Russia is taking place. It is being conducted under the demagogic cover of "returning property to the people that created it".

Gorbachev, who has now retired, confirmed this observation, when he stated:

A transfer of property to the *nomenklatura* as a strata of state power occurred. It used state property, solved its own problems, but the people were left out of this most important process, apart from the question of property.[6]

Gorbachev, however, is mistaken about "a transfer of property". Large-scale property still remains in the same hands as it was during his rule - in the hands of the state. Boris Yeltsin and his team appear to be the main owners of that property. The old ruling class continues to control its own property by slightly different methods. The alleged appearance of 40 or 50 million "new property owners", which turns editors of *The New York Times* and other American liberal media into a stupor of exaltation, is a myth of Herculean proportion.

Vladimir Ilyich Lenin used to boast how he skillfully tricked the masses with his "socialization of land" (that is by allegedly giving land to those who till it), because, as he explained, under the guise of "socialization" the land was nationalized, in other words - appropriated by the ruling clique. In the same way under the guise of "popular privatization" through state-issued "privatization vouchers" the old/new ruling gang of "reformed" Bolsheviks, who *de facto* always controlled all state property, have now turned that control into a *de jure* private possession of that property.[7] Incidentally, such an outcome was predicted way back in the 1930s by the exiled leader of the revolution Lev (Leon) Trotsky.

Because the "proper" and "fair" management of the nomenklatura property and the adjustments in the still continuing redistribution of wealth is currently the main concern of the authorities, they cannot systematically focus on anything else, including Russia's national interests. The vague definition of such interests and many inconsistencies in the pursuit of these interests are hardly surprising. The drive for personal enrichment and happiness by the elite is the overriding goal and pastime of the ruling clan of Russia. The only concerns of members of the governing clique seem to be firstly, how to prevent new drastic changes (corrections) in the distribution of wealth, accumulated by them, that are made inevitable as a result of new parliamentary (1995) and presidential (1996) elections that brought closer to the top representatives of clans that were deprived of their "lawful cut" during the initial redistribution, and secondly, how to guard themselves collectively as a new ruling caste from the populace being ever more pauperized and alienated from the upper strata in the process of "progressive reforms".[8] In other words - how to prolong their stay in power, to "stabilize the regime" as they say, in order peacefully, without much in-fighting, to complete the process of personal aggrandizement.

The 1996 presidential elections, according to the Russian political analyst Viktor Kuvaldin, showed

the ghastly picture of power striving to immortalize itself, using modern technologies of manipulation with mass consciousness and behavior. If the innermost essence of Yeltsin's presidency boiled down to the conversion of post-Soviet *nomenklatura* power into property, then the Russian presidential elections (of 1996) demonstrated how to convert the pocketed property back into power. The circle has been closed.[9]

Another handicap for pursuing national interests is the fact that Russian foreign policy is to a great extent dependent on foreign guidance, especially from the United States. Russia now needs regular foreign financial infusions so she has actually lost any independence in choosing her foreign, and in large measure, domestic policy course. The *sine qua non* of current Russian foreign policy is not to displease Washington as it controls the flow of aid from international financial institutions to Russia. As a result, most major foreign policy decisions for Russia are pre-determined by this indispensable limiting condition that tremendously narrows her foreign policy choices.

While totally engaged in the business of perpetuating their power and further enrichment, the Russian authorities occasionally recall that the dilemma which Gorbachev tried to solve, namely how to feed the masses without undercutting the MIC, remains unsolved. The problem now is more acute: though the flow of supplies for the MIC has been somewhat curtailed, it is presently the only industrial sector that continues to more or less efficiently function in Russia, while the masses have been thrown into an abyss of poverty and destitution. It is so deep that their erstwhile miserable existence under the Brezhnev regime is remembered by the great majority as a life in paradise.[10]

Such feelings breed tempest and the avoidance of such tempest, while continuing wealth accumulation (proceeding even during the gathering storm), constitutes the basic self-centered concern of Russian rulers now - not the pursuit of *national* interests.

Notes

[1] Russia inherited about 60% of the economic potential of the Soviet Union. However, since 1991, Russian GDP has declined by more than 60%, so the economic potential of Russia now would equal 24% of the former economic potential of the USSR. But because USSR economic statistics did not include in GDP calculations the costs of services (even material ones), whilst the present Russian GDP takes into account the share of services (mainly those of financial speculative operations) which equals 50% of the officially calculated GDP, the actual GDP of Russia in 1996 was only about 12% of that of the Soviet Union. (See *Rossiiskii statisticheskii Ezhegodnik* [Russian Statistical Yearbook] (Moscow: Goskomstat Rossii, 1994), p.252, *Izvestia*, 11 December 1996, p.4 and *Itogi*, 17 December 1996, p.14.)

[2] A. Korzhakov *Boris Yeltsin. Ot rassveta do zakata.* [Boris Yeltsin, From Dawn to Twilight] (Moscow: Interbook, 1997), p.394.

[3] The term was coined by Alexander Solzhenitsyn, using the acronym of the official concentration camp administration of the USSR - *Glavnoye Upravleniye Lageryami* [Main Camp Administration] - GULAG in Russian.

[4]Trying to ingratiate himself with the masses Gorbachev conceptually upgraded them from the lowly category of a "work force" or "labor resources" into a more respectable category of a "human factor". Such an "upgrading", naturally, did not add an extra piece of bread or an ounce of meat to their daily diet.

[5] *Nomenklatura* (nomenclature) is a term that was used in inner documents of the Communist Party of the Soviet Union to define a pool of members of the Communist party, selected by the Party governing bodies, that were considered as candidates for appointment (or election) to the selected - nomenclature - jobs in the Party-government hierarchy. There were several levels of the Party *nomenklatura* starting from a district one and ending with the highest positions at the Union level. The highest roster was compiled by the Central Committee of the CPSU. Persons on the roster were those who were considered by the Party bosses as deserving and capable of filling the highest offices of the country (not only in the Party itself but in the government, industry, agriculture, armed forces, academy, public associations etc.). The term was popularized by the Soviet émigré author Mikhail Voslensky in 1984. (See Mikhail Voslensky, *Nomenklatura. The Ruling Class in the Soviet Union.* With a preface by Milovan Djilas. Second revised and expanded edition (London: Overseas Publications Interchange Ltd.), 1990.)

[6]Excerpts from Mark Deich's interview with Mikhail Gorbachev (Razocharovaniya, kotorye byvali i ran'she [Disappointments that used to happen earlier as well]), *Novoye Russkoye Slovo*, 20-21 August, 1994, p.8.

[7]The so-called voucher privatization consisted of allegedly giving every citizen of Russia a voucher, which had a nominal value of 1000 roubles in stable 1991 prices. Due to the "price liberalization" that soon followed and the resulting super-inflation, the vouchers were quickly turned by the state into pieces of worthless paper. The famous Russian liberal economist Larisa Piyasheva estimates that of all the state property designated to be "redistributed", the nominal value of which was 150 billion roubles in 1991 prices, the general public got only 10%. All the rest went to the *nomenklatura*, free of charge (*Nezavisimaya Gazeta*, 27 June 1996, p.5). Very many voucher holders were later lured by various crooks to invest into fake "industrial companies" and "mutual funds", so many vouchers quickly disappeared never to be seen again. As a result, according to most estimates, only about 0.03 percent of the state property (by value) landed in the hands of rank and file people. Because of this fact, Russian voucher privatization ought to be considered as the greatest scam in the 6,000 years history of humanity. Viktor Ilyukhin - the Chairman of the Committee on Security of the Russian State Duma

(lower house of the parliament) - stated that President Yeltsin's economic policy was leading to the "complete legalization of criminal underground capital" and to the creation of "a peculiar criminal state", in which the criminal world "would dominate all the structures, including those of the state power". Mr. Ilyukhin emphasized that "hack privatization" was contributing to such an outcome (*Segodnya*, 13 February 1996, p.2).

[8] The government claimed insufficient means when it did not pay wages to miners, teachers, doctors, military personnel and many other categories of state employees, as well as to pensioners, in the period 1994-1998. At the beginning of 1997 it owed the population the colossal sum of 200 trillion roubles (that is close to $36 billion) according to the statement to the Upper House of the Russian parliament by the Minister of Labor and Social Development, Gennady Melikyan (Channel 1 news on Russian TV, 12 February 1997). At the same time in the beginning of that year "a regular refit of the presidential apartments in the Kremlin was carried out. It cost the treasury US$300 million. While the total annual revenue of the state in foreign currency was estimated to be $43.5 million. In other words it constituted just one seventh part of the repair job in the Kremlin" (*Novaya Gazeta* No. 4 (476), 2-8 February 1998, p.6).

[9] *Nezavisimaya Gazeta*, 19 July 1996, p.5.

[10] "I dare state - and this is principally important", writes Vitaly Tret'yakov, the chief editor of *Nezavisimaya Gazeta*, "that practically all the reforms that have been carried out in Russia, dating at least from the time of Peter the Great (to be exact - from the time of Ivan the Terrible) up until now (including the one carried out by Gaidar), although they had laudable goals, were always carried out exclusively at the expense of the population, that is at the expense of those for whose sake, strictly speaking, all normal reforms are undertaken. I repeat: the Russian - Soviet state has always moved forward at the expense of robbing its own people. This is the gist of reformist and non-reformist activities in Russia" (*NG Stsenarii* [NG Scenarios], the monthly supplement to *Nezavisimaya Gazeta*, No. 9, 1996, p.1).

Chapter One

The Concept of National Interest

Before we can analyze national interests of Russia it is imperative to establish what the very notion of "national interest" is and what it means in the current Russian context.

In a brilliant essay on a term "national interest" in the *International Encyclopedia of the Social Sciences* James Rosenau gives the following definition of the concept of "national interest":

The concept of national interest is used in both political analysis and political action. As an analytical tool, it is employed to describe, explain, or evaluate the sources or the adequacy of a nation's foreign policy. As an instrument of political action, it serves as a means of justifying, denouncing, or proposing policies. Both usages, in other words, refer to what is best for a national society. They also share a tendency to confine the intended meaning to what is best for a nation in foreign affairs.

Although Rosenau admits that a notion of "national interest" will continue to be used in politics for a long time to come, he heavily criticizes the concept. Rosenau shows that the three best known approaches to the concept of national interest are deeply flawed. For example, the "objectivist" one, maintaining that the best interest of a nation is a matter of objective reality, is actually unable to convincingly prove what that reality is and construes the reality subjectively. "To explain that a certain policy is in the national interest, or to criticize it for being contrary to the national interest, is to give an imposing label to one's own conception of what is desirable or undesirable course of action." Even Hans Morgenthau's approach to defining national interest in terms of power (for politics is a struggle for power, according to Morgenthau) lacks the method for determining what a nation's relative power is and what degree of power might suffice.

Another - "subjectivist" - method, which shuns the search for an objective truth and defines "national interest" as a pluralistic set of subjective preferences, allegedly also has inherent limitations, because it cannot explain why this or that mix of subjectively defined "national interests" represents the real expressed and unexpressed interests of a society, especially a multiethnic one. In this respect the "subjectivist" approach comes "perilously close to the objectivist's practice of ascribing his own values to others".

And, finally, the third theoretical approach - the so-called decision-making one - in which "the national interest is what the nation, i.e. the decision maker, decides it is" suffers from the fact that in present-day democratic societies "various officials of a society often hold and assert different conceptions of what the goals of foreign policy ought to be".[1]

Another expert on the problem of national interest - Robert Johansen - states:

The highly acclaimed concept of national interest is not scientifically determined. It is a cluster of goals and strategies derived from more fundamental values. Traditionally foremost among those are the preservation of the security and prosperity of the government and its supporters. This includes maintaining sovereign control over a defined territory and population. The competitive accumulation of military power and, secondly, of economic resources, are the principal means for pursuing the values of security and prosperity.[2]

"Of course", Johansen points out, "one's fundamental values are chosen or assumed, not proven."

All of these valid observations will be taken into account in this study. However, the lack of a better generalizing concept of a nation's aspirations on the world arena, means that one cannot avoid using the concept of national interest in trying to analyze the most basic goals and tasks of a nation in its quest for survival and self aggrandizement. Especially when a nation - contrary to what Dr. Rosenau asserted in 1968 - is not "declining in its importance as a political unit to which allegiances are attached", but, as contemporary events show, is becoming the focal point of allegiances. The main thing is that the concept of national interest is not only an analytical tool of political scientists, but an instrument of political action, widely used by present day governments in defining, explaining, projecting and justifying their policies.

"National interest" of a multinational state

In modern Russian usage the expression "national interest" is difficult to use directly from English. In English, for example, the word "nation" is synonymous with the words "country", "commonwealth", "state". However, in Russian the word *natsiya* (nation) is synonymous not so much with the word "country" or even "people" as with the notion of ethnic community (as in a phrase "national question") denoting one of the key problems of the former Soviet Union's and, presently, Russia's federative organization. The meaning of this word corresponds more closely to the American Indians' usage of the term "nation" than to its common literary use in English as a synonym of people or a state, as in "the United Nations". The latter term, in its proper translation into Russian, should have sounded like "United Countries" (*Obyedinenniye Strany*) or "United Peoples" (*Obyedinenniye Narody*) but instead was translated literally into Russian without any change as *Obyedinenniye Natsii*.[3]

Actually, as Charles Beard one of the first serious students of "national interest" explains, the very notion was born in America in opposition to the original term "state interest" (or "raison d'etat", "reason of state") that was in the wide usage in Europe:

In their resistance to the British government Americans acquired a habit of using terms like "the people", the "nation" or "commonwealth" when speaking of *res publica* in a laudatory sense and of referring to government or state when employing derogatory language. To Americans the state appeared as a "Cold monster"... Dynastic interest and state reason had no roots in the American heritage, and British usage had prepared the way for a transition to commonwealth or national interest.[4]

This observation about the origin of the English-language term is very important because the problem is not just one of linguistic purity or political correctness. We need to consider what kind of interests Soviet scholars had in mind when talking of the "national interests" of the USSR.

The Soviet Union was a multinational state *(mnogonatsional'noye gosudarstvo)*, in a similar way to the Russian Federation today. However, it makes no sense linguistically in Russian to speak about "national interests", unless it is made perfectly clear that the word "national" refers to "state", as in the phrase: "Soviet state interests".

Soviet leaders and scholars were also able to talk of national interests in class terms because the Soviet Union's national interests were, ostensibly, the interests of working masses of the country, represented by its ruling body - the Politburo of the Communist Party of the Soviet Union (CPSU). The theory was that this body represented and pursued identical class interests of Soviet working masses irrespective of their nationality. And since in Russia, socialism had already won "totally and irrevocably", it was no longer possible to exploit classes with particular national interests, as the policies, mapped out by the CPSU, represented the interests of the whole population.

Ostensibly, it was only in the Soviet Union and other states of a similar type, that representatives of the "exploiter classes" were suppressed and destroyed, and where society was allegedly united around the interests and goals of "a working class and a toiling peasantry". In this sense, the term "national interests" could be used straightforwardly, without any caveats.

On the other hand, any government of a capitalist country was not (and, by Soviet specialists' definition was not capable of) expressing real interests even of an ethnically homogeneous nation, because it neglected the interests of its exploited working class majority. That is why the term "national interests", when applied by Soviet authors to describe a capitalist country, such as the United States or France, would always be put in quotation marks in order to emphasize its dubious nature.

But with all the lip-service about "class interests" there was not much difference between the understanding and application of the term "national interest" by the pre-revolutionary Russian ruling dynasty and its post-revolutionary usage by the leadership of the CPSU. The only difference was that communists needed to constantly emphasize their guardianship of national interests to enhance their legitimacy in clinging to power.

Since the ruling body in a totalitarian Soviet state was the self-appointing and self-perpetuating Politburo of the CPSU, composed mostly of ethnic Russians, one could say that the Politburo not so much represented the interests of a multinational Soviet state as the interests of the domineering Russian nation. To a certain extent such a conclusion is correct, unless one takes into account that even the "domineering Russian nation" was itself enslaved by its totalitarian rulers (and suffered most heavily in comparison to other populous nations of the Soviet state during Lenin's-Stalin's murderous "class cleansing" campaigns and wars - the civil war and the Second World War).[5]

All in all, when one spoke of the "Soviet Union's national interests" (up until the end of 1991, when the Union ceased to exist), this largely meant the state interests of the USSR as understood and formulated by the top Russian echelon of the CPSU.

One can question such a conclusion by pointing out that the top echelon of leadership, including the Politburo, always contained some ethnic non-Russians, Jews and Ukrainians being most prominent among them, and for 30 years was headed by an ethnic Georgian - Joseph Stalin. Because of this, with all the talk about "class interests", those interests had to have some multinational aspect, if not coloration. But the fact is that, while being ethnically non-Russian, the aforementioned leaders essentially represented the great-power interests of the leading Russian nation, if not of the nation as a whole, then at least of its politically active communist stratum.

Leading Jews in the immediate post-revolutionary Soviet establishment (like Trotsky, Sverdlov, Kamenev, Zinoviev and others) actually did not give a damn about their nationality: they considered themselves to be above any nationality, as true representatives of the world proletariat.[6] As for the Georgian Joseph Stalin, he was a model Russian great power chauvinist, despite his crimes against the Russian people (along with people of other nationalities) many of whom became victims of his mass incarcerations and massacres.

It often happens that a representative of a smaller ethnic group, who suddenly becomes a senior political figure of the ruling ethnic majority, becomes, so to speak, "more catholic than the Pope". The Chechen Ruslan Khasbulatov, the speaker of the Supreme Soviet of the Russian Federation in 1992-93, and the Jew, Vladimir Zhirinovsky, leader of the Liberal Democratic Party of Russia, are clear examples of such a transformation.

Of course, with all the criminality and brutality of ruling dictators of the USSR (particularly Lenin and Stalin) taken into consideration, it stands to reason that none of them was set either on undermining or destroying the Soviet state. All of them in their policies were trying to build up the Great socialist state, to increase its power, its glory, its international standing, if not the well-being of its people. All of them saw the Soviet Union as a future super state of the world, not only a superpower on a par with the United States but The Superpower - the undisputed leader, if not the boss, of the global community of nations. That was an overriding goal among the set of "national interests" of the USSR: universal triumph of communist system, a communist way of life. However, as they gradually discovered for themselves, they did not want the triumph of communism per se, but the triumph of Soviet-style communism controlled by Moscow. This is why Stalin so brutally installed Soviet-style communism in Eastern Europe after World War Two and that is why Brezhnev was more afraid of independent communist China than of the capitalist United States. Communism, it appeared, despite all Moscow's lip service to internationalism, was essentially a phenomenon of a nationalist, not an internationalist, brand.

All Moscow's other goals were derivatives of this prime goal of destroying Western-style capitalism. They were defined not so much in some positive way, but by the rule of contradiction: whatever was bad for imperialism, especially "American imperialism", was good for the Soviet Union. This amounted to a zero-sum game. It was only in the mid-1970s that some Soviet political scientists, in trying to provide theoretical underpinnings for Moscow's policy of opening up to "imperialism" - the policy of détente - argued that there were parallels between the foreign policy goals of the USSR and the USA, for instance in preventing nuclear war.

The Soviet leaders did everything they deemed necessary in order to achieve the goal of global pre-eminence. Cruelty in treating their own masses was - in their minds - a means to accelerate such an end. All means are moral, if they enhance the cause of (Soviet) communism - was Lenin's dictum.

But they failed dismally! Instead of liquidating the alternative capitalist system, a system of individual enterprise, respect for human rights and democratic rule based on universal free elections of governing bodies, they maimed, ruined and finally destroyed their own "model" state that, according to its Marxist Gospel, was supposed for the first time in human history to do away with exploitation of man by man, with misery, hard toil and downtrodden workers and create a social paradise on earth.

Why and how this has happened is for historians, sociologists, political scientists to debate for several hundred years into the future against the background of the alleged triumph of the Great Liberal Idea of Western civilization, provided that they have enough time before the Great Liberal Idea itself degenerates into something painfully familiar, forced to mimic its erstwhile ugly opponent, when the West, in desperation, will borrow (through a totally democratic process of popular vote) some of the wicked methods of Soviet-style socialism in order to tackle increasing capital crime, the wholesale drugging of population and the onslaught of hungry hordes of ailing people fleeing totally impoverished and ecologically ruined Third and some Second World countries.[7]

However, in a short term, in order to shed some light on the communist legacy, it is imperative to at least sum up, if not to research in depth, some of the most flagrant conceptual and practical blunders and delusions of the communist state in its domestic and foreign policies. It is necessary to do so in order not to slide again into the old Bolshevik path of forcing people into happiness (*nasil'stvennogo oschastlivlivaniya naroda*) under the guise of such fashionable slogans as "marketization", "democratization" etc.

It is also clear that nobody in the Soviet top political command, even the genius of evil - Stalin, was using brutal force and bloody purges simply for the sake of mere enjoyment or even for the sole purpose of keeping power. It was used, first and foremost, to make society malleable for social experimentation.

All revolutions - the joys or the curses of history, depending upon one's outlook - are brutal. The Great October Socialist Revolution in Russia, generated by the Bolshevik's coup d'etat in Petrograd in October 1917, that initially was quite bloodless, but savage further on - was just a continuation of the anti-monarchist coup of February 1917 which toppled the corrupt and decaying Tsarist regime of the Russian empire. The main difference between the two most prominent leaders of the Russian Revolution - Alexander Kerensky, who headed the provisional government in Petrograd and belonged to allegedly extremist socialist-revolutionary party, and Lenin, the head of the main faction of allegedly more moderate social-democratic party, who toppled Kerensky's government and established his own rule - was first of all one of methods. Socialist-revolutionary Kerensky was much more of a democrat and a decent politician than social-democrat Lenin, who was bent on gangster methods in politics.

Since the difference between democracy and most other forms of government essentially boils down to the means chosen for the achievement of certain goals, the victory of "democrat" Lenin with his totalitarian methods trapped Russia for almost 70 years on to the road to a dead end. Actually Soviet Russia was the first ever totalitarian society on the globe. It differed from ancient tyrannies and despotism by the greater scope of government's control over the daily life and fate of individuals.

Everything, except some petty personal property, belonged to the state (that is to the small clique of self-appointed and unchangeable rulers of the country) and the state was also the sole employer. In a situation of modern communications and transportation and pervasiveness of political police, the life of every individual in Russia was literally in the hands of the paramount leader. That explains why it was so easy - in the USSR and, later, in Hitler's Germany - to carry out mass executions of people without any protest from the rest of the population.

Brutal, criminal methods of implementing a more or less reasonable social idea, methods that continued to be used long after the immediate revolutionary period, destroyed the system built on that idea, whatever the idea's original viability might have been. This is one of the indisputable lessons of history. The other is that the very methods of defining social priorities and national interests in the "new socialist state" were totally inadequate. They were defined by a very narrow circle of gradually changing leaders, who appeared to be less and less literate and intelligent almost in inverse proportion to improvements in the provision of free public and higher education of the masses under the Soviet regime. This is one of the paradoxes of a totalitarian system, which promotes leaders not on merit, but in accordance with a degree of sheepishness and obedience a person displays, his readiness to unquestionably follow whatever directions are prescribed from above.

It was observed a long time ago that no great things can be accomplished in a country that permanently dwarfs its people. The Soviet system of promotion of the *nomenklatura* - the ruling strata of the Soviet society (which conceptually played the same role in Russia as the *dvoryanstvo* - the nobility - under the Tsarist regime) doomed the viability and intellectual capabilities of the ruling class. On top of that there was no real feedback between the rulers and the society, there was no civil society as such and there was also a total lack of adequate understanding at the top about what was happening with the economy and social system itself because all information was based on lies, damn-lies and empty slogans that substituted for hard facts. (All such falsifications were designed either to report non-existent progress, or to cover up wholesale stealing.) Mikhail Gorbachev - a Secretary of the Central Committee of the CPSU from 1978 onwards - queried General Secretary Andropov about the real situation with the USSR's state budget, but evidently even Andropov did not have the whole picture![8]

All this finished the system, because ruling mediocrities did not have a "gut feeling" of the sum total of national interests, as a well-established ruling class of any country has. Despite the *nomenklatura* system, there were too many shakeups under Stalin and Khrushchev for a stable solid ruling class to form. It was too young, too troubled, too frightened to feel itself a real "owner" of the country with established norms and traditions. Neither could the ruling clique intelligently reason about national interests, in modern, contemporary terms. They could only blindly follow worn out slogans and myths about their own great role, slogans that gradually became absorbed by the system.

However, because any country is a living organism, and not just some artificial social corral, there were goals, trends and directions in Soviet rulers' domestic and foreign policies that were inherited from the regime they destroyed. Those goals stood above the trifling *melkotravchatykh* (petty, selfish) considerations of the Soviet elite.

"Many of a country's national interests leave, in fact, almost no room for real debate. They are to a large extent predetermined by geography, history, culture, ethnic composition and political tradition", remarked Sergei Stankevich, who was at one time a presidential adviser to Boris Yeltsin.[9]

Whether one likes it or not those interests include the indelible bequests of the old Russian empire, its grand hopes, not yet materialized at the time the revolution occurred. They had their hold on the mentality of Soviet rulers, despite their illiteracy and pettiness. One might say it was like a heartbeat of the allegedly dead empire, conditioning the behavior of the new rulers.

In a more prosaic and cynical way the same idea was expressed by some knowledgeable American Sovietologists, such as Richard Pipes and Seweryn Bialer, who argued that the Soviet regime happened to save the old Empire from annihilation and continue its historic expansionism.

Russian émigré philosopher Nikolai Berdyaev expressed it in a different way by remarking that Moscow under Bolshevik rule replaced the old Russian idea of Moscow as the Third Rome with the concrete practice of Moscow as the Third (Communist) International, which in its outward manifestation was almost the same as the old slogan. The old one presented the Great Russian Idea as a continuation by Moscow of an original Christian mission of proselytizing and of universal salvation after the first two Romes (Rome and Byzantium) fell under the onslaught of barbarians.

The new Great Idea, meanwhile, presented the Russian messianic goal as that of the salvation and unification of the international proletariat - the new "chosen people" of Marxian theology, the only part of humanity worthy of salvation. So there was not much difference between the concepts, especially if one remembers that behind this constant and allegedly universalist drive, both old and new, was hidden a purely Russian, Slavic interest of aggrandizement of the empire, which had nothing to do with real aspirations either of Christianity or of Communism as initial universalist teachings.[10]

Finally - not to be bothered in their pursuit of Epicurean life styles, a pursuit, which began under Brezhnev's "regime of stability", when all the scary things of the Soviet past started to recede into history - the rulers put the system on auto-pilot. As Yeltsin testifies:

In the Politburo, of course, they have been adopting some momentary tactical decisions; it had its own "progressives" and its own "hawks". But the country did not have any special need for their commands or decisions.
People arrived to those plush offices, to that unlimited power as parts arrive to a machine - with the same measure of independence.
The main paradox of Russia consisted in the fact that its state system has been trudging on its own, no one steered it in the final analysis. In fact, a strong leader has been absent in Russia for a long time. Even the reformer Gorbachev was most of all afraid to break, to demolish the system, he was afraid that it will revenge him. In his design *perestroika* should not have touched main mechanisms of the Soviet order.[11]

That kind of governing resulted in the exacerbation of the previously established economic pattern of "production for production's sake", when heavy industry and the military were yearly gnawing more and more at what was left of a civilian economy.

When the last paramount leader of the USSR - Mikhail Gorbachev - tried to squeeze from the lop-sided economy even more military hardware in order not to lag behind the United States in the strategic arms race, the economy collapsed, while the huge bureaucratic superstructure of the state survived through a transformed incarnation as a new *nomenklatura*.

Some Russian sociologists assert that the system under which most of the those currently living endured for a large part of their lives, did not, in fact, collapse at all, but was instead reformed in a quite peculiar way. It was just restructured, to use Gorbachev's pet word. The old communist ideology was discarded as ineffectual and irrelevant to the new tasks of the ruling elite. With the demise of the all-powerful secretive Politburo and the Party totally servile to it, with the easing of the grip of the KGB and other agencies of repression, and with the possibility of economic independence for an individual, totalitarianism mellowed into authoritarianism.

A very important factor here is that the Soviet system of state capitalism, where all the property belonged to the Party in general, but in practice was run by a heavily centralized bureaucratic apparatus under the control of Politburo and its executive Central Committee on a depersonalized basis, was decentralized under *perestroika* and the follow-up Russian privatization reform and passed into personal semi-ownership to those managers who actually ran it on a day to day basis as the Party or the state employees in the old days. On the basis of decentralization, a market system was introduced, though it still operates very poorly among former state enterprises.

"As a result, on the basis of the director corps and local administration there appeared an extraordinary original phenomenon - a class of individual owners of objects of state property." The present system has quite a few features of a "normal" capitalism, while at the same time it is not capitalism as the world knows it but "a direct continuation of the pre-perestroika structure".[12]

Very little has changed in the relations between majority of the people and the powers that be, because the ruling *nomenklatura* was reorganized but not even sufficiently shaken up, and it still continues to exploit the masses. All levers of economic and state governance are in the hands of *nomenklatura*, and government officials are openly stating that reforms have ran their course and that a period of stabilization is beginning in Russia. The main goal of such a "stabilization" policy is to create favorable conditions for entrenching the rejuvenated *camarilla* in power so that it can continue, to put it mildly, to have a good life, and in order to prevent any changes in the distribution of property from those segments of the former communist *nomenklatura* who feel deprived of their fair share. This is undoubtedly the primary goal of the clique, presently ruling Russia.

As to its foreign policy goals, this superstructure, with all its set prejudices and beliefs, despite the superficial borrowing of a new "democratic" terminology, is actively reviving some of the traditional Russian/Soviet international goals. In pursuing these goals, it is helped by objective circumstances: the dissatisfaction of many countries by the present monopoly of American power in the world arena.

In the days of the Cold war any country in the world could manoeuver between the United States and the Soviet Union and in fact to "milk" both for its own gain. Even West European allies of the United States, such as France or Germany, when pressed too hard by Washington, to a limited degree courted Moscow. With all the fear of "communism", Russia was an alternative to many, because it deprived Washington of a monopoly of power in the world arena. There was always a possibility of smaller countries opening up to Moscow. Even some symbolic moves towards Moscow on their part lessened the price of obeying Washington. It was a competitive situation.

Now that the Soviet Union has disappeared, Russia does not have much capability for a deep involvement on the international stage. "Look", Russian Foreign Minister Kozyrev once stated, "when Richard Holbrooke mediates in Yugoslavia he flies on two planes, stuffed with most modern gadgets in communications etc. and he brings with him a big team of geographers, demographers, experts on the region's economy and politics, psychologists etc. While my deputy has to take a commercial flight and can bring along just a couple of assistants!"

Of course, some leverages, namely sales of oil, gas, arms, precious metals, timber, Russia's permanent seat on the UN Security Council do matter. And the longing for an alternative option on the world arena has not disappeared altogether. In conditions, when close U.S. partners, like the countries of Western Europe or Japan, emphatically refuse to assume such a role, Russia emerges again as such an alternative "back up" almost by default - on purely geopolitical, not ideological, grounds. Many countries of the Middle East, Asia and Latin America want to strengthen their ties with Russia, albeit a weakened one, for the sole purpose of gaining greater freedom of manoeuver vis-à-vis the United States. A similar role is increasingly being forced upon China.

The Russian Federation as an heir to the Soviet Union

The Russian Federation until its separation from the USSR through the conspiracy of the three leaders of the USSR's Slavic republics (Yeltsin, Kravchuk and Shushkevich), who tried a coup de grace whilst the Union was disintegrating, was never a full-fledged state within the Soviet Union.

Although Russia, as one of the 15 constituent republics of the Union, had some accoutrements of a nation-state (its own rubber-stamping Supreme Soviet, meeting for three days twice a year, its own Council of Ministers, dealing mainly with local (consumer) industries, while at the same time having no Communist Party organization of its own in contrast to the other 14 republics) Russia was actually intertwined with the USSR in a manner that no other republic was. It was pro-forma one of the co-equal republics of the Union, and at the same time, it was at the apex of power in the USSR: the Union itself!

It is difficult to explain such a peculiar position of Russia, because it was not established formally as held informally. The real leaders of the Union were leaders of Russia as well, Russia's capital - Moscow - was also the capital of the Union and anything that was decided in the CPSU Politburo had the aura of a decision emanating from Russia. Joseph Stalin, who pressed President Roosevelt hard to make him agree that separate seats in the United Nations should be allocated to all the Soviet constituent republics (apart from the seat for the USSR), finally succeeded in securing separate seats for the Ukraine and Belorussia. But it never dawned on Stalin to put Russia into the UN instead of the Ukraine or Belorussia. Russia and the Soviet Union for him (like for millions of citizens of Russia) were indistinguishable.

Nikita Khrushchev, yielding to the stirring of Russian nationalism, created in February 1956 a special Bureau of the Central Committee of the CPSU for the Russian Federation in order "to provide for more effective solutions to the problems of economic and cultural growth of the RSFSR".[13] However, Khrushchev did not know what to do with it and the Bureau soon died a natural death. Thus when Russia separated from the Soviet Union, through the liquidation of the Union, it turned out to be a new Russia, on the one hand, and the truncated USSR, on the other:

- legally (assuming upon itself all the international obligations of the former Soviet Union, all its total foreign debt and all its property abroad);
- territorially (three quarters of the territory of the Former Soviet Union (hereafter FSU), albeit with arbitrarily defined borders that never existed in Russian history);
- economically (60% of the FSU's GNP and 75% of its military-industrial complex);
- militarily (78% of the FSU's armed forces, and eventually, by

agreement with other republics, Russia acted as the custodian of all the FSU nuclear weapons), and

• diplomatically (a UN Security council seat and actually all the former Soviet embassies abroad in its possession).

Most importantly the new Russia seemed to be for everybody around it and for its new rulers, the old pre-Revolutionary Russia from the point of view of the scope of its interests and influence in the "Near Abroad" (*blizhnem zarubezhye*),[14] as well as elsewhere: a nuclear superpower with all its formal clout in international councils, albeit much depreciated because of its economic malaise and social turmoil. On top of all that is the traditional Soviet bureaucracy (Party and state) still prevailing in the higher echelons of state power.[15]

This uniqueness of Russia's position and historical experience to a great extent explains Moscow's inherent impossibility to completely shed its messianic globalist mentality, which is rooted, as stressed above, not only in the expansionist policies of the communist period, but in an indelible legacy of hundreds of years of raising the frontier, to use F. Turner's expression, the empire building by the Russian state.[16] This process started with the "land gathering" by the rulers of the Grand Principality of Muscovy and such a task seems to be again on the current agenda of Moscow's present rulers, following the disintegration of the Union, which is considered a tragedy by every true Russian.

Another point that must be borne in mind when discussing the national interests of Russia is that the current Russian state - the Russian Federation - is, like the Soviet Union, a multinational entity, although its national composition - in contrast to the Soviet Union's, where Russians comprised only 51% of the total population, is heavily tilted towards the predominate Russian ethnic community. This Russian population is more or less evenly dispersed throughout the Russian Federation and represents a substantial proportion of the population even in the national republics within Russia with compactly settled indigenous ethnic groupings.

Out of total population of Russia (approximately 150 million people), ethnic Russians constitute around 120 million or almost 82%. There are only six other ethnic groups, whose numbers in Russia exceed one million: Tatars (5.5 million), Ukrainians (4.4 million), Chuvashi (1.8 million), Bashkirs (1.3 million), Belorussians (1.2 million) and Mordovians (1.1 million).[17]

Of all the big and medium-sized national republics of the Russian Federation there are only four - Chechnya, Chuvashia, North Ossetiya and Tuva - where the indigenous ethnic group constitutes more than 50% of its population.[18]

The question in such circumstances is: to what extent are or can the Russian Federation's "national interests" be representative of the interests of non-Russian republics of the Federation? Or, to formulate the question differently, whose interests does the central Russian government represent?

Up to the end of 1993, it was difficult to give a more or less coherent answer to the second question, because the "central government" in Moscow was dangerously split. President Yeltsin and the executive Cabinet of Ministers under him, pursued one set of national interests, while the Russian parliament, on the other hand, pursued a different course. Neither was able to arrive at a workable compromise in many areas of policy-making.

The Russian Supreme Soviet and the larger and more authoritative body, the Congress of Peoples' Deputies, guided by their wily, but somewhat crazy speaker, Ruslan Khasbulatov, were constantly and deliberately throwing spanners into the works of Yeltsin's policy. Such a confrontation, which by the spring of 1993, had all the characteristics of dual power at the Center and in many provinces, inflamed nationalistic strife within the Russian Federation and also within the Commonwealth of Independent States.

By making territorial demands on the Ukraine, the Russian Supreme Soviet set a dangerous precedent for a free for all revisionism with regard to the former inner borders between various regions. It stubbornly opposed many economic decisions of the President, including privatization of large industries and of the land. It was constantly at loggerheads with the executive on matters of foreign policy, including arms control, sometimes joining forces with the radical non-parliamentary opposition, united on a nationalistic platform (the so-called "Red-Brown coalition") that accused "Yeltsin and his clique" of dancing to the tune of "Yid-Masons" and selling Russia wholesale and retail to the United States and other Western powers.

At the same time, the Supreme Soviet sometimes much more adequately than the government, expressed the particular interests of Russia's 89 subjects of the Federation (regions, territories, republics as well as Moscow and St. Petersburg) and managed to reach some compromise with regional interests. The only point on which the President and the majority of the Supreme Soviet were united was the principle of Russian unity, namely on their opposition to any moves that might lead to the disintegration of Russia.

In such a situation it was difficult to discuss national interests of Russia, because even in elite circles, opinions, especially on policy priorities and methods, greatly diverged.

Though the executive, because of its grip on the mechanisms of state, managed in 1992-93 to preserve a degree of continuity in domestic and foreign policies, its line was not so much a conscious, thought-out course, instead it constituted expedient manoeuvering between political pressures from the right and left in a struggle for its own survival.

After the adoption of the new Constitution in December 1993 and the opening of a newly elected parliament (the Federal Assembly), the differences between legislature and the President (who was given much broader legislative and executive authority by the new Constitution than was the case before) persisted.

However, mirroring the previous situation in the Union (in so far as the more dictatorial powers Gorbachev grabbed for himself on paper, the more dependent he became on conservative forces), the Russian president now has to lend his ear to the voice of the new parliamentary majority, because the latter reflects the mood and opinions of the majority of the population. Nevertheless, the Russian president does wield authoritarian powers. In point of fact, his powers are greater than those of the Russian Tsar in 1906-1917. Because, after Nicholas II issued his famous Manifesto in October 1905 and created a genuine legislative body - the Duma - he could issue decrees (*ukazy*) with the authority of the laws, when the Duma was not in session. But they had to be submitted for approval at the next session of the Duma no later than two months after its opening. In accordance with Article 90 of the new Russian Constitution, the President of Russia can issue *ukazy* which are binding on everybody in Russia, without approval of the Duma.[19] And the President is producing them often and in large quantities (like pancakes, as a Russian would say).

The flagrantly nationalistic line of the majority in the Federal Assembly forced the President and government in 1994-1996 to take a more nationalistic line in foreign policy. Hence it is possible to speak not of some abstractly conceived "national interests" of Russia but of such interests as practical signposts of the Russian Federation's policy being worked out at the top on the basis of compromises or tacit behind the scenes agreements between the President and the leadership of the Duma (the lower House of the parliament).

Assuming that the top leadership of Russia now practically shares some set of national interests, albeit poorly understood, vaguely formulated and haphazardly carried out, one must again ask: To what extent does this set of aims and aspirations reflect the interests not just of ethnic Russians but of all the citizens of the Federation, or, at least, of its overwhelming majority?

There were until recently two extreme points of view on this question:

One school of thought, propagated by some national republics and even by some purely Russian ethnic regions within the Federation, was overwhelmingly negative in tone: it is not possible for the central authority (Moscow) to adequately represent the interests of the subjects of the Russian Federation - its republics and provinces. Some national republics within the Russian Federation, led by Chechnya in the Caucasus, and Tatarstan in mid-European Russia, were actually leading the fight for the right of national republics to be independent within the Federation giving them the right to pursue their own foreign policies.

The answer given by the other dominant school of thought was that Moscow adequately represents on the international arena the interests of all the main ethnic groups that inhabit Russia. It was high time, the proponents of this view declared, that the national republics and provinces were prevented, by default, from gaining more and more rights for themselves. The proponents of this point of view advocate the restoration of the USSR as their final goal. They see demands for the full sovereignty of any ethnic grouping within Russia as an act of a high treason and of gross impudence.

Though Yeltsin's government was fighting such "national-patriotic" forces, it could but take their stance regarding separatist movements in Russia because, whatever their other demands, the opinions of the extreme right and left reflect the dominant attitude of the majority of Russians who are against ethnic separatism.

Manoeuvering between those two extreme viewpoints President Yeltsin and his government took a moderate stance on this issue. While Yeltsin detracted from his initial offer to national republics "to grab as much sovereignty as you can swallow" (addressed particularly to Tatarstan during Yeltsin's fight for a popular vote during 1991 Russian Presidential election), he agreed that the local administrations should retain control over the management of their local economies.

The main line of the Russian government is that in formulating national goals and priorities the federal authorities are guided not just by purely Russian, but by *Rossiiskii* interests, heeding all the citizens of the Federation, irrespective of their nationality, religion, party affiliation, gender etc. This is very important distinction because two different Russian words *russkii* (meaning "ethnic Russian") and *rossiiskii* (the adjective, derived from the Russian name of the country - *Rossiya*, meaning Russia, the commonwealth in the wholeness of all its people, their traditions, cultures and beliefs) are misleadingly translated in all modern Russian-English dictionaries by the same single word "Russian".[20]

Bearing in mind this linguistic problem and my earlier warnings about the inherent deficiencies of the concept of national interests, this book in analyzing national interests of Russia, is based upon the following premises:

Firstly, even bearing in mind differences in public opinion, in the ambitions of different nationalities and the divergent viewpoints of the Russian elite etc., it is still possible to outline both objectively and subjectively, the basic indicators of Russia's national goals. In order to carry out a *Realpolitik* study of Russian national interests, it is necessary to focus upon the mainstream basic interests of Russia, as understood by its establishment.

The validity of such an approach rests on the following assumptions:

Given the remote possibility of the final triumph of Western-style democracy in Russia, Russia now and in the foreseeable future will still be governed in the original Russian way, that is in a more or less authoritarian manner. This is inevitable because the Russian ruling class is still composed essentially of the old Party *nomenklatura* (reformed or unreformed) and by the offspring of its members, who possess an appropriate mind set. It is this stratum (with all the tactical differences within it) that formulates Russian national goals and aspirations and acts upon them. And though the forcible dissolution in Autumn 1993 of the old confrontational Russian parliament did not produce a new pliant Federal Assembly (as all the courtiers of "Tsar Boris" hoped for), there now appears to be greater consensus at the top concerning national interests, mainly because all the Russian political parties have gradually become more nationalistic in matters of foreign policy.[21]

This trend became more pronounced in 1996-98. Thus, although the lower house of the Federal Assembly (the Duma) is presently dominated by national-patriotic forces, led by the Communist party of Russia, they are still cooperating with the President, who himself has become more nationalistic (at least in his pronouncements, if not deeds). The upper house of the Federal Assembly - the Council of the Federation - which in 1994-95 consisted mainly of local top administrators, appointed by the president, is now composed of regional bosses (governors of provinces, presidents of national republics and heads of legislatures) duly elected by the population. Even though they are now more politically independent - and thus less prone to pressure from the top - they still tend to support the foreign policy line of the Russian President.

More democratic and *ipso facto* more complex procedures in formulating national interests, involving inputs from voters, requires a complete generational change and the transition to a society based essentially on private property, which will give individuals real freedom from enslavement by the state.[22]

On every subject there are often conflicting points of view, and conceptually each viewpoint is valid, but this book assumes that Russia's interests are reflected in the practical positions of authorities and in the high level of consensus among the ruling elite. To give just one example: one might argue that the best defense for Russia in the present circumstances is no defense at all:

Let those Western bastards occupy our country without any resistance on our part and let them then feed us and provide for us, like Americans did in Somalia.[23]

Theoretically it is quite viable position.

Inadvertently even Russia's leaders (Gorbachev and Yeltsin) at one time contributed to such a line of thought by asserting that the West somehow ought to be more interested in the USSR's or Russia's survival than the Russians themselves. (A variation on such a theme is Moscow's perennial warnings to the West: "You better help us, or else....!")

But to consider a strategy of voluntary capitulation to the West, and view Russia's "national interests" in this way, means adopting an extreme formalistic argument, while at the same time ignoring the fact that no one in the Russian establishment is openly proposing such a "security option" and all the practical steps of the Russian state in retaining and modernizing its huge war machine, demonstrate a quite different approach to this issue.

On the other hand, the world has already witnessed the flowering of a quite extremist position: "We shall quickly become so powerful that we shall take back Alaska from the United States". But that is typical demagoguery used by a one time *bête noir* of Russian politics - Vladimir Zhirinovsky - in order to ingratiate himself with the desperate and impoverished masses, longing for a miracle.[24]

Whoever occupies the office of Russian President in the foreseeable future (even Zhirinovsky himself, which is highly improbable), he or she will hardly be able to proceed with the adventurous policy Zhirinovsky advocates. The Russian ruling elite (including the top brass) will simply not permit it out of a sense of self-preservation.

Despite the existence of some "dissident" national republics within Russia and even some "dissident" governance in the Russian provinces, it will be counter-productive for them to raise their particular stances at a national interest level. For example, one might surmise that the "national interest" of the present ruling clique (and there is no better word for it) of Tatarstan is to destroy the existing Federation and following its ruin gain "total and complete independence'. But such an interest contravenes Russia's number one priority: survival as a coherent society. Because this narrow nationalistic aim of a certain comparatively small ethnic grouping, which is now enjoying home rule, is not shared by the majority of the "subjects of the Federation", and even by the majority of the people of Tatarstan, such a proposition is important only in the context of debating impediments to the realization of a vital interest of Russia i.e. to survive as a coherent entity.

At the same time it is necessary to treat the desire of Tatarstan and other national republics to keep themselves as separate national entities within the framework of the Russian Federation as legitimate goals which are likely to influence the overall cohesion of Russia. In the same way the basic national interests of *Rossiya* reflect the aspirations, desires and needs not only of the ethnic Russian majority, but also the 100 plus other ethnic groups inhabiting Russia. However the desire for security, peace, prosperity etc. are even greater than the aforementioned issues and interests. To raise every specific grievance or demand of some tiny sub-national group to the level of a national interest of the Russian Federation and to analyze it as such, fundamentally undermines the seriousness of an analysis of Russian national interests.[25]

While discarding extremist foreign policy positions, even of the influential forces in Russian politics, as representing true Russian national interests, it is nevertheless necessary to clearly comprehend the specific contribution of those forces to Russian foreign policy making. For example, if there were no Zhirinovsky in Russia one might have had to invent him for the sake of pursuing Russia's true national interests, just as Mikhail Gorbachev did in 1991 (at least according to popular rumors). At that time Gorbachev, while assuming ever greater dictatorial powers, but publicly supposedly moving towards "pluralistic democracy", ordered the KGB to create a loyal (that is controllable by Gorbachev) opposition (in a similar manner to Tsar Nicholas II, who during revolutionary turmoil in Russia at the beginning of the 20th century ordered his secret police to create a government-controlled workers' trade-union movement). The KGB was quick to comply and just in time for the first presidential election in the Russian Federation, the Liberal Democratic Party, headed by an alleged KGB operative Vladimir Zhirinovsky, appeared on the political scene. In retrospect this was a brilliant master stroke by the KGB unsurpassed in the *perestroika* era.

Of course, in the middle of 1991, even the KGB (not to speak about the CIA constantly blamed by some American profanes for its failure to correctly predict events in the USSR), did not envisage the total demise of the Soviet Union. When this happened, Zhirinovsky with his unbridled verbal extremism, became a proverbial secret weapon of the Kremlin in the struggle to regain some of the prestige and international influence of the former Union - at a time when most of the traditional leverages of Moscow's foreign policy became inoperable. Incessant and vehement threats to the West, emanating from Zhirinovsky, provided the Russian powers that be (Yeltsin first and foremost) with an opportunity for foreign policy manoeuver at a time when Russia was cornered by Washington and some of its allies. It is revealing that all-the "smart moves" of the Russian diplomacy in 1994-95, making Russia appear independent in its foreign policy, following its true national interests, were in fact facilitated by Zhirinovsky's antics: Russia's stance on Bosnia, its response to NATO's Partnership for Peace, its position on the Middle East, its opposition to the expansion of NATO and so forth. On every issue Zhirinovsky assumed an extreme position, unpalatable for the world community, whereas President Yeltsin took a more moderate stand open to compromise and ... won! Zhirinovsky, whatever his critics say, objectively plays a role of a watchdog over Russian national interests. His abject rudeness in stating his blood-curdling goals, misbehavior and his well-deserved reputation as a "crazy politician to be reckoned with", created by his Western haters/admirers, is tremendously helpful. Such a stance also appealed to the Russian voters who in 1993 elections to the 5th Duma mostly supported Zhirinovsky's party.[26] However by the time of the elections to the new 6th Duma in 1995 his electoral support had decreased considerably because most of his former voters saw through the demagogic nature of his slogans and promises.

But the fact remains that the popular appeal of ultra-nationalistic, or as one might say the ultra-patriotic, slogans of Zhirinovsky prompted other Russian political parties, including even pro-government parties such as "Our Home is Russia", to devote more attention to nationalistic themes in their campaigns to potential voters. The party that benefited most from the play on national interests and national pride of Russia in its electoral campaign has been the Communist Party of the Russian Federation (CPRF) - an heir to the CPSU. While being heirs to the old Bolsheviks, the new leadership of the CPRF is presently very close in their outlook to the classical social-democratic parties of Western Europe. The party's leader - Gennady Zyuganov - according to his pronouncements and writings is a typical social-democrat of the West European type. However, the CPRF is badly handicapped - the majority of its followers are elderly people, most of whom consider the old Communist system much better - in the sense that it was more just - than the present one with its explicit lawlessness and total neglect of the needs and the expectations of the rank and file. This is why the CPRF leadership delicately counterbalances pronouncements on private property and on the need for reforms with older, more traditional slogans, presenting the CPRF as a watchdog over the national interests of Russia and its prestige on the world arena, which appeals to its elderly voters. This is one of the CPRF's stronger points. The communists have used the nationalistic slogans of Zhirinovsky but presented them in a more moderate, reasonable way, without any extremist outbursts. Such a stance was to a certain degree responsible firstly, for their success in the December 1995 parliamentary elections, when the CPRF became the largest faction of the lower house of the Russian parliament, and secondly, for the popular appeal of Gennady Zyuganov during the presidential elections of 1996, when he lost to Boris Yeltsin by a narrow margin of 13% (officially, but by much less, if at all, according to unofficial estimates). Following these elections, the CPRF formed a wider coalition of left wing parties and movements -- the National Patriotic Alliance.

Such developments made it necessary for Yeltsin and his clique to exploit nationalistic themes more often - and in the process to camouflage their acts of yielding to the dictates of Washington and foreign financial institutions.

As for Zhirinovsky and his party, it is now clear that any nationalistic rhetoric, is mainly a disguise for their total subservience to the President and his team. It is important to remember that in domestic matters Zhirinovsky and his Liberal Democratic Party have supported President Yeltsin on all the crucial issues: the wording of the Constitution and the timing of national elections, the scope of presidential powers, the shelling of the Supreme Soviet, the federal budgets, the launching of a military operation against Chechnya, the formation of the new government, headed by Sergei Kirienko, in the Spring of 1998 etc.[27]

Nevertheless, in a serious analysis of national interests of Russia, the influence of the foreign policy line, advocated by Zhirinovsky and some other nationalist groupings, cannot be ignored.

Secondly, although conceptualists claim that the term "national interests" largely refers to the external policy goals of a state, while domestic, internal goals are covered by the notion of "public interest", the two aspects are inter-related in Russia's case. Therefore, it will be necessary to review in this study the most basic goals of Russia -- its survival as a coherent state entity and the need to resolve the present economic crisis -- and to examine them from the angle of internal and not only external politics. Russia is currently undergoing a historic transformation in which its very survival is at stake.

Conclusion

All in all, the notion of national interests evolved at the end of the 18th century under the strong influence of the American revolution. It was used to define the totality of interests of a country in the foreign policy arena, though the term also always included the most important political interests of a state relating to its security, such as defense and maintaining independence. Gradually the most important national interests were grouped into the category of vital interests.

The Soviet society that emerged at the beginning of the 20th century and was officially based on the Marxist ideology of a class struggle against the "capitalist oppressors", explicitly equated the notion of national interests with the notion of class interests, those of the working people. Hence the main aim was the destruction of all bourgeois societies in the world and the building of a global Soviet republic of workers and peasants. The transformation of the notion of national interests into the one of class interests made it easy for the essentially ethnic Russians that headed a multinational Soviet state to explain to the multitude of ethnic groups in their country that they were the guardians of the interests of Soviet society as a whole. After the end of the Second World War, when the USSR became a founding member of the United Nations, the term "national interests" was more fully introduced into the official political lexicon with the implicit understanding that in such a combination "national" means "people's".

While Joseph Stalin, with all the brutality and viciousness of his political methods, was, nonetheless, a real statesman devoted to the enhancement of Russian grandeur and might, his successors - the persons of a much smaller political caliber than Stalin - gradually began to lose track of Russia's national interests. Khrushchev and his successors shakeups of the ruling strata in Russia proper, as well as in the national republics of the Soviet Union, prevented the consolidation and entrenchment of the new ruling class, the more or less conservative layer of top bureaucrats that in all countries acts as a natural bearer and guardian of the state's national interests. The increasing illiteracy of Russia's ruling strata (which was the inevitable result of the method of selection of its members by the small group of rulers - the members of a self-perpetuating CPSU Politburo) coupled with the lies spread in official propaganda and unofficial reporting made it extremely difficult for leaders to fully understand the troubles and problems facing Russia, especially in terms of its security and foreign policy needs. They began to act more and more like pipe dreamers reluctantly correcting Russia's course only when the country ran into a dead end. That is why détente with the West, the US in particular, was launched under Leonid Brezhnev. When he and two of his elderly followers at the helm passed away, a new bunch of leaders from the younger generation of Soviet *nomenklatura* came to the top, headed by Mikhail Gorbachev. He in turn launched *perestroika* - a reform movement ostensibly designed to improve the living standards of the population, but in fact it was really a new "Manilov's project" - an attempt to make a lap so that the Soviet Union was economically and militarily on a par with the United States. However, the main efforts of Gorbachev were devoted not to reform but to staying in power and combating any challengers. Being a person of a milder character than Stalin, Gorbachev did not use the police and the Army in order to maintain power. This provided the more wily and energetic leaders of the constituent republics of the USSR, such as Yeltsin, Kravchuk, Shushkevich etc., with the opportunity to destroy the Union in order to take the power away from Gorbachev and become top bosses in their own right in the respective republics of the former Soviet Union. Once the republics proclaimed total and absolute independence, a new page of history opened up in Russia under Boris Yeltsin. He became the official inheritor of the FSU. Unfortunately, Yeltsin's struggle for power and the entrenchment of his rule, meant that Russia's national interests suffered greatly in the early years of transition. Thus the Russian émigré philosopher, Alexander Zinoviev wrote in 1993:

Our crisis could have been overcome by using the internal forces of Soviet society. But what has happened? The Soviet leadership due to phenomenal historic stupidity entered on the path to reform. Senseless reforms. Absolutely absurd reforms. It soon became clear that this policy was doomed. To save their skin the Soviet leadership betrayed our national interests. This is one of the decisive factors of the current situation.[28]

Against this backdrop, the discourse on the national interests of Russia was naturally anything but academic. But it gradually dawned on the rulers of the new Russia that Russia's national interest was a very serious issue which had been neglected for far too long and largely formulated in Washington. Clearly, the Russian leadership could not remain indifferent to the most vital interests of Russia for long, as the following chapter shows.

Notes

[1] James N. Rosenau, 'National Interest' in David L. Sills (ed.), *International Encyclopedia of the Social Sciences* (Macmillan/Free Press, USA), Vol. 11, 1968, pp. 34-40.

[2] Robert C. Johansen, *The National Interest and the Human Interest. An Analysis of U.S. Foreign Policy* (Princeton, New Jersey: Princeton University Press, 1980), pp. 20-21.

[3] Some English-speaking scholars are also not satisfied that the word "nation" is synonymous with the word "state". Thus Adam Roberts notes: "There is a confusion in the very language that not only Americans, but also others use, in describing the world. By a routine and understandable fiction, the word "nation" is regularly employed to refer to any foreign state, whether or not the peoples who inhabit it are a cohesive group with some sense of shared identity. Even the Soviet Union and Yugoslavia were sometimes called "nations". (Foreword by professor Adam Roberts to Senator Moynihan's *Pandaemonium. Ethnicity in International Politics* (Oxford, Oxford University Press, 1993), pp. xi-xii.) For an interesting discussion of the discourse concerning the Soviet usage of the word *natsiya* (nation) see *Nezavisimaya Gazeta*, 5 August 1993, p.5.

[4] W.J. Ashley cited in Charles A. Beard with the collaboration of G.H.E. Smith, *The Idea of National Interest. An Analytical Study in American Foreign Policy* (Westport, Connecticut: Greenwood Press Publishers, 1977), pp.24-25.

[5] "In comparison to other big nations" of the former Soviet Union, because some smaller nations of the USSR as a result of Stalin's "national policy" were on the verge of total physical annihilation by the "great leader and teacher", such as the Kalmyks, Kumyks, Nogais, Balkars and several others. The names of such repressed people were cut out of Soviet encyclopedias, reference books and even from literary fiction (namely the novels of Leo Tolstoy and Bestuzhev-Marlinsky), and in later Soviet editions they were simply substituted by the general name Tatars. Some small ethnic groups of the North, such as the Komi, Nentsi, Chukchi were simply dying from neglect, widespread contagious diseases like tuberculosis, industrial pollution of their habitat and the brutal destruction of their traditional ways of life. Altogether, if one adds up the numbers of people of the Soviet Union who did not die a natural death, who emigrated from the country, plus the number of children that might have been born under normal conditions but were not, the total amounts to 156 million people for the period 1918-55, that is equal to the present total population of Russia. About 80% were Soviet Slavs (Russians, Ukrainians, Belorussians). During this period every fifth person, living in Russia after the revolution, died of unnatural causes! (See Oleg Platonov. 'Russkaya tsivilizatsiya' [Russian civilization], *Russkii Vestnik*, No. 18-20, 1993.)

[6] Actually the first big split in the Russian communist leadership happened in 1918, during the debate on the ratification of humiliating Brest-Litovsk Peace Treaty with Germany. Lenin, as a died in the wool Russian nationalist (though he also was half Jewish), was ready to sacrifice anything as long as the Bolsheviks succeeded in hanging on to power even in a truncated Russian state, whereas devoted internationalists, like Trotsky, were ready to sacrifice purely Russian

interests for the sake of grander interests of a "world proletarian revolution". Lenin's point of view finally prevailed.

[7] Judging by the new tough immigration laws of the United States and France this process has already started.

[8] As Chairman of the KGB in the period 1967-82, Andropov once decided to find out just how big Russian gold reserves were and what the annual production of gold was. "Six different government departments supplied different data classified 'top secret'. The data varied from 1,000 to 10,000 tons. Nobody could coherently explain how much of it was expended annually and for what. The data from the State Bank and *Vneshekonombank* (Foreign Economy bank) were somewhat vague. The International Department of the [CPSU's] Central Committee and its Administrative Department claimed no consolidated report, staff of the Financial Commission of the Supreme Soviet were very frightened, and the Ministry of Finance, citing its own sources, declared that Russian gold stock totalled 2,100 tons and it did not blush. It became clear that the rest could be discovered only with the help of a [police] search" (Igor Bunich, *Zoloto Partii. Istoricheskaya Khronika* [Party's Gold. Historic Chronicle] (St.Petersburg: "Shans", 1992), p.223).

[9] Stephen Sestanovich (ed.), *Rethinking Russia's National Interests* (Washington, D.C.: Center for Strategic and International Studies, 1994), p.24.

[10] "The national idea of Tsarist Russia, for example, was imperial and monarchist... Those conceptions were abandoned, of course, after the Bolshevik revolution. The primary elements of the new national idea became world revolution, social utopia and the welfare state", asserts Stankevich contradicting his belief that national interests were predetermined by objective factors (Stephen Sestanovich (ed.), *Rethinking*), p.24. But he is absolutely wrong in this assertion. "World revolution" was a new term for the continuation of 400 years' long imperial expansion, "social utopia" of working class-ruled state was simply a cover for the totalitarian (or monarchist) rule of the Politburo, and "the welfare state" (a term actually never used officially in the Soviet Union, though in a way it was a welfare state) was a continuation of a traditional paternalistic Oriental society: the state ensuring minimal sustenance for all its subjects, who were treated like slaves (serfs).

[11] Boris Yeltsin, *Zapiski prezidenta* [President's Notes] (Moscow: "Ogonyok", 1994), p.34.

[12] Yuri Burtin and Grigori Vodolazov, 'Vlast otorvannaya. Komu i chemu sluzhit ona v Rossii?' [A power cut off. To whom and to what is it serving in Russia?], *Novoye Russkoye Slovo*, 17 June 1994, p.12. The authors call the new emerging system a "bastardly pseudo-capitalism" or a "nomenklatura capitalism".

[13] *Resolutions and Decisions of the Communist Party of the Soviet Union*, Vol.4. *The Khrushchev years 1953-1964* (Toronto and Buffalo: University of Toronto Press, 1974), p.53.

[14] The very term *blizhneye zarubezhye* is a euphemism specially invented to refer to the non-Russian territory of the former USSR.

[15] By 1994 the floor space in Moscow occupied by various bureaucratic offices and institutions of the Russian government increased ten times (!) in comparison with the last days of the Soviet Union, despite the demise of the CPSU with its tremendous Moscow apparatus and the closing down of all the Union ministries and other departments.

[16] The difference between a Russian movement eastward and Americans moving west in their new country lies in the fact that American settlers for a long time considered the territory west of the Atlantic shoreline a "no man's land", while Russians, holding the same principle when moving east in the northern part of Russia, in the south and south-east, incorporated into the Russian state some old civilizations with their own statehood and cultures.

[17] Ted Robert Gurr, *Minorities at Risk. A Global View of Ethnopolitical Conflicts* (Washington, D.C.: United States Institute of Peace Press, 1993), p.210. The figures, taken from the 1989 all-Union census are rounded up.

[18] *Narodnoe Khozyastvo RSFSR v 1990 godu. Statisticheskii Ezhegodnik* [National Economy of the RSFSR in 1990. Statistical Abstract] (Moscow: Republican Informational and Publishing House, 1991), pp. 77-93. The proportions of the indigenous ethnic population to total population in the most populous national republics of the Russian Federation are as follows: Chechen Republic (Chechnya) - 80%, Chuvash Republic - 67%, Tuva - 63%, North Ossetiya - 52%, Tatarstan - 48%, Kalmykia-Khalmg Tangch - 44%, Mari El - 43%, Yakut-Sakha - 33%, Mordovia - 32%, Buryatia - 32%, Udmurtia - 31%, Komi - 23%, Bashkortostan - 23%, Khakassia - 11%, Karelia - 10%.

[19] It is worth recalling what Boris Yeltsin said way back in 1990, when Mikhail Gorbachev introduced the institution of the President of the USSR and made himself the President with powers that were not as sweeping as those of the current President of Russia. Speaking at the session of the Congress of People's Deputies, Yeltsin declared: "The President of the country is being given unlimited authority. Already today the proposed scope of presidential powers has no analogy in Soviet history. Neither Stalin, nor Brezhnev had such a volume of legally authorized power... Actually the Center strives to secure constitutionally an all-out authoritarian regime that would lead in the final analysis to the constitutional legalization of any tyranny" (Quoted in *Izvestia*, 20 December 1990, p.4).

[20] The author will use the terms "Russia" and "Rossiya" and corresponding adjectives interchangeably.

[21] "The 'answers' that Russia is searching for will be judged - both at home and abroad - less by their intellectual coherence than by their political sustainability", according to the Sovietologist Stephen Sestanovich: "In fact, policies that strike a workable balance may emerge even if a clear set of principles does not. The fact

that Russian foreign policy debate became slightly less rancorous in 1993 than in 1992 is perhaps a sign that this balance is already being struck" (Stephen Sestanovich (ed.), *Rethinking*, p. xi). In 1997 Dr. Sestanovich was made Ambassador at Large and appointed a Special Advisor to the US Secretary of State on the Newly Independent States.

[22] "[A] new foreign policy leadership elite has not yet emerged in Russia....The political and administrative structures of foreign policy are in flux, as are Russia's economic, social and ideological foundations. The circle of the officials able to affect Foreign ministry positions is very small and isolated, while the number of rival participants in actual foreign policy practice is expanding" (Alexei Arbatov, Russia's Foreign Policy Alternatives, *International Security*, Fall 1993, p.7).

[23] Discussing the options open to Boris Yeltsin after he came out as a winner in a confrontation with the State Committee for the State of Emergency (SCSE) which in August 1991 organized the Moscow "putsch", Valeriya Novodvorskaya, the leader of the liberal Democratic Union of Russia, writes in her memoirs: "Were I in his seat... I would summon the troops of NATO and of the United States under the pretext of fighting the SCSE and under their cover would carry out reforms, as Americans did in Japan and Germany in 1945, with decommunization, desocialization and desovietization" (Valeriya Novodvorskaya, *Po tu storonu otchayaniya* [Beyond despair] (Moscow: "Novosti", 1993), p.246).

[24] The author believes that Zhirinovsky picked up the idea about Alaska from a popular humorous Russian song of the 1990s with a lyric that went like this: "Stop playing the fool, America. We aren't going to hurt you a speck. Just return to us dear Alasochka. Yes, do give our own land back!" That was one of the numerous mocking songs composed by anonymous bards to compensate for a national feeling of total frustration and humiliation.

[25] There are, for instance, 60 national sub-groups on the territory of the Federation with a combined population of just 450,000.

[26] Russian parliamentarians decided to establish the new Duma (elected in accordance with the new Constitution of Russia) as a successor to the four Dumas that functioned under the Tsarist regime between 1905-17, after the Tsar issued his Manifesto of 30 October 1905 under the pressure of the unfinished revolution of 1905. The document guaranteed civil liberties to Russians and established a Duma with the true legislative function of passing or rejecting all proposed laws. Wishing to stress the continuity of a democratic process that was started in 1905, but interrupted by Bolshevik rule, the parliamentarians named the first post-Communist Duma, the 5th Duma. As a transitional institution it functioned only for two years. The next one, elected in 1995 for the full term of 4 years, is the 6th Duma. It consists of 450 deputies.

[27] "To sum up, *zhirinovtsy* (the Zhirinovsky crowd-H.T.) turned out to be the most tame and most loyal to the President's party", according to Liliya Shevtsova, a well-known Russian political scientist (*Izvestia*, 22 December 1995, p.3).

[28] A.A.Zinoviev, *Post-kommunisticheskaya Rossiya* [Post-Communist Russia] (Moscow: "Respublika", 1996), p.74.

Chapter Two

The "Tree" of National Interests

At the time of writing, there is no official document, dealing specifically with the national interests of Russia. There are, however, several official documents, pertaining to national interests of the new Russia. The first is entitled *Basic Provisions of the Russian Federation Foreign Policy Concept* which was approved by the Russian Security Council and confirmed by President Yeltsin at the end of April 1993.[1] A second document is *The Conception for the Foreign Policy of* the *Russian Federation*, which might be considered a Russian Foreign Ministry input into the document adopted by the Security Council.[2] In addition, there are two other laws of the Russian Federation - *On Security*[3] and *On Defense*[4] which have a bearing on the subject of this study. For instance, the law *On Security* contains the official definition of the notion of "vital interests" which constitute "the sum total of necessities, the fulfillment of which reliably secures the existence of and the opportunities for a progressive development of an individual person, of the society and of the state". In 1996, the President sent the Federal Assembly a message on national security of Russia, which touched upon some basic Russian national interests.[5] A new Russian military doctrine supposedly appeared in 1993.[6] There are two more documents relevant to this study: *Strategic course of Russia towards the states-members of the Commonwealth of Independent States*[7] and the *Strategy of Economic Security*.[8] On 7 May 1997, the Security council of the Russian Federation, presided over by President Yeltsin, approved the *Concept of National Security of the Russian Federation*. Amazingly, the moment it was approved it was sent back to its authors for a "thorough revision" (!). The presidential press office explained such an unusual move in terms of the impact on Russia of the signing of the Founding Act between Russia and NATO and a Treaty between Russia and Ukraine.[9]

Finally, on 17 December 1997 the President signed the *Concept of National Security* which was more than six years in the making.

The *Concept* proceeds from the assumption that the current situation in the international arena is the increasing trend towards a multipolar world. At the same time in the present conditions there appears to be a growing move by a number of countries to undercut the positions of Russia in the international arena in the political, economic and military spheres. The key national interests of Russia, apart from those of the preservation of sovereignty and national integrity, lie in the economic sphere. At the same time the *Concept* recognizes that the existing military structure of Russia is onerous. It needs to be reformed in the process of a military build up that ought to take into consideration the transformation in the balance of forces in the world. However, it is admitted that "the threat of a large-scale aggression against Russia in the observable future is practically non-existent". The main threats to its national security stem from the crisis in Russia's economy and its social services, the fact that its national economy is becoming more and more dependent on exports of fuel and raw materials and on imports of manufactured goods and agricultural produce, the lack of large-scale investments into the economy, the diminishing intellectual and productive potential of Russia, the centrifugal trends of the subjects of the Federation, as expressed in ethnic separatism, as well as from the increasing meddling of foreign states and organizations in the internal affairs of Russia. The last trend is underscored by the increasing penetration into Russia of foreign intelligence services.

The *Concept* says:

Russia does not intend to enter into a confrontation with any state or an alliance of states, and it does not nurture any hegemonic or expansionist aims. As an influential Eurasian power it will sustain relations of partnership with all the interested countries of the world community.

At the same time, in a sort of resurrection of its former superpower image, the authors of the *Concept* assert that

the interests of ensuring the national security of Russia, as well as the evolution of geopolitical situation in the world, predetermine the necessity for Russia, under appropriate conditions, to sustain its military presence in certain strategically important regions of the world.

The document says that in its military policy Russia will realize "the principle of realistic deterrence, based on the determination to adequately use the existing military might to avert aggression". And, finally, the *Concept* states:

Russia retains the right to use all the forces and means at its disposal, including nuclear weapons, if as a result of an armed aggression a threat to the very existence of the Russian Federation as an independent, sovereign state emerges.[10]

Other important documents, relating to the subject in question, include the annual State of the Nation messages of President Yeltsin to the Russian parliament - the Federal Assembly.[11] There are also some unofficial studies and discussions of national interests by various Russian think tanks, individual scholars and journalists published over the past six years. All those materials provide the basis upon which an assessment can be made of national interests of Russia and her priorities from the point of view of the current Russian leadership. Using all those documents and studies, it is possible to compose a chart of Russian national interests, which will closely match any classified documents.

The gamut of national interests of any country can be imagined schematically as a tree, whose roots and the trunk are its most basic vital interests, and the large and smaller branches of the crown are other important and less important interests. Verbally Russia's national interests from the roots of such a tree upward (that is in diminishing priority) can be presented in the following order. The main aim is to:

- ensure survival of Russia as a consolidated society.
- strengthen national security through political, diplomatic, military, arms control measures and through restoring the health of the armed forces and improving their technical base.
- reverse Russia's economic decline.[12]
- uphold the leading role of Russia in the Commonwealth of Independent States (CIS) and to consolidate the CIS to the extent possible under the patronage of Russia.
- create a peaceful international environment, and not to make enemies, to cooperate with everybody in the interests of peace and economic development of Russia, without any ideological or other prejudice, while at the same time not allowing infringements of the basic interests of Russia.

- significantly improve relations with nearby countries and finally to
- continue friendly relations with the United States, developing them into a partnership, while resisting as far as possible any American encroachments into "purely Russian matters", or US attempts to pressure Russia and/or involve it in supporting policies that run contrary to the national interests of Russia.

In addition, Russian interests in other regions of the globe are as follows:

In Europe:

- Not to permit a new ideological, psychological, economic and military borderline to be established between the two parts of Europe along the Western and South-Western borders of the Russian Federation.
- To take an active part in pan-European cooperation and integration.
- To actively support, strengthen and enhance the role of the Organization for Security and Cooperation in Europe (OSCE).
- To restore some degree of economic and political influence in the former communist belt of East European states (including the Baltics). To continue active engagement with Germany and France.

In Asia to:

- strengthen friendly relations with China, to expand economic cooperation, while taking steps to prevent peaceful Chinese expansion into the Russian Far East.
- improve relations with Japan, to more deeply involve it in joint ventures and investments in the Far East and Siberia.
- continue cooperation with the Republic of Korea, while maintaining friendly relations with North Korea (Democratic People's Republic of Korea).
- sustain close relations with India, including military cooperation.
- widen constructive relations with the ASEAN countries.
- increase economic cooperation with the countries of the Asia-Pacific.
- develop in the region arms markets for Russian military hardware.

In the Middle East to:

- gradually restore FSU positions of influence.

- regain traditional arms markets and to obtain some help (credits, investments) for the ailing Russian economy.
- contribute to the West's efforts to establish secure, lasting peace in the region.

And finally,

In the rest of the world:

While abandoning the drive for messianic expansionism and ideological approach, the goal is to:

- try to find new avenues for spreading influence, expand mutually beneficial commercial relations, open markets for military hardware and utilize other yet unknown opportunities.
- participate actively, wherever possible, in international and regional organizations of states, devote greater attention to economic, political and military cooperation, the protection of human rights, ecology etc.
- use Russia's permanent membership in the UN Security Council as a means of promoting its national interests.

Although the aforementioned goals are positioned hierarchically, it is clear that despite their different weighting, the pursuit of all of them cannot but proceed simultaneously, albeit with different levels of vigor given the uneven allocation of efforts and resources.

Some of these goals/interests are complementary to one another (such as the task of upholding Russian integrity and enhancing its security), whereas others might seem to be at odds with one another. But life itself requires daily choices of how best to dispose of one's own finite physical and mental resources and provide the financial means necessary to improve health and living conditions.

A reader might rightfully ask why the defense and expansion of individual human rights, consolidating democracy, establishing a private sector and market economy are not included in the above list? Surely the Russian government sees these as positive national goals? Formally it does.

In the document of the Russian Ministry of Foreign Affairs regarding policy goals it is stated that the basic priorities of Russian foreign policy include:

- the defense of *rights, freedoms, dignity and well being* of Rossiyans; and

- the insurance of favorable external conditions for the advancement of *democratic reforms* in the direction of formation of a civil society (emphasis in the original - H.T.).[13]

The problem, however, is that in analyzing the national goals of any country in *Realpolitik* terms, it is necessary to distinguish real interests from declared ones.

During the seven years of Gorbachev's *perestroika*, there was no shortage of lip service about the rights and needs of the people. At least one third of the nine volumes of Gorbachev's collected speeches and articles consists of endless highfalutin pronouncements on that score. Allegedly *perestroika* was started mainly for the purpose of improving the living conditions of Russians and enhancing rights of the individual. Thus far there are no published volumes of Boris Yeltsin's articles and speeches, but a similar lip service to people's rights and doing away with special privileges of the ruling elite, also heavily permeates them.

But what is the real situation so far? As things stand today, despite the release from jails of the majority of political prisoners (including the amnesty granted by the Russian Duma to the "putschists" of August 1991 and rioters of October 1993), the introduction of limited freedoms for the mass media, observance by the government of the rights of those of Jewish nationality to emigrate, granted earlier during the Brezhnev era, and the whole chapter of the new Russian Constitution devoted to rights and freedoms of a citizen, the situation with regard to human rights in Russia is not much better today than at any time during the post-Stalin period. For the majority of the Russian population, these rights have almost reached zero under the onslaught of an all-powerful mafia, totally corrupt government and municipal bureaucracy, a disoriented and also corrupted militia (police), an inefficient judicial system, suffocated by the lack of finance and the avalanche of contradictory laws and decrees that often cancel each another out, and finally by the wholesale liquidation of free of charge or cheap state legal and other aid, at a time when more than half of the population exists below the poverty line.

The basic human right, proclaimed in the Russian Constitution, namely to a decent living, is actually unavailable to the great majority of the working people of "the reconstructed democratic Russia". Wages and salaries duly earned, are not paid. Payments are being delayed for many months and the Russian people actually work like serfs, begging the remuneration due them like alms. And it happens in a situation when multiplying thieves, embezzlers and other crooks in senior government positions and in totally criminalized financial businesses, live like oriental billionaires, literally swimming in gold.[14] According to Vladimir Maximov, a prominent former Russian dissident:

Let the waterfall of abuse and accusations once again engulf my greying head, but I, a determined and consistent anticommunist, dare to say that the regime that triumphed nowadays in Russia is worse, more unscrupulous and more hopeless than the previous one, first of all because it offers the society a game without rules, an existence outside of the law, and secondly represents the reign of criminal oligarchy.[15]

But does not the Russian government seek to restore law and order, to improve living conditions, and in the process to enhance basic human rights? Theoretically it does,[16] but, unfortunately, while order (which in Russia is traditionally understood as a police order) is definitely on its agenda, law and the upholding of declared human rights are not, as exemplified by many acts of sheer arbitrariness on the part of the powers that be, protected. There is still a reign of "revolutionary law" when a person can be incarcerated, beaten or forcibly deported without any judicial sanction. The very pounding of Russia's parliament building (with deputies inside the building) on 4 October 1993 with heavy tank gun fire, was evidence of such a "law" in action. In this case one cannot help recalling that in Petrograd in 1917, the Bolsheviks used only one shot from the cruiser *Aurora*'s cannon (and even that was reportedly a blank one) to disband Kerensky's Provisional government. The brutal deportation from Moscow after 4 October 1993 of all persons who did not have Moscow's *propiska* (resident's permit), including refugees from the killing fields in the CIS, is another example of the "revolutionary law" in action. The unleashing in December 1994 by the Russian President, without any parliamentary sanction, of a brutal war against Russia's own province of Chechnya, a war that took the lives of almost 100,000 Russian citizens, is the most vivid unforgettable example of the total lawlessness, arbitrariness and ruthlessness of Russia's leadership.

At last, even Yeltsin has finally acknowledged that the orgy of anarchy and corruption in the higher echelons of power undermines his own position as a paramount leader of "democratic Russia" . During an 8 month period of enforced absence from the job (because of a heart ailment and later a bypass operation on the heart and a recovery.), Yeltsin discovered, in his own words, that the government "appeared to be unable to function without a presidential peremptory shout".[17] He finally understood the need to reverse such a course of action in order for the state and himself to survive. This is why, as if regaining consciousness after a lethargic slumber, Yeltsin in his fourth State of the nation address on 6 March 1997 actually repeated a thousand years old observation taken from the first written chronicle of Russia: "Our land is great and plentiful, but there is no order in it".[18]

Whatever long-term noble aspirations the Russian President and the Russian government might have, human rights as they are understood in the West *are not* on the agenda of the present authorities of Russia despite the mellowing of the regime as compared to the Soviet one. Money ensures human rights for big tycoons and speculators,[19] while high government posts ensure human rights for the top echelon of bureaucracy. This is considered sufficient for the time being by the powers that be, who are content on maintaining power, whatever the means and methods used, instead of upholding law and order and justice for all. The strengthening of order, promised by the President, is unlikely to affect human rights for the average Russian.

Hence anyone embarking upon a serious study of Russian national interests, as understood and pursued by its ruling establishment, cannot include "enhancing human rights" on the agenda of the present Russian leaders. More than that, in a situation where the central Russian authorities tend to use indiscriminate military force against national separatists, devoting too much time to human rights might even be seen as counterproductive. As a result, all the sermons regarding human rights emanating from Washington every time the political temperature in Russia starts rising, are as a rule ignored by those to whom they are addressed.

The same can be said about the notion of democracy. The demise of the CPSU, the appearance in Russia of a multitude of political parties, movements and associations introduced quasi-democracy into Russia. "Quasi" because genuine democracy is only possible in the situation of real economic pluralism, economic independence of an individual and a rule of law, unmarred by "his excellency's" whims, whoever that "excellency" might be. The upholding of democracy also requires a certain degree of general well-being, of culture or tradition for its sustained implementation. Hopefully the process of privatization might lead some day to the real, not just facile, democratization of Russia.

But again the goal of democracy in its Western forms is not on the agenda of national interests of Russia, as composed or perceived by the establishment, in spite of all that is said to please the public and the West. The Russian government's stance on the matter of democracy is best illustrated by such an imagined discourse, which summarizes the prevailing arguments. It goes as follows: "Well, we are not averse to democracy, as shown by the newly adopted Russian Constitution and the multiparty elections to the Federal Assembly in 1993 and in 1995. But we have not yet collected our thoughts on the particular socio-economic system that will finally emerge in Russia. However, there will definitely not be a return to communist totalitarianism. But whether Russia will adopt ways and forms similar to those of the United States or some other democratic country of the West, or introduce other ways and practices of governance and of communication with the population, historically more congenial to Russia, will be determined by future trends in Russian natural societal evolution. So we shall not hurry, we shall experiment, having implemented for starters some basic norms of a state based on government legitimacy given by voters".

When talking about "implanting" democracy in Russia, Western scholars and politicians sometimes treat Russia almost in the same way as it was treated by Communists in their experiments with the country and its people. They almost say: "All right, now the communist phase is over, a new page in the history of Russia will be opened by quickly introducing democracy, which ought to be the prime goal of any reforming society". In this approach they forget that though Russia was under the spell of communism for 70 plus years, Russian civilization is one thousand years old. It is a unique civilization with its own culture, mores and habits, a country which by its historic development, traditions, even by its climate, if you will, is more inclined to communal than to the individualistic approach in its economic and societal pursuits. This is why Russia is a multinational country in which the mixture of people and races is to a certain extent organic, not artificial, as is now the case in the United States or Great Britain. And if it is a parent country, supposedly exploiting the outer regions of the empire, then in the case of Russia this "exploitation" was of a rather peculiar nature, in so far as the purely Russian "core center" impoverished itself, in the process of "exploitation", by giving a great deal to non-Russians in the outer regions. And even now Russia continues to command loyalties of many people of the FSU republics (if not the loyalties of some of their present rulers) because it is still liberally giving rather than taking from them. One might consider a "socialist system" in Russia an aberration, the one aimed at saving the Russian empire by tougher methods of rule and discipline than those used by the Tsarist regime. Nonetheless, this "aberrant regime", with all its cruelty, to a great extent contributed to the process of leveling up non-Russian ethnic territories' industrial and educational development in the FSU with those of European Russia.

As mentioned earlier, despite all the sufferings that befell a number of people in the Union, the CIS is still a living organism and the artificial carving of the Union into several separate ethnic parts, against the expressed wish of the majority of the Soviet Union's population, did not contribute to the health either of the Russian state or of most other national republics. Perhaps this is why the simplistic thesis that Russia should borrow ways and forms of government developed in the West does not ring bells for the people of Russia.

Discussing the subject of transition to democracy, Alexander Solzhenitsyn stated more than 20 years ago:

If Russia for centuries was used to living under autocratic systems and suffered total collapse under the democratic system which lasted eight months in 1917, perhaps - I am only asking, not making an assertion - perhaps we should recognize that the evolution of our country from one form of authoritarianism to another would be the most natural, the smoothest, the least painful path of development for it to follow? It may be objected that neither the path ahead, nor still less the new system at the end of it, can be seen. But for that matter we have never been shown any realistic path of transition from our present system to a democratic republic of the Western type. And the first-mentioned transition seems more feasible in that it requires a smaller expenditure of energy by the people.[20]

Present arrangements in Russia confirm Solzhenitsyn's claim. For instance, Mikhail Smondyrev from the physicists' town of Dubna writes:

Nobody, save our theoreticians, considers the civilization, built in the West, perfect... Basic tasks of a bourgeois revolution in Russia seem to be almost accomplished: the redistribution of property is actively pursued (if it is not already ending), soon the process will encompass the land itself. And that's the end of it. The rich will get richer, and at a qualitatively new level at that, and the impoverished will remain such. The Latin American path is well known, and it seems to suit our financial elite well, which means politicians of the new wave as well. It follows that nobody will need democracy, it already stands in the way. It can be suffered only within a severely limited framework, the one that existed even under a communist government: to the extent that the interests of the powers that be were not infringed upon.[21]

The boasting of certain Americans that Russian legislators spent a lot of time in the Library of Congress refining the latest Russian Constitution is born out of ignorance and may also be evidence of a hard-currency greed of those "founding fathers of the new Russia" (pardon the expression), because any major library in Moscow contains mountains of original legal materials and constitutional projects more organic to Russia than any imported ideas.[22]

In the final analysis the Russian Constitution of 1993 is not very democratic.

To what extent should interests, such as building a free market and other institutions of free enterprise system, figure among the national interests of Russia? One can say that such institutions are figuring now not so much as goals per se, but as a means of achieving an efficiently operating economy.

Furthermore, it is clear to many that no democratic society can be based exclusively on state-owned property, because such an arrangement de facto means that all the property belongs to a ruling clique which inevitably begins to bend policies in order to advance their own private goals at the expense of the larger interests of a society as a whole, as was the case under Soviet socialism. At the same time, it is wrong to assert that the Russian establishment as a whole will adopt the goal of a free market come what may.

The national interests of Russia as enumerated above are presumed to be the interests that the current Russian establishment is guided by. They inevitably differ from some abstract formulation of national interests of Rossiya that might, for instance, be conceived by a group of idealistic Russian intellectuals, on the one hand, or compiled for Russia by Washington or a group of Western political scientists with the best of intentions, on the other. I intentionally made the set of national interests, described above, very pragmatic. It does not include the goals of establishing a flowering democracy and free-enterprise economy, despite a great deal of public discussion on these matters. The Russian ruling class, a leftover from the old Soviet one, has not fully accepted the "classic" democratic ways and institutions. Even whilst attempting to practice the basics of democracy, including the division of state powers, it constantly goes astray.

In the final analysis the conflict between Yeltsin and the Russian Supreme Soviet in 1992-93 was not a dispute between some "newborn democrats" of the presidential camp, on the one hand, and a coalition of "stalwart *apparatchiks*", "unreformed communists" and "fascists", on the other. A more objective analysis would show that the Russian Supreme Soviet (a permanently working body of a larger Congress of People's Deputies, elected in 1989) with all its flaws, did a lot of good work in building the legal foundations for a new society, and sometimes was even too lenient to the government in not curbing some of the latter's very rash acts. Both "camps" had in their ranks "reformed communists", as well as conservative stalwarts and rabid nationalists. The conflict intensified because neither of the two branches of power was happy just staying within its own niche defined by the law. Each branch wanted absolute power in running Russia. Such a tendency was, however, most pronounced on the president's side.[23] The third -- judicial -- branch was unable to sustain an independent position of its own (whatever its formal legal status) and hence leaned to one side or the other. This tendency persists in the new Constitutional arrangement as well, because Russia will require years before it acquires (if ever) the customs and habits indispensable for democratic governance and the real division of powers. It is not for nothing that in all the republics of the CIS the executive branch of the government absolutely dominates over the legislative. The task was much easier to perform for the founding fathers of the United States - many of them were aristocrats by upbringing or outstanding intellectuals in a country not burdened by hundreds of years of feudal relationships. It is much more difficult for genuine first or second generation proletarians, who suddenly made up the Russian top elite, to practice democracy.

As the Russian philosopher Dmitry Galkovsky remarked:

The system, that has formed itself now on the territory of Russia, is not interested in the existence of Marxism, the latter being an outmoded and non-functioning myth. However, the whole system is based on Marxism in a wider sense of the word, on the idea of material gain, cynicism, convenient self-deception. That is why Marxist scholars, who appeared totally bankrupt, feel like fish in the water in the CIS.[24]

And he is exactly right. Whilst rejecting Marxism, the Russian elite continues to think in Marxist terms and to reason according to basic Marxist premises. This approach has made its mark on the definition of policy goals, including national interest.

Of course, there has never been a lack of sweeping rhetoric and lofty metaphors emanating from Russian ruling elites (as it happens elsewhere) indicating how great their policies and how noble their goals are. Thus it was once stated that Russia

is strong enough to defend for her territorial integrity and her interests. Concentrating her efforts on building up peaceful industries for meeting the needs of her own population, keeping aloof from armed interference with the affairs of foreign nations, [it] will seek a peaceful settlement of all conflicts which may arise between her and her neighbors. She will base her policy exclusively on her own interests, which correspond with the interests of peace both in the East and in Europe. But she will know how to defend her vital rights. Those who think that she will sacrifice them because she is afraid of a conflict are just as wrong as those who believe that she will become a tool of foreign interests.

However, this is not President Yeltsin or even Gorbachev speaking. This quotation is taken from a 1932 article by Karl Radek, the editor of *Izvestia*, and a very influential member of Stalin's entourage up to the time of his arrest in 1937.[25] There are enough similar pronouncements to fill a multi-volume publication. But to judge national interests by such pronouncements is as productive a pastime as exorcising ghosts.

One should also take into account that, although national interests are influenced by the basic values and goals of the whole nation, or at least by the goals of the state, the sweep of corruption at senior levels is so ingrained that the pursuit of even the most vital state goals is contaminated or distorted to a great extent by considerations of personal gain, political infighting or the other goals of the ruling group or individuals.[26]

As the Soviet ruling clique has abandoned its earlier desire to create a paradise on earth in the USSR by 1980 (as the CPSU promised in its Third Party Program, adopted in October 1961), any goals pursued today ought to be in the national interests of Russia, not the personal desires of Yeltsin or Lebed. However, this will only be possible in a free and democratic society. But can one create such a society out of a state where the Army disperses parliament with artillery bombardment, where the government troops kill thousands of Russia's own peaceful citizens in order to punish some crazy local boss for misbehavior, where the economy is still largely state (that is government)-owned and where it is the President, who is the sole ultimate judge of a legal status of contending political forces? In other words, one cannot build a democratic society with totalitarian methods, but, on the other hand, in order to shed totalitarianism strong-armed tactics are necessary because all other methods are bound to fail in the face of resistance from well-entrenched and well-equipped forces of totalitarianism. As the Americans would say, Russia is in a "Catch 22".

On no issue is such a dilemma more pronounced than on the first priority of the Russian Federation, namely to ensure the survival of the country as a united society, not a series of separate fiefdoms.

Preserving a unified state

Any true *Rossiyanin*, that is a citizen of Rossiya at large, not just an ethnic Russian, when he thinks about the goals of the new Russia, feels that keeping Russia together is the most vital interest of all the interests of the Russian Federation.

From the point of view of the enlightened sector of the ruling establishment and, especially, from the point of view of the masses, this task is a priority number one.

Everybody in Russia and abroad has witnessed for some time how much Russian politicians vigorously oppose giving back to Japan several small barren islands situated at Japan's northern tip, the islands that never belonged to Russia in the first place. But any public anxiety about the fate of these islands is just a drop in the ocean compared to the difficulties facing Russia itself: the prospect of its disintegration as a cohesive entity under the onslaught of local nationalism and separatism.

"The main threats to security happen to be presently inside Russia, not abroad", according to Marshal Yevgeny Shaposhnikov, who at one time was secretary of the Security Council of Russia.[27]

One can state without hesitation: no top leader of Russia will be able to keep his job for any length of time, if he wavers on the question of unity of the country. This question, the very existence of a great nation with more than 1000 years history, is very important.

In a document entitled *Strategy for Rossiya*, prepared by the Council on Foreign and Defense Policy of Russia (hereafter CFDP), a non-government organization, representing Moscow's intellectual elite (as well as some foreign experts), the authors categorically state:

No strategy of national security, long-term foreign and defense policies can be implemented until one issue is decided: whether Rossiya preserves its territorial integrity and maintains itself as a state. The main priority of the state policy at the present stage should be prevention of disintegration of Rossiya, both with the help of reasonable preventive compromises dealing with the distribution of authority between the central and local organs of power and with the help of tough prosecution within the framework of the law of any officials, political and public organizations, whose activities endanger the territorial integrity of Rossiya. This policy ought to be made public /*glasnoi*/.[28]

This document, published in August 1992, called for an end to the chaotic policy of separate understandings of the Center with local authorities pushing the country towards disintegration. But, unfortunately, that is exactly the case that still persists.

There are some politicians in Russia, at lower levels of government, who without hesitation would disband the great country for the sole sake of clinging on to power. Actually the centrifugal forces that brought the Soviet Union to an end are still working in post-communist Russia. However, the basic difference is that the Soviet Union was formally a contractual affiliation of 15 large ethnic groups, albeit not altogether a voluntary one, while the Russian Federation is basically a homogeneous society, where more than four fifths of its 150 million population are ethnic Russians with only a sprinkling of a few consolidated non-Russian ethnic groupings. In addition, many millions of people of different nationalities are spread throughout Russia via horizontal mobility and intermarriages. Of the consolidated ethnic groups, only three indigenous ethnic groups exceed one million people each. Nevertheless, in a situation of political disorder and economic chaos in Russia, and the upsurge in nationalism and regional separatism, a clear and present danger of Russia's splitting into dozens of "independent" entities undoubtedly exists.

The "man of the millennia", Mikhail Gorbachev, himself a politician, who was absolutely in the dark with regard to a national question in the Union in all its complexity and ramifications, made a substantial contribution to the resurgent nationalism of the leaders of the national republics of the USSR. Gorbachev first tried to whip up Russian nationalism in the non-Russian republics in order to prevent their drive for independence. When Gorbachev realized he was losing to Yeltsin, he began encouraging nationalism among non-Russians within the Russian Federation. His tactic was to elevate all small national entities within Russia, that used to exist as autonomous republics and districts, to the status of the constituent republics of the Soviet Union. In this way, Gorbachev tried to atomize Russia and thus block Yeltsin's drive for Russia's sovereignty. Gorbachev failed in this undertaking as well, but he succeeded in increasing the ambitions of local communist bosses within Russia's autonomous republics and national regions to such an extent that they wanted independence and sovereignty for the localities they ruled.

The first small republic within Russia to heed Gorbachev's prompt was the Chechen-Ingush autonomous republic in Northern Caucasus, which declared independence from Russia in November 1991, while the Soviet Union still existed. A half-hearted attempt by the Russian government to restore order in the rebellious region by sending in 650 troops ended in humiliation for Yeltsin. The Russian parliament voted against the use of force and Russian forces were surrounded in the region and sent home.

This evident acceptance by Moscow of a *fait accompli*, engineered by one of its smaller national republics, created a dangerous precedent. After Russia became independent, many small Caucasian ethnic groups, which created a militant Confederation of the People of Caucasus, as well as the larger ethnic groups in the heartland of Russia, started the move to wrestle more authority from Moscow by claiming sovereignty and independence.

The leader of such a movement became Tatarstan, a former autonomous republic inside Russia with a population of 3.7 million people, 43% of whom were ethnic Russians. Tatarstan's national democrats, headed by the old *nomenklatura*, managed to convene in the capital city of Kazan in February 1992 the All-Tatar *Kurultai* (Congress) purported to represent all the 7 million Tatars who lived in Russia and other republics of FSU (700,000 in Moscow and its region alone). The *Kurultai* elected the *Milli Majlis* as a parliament for all the 7 million of Tatars and this *Majlis* (National Assembly) had to work in tandem with Tatarstan's Supreme Soviet, representing just the population of the Tatarstan republic. As a result, Russian members of the Tatarstan's Supreme Soviet accused the leadership of Tatarstan of "mild apartheid". In March 1992, undeterred by warnings from Moscow of the illegal nature of their activity, the Tatars, voting in a referendum, approved "Tatarstan as a sovereign state, a subject of international law" and advocated that Tatarstan "build its relations with

Russia on the basis of equality".[29]   Tatarstan, as well as the Chechen Republic (Chechnya),[30] later on 31 March 1992, refused to join the other 18 ethnic republics, 10 national regions, 57 territories, regions and two capital cities (Moscow and St. Petersburg) of Russia, in signing the Federal Treaty, establishing new relationships between Russia and its subdivisions, although the Treaty granted to other ethnic republics of Russia essentially the same rights that Tatarstan had appropriated, so to say, on its own.[31]

The main aim of the Treaty was to uphold Russia's statehood and cohesion on the basis of a federal arrangement. The Treaty, which was appended to the published text of the new Constitution of Russia, delineated federal and republican jurisdiction giving the republics much greater powers than those enjoyed by individual states of the United States. For example, Article III of the Federal Treaty stipulated:

The republics within the Rossiiskaya Federation are independent participants in international and foreign-economic relations, agreements with other republics, territories, provinces, autonomous provinces and autonomous districts of the Rossiiskaya Federation in so far as it does not contradict the Constitution and the laws of the Rossiiskaya Federation and the present Treaty.[32]

All this was happening at a time when the power of the Center was weakening on a daily basis due to political infighting in Moscow. In their fight against one another for ultimate authority -- the President and the Supreme Soviet -- were conniving with local provincial and republican authorities, who were also struggling for greater power. In March 1993 Yeltsin met provincial potentates in Moscow, whose support he needed on the eve of the 9th Congress of People's Deputies, and restored the jobs of two governors of Siberian provinces, who had earlier been dismissed for brazen insubordination.   Meanwhile, the Supreme Soviet delegated more and more authority to local Soviets (councils) in an attempt to reduce executive power.

Against this backdrop, the republics managed to gain huge concessions from Moscow, especially as far as federal taxes were concerned. Chechnya also appeared to get away with its declared independence. All the republics managed to procure for themselves special concessions in the new Constitution, including recognition by Moscow of each republics' sovereignty. As a result, they no longer considered themselves bound by any of Moscow's political decisions, and attempted to promote their own sets of "national interests", including foreign policy goals. Furthermore many purely Russian provinces started to tinker with the idea of turning themselves into republics as well, in order to gain greater independence from the center. The pioneer in this case was Sverdlovsk province, which was making legal preparations to declare itself the Ural Republic. This was, of course, the home province of President Yeltsin.[33]

President Yeltsin's main priority was keeping power or whatever was left of it. The competition between the Supreme Soviet and the President of Russia, when each side was looking for support on the provincial level and was ready to pay for that support by making further concessions to local separatist forces, was a golden opportunity for local Communist party bosses. They transformed themselves into "democratic" presidents of national republics within Russia and into heads of government of Russian provinces (which they previously ruled as provincial Party secretaries) and sought to wrestle as much power as they could from the hands of the Moscow government. Yeltsin himself told a group of military commanders that his stand-off with the parliament could have split Russia "into 50 or 60 principalities".[34]

Leaders of the ethnically Russian provinces took an anti-Moscow stand essentially because of their grievances in the field of taxation and distribution of resources by the central ministries (or their present equivalents in the disguise of industrial concerns etc.), which are still very powerful in an economy that continues to be essentially state-owned, in order to demonstrate their strength and ability to represent local interests and thus gain support for their grip on power.

The emasculated Kremlin, not sure about its control over the military forces, had to yield to all these challenges. Moscow even signed an economic treaty with Tatarstan thereby enhancing the latter's claim to independence. However Russia avoided signing 14 other treaties the government of Tatarstan was trying to impose on it.

The culmination of such an unrestrained challenge to Moscow happened after President Yeltsin dissolved the Russian Supreme Soviet and called for new elections on 21 September 1993. In their infatuation with their own power, the rulers of certain regions, started to threaten Yeltsin with secession, if he did not cancel his decree on the dissolution of parliament. For instance, the leaders of local Soviets in 13 Siberian republics, territories and provinces, meeting at a special conference in the Siberian city of Novosibirsk, presented an ultimatum to Yeltsin threatening to declare federal property in Siberia local property, to shut down the Trans-

Siberian railway (as if they themselves were not dependent on it), and to schedule October referendums in their regions on "the constitutional-law status of the geographic areas in the Siberian region".

Representatives of 64 of the subjects of the Federation (out of 89) hastily held a meeting in Moscow.[35] They presented Yeltsin with a new ultimatum. If he did not stop the blockade of the Russian parliament building, cancel his order dissolving the parliament and failed to heed to demands of the "Council of the Subjects of the Federation", that they had momentarily created, then Yeltsin and his government would be subject to "all the necessary measures of economic and political pressure".[36] The main leader of this group was the President of the Kalmyk republic, the young millionaire Kirsan Ilyumzhinov.

Of course, they were not fighting for the salvation of democracy (there is no democracy in Kalmykia now because Ilyumzhinov bought all the votes he needed to be elected) but in favor of keeping their cushy jobs.

There is no doubt that there were quite a few people in the provinces who opposed Yeltsin's action because of its flagrantly anti-democratic, anti-Constitutional nature. But what was surprising during the first move to counter Yeltsin's action, was the provincial and ethnic republics rulers readiness to threaten secession. As if such provinces of Eastern Russia, such as Kemerovo, Novosibirsk, Omsk, Tomsk, Tyumen, and Krasnoyarsk territory, were among the temporary adjuncts to the Russian state and not the core elements of "mother-Russia".

Many bosses soon realized that they had overplayed their card, when it quickly became clear that Yeltsin had won.

Although one might criticize the use by the President of military force against parliamentary chieftains who provoked armed fighting in Moscow, such a response proved to be decisive in arresting the drift toward the Russian Federation's disintegration. It had a sobering effect on the local potentates, even the most militant ones, who at one time thought that they could get away with almost anything. They soon realized that resistance led to opponents being fired from their posts by Presidential decree. Good examples here included the most zealous proponents of local independence, such as the chief administrators of the Amur, Novosibirsk and Bryansk provinces and the head of the unconsummated Ural republic.

This was not just "showmanship". Although there might have been quite serious reasons and grounds (especially on the part of such large national entities, such as Tatarstan) to seek independence from the Center, any realistic analysis of the geopolitical situation demonstrates that, unless global politics dramatically changes, small entities will not be better off after seceding from Moscow. For example, the Russian Maritime territory does not want to be "a vassal of Moscow". This is fine, but then whose vassal will it immediately turn into, having gained independence from Moscow?

In raising such a question, I am pointing to the local potentates' zeal for independence (usually with very little support on the part of the majority of local populations, especially in purely Russian provinces) and arguing that it is not driven by some statesmanlike considerations of a higher order, but by the primitive urge to stay in power as long as possible. The latter enables local bosses to enrich themselves via the semi-legal redistribution of national wealth, accompanied by wholesale thievery and corruption. Such are the real considerations behind all the advertised "noble aspirations", aired by local bosses, the former CPSU leaders of the same provinces, who advocate the creation of Bantustans inside Russia as the best way to "democratically" enhance the federal structure of the country.

But with all the brazenness of their attempts to tear the country apart, most of them at the same time, being true sons of a totalitarian system, are cowards and courtiers by nature. A few years ago it was enough for Gorbachev or Yeltsin to pound upon a table with a fist at a session of the parliament or at a conference to make all those bosses immediately stand to attention. Nowadays fist pounding is insufficient. But pounding "the center of insubordination" with tank shells, while inherently anti-democratic, had a highly sobering effect on provincial challengers to Moscow's authority. As Oleg Poptsov, one time head of the second channel of Central Russian TV and a close adviser of the President put it: "Russia always liked a decisive Tsar".[37]

After that Tatarstan, as well as other rebellious republics, scurried to send Moscow taxes which they had withheld for months with impunity. "At first, we had a euphoria of sovereignty", said Midkhat Faroukshin, a big shot in the Ministry of Foreign Economic Relations of Tatarstan. "Now a new stage is starting, a difficult stage for Tatarstan."[38]

On 15 February 1994, a Treaty on "The Demarcation of Objects of Jurisdiction and the Mutual Delegation of Powers Between the Bodies of State Power of the Russian Federation and the Republic of Tatarstan", was signed. Under new circumstances, Kazan agreed to drop from the Treaty the words "sovereign state" and "subject of international law" in reference to Tatarstan. The republic's authorities abandoned one of the cornerstones of their previous position - a single track budget system (with all taxes collected going into the republic's budget) and agreed to pay federal taxes to the Center. However, Moscow, beset by a number of problems, agreed to yield to the renegade republic somewhat greater powers than in the Federal Treaty that the Federal government had signed earlier with other national republics of the Federation. The hope was that such a pact would ease Tatarstan's separatist tendencies, and it proved to be a sound judgement. But the greater autonomy which Tatarstan gained in contrast to other ethnic regions of Russia encouraged them to seek similar rights. This might seriously undermine Federation's unity in future.[39]

In a seminal development, the rebellious Kirsan Ilyumzhinov suddenly annulled in the spring of 1994 the Constitution of the Kalmyk republic and announced that henceforth the republic would be subject to the basic Great Steppe Code. This Code, which actually restored authoritarian government in Kalmykia, was approved by a hand-picked Constitutional Assembly and became the law of the land. But at the same time the new basic law emphasizes the inviolability of links with the Russian people, acceptance of Russian citizenship etc.

"You exchanged your sovereignty for federal subventions?" a correspondent for a New York Russian-language newspaper asked Ilyumzhinov. (In 1993 the share of such subventions in the revenues of the republic's national budget was 86%!) "What do you mean by 'exchanging'?" - retorted the President. "There was no sovereignty. No real one. There was one just on paper. The republic has been living on (federal) grants."[40]

President Yeltsin, dealing with local leaders from a position of strength, personally cut out of the final draft of the Constitution all references to "sovereignty" of republics and provinces, remarking that "recognition of sovereign rights of some parts of the state makes it [Russia] not a federation, but a confederation."[41] It is in such a form that the Constitution of the Russian Federation was officially approved by a slim margin of 60% of eligible voters out of 106.2 million registered voters of Russia. The law stipulated that the Constitution might come into effect only if it were approved at least by 50% of registered voters.

By the end of Spring 1994 it appeared that actually only 46.1%, or 49 million of the registered voters, had voted for the new Constitution. As was stated in the report of a special investigative commission, appointed by

Yeltsin to check the validity of the voting, 9.2 million votes in the December 1993 referendum were falsified. It appeared that invalid ballots were used in various localities to help local potentates get elected to the Federal Assembly, thus boosting the general figure of those voting above the 50% threshold required for the referendum on the Constitution to be valid. *Izvestia* called the report "political dynamite."[42]

Yeltsin learnt about the real results the next day after the elections but kept silent.[43] Evidently after the special commission report Yeltsin decided to pre-empt the pressure for a new vote. So he appealed for a public accord regarding the "newly adopted" Constitution and the parliamentary election results. Since none of the politicians, who were elected, wanted to go through the election again, Yeltsin's idea got overall approval from a wide range of political parties and movements and many prominent figures. By the end of April 1994, a Treaty on Civic Accord was concocted and on 28 April it was signed by the majority of the leaders of political parties, represented in the Federal Assembly, and by almost all the leaders of the republics and provinces of the Russian Federation.

The compromise Treaty represented a hodgepodge of sometimes contradictory pledges and promises designed to satisfy the demands of various political forces of Russia. The signatories agreed not to demand elections to the federal organs of power ahead of the schedule stipulated in the Constitution and not to organize violent public demonstrations and meetings. They also agreed to bolster international authority and the defensive capability of Russia. The government for its part pledged to stabilize the economy, to lower the rate of inflation and to get it under control; all the governing bodies, including the President and the parliament, committed themselves to stimulate integration in the CIS; trade unions pledged not to organize strikes with demands for the budget allocations, and finally, the president, the Federal Assembly and the government agreed to promote the strengthening of federal structures and at the same time to give more rights to the subjects of the Federation, including their own tax base. All the participants accepted the principle that the source of power in the Federation belonged to multinational people and that no single ethnicity had an exclusive right to control a territory, institutions of power or resources. "The organs of state power", as one of the articles of the Treaty stated, "create the opportunity for political parties, movements, public associations to participate in the elaboration of the concept of national security."[44]

The signing of the Treaty on Civic Accord dampened demands to question the validity of Constitution and the elections in general, and their approval. For the time being, the "Soviet Union's way" for the disintegration of Russia was checked.

The only republic within the Russian Federation that still refused to submit to Moscow's authority and retained its declared independence was Chechnya. It is a small, mostly Muslim republic in the Caucasus mountains, 900 miles southeast of Moscow. Until 22 April 1996, when he was killed, the republic was run by Dzhokhar Dudayev, a former Soviet Air Force General.[45] He came to power in the summer of 1991 with the approval of Yeltsin. In September of that year, he dispersed the Supreme Soviet of the republic, when his henchmen brutally beat deputies.

For almost three years, the Russian government largely ignored the insult and imposed only a symbolic leaky blockade on the renegade republic. The blockade, as it is clear today, was deliberately weak because many influential people in Moscow made a great deal of money on shady deals of the Chechen leadership, first of all on oil, which flowed from Russia to Chechnya without interruption. There were also illegal multi-million financial scams perpetrated through Chechen banks, and the widespread production of fake currency, which went unpunished. The capital of Chechnya -- Grozny -- became one of the most important centers of criminal activity in Russia, including narcotics.[46] The Chechen mafia operated in many major Russian cities with the explicit connivance of central and local authorities.

However, after several brazen shoot-outs and kidnappings by Chechen terrorists in the south of Russia, Moscow's patience finally ran out. However, the main reason for the end of Moscow's acquiescence with the behavior of the Chechen leaders was probably the necessity to make the final decision on the pipeline route for the export of oil from new Azerbaijani and Kazakh oil fields developed with the help of foreign investment. It appeared that from Moscow's point of view, the best and the shortest route for the Caspian oil to the terminal on the Russian Black sea shore was through the pipeline already existing in Chechnya. Hence the urgent necessity to re-establish order in the republic.[47]

By heavily arming the Chechen opposition to Dudayev, clandestinely reinforcing them with Russian military volunteers and providing them with air cover, Moscow in the summer and autumn of 1994 attempted to depose Dudayev and to re-establish its control over the republic. But the military operation of the Russian proxies was poorly planned and failed dismally.

Then on 11 December 1994, Russian armed forces launched their own military operation "to save the people of Chechnya from the criminal Dudayev regime and to restore the law and order in the republic". The operation was also started in a semi-legal way, without the introduction of a state of emergency in the region, as it ought to have been in accordance with the Russian Federation's constitution.[48] President Yeltsin evidently hoped that a victorious *blitzkrieg* against Dudayev would not only bring the region back into Moscow's lap, but also bolster his own lagging prestige and authority as the national elections approached. But the outcome of the operation proved to be quite different.

The Russian High Command, headed by the Minister of Defense and the president's buddy, General Pavel Grachev, botched the whole operation. Russian forces, with overwhelming superiority in tanks and other heavy weapons over Dudayev's irregular, albeit highly trained, warriors, and air support, which the Chechen illegal armed formations did not have, were bogged down for three months, trying to occupy the capital of the republic, Grozny. They eventually took Grozny, totally destroying it in the process with massive air and artillery bombardment. Experts unanimously agree that the operation was a total flop. It showed to the whole world that the Russian army is not combat-ready, lacks intelligent guidance and is in a very poor shape generally. The price for such an inept "restoration of law and order" were many thousands of victims among the civilian population - Russians, Chechens and other nationals of Russia that the Moscow government was set to "protect".[49] Moscow's standing in the eyes of international community sank to a very low level.

It was not until mid-June 1995 that Russian troops occupied all the main towns of Chechnya and forced the irregulars into the mountains, where they were cut off from the main supply routes. The war was almost won. But on the 14th of June one of the Chechen field commanders, Shamil Basayev, with a small group of fighters in the most daring terrorist attack in the history of Russia, seized a large hospital in the city of Budennovsk (in the adjacent Stavropol territory) taking hundreds of people inside - doctors, nurses, patients, including pregnant women - as hostages. In the process of the carnage, 119 people were killed and many more wounded. The action of the special Russian forces against the terrorists was totally botched.

As a result, the Russian government was forced to accept the terrorists conditions, namely to let them go and to start peaceful negotiations with Dudayev's government representatives, despite the fact that Moscow officially viewed them as bandits and state criminals. On 30 July 1995, a Peace Agreement on Chechnya was signed by the heads of the Russian and the Chechen delegations. It stipulated the cessation of hostilities, the release by way of exchange of people forcibly detained by both sides, the disarmament of Chechen fighters (through the *purchase* of *illegal arms* by Russia!!!) and a parallel gradual withdrawal of the bulk of the federal troops from Chechnya.

However, the surrender of arms by Dudayev's fighters was a mockery. A unit of irregulars surrendered only a few automatic rifles (perhaps even antiquated hunting guns) and several grenade launchers, and in return they instantly received weapons back in their new capacity as a "self-defense detachment" of a particular village or town. Thus, without a shot being fired, Dudayev's forces were able to retake the strongholds from which they were being forced out earlier.

The political and military situation in the republic worsened with each passing day - the warriors of illegal armed units were in good shape even in the republic's capital Grozny, controlled by the Federal troops. Terrorist attacks against Russian troops, top Russian political and military figures quickly multiplied.[50]

At the start of January 1996, Chechen irregulars carried out another audacious hostage-taking attack in the adjacent republic of Dagestan. When the Russian federal authorities tried to free hostages and to punish the terrorists, the operation was carried out once again in an inept way. The special operation to save hostages quickly degenerated into a fierce attack by the regular army units against the Chechen terrorists, who, through the stupidity of Russian commanders, were given plenty of time to prepare strong defensive positions in the village of Pervomayskaya, close to the border with Chechnya. To suppress the terrorists, federal forces resorted to indiscriminate bombing of the village from the air, and with multiple rocket launchers, without any regard for the lives of innocent people, including children, who were held prisoner by the terrorists. This operation became a world-wide demonstration of the impotence of Russian military forces and total incompetence of the Russian commanding generals, who constantly lied to cover up their helplessness. (None of the commanding generals, who ruined the operation, were dismissed or demoted by the president - the Commander-in-Chief of the Russian armed forces.) Hence the battle at Pervomayskaya (when the terrorists managed finally to sneak off to Chechnya with a number of hostages, past the alleged three rings of encirclement by the federal troops!) became yet another example of national disgrace and humiliation for Russia. The agony of war was prolonged for one more year, as earlier errors were repeated.

Soon after the attempt to assassinate the new Russian commander of the federal troops in Chechnya, General Romanov, hostilities were resumed and continued in a low key until spring 1996, when Yeltsin's ratings in public opinion polls fell dramatically (with only 6% of those polled approving his policy at the start of his re-election campaign). This forced Yeltsin to play another peace trick.

At the end of May 1996, he invited the new head of "Chechen bandits" Zelimkhan Yandarbiyev (who, after Dudayev was killed, took over the post of the president of the self-proclaimed Chechen Republic of Ichkeria) to Moscow. In Moscow, Yeltsin negotiated with Yandarbiyev another peace in Chechnya. While the stay of the Chechen delegation in Moscow was forcibly prolonged, and its members became the de facto hostages of the Russian government for a day, President Yeltsin, like a petty swindler, made a quick day-long visit to a Russian military base near Grozny. There he solemnly declared that the war had come to an end.[51]

On 25 June 1996, ten days before the second round of the Presidential elections, when Yeltsin led his chief rival communist Gennady Zyuganov by a mere 3% of votes in public polls, he issued presidential decree No. 985, ordering the withdrawal of federal troops from Chechnya. To boost his popularity, Yeltsin finally got rid of the Minister of Defense, General Grachev, who was hated by everybody in the country.

After Yeltsin won the second round on 4 July 1996, with the help of another aspiring President, General Alexander Lebed, who prior to the second round lured his voters over to Yeltsin, he completely forgot about his order to withdraw troops.[52] Nevertheless he appointed Lebed as Secretary of the National Security Council and made him the President's plenipotentiary representative in Chechnya and the chief negotiator.

Finally, after some dramatic military moves from both sides, which greatly increased casualty levels, and the brazen recapture of Grozny by the Chechen forces (on 6 August 1996)[53] Alexander Lebed signed a cease-fire agreement with Aslan Maskhadov - the Chief of Staff of Chechen forces, on 13 August 1996.

On 30 August 1996, Lebed and Maskhadov in the presence of Tim Gouldeman, the head of the OSCE mission in Grozny, signed a Joint statement and the Principles for Defining the Grounds of Relationships between the Russian Federation and the Chechen Republic in the Dagestan town of Hasavyurt. The second document stipulates that the final relationship between the Russian Federation and the Chechen Republic will be defined in accordance with the generally recognized norms of *international law* (emphasis mine - H.T.). The final settlement ought to be reached not later than 31 December 2001.[54]

This was an act of Russian de facto capitulation. The most sacred of Russia's vital national interests, that of the preservation of the country's unity, was thrown overboard. The precedent for the gradual dismemberment of Russia has been established and was confirmed by the warm message of congratulation President Yeltsin sent to Aslan Maskhadov on 28 January 1997 when he was elected President of Chechnya by popular secret ballot in the republic.

Realizing that the population of Russia, though weary of the war and welcoming the end of hostilities, would, nevertheless be highly critical of his policies and ask some unpleasant questions, and taking into account the fact that 30 million people, had voted for the communist opposition in the 1996 Presidential elections, Boris Yeltsin at the end of 1996 decided to replay a trick similar to the 1994 Civic Accord. But this time no one of importance took the bait. So on 7 November 1996 (the old USSR Day of national celebration of October 1917 revolution), Yeltsin issued a Presidential Decree No 1537, which read:

The October revolution of 1917 radically influenced the fate of our country. Striving not to allow henceforth a confrontation, with a view to unity and consolidation of the society of Rossiya, I:
  1. declare the holiday of the 7th of November the Day of Harmony and Reconciliation.
  2. declare 1997 - the year of the 80th anniversary of the October revolution - the Year of Harmony and Reconciliation.[55]

On 12 May 1997, President Yeltsin and President Maskhadov signed a Treaty on Peace and on the Principles of Relations between the Russian Federation and the Chechen Republic of Ichkeria in the Kremlin. This so-called historic treaty might rightfully be called the act of Russian de jury capitulation to Chechnya. It consists of only three paragraphs. The main one - the second - restates the clause of the earlier Hasavyurt agreement, stipulating that both sides will build their relations in accordance with the generally recognized principles and norms of international law. This is nothing but the explicit confirmation by the Russian President of the independence of Chechnya. The first point contains the restatement of the UN Charter clause concerning renunciation of force or threat of force in resolving disputes, and finally, the third paragraph states that the Treaty will act as a basis for the conclusion of other agreements and treaties between the two sides.[56] That's it. This absolutely empty Treaty once again confirmed that President Yeltsin, who sent thousands of poorly trained young Russian recruits to die in Chechnya, betrayed Russia's primary national interest - the preservation of the integrity of the Russian Federation. And he, seemingly, got away with it.

Commenting on this treaty, the well-known Russian MP, Vladimir Lysenko, the leader of the Russian Republican party, wrote:

Moscow "indulged" Grozny in giving it independence and relations between the two states will be based on the norms of international law. It is difficult to understand why one should hurry and sign the treaty under such conditions, unprecedented for a state and its constituent part. Most likely, Boris Yeltsin decided to protect his last three years of presidency from Chechen raids, while caring little about what his successor will have to do with the clause in question in 2001, when he has to sign some paper on the (final) status of Chechnya. Today one has to note, that in Chechnya the criminal-mafiosi state (circa 1991-1994) (and the detention of Russian journalists in Chechnya as hostages during many months is the most vivid confirmation of this) has returned. The difference between then and now is that in the past, Russia did not recognize General Dudayev as the president of Ichkeria, whilst today it recognizes Aslan Maskhadov.
The "appeasement" of Chechnya that is taking place... seems to have only one aim: come what may, the oil pipeline from Azerbaijan through Chechnya has to start functioning... The gigantic profits of oil companies are once again overpowering the state interests of Russia.[57]

Although the Constitutional Court of Russia at the beginning of July 1995 actually absolved the Russian President of any responsibility for the bloodbath in Chechnya by closing the "Chechen case", and avoiding the unpleasant matter of judging the constitutionality of the secret Presidential decree No 2137 that gave the go ahead to military operations in Chechnya, the Russian parliamentary commission that analyzed the sources and the development of the Chechen crisis, placed most blame for the bungled enterprise "to restore the constitutional legality, law and order" in Chechnya directly on the President.[58]

Instead of disciplining some potential separatists in Russia, the military operation against Chechnya widened the divisions and conflicts between various political forces in Russia and better still alienated regional administrations in the South of Russia from the Center, undermining the cohesion of the Federation. Chechnya, meanwhile, proposed the creation of the Organization of Security and Cooperation in the Caucasian region (OSCC) in which it hopes to have a leading role.

What are the prospects for the continuation of the present federal arrangement in Russia? This is one of those "cursed questions" of Russia that is difficult to answer. If Yeltsin remains at the helm until the end of his second term, and manages to set things going with the current parliament (elected at the end of 1995), if the army continues to obey the political leadership (though presently it is at the end of its tether), if the economic situation improves, even a little, and if various economic associations of Russia's provinces strengthen their ties on the basis of inter-dependence, then one can expect that the urge for separatism might subside.

The local elections in the Federation which took place in 1993-98 did not fundamentally change the composition of local power elites. More than 60% of local deputies who were elected, are typical Soviet *nachalniki* (bosses) of the old variety: former local CPSU leaders and chiefs of executive governing bodies, state enterprise and collective farm managers. So members of the old ruling elite have entrenched themselves locally whilst the population remains politically passive (more than half of the potential voters shunned local elections during first rounds of voting!).

Having won locally, the old ruling cliques, who have already managed to appropriate as much state property, as was legally and illegally possible, have quietened down somewhat in their zeal to separate. A great deal will also depend on the Federal Assembly, especially on the upper house (the Council of the Federation), created to represent the specific interests of the republics and provinces. However, the functioning of the Federal Assembly in 1994-98 was disappointing - neither of the houses dared censure the President for the bloodbath in Chechnya! Only in the summer of 1998 the Duma started the preliminary procedure to impeach the President, one of the main accusations being his responsibility for the bloodbath in Chechnya. But the majority of political analysts do not believe that the deputies will be able to consummate their action.

Separatist tendencies in some national republics, as well as in some provinces that have their own unimpeded contacts by land or sea with foreign countries and some natural wealth to sell, will persist, as long as the central authority continues to vacillate on key problems of economic development and real help for the regions.

Though the President and the Council of the Federation have enough power now to settle the problem of relations between the regions and the Center through appropriate legislative work, this problem will remain a thorny one for a long time to come. The prerequisite for the amicable settlement of all the unresolved questions between the Center and provinces (including the republics) will be the revitalization of the economy and the enforcement of the rule of law. As is presently the case, many laws, adopted by the regions and national republics within Russia, contravene federal laws and the Federal Constitution. Such a situation encourages separatist tendencies.

Can a civil war develop in a country that continues to vacillate between socialism and capitalism (free enterprise) without going decisively one way or the other? Such a scenario is improbable due to many factors, including recent history and the specifics of Russian character. Russia is unlikely to have a civil war because the population is too tired and worn out, so that Russians are unlikely to fight each other on a mass scale. But mass protests against the economic policy of the government is another matter.

The more probable scenario as far as the cohesion of *Rossiya* is concerned might look like this: In the absence of decisive results in improving economic performance, gradual regionalization of the country - its decomposition without any secession is likely to occur, namely feudalization of the economy and economic and political anarchy. Russia might arrive at that state of affairs without any explicit desire by sheer drift. When all the efforts of the so-called people's leaders (*vozhdei*) for the past seven years have focused mostly on the struggle for power, and when the vital cords of the country had long been damaged, undermined by years of political abuse, slave labor, the annihilation of a free laborer in the field or in the shop, by militaristic culture, economic mismanagement, stealing, corruption, and by a lack of clear goals and incentives, the time might come when sinking into chaos becomes inevitable.

The tremendous loss of life of the "best and the brightest" during the Civil war after the 1917 revolution and during the Great Patriotic War of 1941-45, the initial mass emigration of population, Lenin's and Stalin's policy of liquidation of entire classes of people, several country-wide famines, the gigantic Gulag concentration camps system of intensive slave labor, when a worker-prisoner stayed alive on the average only for a few weeks, the gradual degeneration of peasantry, which is still kept in a semi-serf state, dismally low levels of medical care, ecological catastrophe throughout Russia and the present under-nourishment of the majority of population, may lead at some point (perhaps Russia has already arrived at this point without being aware of it) to Russia's doom.

The authors of the "Strategy for Russia" add another aspect to the analysis of the same problem:

> The erosion of state authority, especially executive powers, certain consequences of ill-considered economic reforms, indecision and discrepancy within leadership, weakening of traditional factors contributing to the consolidation of the Russian state: external threat and internal political coercion, the rise of nationalism and national-communism, the general world-wide process of weakening of states as subjects of international relations, made the danger of disintegration of Russia real. If that happens, the Lebanonization or Yugoslavization of almost of the whole former USSR becomes virtually inevitable.[59]

Because this worst-case scenario is not taken seriously by many people in the ruling circles, who continue their macabre fight for power and wealth (*aprè nous - la deluge*), this might just become a reality. Even if Russia is not yet doomed biologically and historically, it might decay and disintegrate simply by default, because those with the power to reverse the process, simply dismiss such a possibility. In such a situation, all the conjectures made in the following chapters will become irrelevant. Russia will become a country up for grabs and those Russian neighbors, who happen to be more organized and purposeful, will get the booty.

Consolidation of the CIS under the patronage of Russia

It might seem incongruous that the government of the Russian Federation, while as yet unsure whether or not it will manage to hold Russia together, simultaneously attempts to reinstate the dominant role of Russia throughout the territory of the former USSR. But a closer analysis reveals that these two tasks do not contradict, but rather complement, one another. If Moscow succeeds in maintaining Russian cohesion by itself, it will be easier to maintain order throughout the CIS.   On the other hand, if Russia manages to consolidate the CIS under its own patronage, it will thus create a sort of external hoop that will help maintain the cohesion of Russia. Many Russian government documents, first and foremost the President's decree of 1995 on the strategic course of Russia toward the CIS republics, stress that the management of relations with the CIS is a major priority of Russia's foreign policy.

Speaking at the conference of Russian ambassadors in the CIS republics that took place at the end of July 1996, Russian Foreign Minister, Yevgeny Primakov, called the CIS the main field for Russia's foreign policy activities.[60]

The fact of the matter is that soon after Yeltsin, Shushkevich and Kravchuk engineered quite quickly and seemingly painlessly, the dissolution of the USSR in December 1991 and each then went to his own country to enjoy newly won freedom and power, the task to assess the implications of the whole affair was left with the Russian authorities and Boris Yeltsin personally.

Boris Yeltsin was absolutely sure that after he and the two other conspirators removed the power from Gorbachev and became "peers in their own right" in their respective republics, they would quickly restore a more or less cohesive Union on the basis of the democratic Commonwealth of Independent States. In theory, unified economic activities, a single economic and security space, and all the infrastructure where supposed to remain intact, with the same unified armed forces in place to defend the outer borders of the FSU.

But Yeltsin miscalculated. The centrifugal forces of nationalism appeared to be too strong for cohesion to be reinstated. But if some republican leaders did not care about the legacy of the "monster super-state", as soon as they became Presidents of independent Ukraine, Belarus, Georgia, Uzbekistan etc., the new leader in the Kremlin could not afford to continue such a stance because his seat of power is the Kremlin.

Whatever he might privately plan or think, the burden of imperial responsibility could not be evaded by a person who put on the Monomakh fur crown, even if he were a dyed in the wool democrat.[61] And Yeltsin is not. As a former member of the CPSU Politbu020 - a collectivist Tsar of Russia - Yeltsin, like his predecessor Gorbachev, is bound by the lofty legacy of the throne, the old tradition of a unified state and by the mystique of Moscow's historic mission to be the guardian of Holy Rus'.

This is why, after the fever of settling into power subsided, Yeltsin and his advisers started to think anew about the problems of restoring, to a certain extent, a unified state like the Soviet Union was. They, of course, understood that a return to the centralized arrangement based on Moscow's complete dominance was absolutely out of the question. But at the same time, they saw that the new mechanisms of the Commonwealth of Independent States, which were created to continue cooperation among the members of the FSU, were not working properly.

Enchanted by their new power and new presidential titles, which formally put them on a par with any world leader, the new rulers of the eleven former Soviet Republics that initially formed the CIS[62] were frantically trying to divide the property of the former Union without actually thinking what they would do with their newly acquired assets. The biggest joy of all was that they no longer needed to pay a tribute to Moscow and could gain additional profit from their own republics, as if they have not grabbed enough before, under Brezhnev, when most of those local sheiks and khans, masquerading as General Secretaries of republican communist parties, ruled their republics like their own personal fiefdoms.[63]

This explains why national republican leaders were not very eager to strengthen and develop cooperation and coordinating institutions of the CIS, on the one hand, or to seriously improve and promote further CIS-wide economic integration with due regard to the emerging new forms of property and methods of doing business, on the other. And all of them - some openly, others less so - denounced Russia as the oppressor, a callous gendarme etc., actually forgetting the peculiar form of Russian "colonialism". Such "colonialism" boiled down to the fact that the outlying republics of the USSR achieved similar levels of development to Russia at the expense of degradation of "the core Russia" - its central European provinces which were ransacked by the central authority to help increase economic potential and standards of living of the non-Russian republics.

A Western observer might say that those standards of living were rather low by Western standards, which is true. But we are not talking about some abstract indicators: everything in the Soviet economy, based essentially on slave labor, was sub-standard in comparison to the West. But when one compares the standards of living of the masses and their educational levels, say, in the former Central Asian Muslim republics of the USSR with similar Oriental states across the border (Iran, Afghanistan, Pakistan, India), the former would come out on top.

The people in the non-Russian republics paid dearly for any progress made: the gradual disappearance of the Aral sea, tremendous pollution of the Caspian sea, not to say radiological contamination of large sections of the territory of Kazakhstan, these are but a few glaring examples of such a retribution. But this did not happen just to them: the whole territory of the Union under communist rule was turned into one big poisonous dump.[64]

The fact is that it was not only Yeltsin, but other republican leaders as well, who, after they started to tackle the problems connected with independence, began to have some doubts about the wisdom of a total break with Russia. The more far-sighted of them, such as Kazakhstan's President Nursultan Nazarbayev, were from the very beginning in favor of greater unity with Russia - not out of a fear that Russia might use her substantial Russian minority within a republic to reclaim its imperial role, but out of a belief that without close cooperation with Russia, there might be a slight possibility of economic progress in their particular territories.

For some republics, such as Tajikistan and Turkmenistan, the necessity of close cooperation with Russia, was dictated by a danger from across their southern borders. In other cases (Azerbaijan and Georgia), it was Russia's role as a mediator and supporter of the central government in trouble that became the main reason for rapprochement. (Georgia, which initially rejected the CIS, joined it at the end of 1993, when its wily leader Eduard Shevardnadze came to the conclusion that without Russian help Georgia would be simply torn apart by the clan struggle, and Azerbaijan, which initially joined the CIS and then opted out, rejoined it again in 1993, when the new leader of the country - the old CPSU boss and the KGB General Geidar Aliev - decided that without Russian help and arbitration, Azerbaijan would not make it in the war with Armenia over Nagorno-Karabakh.)

The majority of the population of Belarus was never happy with what it considered a purely artificial separation from Russia. So it became a very popular action for both Belorussians and Russians, when on 2 April 1996, the Presidents of the two republics signed a Treaty establishing a Union of Sovereign Republics (USR) of Russia and Belarus within the CIS. The treaty stipulates coordination of foreign policies, interaction in the field of security, the defense of frontiers and in fighting crime. Both republics pledged to form a single legal base and to carry out measures to unify monetary, budgetary and taxation systems. They liquidated customs on their common border and thus laid the groundwork for the creation of a single economic space. Actually Belarus peddlers are now supplying the Smolensk and the Bryansk regions of Russia with food produce and a wide choice of durable goods at competitive prices.

On 23 May 1997, Russia and Belarus signed a new treaty -- *The Charter of the Union of Belarus and Russia* -- that further develops and deepens the integration of the two republics. Though President Yeltsin, while editing the text of the agreement, made certain concessions to the mighty pro-American lobby in the Kremlin that made tremendous efforts to prevent any further consolidation of the two republics, he plucked up enough courage to counter the Charter's opponents. According to the Charter:

The prospects of the Union's development are connected with the successive movement towards a voluntary unification of the states - members of the Union on the basis of free expression of the will of their peoples.[65]

It was ratified by the parliaments of both republics in June 1997.

On 29 March 1996, the four republics of the CIS -- Russia, Belarus, Kazakhstan and Kirghizia -- formed a customs union with the goal of creating a unified market for goods and services. The four countries also envisage the conclusion of a payments agreement, which will permit the banks of all four republics to operate within a single customs space. This will act as a further step towards the formation of a unified financial market. Such advanced cooperation between the four republics will facilitate multi-speed integration within the CIS. This notion is shared by all the member-states of the CIS.

Even Ukraine, whose first President, the cunning Kravchuk, was the odd man out in the CIS under the pressure of ultra-nationalist forces based in Western Ukraine (somewhat like De Gaulle used to behave in the Atlantic Alliance), finally realized that without closer cooperation with Russia, the Ukrainian economy would simply collapse. In the elections in the summer of 1994, the majority of Ukrainian voters chose President Leonid Kuchma, who has consistently advocated closer ties with Russia.

At the end of May 1997, during visits to Ukraine by Russian Premier Viktor Chernomyrdin, followed by President Yeltsin, most of the unresolved problems between the two republics were settled, especially the painful problem of the division of the former Soviet Black sea navy, which had plagued both counties for 5 years. The Navy was divided (with the biggest groups of ships going to Russia) and the most thorny problem, where to base the Russian part of the navy, was solved by the agreement of Ukrainian government to lease to Russia several bays with the appropriate shore facilities, including Sevastopol bay.[66]

President Yeltsin and President Kuchma also signed *The Treaty of Friendship, Cooperation and Partnership* between the Russian Federation and Ukraine, which *inter alia* removed all the territorial claims of Russia to Ukraine. This opened greater prospects for strategic cooperation between the two republics.

Thus when analysts in the West attribute the centripetal tendencies in the CIS exclusively to Moscow's pressure, to its imperial designs, they should know better because for the time being Russia is the only one of the CIS republics that can avoid cooperation with the others and still be economically sound. Most of the other members of the CIS are compelled by circumstances to stick with Russia.[67]

Russia, for its own part, wants to be a patron and a guiding spirit of the CIS states and to preserve its "near abroad", at least as a sphere of influence. Though, in actual fact there is also an uncontrollable urge to go even further in reinstating the unity of the territory of the former USSR or the erstwhile Russian empire (granted that present Moscow leaders and most of the politicians do not aspire to include the Baltic countries in this arrangement). This is considered by the present Russian leadership to be a vital national interest of Russia and no amount of criticism on the part of the West of its political line in the "near abroad" will change Russia's mind.

There is no Russian politician or political analyst who would not recognize that the preservation and further deepening of economic, humanitarian, cultural and security interdependence among the former Soviet republics is one of the most vital of Russia's national interests. The only difference between liberals and moderate conservatives in Russia is that conservatives believe in a more assertive policy on the part of Moscow in this regard, whilst liberals caution that interdependence (an objective reality of the CIS) "should not be forced on one state by another".[68]

However, one Russian Foreign Ministry document on foreign policy priorities states quite unequivocally (albeit in communist *newspeak*) that even military force can be used to achieve the consolidation of the CIS:

The formation of the foreign policy of a number of CIS states is influenced by an exaggerated distancing from Russia, typical for the period of independence-building, by territorial quarrels, fanned by nationalism, including claims against Russia, and also by a sort of allergy to everything that might remind them of past dependence on the Union structures. The realization of the objective reality that the reliance on connections with a regenerated Russia will simplify the solution of their national tasks will not come at once...

Thus a complicated process with regard to Russia's closest geopolitical environment is underway. Its outcome will to a great extent depend on our ability through persuasion, *and in extreme cases through the use of power*, to affirm the principles of international law, including the rights of minorities, and to strive for stability and good-neighborliness (emphasis mine - H.T.).[69]

As mentioned above, the preservation of Russia's own security is unthinkable without the cooperation of other CIS republics, especially when Russian conventional armed forces are seriously weakened, while potential threats from across the CIS outer borders are growing.

Muslim foreign neighbors of the CIS republics, emboldened by the turmoil and chaos on its fringes, are itching to secure some *place d'armes* in the FSU states. Militant Muslim fundamentalism is overflowing the borders of some of them.

Although Western statesmen are advising Moscow to refrain from getting involved in the defense of some of those borders, no Western nation or a coalition, such as NATO, is going to do anything to help a CIS republic defend itself from intrusions from the outside. 60,000 Russian troops, that are, by Western estimates, presently deployed in Russia's "near abroad", are stationed there not for sheer pleasure or for domineering purposes. They actually constitute the first line of defense not only for those republics, where they are situated, but for Russia itself, because there are as yet no internal borders between Russia and other republics of the CIS in the proper sense of defensible, secure and non-transparent ones.

At the same time, it should be noted that the invocation by Moscow of concern for the fate of Russian minorities in other republics is done not only to apply pressure, but out of a real anxiety for the deteriorating conditions of many Russians and Russian-speaking populations in other republics.

There are an increasing number of instances of the rough treatment of Russian people in many Central Asian republics, despite the fact that most of those republics need Russians as qualified specialists working in key industries and as officers in their armed forces. While the official authorities assure Moscow that there is no discrimination against Russians in terms of jobs, education etc., there is now a wealth of accumulated evidence concerning the squeezing of Russians out through subtle and not so subtle pressure and discrimination. For example, more than 100,000 Russians emigrated from Tajikistan alongside all the Germans and Jews that have lived there for ages. Uzbekistan banned the activities of Russian, Ukrainian and Belorussian cultural centers, while permitting the existence of such centers for non-Uzbek Muslim ethnic groups. In addition, Kazakhstan is spreading the practice of settling Kazakh immigrants from Mongolia and China in the northern regions of the republic, where the local population is mostly Russian. In Ukraine the authorities have been trying, albeit unsuccessfully so far, to ensure "national cohesion" by presenting Russians as the main enemy. The government forces local TV stations to translate all telecasts from Russia into Ukrainian, while the native language of the majority of viewers in Eastern Ukraine is Russian. In the Trans-Caucasus, Russians are blamed for everything, even if Russians have nothing to do with many of the local problems. (Armenia with its traditional loyalty to Russia is an exception to this rule.) Discrimination against Russian speaking people in Latvia and Estonia has achieved such a high magnitude that even international human rights organizations are expressing concern.

Evidently, many leaders of national republics, having initially whipped up nationalism for their own ulterior motives, are now unable to cope with it. Furthermore, playing on ethnic passions helps the rulers to distract people's attention from more mundane problems of a daily nature. Actually the same tactics are used by the authorities of Russia as well.

During the past five years, Russia has given refuge to more than three million people from the Former Soviet Republics. Four more million are expected to flee into Russia from these republics over the next few years.[70]

However, if the old republics consolidation continues essentially on ethnic principles and on Russian-baiting it will be a tragedy, because with all the multi-culturism and traditional genuine (not just Marxist) internationalism of Moscow, Russia has its limits, and its patience will eventually run out.

In the period 1994-96 some progress was made in the CIS towards greater integration, especially an economic one. An agreement was reached to create a free trade zone within the CIS framework. An Inter-State

Economic Committee was set up. Without waiting for a general arrangement, several chains of interdependent factories in the CIS have concluded cooperation agreements. The CIS states have also agreed to create a joint system of anti-aircraft defense and thus made a big stride towards the revival of a single air space over the CIS.

At the same time, the trade turnover among the CIS republics in 1995 constituted only 26% of their general foreign trade turnover and actually fell by 17% in comparison to 1994.[71]

Summing up the situation in the CIS one can say that current evaluations of the progress made by the CIS during five years of its existence and its prospects for the future vary from highly positive to absolutely negative. Those who believe in the usefulness of such an arrangement emphasize that the world trend nowadays is geared towards integration and from this point of view, the CIS is a successful union that helps its members overcome the difficulties of transition from planning to market economies. They point out that the CIS has facilitated the restoration of old forms and the creation of new forms of economic cooperation both on bilateral and multilateral levels. There is a movement, albeit not very fast, towards greater military cooperation. The most important step in this regard was the signing in May 1992 of the Tashkent Treaty on Collective Security by nine members of the CIS (Ukraine, Moldova and Turkmenistan preferred to stay out of the Treaty).[72] The CIS has been recognized by the United Nations as a regional organization, and as such, is useful to its members in contacts with the OSCE over the rights of national minorities and to fair elections.

The main thing is that the people of the FSU are encouraged by the existence of the CIS as a symbol of the preservation of close ties among former citizens of a great country as well as a signpost to a better future for their children and grandchildren.

At the same time, many political analysts, who favor the existence of the CIS and are working on ways and means to develop it into something more cohesive, emphasize that those, who support integration, do so only because it might ensure uninterrupted deliveries of Uzbek cotton for Russian weaving mills or some such "reciprocity", are actually working against the future of the CIS. They believe that the CIS has a chance to survive only if its constituent republics, combining their most advanced industrial facilities, scientific achievements and capabilities, and labour skills, strive to carve their own niche in developing and restructuring its present and future global market in such fields as space missiles and satellites, aviation, computers and communication equipment.

In order not to lose out in competition with foreigners, who are trying to replace Russia in the other CIS states, Russia should use its invaluable capital of science, culture, and information networks that in some way keeps various parts of the FSU closer together.

There are many sub-variants of integration. Thus Adjar Krutov comments:

Capricious Dame Clio has not yet made her choice. She is still waiting... Considerations such as the price of a mistake, the cost of indecisiveness, immediate concerns, the personal ambitions of individual politicians make no difference for her. But for Russia and its security they mean a lot.[73]

At the same time, however, there are politicians who believe that the real integration in the CIS is yet to come. "We are talking about integration, but nothing of the kind exists",[74] stated Aman Tuleyev, one time candidate to the Russian presidency and later, Minister for Cooperation with the CIS Countries. In January 1997, he informed the public that there were around 1,300 signed agreements and other documents within the CIS framework, but only about 300 of them were operational.[75]

Russia's ambitious and educated "reformers", such as Yegor Gaidar and his team, according to President Nursultan Nazarbayev of Kazakhstan,

knew what to do, but did not know how to achieve integration. After the demise of the USSR their approach to integration was based on the sole principle: Russia should get rid of the "ballast". When speaking of "ballast" they meant the majority of the FSU republics.

In a harsh, often humiliating manner, pushing neighbors off, the then Russian government thought that it could beat everyone on the road to reform. The neighbors, by their calculation, were to be left "on their knees" to degrade, and then to queue up for the right to attach their "little carriage" to the Russian locomotive of reform...

Perhaps in this way the young team of Russian reformers got some tactical gain, but they lost strategically in the political field. The Russian government's "economic egotism" of those times was connected first of all with the renunciation of a single currency and of a united industrial and agricultural complex. This produced an irreparable impact upon the process of integration...

Today, frankly speaking, the Russian locomotive is hardly pulling, if at all. Who would recklessly want to be driven by it?...

The main conclusion, stemming from my musings over the five year history of the CIS, boils down to the following: today it is necessary to radically reform not only the CIS itself, but Russian policy towards its neighbors as well. Until Russia becomes really responsible and friendly - naturally I am in no way calling upon Russia to give up her national interests - the direction of attention of the CIS countries towards other geopolitical centers of gravity will persist.[76]

It appears that one of the greatest obstacles to deeper consolidation of the CIS space is the bossism of Moscow, its unwillingness to behave as an equal towards the other CIS partners. Until mid 1997, Ukraine, despite the demise of Kravchuk, continued to act as the main brake on all the joint ventures, which brought it some additional benefits from the United States. However, the growing realization in many CIS capitals that no single republic, save Russia, can really survive as a going concern without extended cooperation with its CIS partners, is the main reason for most moves towards greater consolidation.

Conclusion

This general overview of Russia's national interest shows that their range embraces many global directions and spheres: political, economic, military and others. Their scope fits the criterion of the interests of a great power. But Russia today is too weak economically, politically, morally to conduct a true great power policy. On top of this, its ruling class does not have the guts or the desire to promote its interests. Superficially, however, Russian leaders behave as if they still have in their hands the leverages of the old and mighty Soviet Union.

The most vital interests of Russia today are the preservation of the country's integrity and the consolidation of the Commonwealth of Independent States, a weak shadow of the former Union.

The task of maintaining the integrity and stability of Russia is a very difficult one for the powers that be because of the growth of nationalism in the various ethnic republics within Russia and the absence of many powerful central leverages to influence the course of events in various parts of Russia. For the first two years after the collapse of the Soviet Union, senior Russian leaders were engaged in a major power struggle between the newly elected president of Russia, Boris Yeltsin, and the Supreme Soviet - the leftover parliament of the previous Soviet regime.

The duality of power in Moscow slowed down the development of new state institutions and the progress of reform in Russia.

The conflict was finally solved in a classical totalitarian way: President Yeltsin used tanks to tame an uncooperative parliament. The President's victory gave him the freedom to promote a new Constitution, which made considerable changes in the structure and composition of the central authority. Russia actually became a presidential republic with a comparatively weak parliament - the Federal Assembly. Its lower house is the Duma, whose deputies are elected essentially by parties lists and the upper house - the Council of the Federation – which is composed of governors of the regions, presidents of the ethnic republics and the heads of their respective legislative assemblies (two persons from each of the 89 subjects of the Federation except Chechnya, which refuses to send its representatives to the Federal Assembly). Even the main authority of the parliament - its power to adopt laws of the land is circumscribed by the authority of the President to issue decrees substituting for laws. Such a mix up makes the legal system of Russia rather murky.

The Russian President, who according to the Constitution, is the main guardian and champion of its national interests, has failed to uphold the most vital interest of the country -- the maintenance of its integrity. Because of the absolutely inept, fallacious policy and absolutely incompetent, if not to say criminal, handling by the top brass of military operations against Chechnya - Moscow was forced to officially recognize Chechnya's self-proclaimed independence. Such a precedent enhances dangerous centrifugal tendencies in the Russian Federation, with the prospect that many subjects will demand more authority and privileges -- political, economic (fiscal) and commercial.

One of the mechanisms that to a certain extent helps Moscow to restrain centrifugal tendencies is the existence of the CIS, which in some way acts as an external hoop against the outlying subjects of the Federation.

The CIS republics - the so called *near abroad* of Russia - are very important for Russia for security reasons, as no strictly demarcated and guarded borders between Russia and the FSU republics surrounding it, currently exist. In many places, the outer borders of the CIS, function as the de facto external borders of Russia: troops, supplied by Russia, help guard those borders.

The Soviet Union was a country with a well developed infrastructure and inter-republican industrial and agricultural cooperation. Sheer economic necessity means that the FSU republics are likely to continue economic cooperation and to a certain extent to restore their erstwhile interdependence, which they initially almost destroyed in the euphoria of newly gained freedom. Now it is time for much closer inter-republican economic and political cooperation for the sheer sake of a survival as independent entities in the present highly competitive world. This necessity is to a large extent based on three important factors:

Firstly, the absence in almost all of the successor states, except Russia, of complete production cycles for many goods that used to be produced in those republics. They have either to close down many of their factories or cooperate with neighbors;

Secondly, the poor competitiveness of many products, manufactured in the CIS (due to poor quality or obsolescence), on the international market. At the same time, most of these products are still marketable within the CIS and in Third world counties; and

Thirdly, the need to use Russia's help and mediation to combat local ethnic separatism and to defend outer borders.

In this way, the national interests of some newly independent countries (NICs) coincide with those of Russia. This is clear from the pronouncement of President Nazarbayev, cited above. But many leaders of the CIS republics are displeased about Moscow's alleged arrogance or intrusion into their internal affairs. And, given Moscow's weak vacillating leadership, the building of the CIS into a strong and prosperous community of nations is highly unlikely.

Notes

[1] The main points of the document were summarized by Vladislav Chernov, the then Deputy Head of the Department of Strategic Security of the Security Council of the Russian Federation, in *Nezavisimaya Gazeta*, 29 April 1993, pp.1,3.

[2] It was published in February 1993 as a special supplement of *Diplomaticheskiy Vestnik*, an official publication of the Ministry of Foreign Affairs of the Russian Federation (hereafter referred to as *The Conception*).

[3] See *Rossiiskaya Gazeta*, 6 May 1992, p.5. The law "On Security" was adopted by the Russian parliament and came into effect on 5 March 1992. This law defined the status, functions and the composition of the Security Council of the Russian Federation, chaired by the President of Russia. The law has been re-edited several times since then. It defines security (*bezopasnost*) as "the situation, when vital

interests of a person, of the society and of the state, are protected from internal and external threats".

⁴ See *Sobraniye zakonodatel'stva Rossiiskoi Federatsii* [*The Compilation of Legislation of the Russian Federation* - hereafter - *Compilation*], No. 23 (3 June 1996), pp.5685-5700. The first law "On Defense" was adopted by the Russian parliament in 1992. In 1996 it was replaced by a new law. One of the main differences between the two texts is that in the 1992 version the majority of functions relevant to the defense of the republic belonged to the parliament. The 1996 law concentrates almost all powers in the hands of the president.

⁵ 'O natsional'noi bezopasnosti [On National Security]. The message of the President of the Russian Federation to the Federal Assembly'. *Nezavisimaya Gazeta*, 14 June 1996, p.7. "[T]he world", stressed the President, "did not turn into one without conflicts. International system is groping for a new footing, the balance in the three global spaces: geopolitical, geostrategic and geoeconomic. As one of the world centers Russia is participating in reciprocal moves toward a new stable global equilibrium."

⁶ The doctrine was promulgated by the presidential decree No. 1833 of 2 November 1993. It was soon published as "Osnovniye polozheniya voennoi doktriny Rossiiskoy Federatsii" [Basic principles of the military doctrine of the Russian Federation] (*Izvestia*, 18 November 1993, pp.1,4). Much later it was disclosed that in fact only basic principles of the doctrine were formulated and approved in a hurry under pressure from the top brass after the dispersal of the Russian Supreme Soviet, while a complete doctrine has yet to be elaborated. The document that was approved in the Autumn of 1993 "almost from the start was recognized as essentially a political declaration, rather than a guidance for the reform of the military organization of Russia. It has been elaborated within the Ministry of Defense. However, in the process of coordinating the text with various ministries and departments, concerned with the problem, the document was 'impregnated' with phraseology, that fuddled reference points for military professionals. The basic thesis about the necessity to be prepared for defense of the country from all directions nonplussed commanders and staffs at all the levels, for the focus of their work on how to organize combat operations was always geared towards answering the question: 'Who is the adversary and how can one fight him?' Regular officers felt that the concrete problems of enhancing the defense capabilities were sacrificed to the existing political situation; military reform has been skidding" (Vladimir Solov'yov, 'Second military doctrine. Defense Council is preparing it for a speedy approval', *Nezavisimaya Gazeta*, 6 November 1996, p.1).

⁷ See *Compilation* No. 38 (18 September 1995), pp.6844-6849.

⁸ *Ibid*. No. 18 (29 April 1996), pp. 4594-4601.

⁹ The newspaper *Nezavisimaya Gazeta* which revealed this fact commented: "If it is really so, then it speaks about only one thing: Russia concludes international

agreements not proceeding from the approved concept of national security, but the concept itself is being transformed and adapted to correspond to treaties being concluded" (*Nezavisimaya Gazeta*, 7 June 1997, p.2).

[10] *Rossiiskaya Gazeta*, 26 December 1997, pp.4-5.

[11] 'Poslaniye Presidenta Rossiiskoy Federatsii Federalnomu Sobaniyu. Ob Ukreplenii Rossiiskogo Gosudarstva (Osnovniye napravleniya vnutrennei i vneshnei politiki)' [The Message of the President of the Russian Federation to the Federal Assembly. On the Strengthening of the State of Rossiya (Main directions of Internal and External Policy)]. *Rossiiskaya Gazeta*, 25 February 1994, pp.1,3-7; 'O deistvennosty gosudarstvennoy vlasti v Rossii. Poslaniye Presidenta Rossiiskoi Federatsii Federalnomu Sobraniyu' [On the Effectiveness of the State Power in Rossiya. The Message of the President of the Russian Federation to the Federal Assembly]. *Rossiiskiye Vesti*, 17 February 1995, pp.1,3-7; 'Poslaniye Prezidenta Rossiiskoy Federatsii Federalnomu Sobraniyu. Rossiya za kotoruyu my v otvete' [The Message of the President of the Russian Federation to the Federal Assembly. Russia which we are Responsible for]. *Rossiiskiye Vesti*, 24 February 1996, pp.2-7; 'Poryadok vo vlasti - poryadok v strane. Poslaniye Prezidenta Rossiiskoy Federatsii Federalnomu Sobraniyu (O polozhenii v strane i osnovnykh napravleniyakh politiki Rossiiskoi Federatsii' [Order in the State Power - Order in the Country. The Message of the President of the Russian Federation to the Federal Assembly (On the Situation in the Country and Main Directions of the Policy of the Russian Federation)], *Rossiiskaya Gazeta*, 7 March 1997, pp. 5-12; 'Poslaniye Prezidenta Rossiiskoy Federatsii Federalnomu Sobraniyu. Obshchimi silami – k podyomu Rossii (O polozhenii v strane i osnovnykh napravleniyakh politiki Rossiiskoy Federatsii) [The message of the President of the Russian Federation to the Federal Assembly. By joining hands – towards the upsurge of Russia] (On the state of the country and main directions of the Russian Federation's Policy). *Rossiiskaya Gazeta*, 24 February 1998, pp.3-6.

[12] That task may or may not include improving living standards of the population. Thus far the Russian central authorities have not been particularly absorbed with that goal.

[13] *The Conception*, p.9.

[14] "If one takes as the poverty line an income of $4 per day, then the number of poor people in the region of the former socialist camp from 1988 to 1994 increased from 14 to 119 million. Half of the last figure comprise Russian citizens" (*Izvestia*, 17 June 1997, p.1, quoting the 1997 UN report on Human Development).

[15] Vladimir Maximov, 'Igra v krovavuyu kopeyechku' [A game of a bloody little kopeck]. *Pravda*, 31 March 1994, p.2. Maximov died in Paris in 1995.

[16] In his State of the Nation speech before the Council of the Federation - the upper house of the new Russian parliament - on 24 February 1994, President Yeltsin said: "A strong state is necessary above all in order to curb crime. That is the most

important problem of the year" (*Rossiiskaya Gazeta*, 25 February 1994, p.1). Since that time there have been many other similar declarations and solemn pledges on the part of the President to put an end to raging crime. However, criminal activities in Russia continue to   dramatically increase. In 1996   more than 2.6 million offenses were officially registered, more than 60% of those being violent crime. "Particularly alarming is the growth of banditry, assassinations by hired killers, explosions and other manifestations of terrorist activities" - stated the Procurator-General of Russia Skuratov in his report to the Upper house of the Russian parliament at the beginning of 1997. And he continued:. "Smuggling of narcotics into Russia increases annually by 1.5 times... 43% of heavy violent criminal acts have not been solved" (cited in *Nezavisimaya Gazeta*, 19 February 1997, p.5). As far as purely economic crime is concerned it has actually impregnated all layers of society and government apparatus. The "shadow" (underground) economic activity (from which the state gets no taxes) now accounts to 40% of Russia's GDP. The annual increase in economic crime amounts to 12.5% according to official estimates, while most experts consider the rate of increase to be three to four times higher. The amount of foreign currency illegally transferred abroad is thought to be in the range of 150-300 billion (from the official report of the Russian Ministry of Internal Affairs cited in *Nezavisimaya Gazeta*, 17 January 1997, p.5).

[17] *Rossiiskaya Gazeta*, 7 March 1997, p.3.

[18] In introducing his Message to the Russian parliament Yeltsin said: "Russia must be governed by the authority in power, not by circumstances. It is high time to establish order. First of all - in state power. And I shall do it" (Ibid.).

[19] The same way as, say, the US$5 million that O.J. Simpson, a well-known US football player, spent on his legal defense team in a murder trial in California ensured for him human rights, a "fair trial" and the acquittal against all evidence to the contrary.

[20] Alexander Solzhenitsyn, 'As Breathing and Consciousness Return' in *From Under The Rubble* (London: Collings & Harvill Press, 1975), p.24. Assessing the situation in Russia, as far as democracy is concerned, 22 years later, Solzhenitsyn, now living in Moscow, says that the system of central authority created in Russia "is as uncontrolled, unaccountable to the public and acts with the same impunity as the former communist power. As much as one would like to refer to it as democracy it cannot be termed so. All the important motivations, decisions, as well as transfers of personnel, are executed in absolute secrecy from the masses, and only the final results come to light... The moral imperative of the powers that be is: 'we don't hand over our own and do not disclose their guilt'. So, from the dexterous representatives of the erstwhile top and middle echelons of the communist power and from the ranks of swindlers who enriched themselves with lightning speed, a stable and closed oligarchy of 150-200 people emerged that decides the fate of Russia" (*Zavtra*, No. 3, January 1997, p.4).

[21] Mikhail Smondyrev, 'Rossiya: 1937-1993'. *Nezavisimaya Gazeta*, 28 October 1993, p.5.

[22] As a Russian scholar, who has spent a lot of time in the former Lenin Library in Moscow (now - Russian State Library - an equivalent to the U.S. Library of Congress), the author does not believe that there are some documents of a general nature relating to constitutional law (including the American one) kept in the U.S. Library of Congress that cannot be found on the shelves of that Moscow library. His own experience also shows that there are quite a few historic *American* documents that are easier to retrieve from the storage in the Lenin library than from the confines of the Library of Congress.

[23] As Len Karpinsky and Lilliya Shevtsova of *Moscow News* correctly asserted, the struggle between the president and the parliament was evolving "inside a totalitarian paradigm of politics, for which undivided authority and monopoly on power is the only possible form of existence" (quoted in *Novoye Russkoye Slovo*, 11 February 1994, p.29).

[24] Dmitry Galkovsky, 'Broken Compass Shows the Way', *Nezavisimaya Gazeta*, 27 April 1993, p.5.

[25] Karl Radek, 'The War in the Far East', *Foreign Affairs*, July 1932, p.557.

[26] So far one interesting fact surfaced from an amazing story connected with the adventures of Dmitry Yakubovsky - a young Moscow lawyer, who suddenly skyrocketed into the top echelon of the Soviet government and received the rank of an army colonel. His life story beats the best whodunnits and surely will eventually be made into a thrilling movie. At one time Yakubovsky managed to convince the Soviet Minister of Defense Dmitry Yazov that, instead of threateningly pounding tables with their fists while negotiating with the Bonn authorities the fate of huge Soviet property holdings in Eastern Germany (GDR), the Soviet military should study West Germany's (the FRG's) laws and profit from their application. For example, one piece of German legislation prohibits private claims of restitution with regard to property that belonged to former Nazi organizations, namely the bulk of property Soviet forces in Germany possessed as a result of Second World War. The property could therefore have been sold back to the German state or private businesses for billions of Marks. The Minister of Defense was very enthusiastic about such a plan and appointed a high level working group to deal with this issue. But when the plan was reported by the then Speaker of the Soviet parliament, Anatoly Lukianov, to Gorbachev the latter advised him to stay away and evidently terminated the project because he had "his own agenda with [Chancellor] Kohl". "We appear to be on the periphery of some grand political ploy" commented Lukianov to a puzzled Yakubovsky (see Edward Topol, Alexander Grant 'Kremlin's Prisoner', *Novoye Russkoye Slovo*, 9 November 1993, p.9; 24-26 December 1993, pp.19-20). "Expert analysts have found that the Soviet Union derived no advantages from these changes (in GDR - H.T.), and did not even

take the trouble to protect Soviet property in that country" according to Gorbachev's chief of staff (Valery Boldin, *Ten Years That Shook The World. The Gorbachev Era as Witnessed By His Chief of Staff* (New York: Basic Books, 1994), p.141).

[27] *Novoye Russkoye Slovo*, 26 August 1993, p.7.

[28] 'Strategy for Russia. Some theses for the report of the Council on Foreign and Defense Policy', *Nezavisimaya Gazeta*, 19 August 1992, p.5.

[29] *The Washington Times*, 23 March 1992, p.A7.

[30] In 1991 Chechen-Ingush Republic was divided into two republics: Chechen Republic (Chechnya) and Ingush Republic.

[31] The official title of the Treaty is: "Treaty on Demarcating Objects of Jurisdiction and Powers Between the Federal Bodies of State Power of the Russian Federation and the Bodies of Power of the Sovereign Republics Within the Russian Federation" (see *Konstitutsiya Rossiiskoi Federatsii* [The Constitution of the Rossiiskaya Federation], Moscow: Yuridicheskaya Literatura, 1993, pp.63-70). As supplements to the text of the Constitution, there appear to be three more or less similar treaties demarcating objects of jurisdiction and power between the Federal bodies of state power and the bodies of power of a/ Sovereign republics; b/ Territories and provinces, as well as the cities of Moscow and St.Petersburg; and c/ Autonomous provinces and autonomous regions within the Russian Federation. The main difference of the Treaty that deals with the rights of the republics and the two other treaties is that republics, in contrast to territories, provinces, autonomous provinces and regions, are treated as sovereign states, possessing full state power. The leaders of mostly ethnically Russian territories and provinces vigorously objected to such a differentiation and started to demand equal status for all the administrative units of the Federation.

[32] *The Constitution*, p. 67. After the 1993 elections to the state Duma (lower house of the Russian parliament) the central authorities *de facto* renounced the Federal Treaty and started to conclude separate agreements on demarcating objects of jurisdiction and powers with ethnic republics within the Russian Federation and similar agreements with purely Russian regions and territories as well.

[33] It is interesting to note a specific Russian phenomenon that has developed lately: when the name of the capital of a province is changed from the one given it in Soviet times back to its old pre-revolutionary one, the province somehow keeps its Soviet name. For instance, the capital city of the province is now Yekaterinburg, but the province is still Sverdlovsk. The capital city is now St. Petersburg, but the province is still Leningrad etc.

[34] *Newsweek*, 5 April 1993, p.21.

[35] They were mostly officials of the local Soviets, who by the Soviet Union's tradition of "democratic centralism", still considered themselves subordinates to the top body - the Supreme Soviet of Russia - that Yeltsin dissolved.

[36] *Segodnya*, 30 September 1993, p.2; *Novoye Russkoye Slovo*, 19 October 1993, p.8.

[37] Oleg Poptsov, *Khronika vryemen tsarya Borisa* [The Chronicle the Times of Tsar Boris] (Moscow: edition Q Verlag-Gmbh. and "Sovershenno sekretno", 1996), p.318.

[38] *The Washington Post*, 22 November 1993, p.A14.

[39] After Tatarstan, six other national republics within Russia managed to wrestle from the federal government a similar enhanced status of a state *associated* with the Russian Federation. On the eve of the 1995 parliamentary elections, the then Russian prime-minister Viktor Chernomyrdin in a move to ingratiate local bosses (whose support was vital for the prime-minister's party *Our home is Russia*) promised that the central government would sign similar agreements with all the republics, territories and provinces of the Federation. The first purely Russian province on the list became Yeltsin's own, Sverdlovsk province, headed by governor Edward Rossel, whom the President earlier fired from his post after his attempt to create the Ural Republic and thus ensure the same rights which the national republics within Russia got. Mr. Rossel won in the elections for governor of the province in 1995, upstaging the incumbent governor, who represented the party of the Russian prime-minister. By the end of 1998, Moscow signed the agreements on the demarcation of objects of jurisdiction and powers with most of purely Russian regions. Because each such treaty is unique, containing specifics lacking in other such documents, many experts and politicians are worried that such a process might eventually turn Russia from being a federation into a confederation. There is a growing feeling that central government has to return to a single universal document, governing its relations with the 89 subjects of the Federation. But the President and the government in the process of their negotiations with local authorities lost a number of leverages previously used to bring the regions into line. Because the bosses of all the provinces and republics (governors or presidents and heads of the legislative bodies) are now popularly elected and in their totality constitute the Upper house of the Russian parliament (the Council of the Federation), it is much more difficult nowadays for the President and the Prime-Minister of Russia to check the actions of regional chiefs undermining the cohesion of the Federation.

[40] *Novoye Russkoye Slovo*, 28 April 1994, p.6. The journalist Vadim Kegeles wrote: "One would think that Kirsan Ilyumzhinov was prompted to make such a step not so much by a concern about 'greatness and indivisibility of Russia' as by the difficult economic situation in the republic" (*Novoye Russkoye Slovo*, 11 April 1994, p.4). There was also a so-called black oil affair, connected with an illegal sale of this type of fuel oil from Kalmykia. Federal authorities long ago compiled a file on the deal, implicating Ilyumzhinov, but opened it only after a former "personal friend" of Yeltsin became a turncoat. After the Kalmyk President

changed his attitude to Russia the case was closed without much ado. More than that, in 1995 President Yeltsin supported the election of President Ilyumzhinov to the post of the President of International Chess Federation. In the summer of 1998, after the editor of the only independent newspaper in Kalmykia had been assassinated, Russian media finally started to describe Ilyumzhinov's rule as absolutely authoritarian.

[41] *The Washington Times*, 9 November 1993, p.A10.

[42] *Izvestia*, 4 May 1994, p.4. See also *The Washington Times*, 10 May 1994, p.A14, 19 May 1994, p.A7.

[43] The former Press Secretary of President Yeltsin, Vyacheslav Kostikov, tells the following story in his memoirs: On the morning of 13 December, the head of the Central Electoral Commission, Nikolai Ryabov, reported the results of the vote to the President. He was very agitated. To please the press secretary, Ryabov showed him the document of the Commission entitled *Preliminary Results*. "After the appropriate statistics, writes Kostikov, the text concluded: 'The Central Electoral Commission states that more than 50% of the electors, that took part in the voting, voted for the adoption of the Constitution...'. Ryabov then went into the office of the President...". "Two or three hours later the same day, in the official information bulletin of the TASS news agency, a communiqué appeared that somewhat perplexed me. It stated: 'The Central Electoral Commission confirmed today that... from the 55% [of potential electors -H.T.] who came to the polls about 60% approved the basic law'. Thus the earlier phrase 'more than 50%', who voted for the Constitution, had now become 'about 60%'. The altered figure later appeared in all official documents. My first thought was that, probably, during the numerous hours that had elapsed between the time of Ryabov's conversation with the President, new, more accurate data, appeared, and the Commission quickly took it into account. However, after a few days, I happened to see a copy of the same document that Ryabov initially brought to the President. The correction mentioned above was inserted with a fountain pen. It probably would not be difficult for a graphologist to establish who had made the said correction. But I am not a graphologist" (Vyacheslav Kostikov, *Roman s presidentom* [Love Affair with the President] (Moscow: "Vagrius", 1997), pp.266-267).

[44] *Rossiiskiye Vesti*, 29 April 1994, p.2.

[45] Reportedly Dudaev was killed by a missile precisely targeted to the spot he was on through direction-finding of the antennae emission of his cellular telephone. Another version of these events suggests that Moscow finally persuaded Dudaev to get the super-secret communication equipment in order to establish a confidential channel of peace talks with Moscow. He agreed and the communication was delivered to him by a special messenger, the officer of the Russian Federal Agency of Government Communications. Even that officer did not know that the equipment supplied to Dudaev was an actual mine that would explode at the required moment.

It was an operation of the type the Israeli security services used to assassinate the Palestinian extremist called "engineer". Allegedly the Russian officer perished together with Dudaev (*Nezavisimaya Gazeta*, 28 May 1996, p.3).

[46] Through fake letters of credits, Chechen mafiosi stole about 4 trillion roubles from the Russian banks. Almost half of the forged banknotes withdrawn from circulation on the territory of Russia were of Chechen origin, thousands of containers and railway cars were annually robbed clean in Chechnya and all income from the sale of oil, the only export commodity of Chechnya, landed in the pockets of criminal bosses and the leaders of Chechnya, who, as is now absolutely certain, shared their illegal income with some big shots in the Moscow hierarchy (*Izvestia*, 8 February 1995, p.4; 23 August 1996, p.2; 26 September 1996, p.5).

[47] But it was not only a matter of choosing the route for oil. The task was also to keep criminal enterprise going. The Russian politician, Nikolai Gonchar, the deputy of the Duma writes: "Actually Russia has been fighting for the right to continue to invest trillions of roubles, earned by the sweat of her brow, into the insatiable jaws of local *bandocratia*. There are no other real Russian aims in Chechnya. By the way, they were lacking for the USSR in Afghanistan and Africa... Whether Chechnya is within Russia, or it is an 'independent state', all the same money from the export of the Chechen oil was going, is going and will be going solely and exclusively to Grozny. The question of whose pockets that money has been filling and who in Moscow gets their share of the money in the form of bribes is a quite different matter. The only thing that is absolutely certain is that no average inhabitant of Chechnya, nor the Russian budget sees that money and never will" (*Moskovskii Komsomolets* (hereafter simply *MK*), 18 July 1995, p.4).

[48] The operation was also in flagrant violation of the Code of conduct relating to military and political aspects of security that was adopted only a few days before at the OSCE summit meeting in Budapest. Article VIII - 36 of this Code requires of the participating countries that, when a decision to use military forces of the state is made to ensure internal security, it ought to be made in accordance with Constitutional procedure and hence those military forces must adopt the measures necessary to avoid causing harm to civilians and their property. That was simply not done. However, at the end of July 1995, the Constitutional court of Russia, acting on an inquiry from parliament, unexpectedly justified the decree of the President No. 2137 of 30 November that started the military operations in Chechnya. The Presidential decree created a high-level group to introduce a state of emergency in Chechnya, while cunningly not calling into question the compatibility of military intervention with Constitutional provisions. The Presidential decree was in fact a secret, which also contravened the relevant legislation. Nevertheless, the court found no infraction of the law in the Presidential decree and thus actually considered the carnage in Chechnya legal, even without the declaration of a state of emergency.

[49] Actually nobody knows the exact figures for the victims of the war against Chechnya. In the Autumn of 1996, Alexander Lebed, the then Secretary of the National Security Council of Russia, stated that the number of people killed in Chechnya, totalled 80,000 with more than 240,000 people wounded and maimed (*Izvestia*, 9 September 1996, p.1). The number of refugees from Chechnya is estimated at half a million. The cost of military operations is said to be around US$5-6 billion. An additional US$6-8 billion will be needed for the restoration of everything that was destroyed. Indirect confirmation of the colossal costs of the war is the fact that just between March-August 1995, the gold stock of Russia diminished by 97 tons, whilst no emergency repayments of foreign debts or huge purchases from abroad were made by the Russian government (*MK*, 8 August 1995, p.1). "Isn't this too high a price to cover up a couple of dozen of high-placed criminals?" asked the newspaper (ibid.).

[50] On 20 September 1995, Chechen terrorists just by mistake missed the car of the President's representative in Chechnya, the Secretary of the Russian Security Council Oleg Lobov, and instead with a remote control mine blew up the escort car. On 6 October, they blew up the car of the Commander-in-Chief of the Russian federal forces in Chechnya, General Anatoly Romanov, who stubbornly stuck to a peaceful solution to disputed issues. The General was seriously wounded with probable irreversible brain injuries.

[51] "This was a sheer propaganda action", recalls General Lebed. "It was like a movie. There were 39 aircraft in the air, securing the landing of the presidential plane. He (Yeltsin) landed at *Severny* [Northern] airport. All around it was cordoned off by regiments and divisions. He was brought to a model military post, which was serviced by the special militia troops, that had been flown to the base two hours before the arrival of the President. All men well-fed, smart looking. He asked them: 'How are things going?', 'Perfectly well', they answered, being fully aware that in two hours after the departure of the President they will also depart." (*Noviye Izvestia*, 21 January 1998, p.4.) At a heavily guarded meeting at the airport, Yeltsin said that "the criminal regime that seized Chechnya (the regime with which the President was negotiating in Moscow -H.T.!) ought to be liquidated for the sake of the defense of the [Chechen] republic's population, the restoration of legality and peace on its territory, public tranquillity in the Northern Caucasus and the preservation of the unity of Russia" (*Nezavisimaya Gazeta*, 29 May 1996, p.1).

[52] Very many people in Russia (including experts) doubt that Yeltsin really won in the second round. His opponent in the elections, the leader of the Communist Party of Russia, Gennady Zyuganov, when asked in an interview on the first anniversary of Yeltsin's "victory" why he did not protest, said that it was very difficult for him and his party to recognize the official results of elections because they knew of the tremendous scope for the falsification of electoral results. But they

understood that if they started to protest too strong, Russia might split in half between the north (voting for Yeltsin) and the south (voting for Zyuganov), so they decided not to protest, "because only the people, who hate their country, can throw it into a conflagration of civil war for the third time this century" (*Nezavisimaya Gazeta*, 4 July 1997, p.5).

[53] This was one of the most shameful defeats of the Russian armed forces in all their history. Chechen irregulars occupied the city without fighting, though the correlation of Russian troops in the city and incoming Chechen warriors was 4:1. Besides, Russian armed forces had more than 200 armored vehicles that Chechens did not have, and there were quite a few Russian military units based around the city. Commenting on this inglorious event on its second anniversary *Nezavisimaya Gazeta* wrote: "The most perfunctory analysis of the events of that August makes one to conclude that the cause of tragedy was the greatest betrayal. Otherwise it is impossible to understand how the army of separatists could without fighting get into the city filled to overflowing by Russian troops and defeat them, despite tremendous preponderance of the federal forces in numerical strength, firepower and technical might". However, added the newspaper, "though the betrayal definitely occurred, the gist of the matter seems to be that the people of various ranks and titles, that in the summer of 1996 constituted the Russian military machine in Chechnya, were as a whole absolutely reluctant to fight" (*Nezavisimaya Gazeta*, 6 August 1998, p.1).

[54] On 19 August 1996, President Yeltsin officially ordered Lebed "to restore law and order on the territory of the Chechen republic, including its capital, Grozny, as it existed on 5 August 1996 (that is, before the capture of the city by the Chechen forces - H.T.)" (*Segodnya*, 20 August 1996, p.1). This was the most bizarre assignment because the President refused to make Lebed the commander of the federal troops in Chechnya and the cease-fire was already operating. Evidently, by that time, the President due to his illness, was not in full control of the situation and this and some other controversial orders, to put it mildly, allegedly signed by him, were actually the "products" of his immediate staff, headed by Anatoly Chubais. Such a crazy directive can properly be considered *ex post facto* as another attempt by the "war party" in the Moscow establishment to disrupt peace negotiations. Such a conclusion is also confirmed by the fact that, when Lebed and Maskhadov eventually signed the aforementioned agreements, President Yeltsin showed no public reaction to this achievement. For several days, he refused to talk with Lebed even over the telephone! There might also be another explanation: to hell with Chechnya, the most urgent task was to dispose of Lebed, who had become very popular on the eve of a rather risky bypass operation on the President's heart, which might have made new Presidential elections necessary.

[55] *Compilation*, No. 46 (11 November 1996), p.10252.

[56] *Izvestia*, 14 May 1997, p.1.

[57] *Nezavisimaya Gazeta*, 11 June 1997, p.2.

[58] "When in the spring of 1991, Boris Yeltsin, then a candidate for the post of the President of Russia, visited the then Chechen-Ingush Republic he supported the sovereignty of the republic by repeating his well-known call "Take as much sovereignty as you can swallow". It is difficult to believe that Yeltsin, by repeating his infamous phrase about sovereignty during the heat of the election campaign, did not understand how it would all end. It follows that he gave promises with the sole purpose of getting (at any price) people's votes. And so it happened. At the presidential elections of 1991, Yeltsin got 80% of votes in the Chechen-Ingush Republic, a much higher percentage than in Russia as a whole. This was what we call "dirty politics", i.e. personal gain at any price, even to the detriment of the state interests... Chechnya clearly demonstrated the character of the ruling regime of Russia, which provided a unique opportunity for mass plunder of its own country, for the creation of fighting units from criminals, released from prisons, and for the organization of genocide of its own people" (Gosudarstvennaya Duma. Komissiya po rassledovaniyu prichin i obstoyatel'stv vozniknoveniya crizisnoy situatsii v Chechenskoy respublike. *Itogovii Otchet.* [The State Duma. Commission on Investigation of the causes and circumstances of the origin of the crisis situation in the Chechen republic. The Concluding Report] (State Duma. Moscow, October 1995, pp.14,54). The Commission is known as "the Govorukhin Commission" after the name of the deputy who chaired it, a well-known Russian director of documentary movies).

[59] *Nezavisimaya Gazeta*, 19 August 1992, p.5.

[60] See *Nezavisimaya Gazeta*, 30 July 1996, p.2.

[61] Kievan Grand Prince Vladimir Monomakh (who ruled between 1113-1125) was uniting the separated principalities of Kievan Rus'. The Monomakh gabled gold crown decorated with precious stones, a cross and trimmed with sable fur is the earliest Tsarist regalia kept on display in the Kremlin. It is commonly known as *shapka Monomakha* (Monomakh's fur hat).

[62] All the FSU's republics minus the three Baltic countries and Georgia.

[63] "All these toy 'Presidents' of other republics - actually first Party secretaries...finally had the prospect of unlimited rule at home", according to the well-known Russian author, Tatyana Tolstaya. "They would not be accountable to 'Moscow', have to crawl on their bellies, to send tithes: rugs, diamonds, cognac, money, porcelain vases of human height with portraits of the Great Russian Boss..." (Tatyana Tolstaya, 'Boris the First', *The New York Review of Books*, 23 June 1994, p.4).

[64] Post-communist scoundrels, posing as businessmen and unhampered by the bribed authorities, are now only too eager to widen that dump by collecting poisonous and contaminated industrial waste from Europe and the USA. They are willing to bury it for money in Russia and other CIS republics.

[65] *Izvestia*, 24 May 1997, p.2.

[66] *Izvestia*, 3 June 1997, p.2. In answer to the question about the rent, Moscow politicians replied: "Slightly less than $100 million a year" (Ibid.). This means that Russia will pay to Ukraine no rent for 20 years to compensate for the Ukraine's debts to Russia.

[67] The aggregate CIS republics debt to Russia at the beginning of 1997 was close to 15 trillion roubles or US$2.6 billions (*Segodnya*, 28 February 1997, p.2).

[68] Alexei Arbatov, 'Russia's foreign policy alternatives', *International Security*, Fall 1993, p.29.

[69] *The Conception*, pp.3-4.

[70] *Izvestia*, 23 April 1996, p.1.

[71] *Segodnya*, 13 April 1996, p.1. According to the Prime Minister of Russia, the share of the CIS countries in the world export trade equals 2%. In the main, it consists of raw materials. This is one more valid argument in favor of increased intra-CIS trade.

[72] Signatories pledged to refrain from the use or threat of force in disputes among themselves. They have also undertaken not to join any military alliance or to participate in any activities that are directed against any other signatory state. They have pledged to coordinate efforts in the event of a military threat and to provide military assistance to any signatory state i.e. the victim of aggression from the outside. (See Dogovor o kollektivnoij bezopasnosti [The Treaty on Collective Security], *Diplomaticheskii Vestnik*, 30 June 1992, pp. 9-11.)

[73] Adjar Krutov, 'National Security of Russia Depends on the Rate of Integration of the CIS States', *Nezavisimaya Gazeta*, 15 January 1997, p.5.

[74] *Nezavisimaya Gazeta*, 10 September 1996, p.2.

[75] A. Tuleyev in the interview on the First Channel of Russian TV (6 o'clock evening news on 27 January 1997).

[76] Nursultan Nazarbayev, 'Rossiya mogla by stat sterzhnem Sodruzhestva, no ne stala' [Rossiya might have become the Pivot of the Commonwealth but it hadn't], *Nezavisimaya Gazeta*, 16 January 1997, pp.1,3.

Chapter Three

The Problem of National Security

A long time before the demise of the Soviet Union, the main preoccupation of its government, as presented in all the CPSU official documents and speeches of its leaders, was to ensure Russia's security in the face of a nuclear threat from the "warmongering Western nations". This bogy of an extreme "threat from the outside" was actually the main motivation which kept the Soviet machine running. This is also why the Soviet people were given the "leftovers" in the form of consumer goods manufactured from what was not used by military industry. This "leftover" principle reached its peak when the people themselves were turned not just into residual elements of the production process, but into mere cogs, to use Stalin's definition, in a colossal military machine. Such an arrangement of Russian economics and life led to the demise of the Union.

The "mortal threat from the outside" for both the Soviet Union and the United States was initially largely a psychological image created by the leaders of both countries (although it must be acknowledged that Joseph Stalin bears more responsibility than Harry Truman for the start of the Cold war). With a passage of time and the continuous non-stop arms build up on both sides, this threat gradually turned into a self-fulfilling prophecy.

However, in contrast to the United States, where a democratic political process in one way or another put a limit on the amount of resources (human and other) that were to be sacrificed to the military, in the Soviet Union after World War Two it was the military establishment itself that determined what it needed. As a result it claimed unlimited amounts of resources plus a little bit more!

A relatively small Russian ruling elite (including the top military leadership) and the personnel directly servicing it (altogether no more than 8% of nearly 300 million population), ensured, through a system of specialized distribution of consumer goods and services, which were not accessible to the general public (special clinics, health resorts, stores, food supplies, housing complexes, country villas, hunting lodges, swimming pools, advanced priority bookings for travel, entertainment - you name it), that they received everything they needed. (By the way, this system of privileges for the ruling elite is still intact!) The rest of the population was left to live in absolute poverty.[1] All other resources were consumed by the military-industrial complex (MIC).

By the mid 1980s, a tense atmosphere existed between the United States and the Soviet Union and the world was steadily drifting into a nightmare of nuclear catastrophe, with superpower strategic arms control agreements doing little to decrease tension.

Gorbachev, when he finally realized that the Soviet economy was unable to sustain an intensifying arms race, called it quits and by the series of moves in the realm of foreign, arms control and military policy defused the atmosphere. Those moves are well-known, so it is unnecessary to dwell on them here. Their main thrust was that Russia should enhance her security mainly through political, diplomatic and arms control measures, thereby creating a more friendly international environment. This approach was fully in line with the Russian word for security (*bezopasnost*), which literally means "an absence of danger". Since the "imperialist war threat" was mainly the creation of Soviet leadership's imagination and of the corresponding mass propaganda, it was not difficult to drastically reduce that threat, almost overnight, by simply downgrading official descriptions of the threat.

The drastic downgrading by Moscow of the American and NATO threat to the Union (coupled with friendly moves on the part of the West towards a changing Soviet Union) put the problem of protecting Russia's security onto a quite different plane, and turned it from the most vital issue into something that could be dealt with like any other matter of state, not as a permanent emergency issue. This change in threat perception theoretically allowed for some redistribution of resources from the military into the civilian sector of the economy. The military doctrine of "strategic sufficiency" with its main emphasis on a defensive military posture was announced.

For the West, a drastic decrease in the Soviet military threat was confirmed not only by all the steps towards the de-militarization of foreign policy, undertaken by Moscow in the period 1987-1990, but also by the collapse of the Soviet empire in East Europe and, finally, by the demise of the Union itself. The Soviet Union, and later its main inheritor Russia, were officially seen by Western leaders as no longer a threat (except in the narrow sense of concerns on both sides about the use and control of the thousands of nuclear weapons).

New importance of geopolitics

The perennial hope of humankind after the end of some dark, awful, tragic period in its life (a plague, a global famine, a bloody war,) is the need for a new beginning: a real brotherhood of nations, a world "safe for democracy", a golden era of peace, an end to all strife, or even an end of history itself with all its painful past.

Regretfully, history repeats itself. This is what, evidently, is happening to the great expectations of humankind after the end of the Cold war (if it has really ended). New gory conflicts across the globe, new fratricidal strife, rearrangements of power alliances and new moves for better positions in the battles of the future are taking place simultaneously with intensified pious preaching about a "New World Order".

The geopolitical situation in Eurasia and, as a result, in the whole world, is in the process of accelerated change with consequences difficult as yet to forecast. This change, however, started long before the demise of the Soviet Union. It actually started with the disappearance at the end of 1960s of the Sino-Soviet monolith, which for more than a decade menacingly towered above the Eurasian landmass, and signified the peak of communist global influence.

This momentous development was duly appreciated by Washington, which began to practice anew its traditional balance of power politics in the Eastern hemisphere because the world was ceasing to be bipolar. Hence President Nixon's opening up to China and the increasingly complex triangular relationships among the USA - China - USSR.

Russian scholars and strategists, who were educated to believe that geopolitics was a "fascist invention", initially simply did not understand the conceptually momentous implications of a Moscow-Beijing rift for global politics. (I personally sat in on many internal foreign policy discussions in Moscow and was punished by the authorities for predicting such a possibility earlier in a *private* conversation.) Nonetheless, intuitively and out of an exaggerated fear at the time of the "Yellow peril" (a fear organically present in the Russian psyche since the days of the 200-year long Tatar-Mongol rule over Russia), Leonid Brezhnev and his colleagues favored détente with the United States. This was one of the first consequences of an emerging Sino-American détente.[2] The balance of power politics suddenly became everybody's business, that of the United States, the Soviet Union, China, and Western Europe.

But Russian leaders at the time, given that they were illiterate *muzhiks* (peasants), as usual over-reacted. They not only exacerbated the split with China, but enabled it to become more entrenched as a result of the total militarization of the Soviet Union's border with China. They also launched a military intervention into Afghanistan in an attempt to provide an "object lesson" in Soviet might to "foreign enemies".[3] This unsuccessful intervention backfired and the USSR's standing on the world stage was weakened, not enhanced.

However, despite its misadventure in Afghanistan (like the United States' earlier misfortunes in Vietnam), the Soviet Union, in the appreciation of outsiders (including the American CIA), was still "going strong" and a mighty force in Eurasia which needed to be delicately handled.

The demise of the Union in 1991 further altered the picture.

Theoretically, inner Russia still remains the geographic "heartland" of the global landmass. But what was at the time of Halford Mackinder a crucial geopolitical factor defense-wise, does not have much significance in the nuclear age. More than that, the very core of the "heartland" - Russian Siberia - remains, after 50 plus years of Soviet policy of total industrialization, an underdeveloped, sparsely populated territory, which, despite its underdevelopment, is totally polluted, and its ecosystem has been heavily damaged by the widespread exploitation of its natural resources.[4]

However, Russia remains a nuclear superpower, with all the nuclear weapons of the FSU (including around 7,000 strategic nuclear warheads) on its territory. However according to other criteria (population, economic potential, per capita GNP) Russia is now a medium power, albeit with a colossal military and supporting industries.

The important thing is that, despite its territorial shrinkage and major economic difficulties, Russia, per force its location in-between the two different global civilizations -- Oriental and Western (being at the same time a peculiar civilization of its own) -- still remains one of the main elements of the Eurasian and the global geopolitical picture. Russia still occupies the position of civilizational equilibrium, and remains a pivotal weight in the global balance of power. Its role in the multipolar balance of power is no less crucial than the Soviet Union's role as the second "superpower" in the Cold war period of bipolar global confrontation. But, while the latter was frigid and inflexible, this new balance is delicate and flexible because moves by one or more chief players in the new global balance of power-game can lead to a profound rearrangement in the balance, which is presently characterized by the following dynamics:

- China is gradually becoming the number one industrial giant of the world under increasing pressure of overpopulation, which needs to be vented.
- Japan has emerged as the present second-ranking global industrial power and is looking for its own international identity and role, not marred by the United States' patronage.
- The center of global economic activity has shifted to the Asia-Pacific region.
- On the other side of Eurasia, a new politico-economic European Union has emerged that is clearly in the process of being dominated economically by the unified and ever more assertive Germany, whose economic aspirations are aimed eastward.
- The United States military presence in Europe is gradually diminishing as well as its influence over Japan and China.
- The so-called military vacuum of the successor states of East Europe, including the Baltic republics, has became the main zone of contention for influence between the East and West.
- Russia itself has become separated from Western and Central Europe by the Baltic states, Belarus and Ukraine. Though Russian borders with the last two countries have not yet taken the form of strictly international borders, Russia's military planning has to treat these countries as foreign states.
- In a volatile European South East, Russia now has to compete for influence in the Transcaucasus republics of Georgia, Azerbaijan and Armenia with an increasingly active Turkey and Iran (with Armenia being the only one solidly pro-Russian republic).
- In the former Soviet Central Asia all the indications suggest that the region (together with former Soviet Union's Transcaucasus) might turn

into a new unstable Middle East of the globe, with Muslim influence on the rise and with many outside powers strongly competing for control of the region.

• In its Asian south west, Russia now borders on Kazakhstan, where the Russian population nearly equals the numbers of indigenous Kazakhs (around 40% for each group), while in the Kazakhstan's northern border regions, Russians significantly outnumber Kazakhs. Kazakhstan and four other Muslim republics of the FSU (Uzbekistan, Kyrgyzstan, Turkmenistan and Tajikistan) do not have strong military forces, and are not in any way a danger to Russia at least for the time being. More than that, their military forces are essentially still under the control of Russian officers. The danger lies in the fact that these five republics with a combined population of 45 million and a territory of more than 1.5 million square miles, nowadays represents a proverbial "geopolitical vacuum", very tempting for militant Muslim states such as Iran, Afghanistan and Pakistan, as well as for China which has a common border with Tajikistan, Kyrgyzstan and Kazakhstan and quite a sizable population of Kazakh and Kyrgyz in its own Xinjiang province.[5]

• Thus far Russia is filling that Central Asian vacuum by providing troops to guard the troublesome Tajikistan-Afghanistan border and military officers for fledgling armies of other Central Asian FSU republics. The Tashkent Treaty on Collective Security, signed on 15 May 1992 by the representatives of Kazakhstan, Kyrgyzstan, Tajikistan, Uzbekistan, Russia and Armenia, provides a legal basis for the Russian military presence in the area.[6]

• While Russia has settled its own 2725 mile border with China,[7] responsibility for the demarcation of the borders between China and the three other ex-Soviet republics is now a subject of bilateral negotiations between the corresponding parties. As Gerald Robbins notes this amounts to a tacit understanding between China and Russia concerning the "rearrangement of their zones of influence".[8]

• At the same time a long-term territorial dispute exists between Japan and Russia regarding the South Kuril islands (the "Northern territories" according to Japan's definition) that were occupied after the Second World War by Soviet troops. At the time of writing the dispute remains unsolved, while the general weakening of Russia makes the Japanese hopeful that time will work in their favor.

We shall discuss later numerous possible future political combinations for Russia based on her security considerations, but because of the aforementioned factors, the new Russia continues to act as a "mediator" (balancer) in the new geopolitical situation in Eurasia. More than that, in certain respects, the geopolitical importance of Russia now is greater for the fate of the world than during the years of the global bi-polarity, when not only minor, but quite a few major political and economic changes, and large-scale local wars failed to alter in any significant way the global geopolitical picture that emerged as a result of World War Two. This war itself was triggered by the accumulated geopolitical change stemming from the rise of Nazi Germany, Communist Russia and a militaristic Japan, and from the serious weakening of Britain and France.

However, as Dr. Joseph Churba, the President of the U.S. International Security Council, aptly remarks, a period when a substantial geopolitical transition on a global scale is taking place, similar to the one nowadays, is always closer to war than to peace. This is why the security of Russia in its present dual incarnation of a single state and as the unofficial leader of the Commonwealth of Independent States (now incorporating all the ex-USSR minus the Baltic republics) is not just a particular problem for Russia, but one of global significance. It is doubtful that all the world-wide implications of this problem are as yet fully appreciated and thought through by Moscow itself. Perhaps for this reason, the Russian Duma (under the prodding of Zhirinovsky) established a special parliamentary Committee on Geopolitics.

The fact is that Soviet/Russian political leaders and military strategists, who for more than a generation focused their attention on the United States and NATO, and who did so within the framework of East-West bipolar confrontation, adopted a quite different continental and global outlook, when pathways to security are not as clearly defined as before, and when a number of things depend on the right geopolitical choices. This process of a necessary accommodation to the new strategic environment is a difficult one, especially in a situation whereby the Russian leadership (both political and military) has concentrated on the internal struggle for power over the last six years.

What kind of existing and potential military dangers from the outside and other circumstances, when Russian troops have to or might be used, has Russia to consider in the immediate and near future?

If one takes into account all the potential (theoretical) threats and other situations that might necessitate the use of Russian armed forces (without arranging them in accordance with the degree of their probability) the list might look like this:

- A strategic nuclear threat from the United States and NATO.
- A nuclear threat from a non-NATO country.
- A threat from a CIS republic.
- A non-nuclear threat from a non-CIS country.
- Russia's involvement in the CIS, the UN, the OSCE and finally, even in NATO's peace-keeping operations; and
- Internal security threats - the need to use troops within Russia, in the event of large scale popular unrest, uprisings, and/or dangerous secessionist moves by one or more of its provinces or republics.

What is absent from this list is a situation requiring the dispatch of Russian troops overseas not on a UN or some other mission, collectively supported by the members of the world community. However, at least for the time being, an exhausted Russia, in contrast to the FSU, has no urge and no commitments to act in the Third world as a military "guarantor", "balancer", assisting a particular regime or movement.

The authors of the document *Strategy for Russia* summed up the reasons for such restraint quite well. They state:

It is sufficiently clear that financial limitations, economic interests, a lack of opportunity for the sizable export of capital and a high self-sufficiency in resources dictate the necessity for Russia to return to its traditional continental strategy, and to totally renounce a global involvement in the affairs of the whole world, which was imposed upon the USSR by communist proselytizing and by the vagaries of history. This underscores the urgency of a further reduction, at least for the observable future, of geo-strategic ambitions, of overseas commitments and of the forces and means needed to sustain them (first of all an oceanic navy).[9]

This assessment, however, is, evidently, not shared by some sections of the Russian military establishment, who still consider it necessary for Russia to engage in overseas ventures. Even the well-known Russian General and aspiring President, Alexander Lebed, had this to say:

As soon as Russia begins to break out of the systemic crisis and becomes economically (and politically) more independent, it will have to assert its national and state interests beyond its own territory.[10]

So, it seems, such sentiments cannot be reduced just to the expansionist demagoguery of Zhirinovsky.

Strategic threat from the United States and NATO

Whatever the current Russian leadership says regarding its partnership, as partner, with the United States, theoretically the nuclear threat from the United States still exists simply because of the existence of deployed American strategic weapons (nuclear weapons-carrying strategic bombers, intercontinental ballistic missiles (ICBMs) and nuclear missile-carrying submarines). Most of these weapons were targeted on key points within Russia. The bulk of Russia's strategic forces was also aimed at targets in the United States.

Of course, it is now clear (as it was even before the demise of the Soviet Union) that neither Russia, nor the United States have any intention to attack one another. More than that, the two strategic arms reduction treaties concluded between them (START I and START II) envisage a reduction in strategic armaments on both sides to 3,000 - 3,500 warheads for each side by the year 2003. But even if and when those drastic reductions are realized, the mutual threat (at least in the form of accidental or unauthorized launch) will still persist, until and unless it is eliminated by some future global agreement to ban all nuclear weaponry. So the situation of mutual deterrence still exists despite the drastic decline in feelings of danger on both sides.

In an important gesture of mutual trust, President Yeltsin and President Clinton signed an agreement in Moscow on 14 January 1994 stipulating that by 30 May 1994 none of their strategic missiles would be targeted at each other, or for that matter at any other country. The key points would be somewhere in the Pacific Ocean. Serge Schmemann of *The New York Times* commented:

Officials agreed that the measure was more symbolic than practical, since it carried no verification procedures, and since missiles can be rapidly re-targeted. Besides, Mr. Yeltsin has already declared that no Russian missiles are targeted on the US.[11]

However symbolic, this agreement had a positive effect, which was not only psychological because an ICBM of either country, launched without the proper authorization, will not hit another country, but will land in some deserted region of the World Ocean. The agreement actually gives the United States an additional assurance against the possibility that some desperadoes might try to provoke a nuclear exchange between Russia and the United States by launching an ICBM or several of them toward the United States.

On the appointed day - 30 May 1994 - both the Pentagon and the Soviet High command reported that they had completed the process of re-targeting their respective strategic missiles away from points inside the territory of the other country.[12]

It should be noted that all solemn pledges and obligations of this kind, so-called confidence - and security - building measures, are, as a rule, undertaken by parties deeply suspicious of each other, and no one ever proposed mutual pledges of this kind between genuine partners, such as the United States and Great Britain.

While Russian military commanders publicly agree that a nuclear threat to Russia from the United States has drastically diminished, in their hearts they still have some apprehensions about the United States. Years of indoctrination about "insatiable aggressive imperialism" cannot be easily wiped off the memory of marshals and generals of a former totalitarian regime. Even the eradication of such thoughts from the minds of their counterparts in the United States, who have lived under conditions of freedom and sophisticated intellectual debate, requires a great deal of effort. Also, in view of the tremendous domination in the FSU and, presently, in Russia of industries producing weapons, who are actually the backbone of all Russian economics, it is virtually impossible for the Russian leadership to totally abandon in internal debates some speculation with regard to a "potential American threat", because such a speculation justifies the need to maintain a strategic nuclear arsenal, and to keep up - qualitatively - with the American Jones', who, evidently, are also modernizing their strategic arsenal.[13]

Of course, the opportunities for modernization in Russia are now becoming more narrowly defined, more limited and less money is available to finance this strategy. There is no more fiscal largesse of old times and free for all designers approach, which tended to act as a substitute for the absence of real economic competition in the FSU among weapons makers.

But pressure from a powerful arms manufacturing lobby, which has close links with the President and his entourage, will persist, swallowing up tremendous human and industrial resources and thus slowing down the actual transformation of the Russian economy toward more efficient production geared to the needs of an individual private consumer, not to the requirements of industrial consumption.[14]

Russia has managed to curtail production of some weapons systems. But at the same time there are persistent reports about new weapons systems being developed. The Russian MIC is engaged in the construction and production of new road-mobile and fixed site land-based ICBMs. At the end of December 1994, a new solid-fuel ICBM "Topol-M" was successfully tested in Russia, and on 24 December 1997 two such missiles were installed into silos in the Saratov region of Russia. This ICBM, which is made exclusively of parts manufactured within Russia, will eventually replace most of the seven types of Soviet-built strategic missiles that are currently deployed in Russia. While it is designed to carry a single nuclear warhead, it can be quickly fitted out with multiple warheads. It can be deployed either in silos, or on mobile launchers. In Severodvinsk a new generation attack submarine was built, with priority financing. The Baltiiskii shipyard in St. Petersburg finished construction of a heavy cruiser *Pyotr Velikii* (Peter the Great). The Sukhoi aircraft design bureau created a new frontline fighter-bomber SU-34, a super-modern fourth generation plane, that is put into mass production. It also produced a new fighter SU-37, which is considered to be the best in the world at this moment in time. On the verge of mass production is a new generation of "smart" long-range cruise missiles produced on stealth technology for strategic bombers. In September 1995, a new model of tank (T-90) was shown in Russia. The head of the Russian State armaments agency also announced that the designers will soon produce a conceptually different tank.[15]

Russia can live with the so-called residual American threat, especially if both Russia and the United States, continue on the road to arms reductions. This is evidently what the forces now in control of the Russian government are interested in. But their freedom of manoeuver is circumscribed by the current correlation of political forces in Russia, by the strong and growing influence of nationalistic factions in the Russian parliament and by the corresponding movements outside of it.

If the West, the United States in particular, tries to meet the resurgence of nationalism in Russia with some measures that would demonstrate to Russians an American swing towards increased military preparedness, this in turn will generate even stronger apprehensions on the part of the Russian leadership and, especially, of the military. Such a trend will lead the Russian military high command to draw negative conclusions about the real strategic designs of the United States, and this might end in heightened international tension. It is clear, however, that in its present socio-economic condition, Russia cannot physically restart a new round of arms competition with the United States.

Finally, it is doubtful that the present Russian civilian and military leadership is in any way worried about the nuclear potentials of France and Britain. Their arsenals cause concern only as part of the overall apprehension by any nuclear state regarding the possibility of the unauthorized or accidental launch of a nuclear missile. Otherwise it is clear to Moscow that the only circumstances when Britain and/or France might use their nuclear weapons against Russia will be either to respond to Moscow's nuclear attack or in conditions of a global warfare generated by the Russian-American military clash. So, to all intents and purposes, it is in the national interest of Russia to downplay the danger from these weapons.

It will be a quite different situation, however, if Germany all of a sudden were to stop being in a non-proliferation regime and start making its own nuclear weapons. And though there are some American scholars who envisage such an eventuality,[16] it will hardly materialize within the time frame dealt in this book, especially if the conditions of the Non-Proliferation Treaty continue to remain in force.

There is one more worry in Russia today. This stems from the eastward expansion of NATO that started in earnest at the Madrid NATO summit in July 1997, when the first three East European counties - Poland, Hungary and the Czech republic - were invited to join the Alliance. A hypothetical possibility of stationing of some of the bloc's tactical nuclear weapons, as well as additional troops, on the territories of the new NATO members is extremely worrying for the military commanders of Russia, if not to its pro-American leaders. Such apprehensions have been repeatedly expressed by the Russian leadership, though the fact is that NATO officially promised not to deploy nuclear weapons on the territories of NATO's new members. However, the main thing is that for many reasons (including the inevitable retaliatory deployment of short range nuclear weapons by Russia, given a volatile situation in certain East European countries) it will be sheer madness strategically for NATO to do that in peacetime. Such a step would increase the possibility of a limited nuclear war in Europe, which is not in the interests of any European country.

Nuclear threat from a non-NATO country

This is a universal threat for all the countries in the world, a threat which is slowly but gradually growing in view of the appearance on the world stage of new nuclear countries like Israel, India, Pakistan and what one might call terrorist nuclear states, such as Libya or North Korea. It is highly unlikely that a civilized international community, either through the UN Security Council, or simply as a group of states extremely worried by such developments, and by implicit and explicit threats, emanating from a potential nuclear power, will make some decisive pre-emptive military moves geared towards liquidating the appropriate illicit facilities on the pattern of Israel's bombing of the Iraq nuclear reactor in 1981. The United States' vacillating stand in its negotiations with North Korea in the period 1991-95 regarding international control over the latter's nuclear facilities (North Korea is a party to the NPT) proves my point beyond reasonable doubt.

A devastating counter attack from any nuclear country attacked by a nuclear outlaw state is quite probable, but it will be an act of retaliation, not a preventive strike.

So the two feasible options for the leading industrial countries to neutralize such a potential threat are, firstly, to use political and economic leverages to compel the countries in question to observe the non-proliferation regime and, secondly, to develop (collectively or separately) tactical or limited strategic anti-missile defense, as advocated by the United States government, which is slowly switching from a sweeping SDI research to the development and deployment of advanced theater missile defenses (TMD), whose potential capabilities extend into the strategic sphere.

Previous international responses by the Western countries vis-à-vis so called "outlaw states" in crisis situations, vividly demonstrates that some hidebound (though often trivial) "national interests" often outweigh the impulse for a unified approach to such situations, even among a group of very close allies.

For the time being Russia is following both tracks in trying to contribute to the strengthening of the non-proliferation regime[17] and in cooperating with the US on TMD.[18] At the same time, Russia might involuntarily contribute to a growing danger of nuclear terrorism by being unable, in the present chaos, to effectively control transfers abroad of some of its fissionable materials, as well as movements of its highly qualified nuclear arms scientists and engineers, who are lured by big money in hard currency offered by likes of Libya, Iran and other states.

The Russian government is attempting to tighten such controls, but it is far too optimistic to expect Moscow to be completely successful in curbing transfers of appropriate materials and know-how, especially so in a situation when, on the one hand, one can transfer some know-how and designs electronically across the borders and, on the other, when some other republics of the CIS possess nuclear-weapons materials in large quantities. So, in a way, Russia itself might contribute to the growth of a nuclear terrorist danger. This is in direct contrast to the previous situation when the Soviet Union was one of the states with the most stringent control over nuclear facilities and very tight rules against the transfer of any blueprints, materials or manufactured products that might be used in making nuclear weapons.

Excluding any hypothetical threats from some emerging nuclear terrorist state, one can foresee so far only one "legitimate" non-NATO nuclear nation, that has deployed strategic ballistic missiles, namely China. As is well known, China has gone full steam ahead with its nuclear weapons development program and it was the last to stop nuclear weapons tests. The so-called China threat to Russia is a very delicate subject to be openly discussed by a Russian author. One can only say that the potential, hypothetical Chinese threat to Russia (understood not as a deliberate posture of the Peoples Republic of China, but simply as a huge and growing nuclear potential of a country in close proximity to Russia, that might under certain conditions become unfriendly) cannot but increase with the passage of time. And all this is happening at a time when the military preparedness of Russia and the general state of its armed forces has not significantly improved, and when Russia's existing strategic forces were geared towards countering an American strategic threat. This situation deserves more attention today than it was given during the 1960s and '70s. At that time Moscow's leadership, through sheer stupidity, tremendously boosted the "Chinese threat" and contributed to raising and entrenching tensions with its great southern neighbor by deploying 40 divisions of ground forces along the Soviet-Chinese border, doubling the size of the Soviet Pacific navy, significantly strengthening the Russian tactical and strategic air force in the Far East and moving some of the newest Intermediate Nuclear Forces (INF) missiles (now banned) into Siberia.

It is difficult to conceive of a "bolt out of the blue" nuclear strike on the part of China, given the Russian strategic nuclear potential, all present and future reductions considered. On the other hand, the possibility of nuclear escalation through a non-nuclear conflict cannot be entirely ruled out under certain scenarios, for example in a situation whereby the CIS southern Central Asia has become an area of political, religious and military struggles. To put the matter more bluntly, one can say that out of all the thinkable and unthinkable scenarios of a clash between any two nuclear powers of the world, that might be construed, the Sino-Russian one is the most likely.

Speaking in December 1996 at a conference of the CIS countries, devoted to their further military and political integration, Igor Rodionov, who was Russian Minister of Defense at the time, emphasized Russian concern about attempts by certain Asian countries to radically increase the offensive capabilities of their armed forces. Rodionov pointed in particular to Turkey, Iran, Pakistan, Japan and China. All of them, according to the Minister, seek to expand their zones of influence and to diminish the political relevance of the CIS countries as a solution to key regional problems.[19]

Later on Rodionov retracted his statement about the threat from China, and during his visit to China in mid-April 1997, he agreed with his Chinese counterpart, Chi Haotian, to develop a bilateral partnership "aimed at strategic cooperation in the twenty first century".[20]

On 24 April 1997, during an official visit to Moscow by Jiang Zemin, the Chairman of the People's Republic of China, he and the heads of the four CIS states (Russia, Kazakhstan, Kirghizia and Tajikistan) with a common border with China signed a five-power agreement on the reduction of the armed forces in the vicinity of the border. The agreement established ceilings on the numerical strength of the land forces and the quantity of armaments of the participating countries, as well as on their frontal aviation and aviation of the AA defense within a 200 kilometer zone across both sides of the border. The total permitted numerical strength for all land forces in the area was set at 240,800 men. Half of this quota belongs to China. The four CIS republics ought to divide between themselves the other half (120,400 men). Reportedly the bulk of this quota goes to Russia.[21] The agreement does not affect strategic missile forces, navies, strategic aviation and missile units of an AA defense variety.

Russian military doctrine considers one of the potential sources of military danger from outside to be

the spread of nuclear and other types of weapons of mass destruction, delivery vehicles and the latest technologies of military production in combination with attempts by individual countries, organizations or terrorist groups to realize their military and political aspirations.

In addition, we are also concerned about

the possibility of the undermining of strategic stability as a result of the violation of international accords in the field of arms limitation and reduction and of qualitative and quantitative arms build-up by other countries.[22]

Such a broad definition of what might represent a military danger to Russia might prove to be unsettling for some other countries, thus contributing to an increase, not alleviation, of international tension. This is the problem that the Russian political leadership must recognize before it again appears, as it happened with the USSR, that almost everybody is a "natural enemy" of Russia.

Threats from the CIS republics?

Thanks to the efforts of Russia, support from the United States and to the realistic, far-sighted policies of the leaders of the three FSU republics that, beside Russia, remained in possession of nuclear weapons after the collapse of the Soviet Union, the problem of the de-nuclearization of these states was successfully resolved by the beginning of 1997.[23] Now among the 15 successor states, only Russia remains nuclear judging by the quantity and quality of its nuclear weapons stockpile.[24]

After all the tactical nuclear weapons of the FSU, kept in various storage depots scattered throughout the ex-USSR, were transferred by July 1992 to the territory of Russia proper, only three former Soviet republics, besides

Russia, still had nuclear weapons (including means of delivery) on their territories: Belarus, Kazakhstan and Ukraine. In accordance with the Lisbon Treaty, signed by all of them (together with Russia and the United States) on 23 May 1992, all three pledged "to adhere to the Treaty on the Non-Proliferation of Nuclear Weapons of 1 July 1968, as non-nuclear weapons states in the shortest possible time...",[25] and they fulfilled their pledges.

Belarus had 81 road-mobile SS-25 (Russian designation RS-12M) single-warhead ICBMs with the range of 6500 miles and a 550 kiloton (hereafter kt) warhead. In accordance with the agreement between Belarus and Russia, all these missiles were supposed to be moved onto Russian territory at the end of November 1996. Some people suspect that a slow-down in the missiles withdrawal was a Moscow-Minsk response to the eastward expansion of NATO.

Kazakhstan was the first of the three republics to get rid of its nuclear weapons, despite the fact that Russia and Kazakhstan had an agreement allowing Kazakhstan to keep its nuclear weapons until 1999. It had 104 SS-18 (Russian designation - RS-20) MIRVed ICBMs - the biggest in the FSU arsenal - with ten 550 kiloton warheads each and a range close to 7,000 miles. The missiles were deployed at the two ICBM bases in Northern Kazakhstan where the Russian population predominates. It also had 40 Bear-H (TU-95MS) strategic bombers armed with air-launched cruise missiles.

On 13 December 1993, Kazakhstan's parliament by a 283 to 1 vote ratified the nuclear Non-Proliferation Treaty thus committing the Republic to doing away with all the nuclear weapons on its territory.

In March 1994, the last big dispute between Russia and Kazakhstan, relating to rocketry, was solved. The two largest republics of the CIS signed an agreement allowing Russia to rent the Baikonur cosmodrome in Kazakhstan for 20 years. In line with this agreement, Russia took full charge for what had been the Soviet Union's principle space-launching center and the only one in the FSU allowing Russia to put satellites into a geo-stationary orbit. In exchange, Russia agreed to pay an annual rent of about US$115 million, which, for the near future, would in fact be deducted from Kazakhstan's debt to Russia. Russian control of Baikonur made it possible for Russia to go into a full-scale cooperation with the United States in building a new orbiting international space station.

By the end of 1995 all nuclear warheads located in Kazakhstan were transferred to Russia. At the beginning of September 1996, the last missile silo on Kazakhstan's territory was blown up. (Incidentally, the dismantling of silos in the republic was carried out by Brown and Ruth of Houston, Texas, in conjunction with another foreign firm.) All the missiles had been transported earlier to Russia. The US inspection team later certified the liquidation of all the strategic missile silos in Kazakhstan. All strategic bombers in Kazakhstan were re-deployed to bases in Russia as early as the summer of 1994.[26]

Ukraine, due to its policy of equivocation and outright reneging on its Lisbon commitment, until 1994 was rather vague about the fate of the FSU's strategic nuclear weapons on its territory, which was third largest arsenal in the world! The Ukraine had 176 ICBMs: 130 silo-based SS-19 (RS-18) MIRVed ICBMs with six 550 kt warheads each and a range of 6,000 miles, and 46 of the most modern SS-24 (RS-22) MIRVed ICBMs with ten 550 kt warheads each and a range of 6,000 miles. Although some of the SS-24 ICMBs were produced as rail-mobile, those deployed in Ukraine were silo-based. Ukraine has also been a sole producer of heavy SS-18 ICBM, though it lacks its own facilities for the production of nuclear warheads, and all ICBMs silos on Ukrainian territory are unfit for the SS-18. Presumably all the ICBMs deployed on Ukrainian territory were targeted on the United States before they were zero-targeted by Moscow, in accordance with the U.S.-Russian agreement of January 1994.

Ukraine also deployed 46 strategic bombers, including 21 Blackjacks (TU-160s), each capable of carrying 16 nuclear-tipped cruise missiles with a range of more than 2000 miles. The total nuclear arsenal of the Republic consisted of 1,910 warheads (including 564 on cruise missiles) with a yield between 300 and 550 kiloton each.

Though the Ukrainian leadership solemnly declared many times that it was not aspiring to have its own hand on the nuclear button, the manoeuvering of Kiev up until the end of 1993 around its nuclear weapons, as well as the establishment of Ukrainian administrative control over them (although operational control remained in Moscow's hands), did alarm Russia, the United States and many other countries. Due to inadequate storage and servicing, some of the nuclear warheads were approaching the dangerous stage, when even dismantling them might have proved problematic.

In September 1993, Russian president Boris Yeltsin and Ukrainian President Leonid Kravchuk reached an accord on the transfer of Ukrainian nuclear warheads to Russia. In exchange, the equivalence of the nuclear fuel for 6 atomic power stations was to be shipped from Russia to Ukraine. But a few weeks after the accord was reached the Ukrainian leadership declared that it was not bound by it and that it wanted to keep some of the nuclear weapons, namely the modern SS-24 ICBMs.

On 18 November 1993, the Ukrainian parliament by 254 to 9 votes ratified the START I Treaty, but attached 13 preconditions on Russia and other countries before Ukraine would give up all the nuclear weapons on its territory. One of the stipulations was that in the initial stage only 42% of the nuclear warheads were to be removed or destroyed (as required by the START I Treaty); whilst another condition disavowed article 5 of the Lisbon Protocol, which required Ukraine to give up all its nuclear weapons. Declaring that they treasure nuclear weapons not as weapons, but as "material wealth", the Ukrainian leaders demanded compensation not only for the strategic weapons to be dismantled but also for tactical nuclear weapons that were earlier transferred to Russia.

After the United States increased its pressure on both republics, and then the US Congress approved US$350 million in Ukrainian aid to enable denuclearization to take place, the three countries finally worked out a compromise agreement on the fate of the Ukrainian missiles. The accord, signed by Presidents Clinton, Kravchuk and Yeltsin on 14 January 1994 during President Clinton's official visit to Moscow, stipulated that all the warheads remaining in Ukraine following the collapse of the Soviet Union would be dismantled and the highly enriched uranium within them processed in Russia into nuclear fuel for civilian use. The agreement set a "sequence" for the deactivation and destruction of those weapons.

Ukraine's large debt to Russia for oil supplies was to be forgotten, and Russia agreed to supply Ukraine with nuclear fuel for its atomic power reactors. (It has already started doing this.) Both the United States and Russia provided Ukraine with security guarantees, with Russia, for example, pledging to respect Ukraine's territorial integrity. The other nuclear-weapons states-signatories to the Non-Proliferation Treaty, made official pledges that they would not attack Ukraine. The Organization on Security and Cooperation in Europe also guarantees Ukraine's borders.

On 4 February 1994, the fractious Ukrainian parliament endorsed the trilateral Moscow nuclear disarmament accord and unconditionally ratified the START I Treaty, which became "a major step toward surrendering its inherited Soviet nuclear weapons".[27] In November 1994, the Ukrainian parliament (*Rada*) adopted a special law to join the Non-Proliferation Treaty.

In early 1994, Ukraine started dismantling its ICBMs. By the summer of 1996, nuclear warheads had been removed from all the Ukrainian ICBMs and transferred to Russia. Russia also bought from Ukraine 32 SS-19 ICBM's and intended to buy 25 strategic bombers.[28] On 5 January 1996, the three defense ministers of Ukraine, Russia and the United States symbolically blew up a missile silo at one of the Ukrainian missile bases. By the end of 1997 Ukraine had eliminated all but 20 missile silos on its territory. The rest will be destroyed in 1998. It has been reported that the United States promised Kiev more money to help finish the dismantling process. Initially, Ukraine demanded that the West pay it US$3.8 billion for this purpose.

Hence, at the time of this writing, Ukraine has also joined the ranks of non-nuclear states. Ukraine, Belarus and Kazakhstan became parties to the Non-Proliferation Treaty as non-nuclear states and opened their nuclear facilities to IAEA inspections.

In other words, the problem of denuclearization of the three nuclear republics has been successfully resolved.

Are there any other problems that might lead to a military conflict between Russia and any other newly independent country (NIC)? The answer to this question is "no". Of course, the FSU has already witnessed not only political conflicts, but even little wars in various territories that were formerly united in the Soviet era: an Armenian- Azerbaijan war over Nagorno Karabakh, the war in Georgia that resulted in the separation of Abkhazia as well as hostilities that ended up in semi-separation of South Ossetia from Georgia, military confrontation between two parts of Moldova that brought into existence the self-declared Dniester republic, populated mostly by ethnic Russians, that no country officially recognizes, and so forth.

Such wars, clearly spoil the atmosphere of friendship and cooperation that existed among formerly sister republics of the USSR, and this raised tensions in many parts of the FSU. Ethnic separatism, combined in some places with clan struggles and exacerbated by the stubborn attempts of the former CPSU elite to stay on top, at least locally, greatly complicated the tasks of economic, military and political cooperation among the newly independent countries (NIC's) and of preserving larger entities with their former administrative borders intact.

It will take a great deal of time and effort, including some outside help (such as that of the United Nations) to quell the passions of struggles and hatreds they generate. But one thing is absolutely clear: with all the skirmishes in its surroundings and outlying districts, no FSU country in any way threatens Russia. Quite the contrary: most of them appeal to Russia asking her to act as a political arbiter, thus enhancing the importance of the CIS arrangement.

As for Russia itself, its most acute political conflict within the CIS has been the fracas with Ukraine over the ex-USSR Black Sea Navy, which both countries agreed to amicably divide, but for several years could not agree on the method of division of land-based facilities and on the sites for basing the divided Navies. The question of bases was connected with the traditional main military base on the Black sea - the port of Sevastopol. Many in Russia, including those occupying top government positions, did not want to pay Ukraine for leasing some port facilities. The mayor of Moscow and many of his supporters claim, referring to official documents, that Sevastopol still belongs to Russia despite the fact that the Crimean peninsular was transferred from the RSFSR to Ukraine, then a constituent republic of single country - the USSR - on 19 February 1954.[29]

All this heated up the controversy, which the Presidents of the two republics allegedly solved several times, but the issue remained unresolved until May 1997 when, as was mentioned earlier, the visits to Kiev by Premier Chernomyrdin and President Yeltsin resulted in the solution to this issue, which appears to be almost final. In a twist of the navy drama, Georgia made an attempt to break into the dispute, by claiming that as a Black Sea country it should also have its share of the former Union Navy. However, its claim went unheeded.

Taking all of the above into account, it would be a mistake to think that heated debates about the Navy and Sevastopol in the media and in the parliaments of Russia and Ukraine could have ended in a military clash between the two countries. It is known that a number of think-tanks in the West carried out war games on a scenario of a military conflict between Ukraine and Russia. I personally took part in one such exercise at the RAND Corporation. Initially the bone of contention was said to be nuclear weapons. Later, when that problem was amicably resolved, the trigger for the hostilities was said to be the quarrel over the division of the Navy or over its base. The United States government, which has played a major role in exacerbating tensions between Kiev and Moscow (in order to have some more leverage against both capitals), has been trying to fan the passions, promoting joint NATO-Ukrainian navy exercises in the Black sea of the "Sea Breeze-97" type which were purportedly designed to polish a possible joint action of Ukraine and NATO Navies to suppress a separatists' uprising on an unnamed peninsular against the lawful authorities.

Though some of the imagined *casus belli* look plausible at first glance, the events would really need to get completely out of hand in either country for the scenario of a military clash between Ukraine and Russia to become a reality. With all their bickering the leaders of the two Slavic republics fully understand that the most fatal mistake they can make, a mistake that will mark doom for both countries, is to allow a military clash between Ukraine and Russia. This is why such an eventuality is unlikely to happen in the foreseeable future.[30]

Whilst the idea of Russo-Ukrainian war over Sevastopol or the Black Sea Navy seemed far-fetched from the beginning, a new Chernobyl type disaster, stemming from inadequate servicing of the equipment at an atomic power station, cannot be ruled out. If this occurs, God forbid, Russia and Ukraine will surely pool efforts to contain the consequences.

Vagueness and confusion in the official treatment of the problem of external threat exists, because the very notion of "external threat" is not clearly defined. In theory, although non-Russian republics of the CIS are now officially considered as foreign sovereign countries, in reality the states of the Near Abroad are still treated as internal subdivisions of some unified entity because there is a single strategic space over the CIS and the borders between the CIS republics are actually transparent.

The current Russian military doctrine admits that under the present conditions the immediate threat of outright aggression being unleashed against the Russian Federation has been considerably reduced. The main existing and potential sources of non-nuclear military danger from the outside are said to be as follows:

- territorial claims of other states against the Russian Federation or its allies;
- existing and potential areas of local wars and armed conflicts, especially those in close proximity to Russia's borders;
- the possible use of some weapons of mass destruction other than

nuclear;

- the possibility of strategic stability being undermined, as a result of breaking international accords in the field of arms control and arms reductions or as a result of quantitative or qualitative arms build-ups by other countries;
- interference in the internal affairs of the Russian Federation, to destabilize its internal political situation;
- suppression of the rights, freedoms and legitimate interests of citizens of the Russian Federation in countries abroad;
- attacks upon military installations of the Russian Federation by armed forces deployed in foreign countries;
- the expansion of military blocs and alliances to the detriment of interests of military security of the Russian Federation; and
- international terrorism.

This is not a complete list. Furthermore, the classified document contains more definitions of potential dangers. But even from this list, it is clear that the Russian military perceives almost any development outside the borders of the Russian Federation as a potential source of danger to Russia. Yet at the same time, it is evident that the external threat is considered by the top brass to be essentially a threat coming from outside CIS borders.

As to the factors which might turn existing and potential dangers to Russia into an immediate military threat, the document on Military Doctrine mentions the following:

- an increase of groupings of troops (forces) near the borders of the Russian Federation to levels, that violate the established balance of forces;
- attacks on installations and structures on the Russian Federation's state border *or the borders of its allies* (my emphasis - H.T.), and the unleashing of border conflicts or armed provocation;
- the training on the territory of other states of armed formations and groups aiming to cross into the territory of the Russian Federation or its allies;
- the actions of other countries that impede the functioning of Russia's systems of safeguarding strategic nuclear forces and of state and military administration, especially the space component of these systems; and
- the introduction of foreign troops onto the territory of states

contiguous to the RF (if this is not associated with measures to restore or maintain peace in accordance with a decision by the UN Security Council or a regional body of collective security that has the consent of the RF).[31]

From all those definitions it is clear that firstly, Moscow continues to view the space of the former Soviet Union as its immediate security zone, and secondly that the Russian military will not be short of plausible justifications when undertaking military action within that space or on its outer borders.

Russian national security, according to these definitions, is inseparable from the security of near abroad states, that is the republics of the former Soviet Union, and the Russian military actually consider that they ought to have a free hand in actions within those perimeters. As the document on military doctrine unequivocally states:

The interests of security of the Russian Federation and other states of the CIS might require the deployment of troops (forces) and means beyond the territory of the Russian Federation, and also involve, as a rule, the creation of mixed military formations, manned by the servicemen of the CIS states on a contractual basis.[32]

This was also the essence of the Russian Foreign Minister's statement before the United Nations General Assembly in September 1993, when he insisted that it was solely Russia's job to maintain order in the former Soviet Union and that the rest of the world should help to pay for it. Earlier, President Yeltsin formulated what one might call the Yeltsin doctrine, namely that Russia ought to be the guardian of security of the former Soviet republics.[33] The Western media quickly dubbed that statement as the "Monroeskii doctrine".

However, at the time of writing, the efforts of Russia to obtain official recognition of its special role within the territory of the FSU, has not succeeded. The Rome meeting of the 53 states-members of the Conference on Security and Cooperation in Europe at the end of 1993, did not sanction such a role for Russia. The most vehement opponents were the former Soviet republics and satellites themselves. "We are against a new re-carving of Europe, against a new Yalta", declared the Foreign Minister of Estonia, Trivimi Velliste.[34] Most of the Western states at the meeting, however, expressed some understanding of Russia's problems, though there is growing criticism in the West, and in the United States in particular, of American and NATO alleged permissiveness in allowing

Russia to behave as a patron and in a way like a boss of the CIS republics.

But whatever position foreign statesmen take in respect to Russia's claim for its special peacekeeping role within the borders of the FSU, they are hardly capable of changing or challenging it.

First of all, it is clear that no NATO members are willing to get involved in ethnic strife within the FSU or on its borders[35] and second, a number of security treaties now exist between Russia and other former republics of the Soviet Union. In addition, there is the 1992 Tashkent Treaty on collective security (involving 9 republics), legalizing the joint use of military forces in repelling aggression, as well as Russia's military presence within the borders of these states. Russia will abide by these agreements, especially as many other republics of the CIS simply do not have adequate military forces to defend themselves, even against small-scale military aggression.

It is clear that given the existing situation of almost total transparency of borders between Russia and other republics of the CIS, Moscow still views its real security borders as CIS borders with non-CIS countries. More than that, Moscow, evidently, still considers even the Baltic countries as belonging to its lawful security zone.

Of uppermost significance to Moscow are the radar stations of the FSU missile attack warning system (MAWS), which are indispensable for maintaining Russian security proper and a single space system over the CIS. These stations are now located in six independent states (Latvia, Belarus, Ukraine, Azerbaijan, Kazakhstan and Russia) but controlled by the Russian military. Whilst the Russian authorities understand that some of these stations might be closed in the future and rebuilt within the borders of Russia proper, at present maintaining this system in operational order is very important to Russia so any attempts to appropriate one of these stations by hostile forces might be considered by Moscow a *casus belli*. This is what the document on Military Doctrine describes as impedance of the functioning of Russia's systems of safeguarding strategic nuclear forces as an immediate military threat.

But that document, adopted in 1993, did not anticipate that in 1997 the area, covered by the ABM Treaty of 1972 with all its appropriate prohibitions, would not - through criminal stupidity of Russian authorities - include the territories of 11 FSU countries (see footnote 18). Such a new situation, for example, means that the United States, by an arrangement with one or more Baltic countries (with which it already signed a special

Charter on security questions), could deploy on their territories (or just lease to them to deploy) one or more of its newest TMD systems (even if these republics continue to stay out of NATO). One does not need to be a military expert to understand that such systems, being deployed at a 600 - 1300 mile distance from the main bases of the Russian strategic missiles (and having no limitations on the velocity of their interceptor missiles!), can easily destroy all Russian strategic missiles at the initial stage of their journey. Such deployment can also take place, say, in Poland, which is joining NATO, and in fact it is already taking place in Germany, where Americans are creating a nucleus of the NATO TMD system.

Another point which is emphasized in the same document as a source of military danger is the suppression of the rights and lawful interests of citizens of Russia in foreign states. This concern has already led to Russian interference in situations outside its own borders and will definitely be used many more times in the future.

Speaking at the conference in the Ministry for Foreign Affairs devoted to Russia's relations with the rest of the CIS states and the Baltics, the then Russian Foreign Minister, Andrei Kozyrev, emphasized the problem of mistreatment of Russians and the infringement of their human rights in some CIS states and the Baltic republics, and noted that Russia does not intend to remain indifferent: "We shall react in tough ways to violations of human rights. If any attempts are made to increase tension and to destabilize Russia, of course, we will not stay silent and, if necessary, strong measures, including economic sanctions, will be employed." "I would like", added Kozyrev, "to note that our partners in the West react seriously to this, for there should be no double standards in the defense of human rights".[36]

Russia's desire to defend the life and well being of its citizens abroad is quite lawful and understandable. If the United States is ready and willing to intervene militarily in a situation when the lives of a dozen or two of its citizens are endangered, why cannot Russia, especially as Russian citizens abroad number in the millions? But, of course, speaking frankly, it will not be always easy to determine in what cases such concerns might be real ones and in what sense they are simply used as a plausible pretext for interference. As a general rule, one might expect that, if internal conflicts in the republics of the CIS do not explode into large scale wars with international implications, then Russia will probably not meddle militarily, although a lack of discipline within the Russian military, combined with the desire to earn more money, does not preclude the possibility of Russian military personnel involvement (in groups or units) in local conflicts within the CIS, as in earlier instances in Moldova, Georgia and Azerbaijan.

However, one should clearly understand that, due to the economic, infrastructural, and organizational dependence of the majority of the CIS republics on Moscow, and the tremendous "weight" of Russia vis-à-vis every other republic of the FSU, large scale military conflict between Russia and a CIS republic is highly unlikely in the foreseeable future. Only some absolutely outrageous provocation, for example, the widespread massacre of Russians in some republic, will trigger real Russian military moves against the perpetrator.

At the same time, there are quite a few CIS republics where events might develop or have already developed along the lines of a Yugoslav model: Moldova, Azerbaijan, Georgia, Ukraine, Kazakhstan and some other Central Asian republics are all cases in point.

In Moldova, the Russian 14th army has been guarding the Russian population in the Dniester republic, carved by the militant Russian nationals out of Eastern Moldova. Since the army took an active part in the hostilities that sprang up between two parts of Moldova in 1992, many wanted the 14th army to stay on to guard that illegal republic. However, this is not the case. In the summer of 1994, an agreement was reached between Moscow and the government of Moldova on the withdrawal of Russian troops by 1997. Moscow gradually reduced the strength of the army, before turning it into an operational grouping of troops, and it is now ready to withdraw completely. Such a step was facilitated by the agreement reached in the spring of 1997 between the authorities of the self-proclaimed republic and the government of Moldova, under the auspices of Russian Foreign Minister, Yevgeny Primakov. The authorities of the so-called Dniester republic agreed to continue negotiations with the government of Moldova regarding their status, with the understanding that their territory is an integral part of the republic of Moldova.

If Ukraine suddenly disintegrates under the weight of its tremendous economic misfortunes and, as a result, political clashes between Ukrainian ultra nationalists (based in the Western Ukraine) and its Russian population (concentrated in Eastern Ukraine and in the Crimea)[37] grow into a civil war, one cannot expect Russia to remain aloof. Russian actions in this case might strongly resemble the behavior of Serbs in the conflict in former Yugoslavia.

There is also a potential that the Crimea, whose population consider themselves citizens of Russia, might plead with Moscow to protect them against Kiev if the latter tries to severely curtail the autonomy of the peninsula, which Khrushchev presented as a gift to Ukraine more than forty years ago.

One also cannot totally exclude some conventional skirmish on the Russian-Ukrainian border, though it is hard to imagine such a local encounter developing into a full-scale war.

Azerbaijan, which lost 20 percent of its territory in 1992-93 during the war with Armenia over the predominantly Armenian enclave of Nagorno-Karabakh, is heavily dependent on Russia as a moderator in that conflict. Besides, it is constantly undermined by the in-fighting between various clans which resulted in several turnovers of forces that govern the republic. It seems almost inevitable that Baku will continue its rapprochement with Moscow in order to maintain some stability in the republic, the shortage of which has been undermining the efforts of Baku to clinch long-lasting deals with foreign investors in the Azerbaijani oil industry. In all probability, it will have to pay the price of re-inviting the Russian military into the republic to maintain law and order.

Since the demise of the Soviet Union, Georgia finds itself in a state of constant internal conflict. Two types of conflict run in parallel: the first, within the 70% Georgian majority of the republic as its clans fight for government leadership; whilst the second type of conflict consists of secessionist aspirations and movements among its minorities, the Ossetians, Abkhaz and Adzhars. With some Russian help, albeit unauthorized by Moscow, the Abkhaz managed to a great extent to separate themselves from Georgia, though nobody in the world has yet recognized the independence of Abkhazia. The same urge by the Ossetians is contained by the peacekeeping forces of Russia and Georgia. The republican leadership recognizes that it can actually keep the country together only with Russian assistance, and Russia obliged after Georgia, exhausted by the internal strife, decided to join the CIS, invited Russian troops to guard its external borders and allowed Russia to create military bases on its territory.[38]

Non-nuclear threats from non-CIS countries

Conflicts along the perimeter of the CIS are much more feasible grounds for Russian military intervention, as is now the case on the border between Tajikistan and Afghanistan, where Muslim refugees, squeezed out of Tajikistan by its communist government, formed into military units to fight the continuing civil war in Tajikistan.

Probably the entire Southern border of the CIS, starting from Moldova's border with Romania in the West, and ending with Russia's own border with China in the East, is now to a certain extent transparent and endangered, either by some conflict or simply by turmoil and mass border crossings.

Today 530 divisions are concentrated, along the borders with Russia including 42,000 tanks and 12,000 military planes. This is an impressive instrument of war. It is difficult to determine how politicians might use it. It is dangerous either to whip up an "enemy image" of states that have the right to possess their own armed forces, or to serenely contemplate such a military might.[39] To answer such a potential threat Russia made two steps in addition to the deployment of its military forces in many southern CIS republics.

The first step was the re-formulation of its stance regarding the use of nuclear weapons. Breaking with the well known Brezhnev pledge of 1982 that Russia will not be the first to use its nuclear weapons, the current Russian military doctrine states that:

The Russian Federation: will not use its nuclear weapons against any state-party to the Treaty on Non-Proliferation of Nuclear Weapons of 1 July 1968, which do not possess nuclear weapons, except in the cases of: firstly, an armed attack by such a state, linked by an alliance agreement with a state that possesses nuclear weapons, on the Russian Federation, its territory, its armed forces and other troops or on its allies; and secondly, joint activities of such a state together with a nuclear-weapons state in carrying out or sustaining the invasion of or an armed attack on the Russian Federation, its territory, its armed forces and other troops or on its allies.[40]

Some politicians and experts in the West believe that such a position on nuclear weapons was designed to discourage former Warsaw Pact countries and some FSU republics from joining NATO, and they immediately viewed Russia as a "new menace". According to Jonathan Lockwood, a former U.S. Defense Intelligence Agency analyst:

The new Russian strategy is really a move backward to the traditional Soviet type of military doctrine. It's a very ominous development.[41]

However, mainstream public opinion in the West did not see much menace in the new Russian doctrine, which clearly and unequivocally for the first time embraced the concept of nuclear deterrence. US Secretary of State, Warren Christopher, correctly remarked that the new Russian nuclear strategy made Moscow's doctrine "not very different from our own".[42]

The new approach to the use of nuclear weapons was also influenced by the pitiful state of the Russian conventional forces. However, the state of the strategic nuclear forces, despite all the official reassurances, seems also not to be flawless.

Speaking at a meeting with journalists in Moscow in February 1997, the Minister of Defense, Igor Rodionov (now retired) made the following puzzling statement:

No one today can guarantee the reliability of our control systems. Russia might soon reach the threshold beyond which its rockets and nuclear systems cannot be controlled.[43]

Such a statement, coming from a person who knows the problem at first hand, is especially worrying in a situation whereby Russian military strategy envisages a launch of its strategic missiles, if there is a warning of an incoming attack (*otvetno-vstrechnii udar*).[44] Many Russian early warning stations are now situated abroad in Latvia, Ukraine, Kazakhstan etc., which makes one doubtful about their smooth operation. So it is not so much the doctrinal readiness of Russia to use nuclear weapons, as its intended tactics of their use, which is unsettling under the current state of control over them.

Nevertheless, the implicit possibility of Russia resorting to using nuclear weapons for its defense is a sound deterrent to any aggression against it. In their writings, published after the announcement of the new military doctrine of Russia, Russia's military and civilian analysts quite explicitly stated why it was so important for Russia nowadays to rely on the nuclear deterrent:

The majority of analysts, investigating the problem of war prevention, agree that nuclear deterrence preserved peace during the last few decades, despite fierce confrontation between the two global systems. Universal realization of the impossibility of achieving any goals in global nuclear warfare due to its catastrophic nature is a deterrent factor in contemporary conditions as well. What is stated above allows one to conclude that *nuclear deterrence as a military way of preventing global warfare has no alternative....*
If today Russia's nuclear potential ensures deterrence to a global or a "limited" nuclear war, the potential for deterring large-scale war on the basis of conventional weaponry runs into a number of problems. First, with the dissolution of the Warsaw Pact strategic military situation of Russia became severely complicated... Second, the state of the Russian economy is drastically limiting Russia's capability to deter large-scale warfare... That is why the maintenance by Russia of the existing nuclear potential, that requires, by some estimates, 10-17 percent of the budget, is the most rational solution. (Emphasis in the original - H.T.)[45]

With such a premise in mind, the Russian military announced in the autumn of 1993 the second step, namely that the numerical strength of the Russian armed forces must be curtailed and frozen at 2.1 million men[46] (at the middle of 1994, they still numbered 3 million),[47] and that as a result of the reorganization of Russian fighting forces, their core would consist of mobile troops. The first echelon of such troops was to consists of rapid deployment paratroop forces with 10-hour combat readiness and the second of quick reaction motorized infantry units with appropriate support forces which can be combat-ready within a few days.

However, these military plans have not been realized. By Order No. 070 of 26 December 1995, the Minister of Defense transferred the command over twelve large formations (two divisions and ten brigades) of crack paratroop forces from the Commander of the Paratroop forces to Army Generals - Commanders of military districts, where the units were stationed. This boiled down to a partial disbandment of the most mobile, highly trained and combat ready forces, as a special arm of the service. Commenting on the idea of mobile forces as the main fighting component of the Russian armed forces, General Alexander Lebed (a former paratrooper), stated at the beginning of 1996:

It is not even mentioned nowadays. More than that, in the General Staff and in the paratroop forces (which were supposed to form the core of those forces), the very term - mobile forces - is banned.[48]

It was clear that the idea of mobile forces was killed off not by the Minister of Defense but by the political authorities and personally by the President. But that was only the first step of a drama based on the deep fear of the underfed and poorly financed Army by the current political leadership of Russia.

As is well known, Boris Yeltsin won in the second round of the 1996 Russian presidential elections thanks largely to the support of General Lebed, who was also running in the elections as a presidential candidate. Before the second round Lebed withdrew from the race asking his electorate to vote for Yeltsin. In return, Lebed was appointed Secretary of the Security Council of Russia. The colossal rise in the popularity of Alexander Lebed, after he managed to negotiate a real cease fire in Chechnya, whilst Yeltsin was seriously ill (this only became public after the elections), frightened the President's *camarilla* who ran Russia after Yeltsin became incapacitated. The possibility of Yeltsin's retirement or passing away became very likely, as did Lebed's election as the new boss of Russia. This sealed Lebed's fate. Despite his great achievement of securing peace in Chechnya, he was summarily dismissed by the ailing President on 17 October 1996 on the flimsy pretext of plotting an alleged *coup d'etat.*

Alongside the conspiracy against Lebed, new steps were taken to further incapacitate crack paratroop forces. For example, they were taken out of direct subordination to the General Staff, their strength declined further and separate units of paratroop forces were sent to different military districts of Russia and subordinated to local commanders of land forces.[49]

After a while, it become clear that the Russian political leadership was deliberately cracking down on the Russian Army because it was not sure of its loyalty. The Kremlin started to use the pretext of "forthcoming military reform" in order to de facto deprive the Army of fighting efficiency. The authorities switched their support to Ministry of the Interior (MVD) forces who now have better resources and are better paid. They number around 1.5 million personnel. This force exceeds the combined numerical strength of the KGB and MVD in the former USSR![50] While scaring the population with a "new threat from NATO", the top leadership of Russia has actually been deliberately destroying conventional Russian armed forces. This change in policy was confirmed by Pavel Grachev's replacement as Minister of Defense, Igor Rodionov.

At a meeting with representatives of mass media on 6 February 1997,

Rodionov made several shocking, puzzling statements. He pointed out, for example, that he wrote a letter to the President and the Prime Minister, reporting "the awful condition of the armed forces of the country". The minister bitterly remarked that:

Reform in the armed forces has turned into a struggle for their survival, a struggle against disintegration. There are no coordinated efforts to prevent the destruction of Russia's defense potential. The whole horror lies in the fact that, as Defense Minister, I am becoming just a spectator of the destructive processes in the army and navy[51] and can do nothing about it.[52]

What is the explanation for such a state of affairs?

The fact is that during the August 1991 "coup" in Moscow, a precedent was created in the Soviet armed forces that it is not only possible but sometimes even quite honorable and profitable (politically, financially and otherwise) to disobey the orders of one's superiors. Many of those who are now in command of the Russian armed forces actually moved to the top on the strength of their refusal in August 1991 to obey the orders of the then Minister of Defense of the USSR. The most prominent of the mutineers was the Commander of the paratroop forces, Pavel Grachev, who, by siding with Boris Yeltsin, actually decided the outcome of the confrontation between Yeltsin in the Russian "White House" and the "putschists". This precedent enabled President Yeltsin to use force in dissolving the Russian parliament in the Autumn of 1993,[53] as he persuaded his own appointees in the top military command to act against the parliament. However, Yeltsin knew that he could not rely on the loyalty of the Russian Ministry of Defense in other circumstances. This was evident during military operations in Chechnya. Some Deputy Ministers of Defense publicly criticized the actions of Pavel Grachev, the Minister of Defense at that time, and some highly placed commanding Generals refused to take part in the Chechnya operation. All such actions demonstrated to the whole world a total break up of military discipline in the armed forces of Russia.

Against this background, increasing public wrath against the government for its social policy, long delays in the payments of wages to workers of state enterprises, to scholars, doctors, schoolteachers and other employees of institutions financed from the state budget, and against similar delays in payments of state pensions to millions of elderly people, convinced the Russian authorities that they could no longer count on the continued loyalty of the Army, in which the sons and grandsons of destitute Russian workers serve as reluctant recruits. This is why Yeltsin and his minions under the guise of military reform, are deliberately destroying the army, or, to put it mildly, are incapacitating it, while hoping that in the worst case scenario of aggression from the outside, they could rely on atomic weapons, or on the threat of their use.[54] If and when internal popular unrest reaches intolerable levels, Yeltsin can use the well-oiled MVD forces to suppress opposition.

While making the Army inoperable for a while, the authorities still try to bribe it, evidently as the only possible way to maintain its loyalty. For example, the President exempted the military from paying personal income tax, constantly increases their pay, fringe benefits and other perks to the officer corps and so on. Yeltsin also turns a blind eye to the tremendous thieving in the armed forces, when not only small arms but large vehicles, grenade launchers and ammunition, are sold in bulk to criminal organizations. Many soldiers sent to hot spots to fight are recruited on a contract basis with much higher pay. However, corruption, lack of discipline, ethnic friction, split loyalties of personnel, diverse nationalities, poor living conditions, low quality of food, widespread brutality, the violation of the human dignity of young recruits by older soldiers (*dedovshchina*) and poor consumer supplies, all erode the armed forces and their morale, and hardly make Russian soldiers fit for real large-scale fighting. So to be on the safe side, the present ruling clan of Russia has been trying to keep the Army paralyzed for a while, especially in the Moscow and Leningrad military districts, while further curtailing the size of the armed forces to 1.2 million men in 1997.

With the anticipated level of conventional forces and armaments, there is no foreseeable armed conflict that might arise along Russian or CIS borders in the West and South that Russia would not be able to cope with on her own without resorting to the use of nuclear weapons, with the sole exception of military conflict with China.

At present, the main worries of the Russian leadership regarding the use of military forces for local conflicts around Russia do not so much focus on the size of the Russian forces or on the adequacy of their technical base, as much as on their cohesion, manning and ostensibly their control by the civilian leadership. This last problem the Kremlin "solved" by making Igor Rodionov officially retire from the armed forces, while continuing to keep him for a while in the job of Minister of Defense, allegedly as a civilian.

Yeltsin knew full well that any real civilian would have absolutely no authority in the present Russian army, so he used the gimmick of the Minister changing clothes to create the impression (designed especially for Western eyes) of a civilian command in the Ministry of Defense. But the President was still not sure of Rodionov's loyalty, because the latter was allegedly Lebed's appointee. The theme of Rodinov's disloyalty has been spread by Yuri Baturin, who was at that time the civilian secretary of the Defense Council and the President's chief adviser on military matters. Baturin wanted Rodionov dismissed because he refused to dance to Baturin's tune, and to appoint someone else instead who would be much more docile. This corresponded to the wishes of the new government team in charge of Russia since 1997 (though camouflaged as the "old government" because the only important person in it who had not been replaced until spring 1998 was Viktor Chernomyrdin, a figurehead Prime Minister).

To dismiss Rodionov, Yeltsin used a truly Jesuit trick. He accused Rodionov of undermining the strength of the army by destroying the paratroop forces! Poor Rodionov thought that by disbanding the paratroop forces he was executing the express wish of the President and his closest advisers, who hated paratroopers, because they were said to be loyal to General Lebed, a paratrooper himself, who was tremendously popular in their ranks. In May 1997, there was a twist: Rodionov was publicly reprimanded by the President and ordered "to stop the hasty reorganization and reduction of paratroop forces".[55]

At a meeting with the Minister, which took place a few days after and was covered by Russian TV, Yeltsin said to Rodionov: "My appreciation of your work is extremely low. I am not just dissatisfied, I am outraged by the way the reform of the Army is being carried out and by the general condition of the armed forces".[56] This was a great humiliation for one of the most experienced and well-educated Russian Generals. On 22 May 1997 at a meeting of the Defense Council, the President dismissed Rodionov from his post.[57] Forgetting all his previous talk about the necessity for civilian control of the Defense Ministry, Yeltsin appointed General Igor Sergeyev, the 59 year old Commander of the Strategic missile forces, as the new head of the Ministry of Defense. Thereafter, a few well-known generals retired. Colonel-General Anatoly Kvashnin, one of those high military commanders who can rightfully be considered responsible for the defeat in Chechnya (during that war he was the Commander of the

North Caucasus military district), was appointed as Head of the General Staff of the Armed Forces.

Following General Sergeyev's arrival at the Ministry of Defense, the initial concept of creating in the process of the army reform, highly mobile, well equipped and trained units as the core of conventional armed forces, was buried for good.

The deliberate destruction of the Army by the government could not pass unnoticed by a wider circle of Russian politicians and public opinion makers. On 14 February 1997, the *Nezavisimaya Gazeta* published a report of the Russian Council on Foreign and Defense policy, which stated:

The present state of the Russian army can only be described as a catastrophe... It will shortly develop into *a nation-wide catastrophe* unless, at last, the society and the state responsibly and in a consolidated manner proceed to avert this approaching threat.[58]

But the scandal flared up even more when a leading military expert, widely respected General Lev Rokhlin, who headed the Defense committee of the Russian Duma, publicly accused President Yeltsin of ruining Russia's armed forces, and stated that as a consequence Russia risked losing all its territory East of the Urals. In an open address to Yeltsin, General Rokhlin, who, by the way, belonged to the government's party "Our Home is Russia", declared that the President as Commander-in-Chief had "done nothing over the past six years for the country's military security". Rokhlin went on:

One might have agreed with the reduction of the Armed forces, if they were cut together with other force structures. But the latter were not reduced, but are constantly growing. They already are on a par with the Armed forces. After the size of the army is reduced, they will be much bigger numerically. Russia is turning into a police state. The regime does not need an army, because the army is hungry, discontented and untenable to the West. The regime needs police forces that are well provided for and well treated in the hope that they will support it, when it comes to dealing with angry people. [59]

Rokhlin also stated that it was the International Monetary Fund that had guided the nature of military reform in Russia and set the parameters of military appropriations. He also appealed to Russian officers, remarking that the greatest danger to Russia is the likelihood of social liquidation of the officer corps, the ruin of defense industries and the destruction of strategic nuclear forces. A substantial part of Rokhlin's message was devoted to the social insecurity of servicemen. He urged officers to fight government plans seeking to destroy the armed forces. His appeal was enthusiastically welcomed in the Army and terribly frightened Yeltsin and his staff. The initial reaction of the President to Rokhlin's message was a directive to then Prime-Minister Chernomyrdin, to pay off all the government's debts to servicemen within two months.[60]

Later a tremendous defamation campaign against General Rokhlin was orchestrated in the government-controlled media (and in Russia almost all the so-called independent media are government-controlled). But the new Minister of Defense of Russia, while speaking in the upper house of the Russian parliament, actually confirmed that Rokhlin was correct in many ways. Igor Sergeyev described the situation in the armed forces of Russia as critical. Only the Strategic Missile Forces, Paratroopers and some separate units of the land forces, were, according to Sergeyev, combat-ready. Battle training in the Army and in the Navy is not financed. Payments to servicemen and civil personnel of the armed forces are constantly delayed. The prestige of the military service is at its lowest and the number of suicides among the officer corps is increasing.[61] So evidently the wrath of the powers that be, in relation to Rokhlin's message, was mainly directed at his sharp criticism of the President and his appeal to officers to fight for their rights and against the destruction of the Army.

For the purpose of defending the rights of servicemen and those who are employed in military industries Rokhlin created the Movement in support of the Army and Navy, defense industries and military science and soon became the most popular politician in the eyes of servicemen.

In the beginning of June 1998 at the height of new Yeltsin's confrontation with the Duma and against the background of deepening economic crisis and a new countrywide wave of miners' strikes, the Movement on the initiative of Rokhlin decided to organize mass protest sit-downs along the Moscow ring road. In the night of 3 June he was assassinated in his own house near Moscow.[62]

In accordance with the military doctrine of Russia, special attention is devoted to armed conflicts that arise in Russia, on its borders, and on the territory of the FSU "on the grounds of aggressive nationalism and religious extremism". As the President of Russia admitted:

Regrettably, the present armed forces, that historically were composed in anticipation of a world war or large regional conflicts... are inadequately prepared for ensuring the interests of Russia's security in conflicts of a local character...
Legal and organizational arrangements for the use of armed forces in the event of attempted armed insurrection on the territory of the Russian Federation have not been worked through.[63]

This was an ominous statement indicating that the powers that be want to prepare the armed forces of Russia to fight their own subjects. And such statements are made after repeated oaths that the Russian army will never be used to fight the people of Rossiya.

Though, as the current document on the Russian military doctrine admits, the legal status of the presence of armed forces and other troops of the Russian Federation outside its borders has not been completely settled, Russian troops are still used by the President of Russia in a variety of ways in the "near abroad".

They guard borders and actively engage with the opponents of a regime, who are trying to carry out an armed struggle against the government. That is how the Russian troops are used in Tajikistan. Sometimes they are just officially present, as in South Ossetia or Abkhazia, performing a peace-keeping role without much fighting. Russian officers also command and train local units, as is the case in Kazakhstan and Turkmenistan, though Turkmenistan refused to sign the Tashkent treaty on collective security to which all other Central Asian CIS states adhere. Some Russian troops just guard the communicational infrastructure of a republic, as in Georgia on the request of the Georgian government. Or else they fight unofficially, allegedly without any sanction from their superior command, as they did in Azerbaijan or initially in Abkhazia. They can perform a *de facto* stabilizing and peace-keeping role without Moscow officially acknowledging such a role, just as Russian 14th army did in the so-called Dniester republic. In addition they can be shuttled across a republic, where there are no Russian troops, in railway cars and in road vehicles in frequent redeployment etc., as in Lithuania, which plays a role of a military bridge between Russia and the Russian enclave of the Kaliningrad province (former East Prussia). Combined with other kinds of sticks and carrots such practices will undoubtedly continue.

The use of Russian troops for the UN or the OSCE
peace-keeping operations

The current military doctrine of the Russian Federation stipulates that one of the tasks of the Russian armed forces is to carry out peacekeeping operations in accordance with the directives of the UN Security Council or international obligations of the Russian Federation.

So far, as we saw earlier, Russian peacekeeping and peace-restoring operations in the CIS zone, except those in Georgia, were not sanctioned by the UN Security Council, though, on the other hand, the United Nations or its Security Council did not explicitly object to Moscow's actions to defend Tajikistan's outer border or to maintain stability in other regions of the CIS were armed conflicts are raging.

In 1997, 22,000 Russian servicemen forming 17 motorized infantry and 4 paratroop battalions, trained to perform peace-keeping operations, were available for such duties. Some of these forces are participating in four peace-keeping operations on CIS territory: in Tajikistan, South Ossetia, Abkhazia and Moldova. In all these situations, Russia does not impose its peacekeeping services but acts only at the request of the legitimate governments of the countries concerned.

At the time of writing one battalion of Russian peacekeeping forces is deployed in the Dniester region and another in South Ossetia. Three battalions of Russian peacekeepers are stationed in Abkhazia. In Tajikistan peacekeeping functions are performed by the 201 motorized infantry division of the Russian Federation (about 6,000 men). The division is a part of collective CIS peacekeeping forces in Tajikistan. From 1992 until the end of March 1997, 86 Russian peacekeepers had been killed and 80 wounded.

At the same time, Russian contingents take part in peacekeeping operations in former Yugoslavia. Their total number is over 2,000. These Russian forces include a paratroop battalion in Slovenia and a paratroop brigade in Bosnia. All of them represent nowadays a component of the multinational Stabilization Forces (SFOR).

Although Russian units are acting as a component of the UN blue helmeted troops in Yugoslavia preserving a strong neutrality in relation to warring parties, there were reports that Russian soldiers and officers were secretly conniving with Serbs, sometimes even helping them to get arms out of UN storage facilities.

More pronounced Russian peacekeepers' siding with Serbs, occurred in February 1994 after the NATO Council's decision to bomb Bosnian Serbs' artillery positions around Sarajevo, if they did not comply with the NATO demand to withdraw all the Serbian artillery around Sarajevo beyond the exclusion zone of 12 mile radius or to surrender such equipment for safe-keeping to the United Nations forces by midnight on Sunday 21 February 1994. Serbs finally did comply with the demand, but they have in a way been bailed out of deep humiliation by Russian diplomacy. Moscow, allegedly incensed that NATO did not consult with Russia when issuing the ultimatum, offered to send an 800-strong contingent of its own UN troops to Sarajevo. Thus in a way Moscow was assuring the Serbs that it would not allow any bombing to happen. Since the Serbs eventually complied with NATO's ultimatum, the sudden initiative by Moscow, though irritating for NATO leaders, was welcomed as a "constructive step". Serbian fighters around Sarajevo welcomed arriving Russian troops almost as liberators!

Apparently, President Clinton and his Western colleagues, were in this particular case relieved by Russia's action as it saved them from proceeding with the bombing option which no one was enthusiastic about, because such a decision was imposed on them against their will by the force of Western public opinion.

So at the end of February 1995 everybody was happy, including the Bosnian Muslims, who for a period had a respite from heavy pounding by Serbian artillery.

But the strain of Moscow - NATO initial "misunderstanding" shows how shallow the roots of partnership between Russia and the West still are. Russia used its peacekeeping presence in Yugoslavia to impose its own variant of a "solution", while the Western allies had to take into account Russian sensitivities on the Serbian issue. The allies reluctantly praised Russian interference into NATO's confrontation with Serbs (sanctioned by the UN Secretary General, Mr. Boutros-Ghali). More than that, they had to make Russia a member of the so-called contact group that acts as a mediator between Serbs, Bosnians and Croats.

In the final analysis, however, it was NATO, not Russia, that negotiated the peace accord in Yugoslavia, after heavily pounding Serbs from the air, despite Russian protests. Offended Russian leaders and the media made a great fuss about NATO's "genocide" against the Serbs, but finally had to acquiesce and accept an American-brokered peace.[64] At the same time,

Herculean efforts were taken by the Russian leadership to prove that it was not the US but Russia that made the biggest contribution to the settlement. All the incessant self-praise in Moscow about the "great Russian contribution" to the solution of the conflict demonstrated to the entire world how deeply wounded the Kremlin really was. In such a state, Russia can become unpredictable, so the Americans wisely refrained from a public debate about the dimensions of each country's contribution to the final settlement. The problem of the further presence of Russian peace-keepers in Yugoslavia after the withdrawal of UNPROFOR (United Nations protection forces) and the introduction of the so-called Implementation Force (IFOR), composed essentially of the NATO-supplied troops, but with contributions from 15 other nations, was finally settled during negotiations between US Secretary of Defense, William Perry, and Russian Defense Minister, Pavel Grachev. About 1,500 Russian troops were participating in the IFOR mission in Bosnia-Herzegovina as a *de facto* part of an American brigade, but formally receiving their orders from a Russian General who became the Deputy for this mission to NATO's Supreme Allied Commander Europe, American General Joulwan, who had operational control over IFOR.[65] The same arrangement continued after the IFOR forces were transformed into SFOR.

However, the main peacekeeping operations of Russian troops (in conjunction with the forces of other CIS republics and/or troops from other UN member-countries) are taking place in the volatile regions of the CIS.

The overall development of the CIS, according to President Yeltsin,

is the sphere of special responsibility and the particular mutual interests of Russia and its neighbors. Our country is connected with them much more intimately than is the usual pattern of neighborly connections... Practice shows that no one, except Russia, is ready to take upon itself the burden of peacekeeping within the former USSR.[66]

Speaking at a session of the UN General Assembly in September 1994, President Yeltsin again stressed that Russia's priority interests lie in the newly independent states of the FSU and he served notice that Moscow believes it has prime responsibility for ensuring peace and stability among its neighboring states. "Russia's ties with them", Yeltsin said, "are closer than traditional neighborhood relations; rather, this is a blood tie".[67]

At the same time, the Russian President called on other nations to be more active in UN peacekeeping operations and stated that Russia was prepared to designate troops for a stand-by UN force. The UN has long requested the creation of such a rapid-deployment force that could respond to emergencies without the United Nations first having to ask for troop contributions, a process that usually takes months.

Internal security threats

The Russian document on military doctrine also considers the basic internal sources of military threats that the armed forces or other troops of the Russian Federation may be used to counteract.

They are:

• the unlawful activity of nationalist, separatist or other organizations aimed at destabilizing the internal situation in the Russian Federation and violating its territorial integrity, via the use of armed force;

• attempts at the forcible overthrow of the constitutional structure and the disruption of the functioning of bodies of state power and administration;

• attacks on nuclear power installations, chemical and biological production facilities and other potentially dangerous installations;

• the creation of illegal armed formations;

• increases in organized crime and smuggling activity to levels that threaten the security of Russian citizens and society;

• attacks on arsenals, weapons depots, arms-producing enterprises, military and special equipment and property, and organizations, institutions and structures possessing regular-issue weapons with the aim of seizing those weapons; and

• the illegal distribution on the territory of the Russian Federation of weapons, ammunition, explosives and other means of carrying out sabotage and terrorist acts, as well as the conduct of unlawful trade in narcotics.

This is a sufficiently complete roster of the potential domestic troubles that might endanger the cohesion of Russia or its security. Some of the activities enumerated above do take place in Russia - thefts of weapons from military depots and their illegal sales, rampant organized crime, increasing trade and transportation of narcotics and some illegal demonstrations by nationalists in the big cities. The latter   are combated mostly by local militia (police), with the exception of the anti-government riots in Moscow on 3 October 1992, generated by the former parliament's leadership, when special troops and army units were involved. Army units are occasionally used to fight organized crime. The only case so far of the direct use of regular troops against secessionists was the inglorious operation in Chechnya, which evoked strong criticism of the government from the Russian public and from abroad. Even those Russian citizens, who in principle supported the idea of strong arm action against the Chechen separatist leadership, were appalled by the ineptness in the use of force. The heaviest blows of this gory operation fell upon peaceful citizens of Chechnya, not Dudayev's bandits.

It became absolutely clear that the High Command of the Russian armed forces had neither strategy, nor the tactics of conducting pacifist operations within its own territory. Actually the "license to kill", which President Yeltsin issued to himself during the tank onslaught on the Russian parliament in October 1993, was used in a much more brutal and unrestrained way in winter-summer of 1994-95. Despite strong criticism of this action on the part of some members of the Russian parliament, neither chamber managed to get a majority to censure either the President or the government for the massive slaughter of innocent people. The Chechen adventure will have deep long-term repercussions across the whole of Rossiya. Instead of unifying the regions around the Center, the brutal barbarity of the Chechen campaign actually increased secessionist impulses among the people of the Caucasus.

The Northern Caucasus region is a plethora of small ethnic groups and for centuries was the trouble spot of Russia. The fact is that all these tiny ethnic groups can hardly exist as fully independent modern states, and will always have to rely on Russia. Even the Abkhaz people in the Transcaucasus, fighting for independence from Georgia, demanded nothing more than the right to be an autonomous region of Russia. But the approach to settling disputes and disagreements ought to be more delicate and the use of armed force should be only the matter of the last resort. This is the consensus of opinion of the majority of political parties and groupings of Rossiya. The most effective way to suppress a separatist uprising is to improve the economic situation in Russia and to entrench the democratic institutions of self-government at a local level.

However, the one lesson of the tragic war in Chechnya is that, if, before it, the majority of Russian citizens have unquestionably supported the use of armed force against any separatists, henceforth such support cannot be guaranteed. The tremendous loss of life in peacetime of both non-combatants and combatants, especially young recruits, seems to have changed the mood of the silent majority of Russians. It is one thing if some administrative entity situated deep within Russia, such as Tatarstan, tries to secede. The majority of the people will hardly accept this and are likely to demand some resolute action by the government to stop it. But it is almost certain that if some sub-national grouping on a fringe of Russia, suddenly decides to separate and, especially, if it formalizes such a choice by some democratic vote or a referendum, there will be an no outcry in the rest of Russia against such a development.

Conclusion

The Soviet economy, and to a great extent the Soviet system itself, were ruined by the inordinate amounts of money devoted to security and foreign policy adventures in the Third world, though the real threat to the Union was not as great as has been imagined by the frightened Moscow practitioners of the Cold War.

Mikhail Gorbachev, when he became the leader of the Union, somewhat downgraded the external threat, which theoretically allowed the redistribution of resources in favor of the civilian sectors of Russian economy. But the measures adopted were too late and far too narrow: the Soviet Union disintegrated under the weight of unbearable military expenditures and through the ambitious aspirations of the leaders of its constituent national republics, who sensed the opportunity to become "peers in their own right" by ruining the Union.

The demise of the Soviet Union, that was considered by the Western public and statesmen to be a very aggressive state, drastically diminished their perception of threat. Earlier, it was already somewhat decreased by the rift between Moscow and Beijing and the consequent disappearance of the Sino-Soviet monolith from the international arena.

But while Russia, the main inheritor of the Soviet Union, came to be a smaller state territorially and demographically, it still continues to occupy the heartland of the Eurasian landmass which gives it certain geopolitical advantages in the game of nations on the world stage. Due to its geopolitical location, Russia remains a natural holder of the equilibrium between the East and West, and its role in the global balance of power is pivotal. It is also still a nuclear superpower, that possesses a nuclear missile potential equal to that of the United States.

At the same time, Russia has to adapt to a new geopolitical situation in the world that emerged after the liquidation of the Warsaw Pact, the collapse of the Soviet Union, NATO expansion eastwards, the economic and military growth of China etc.

The Russia that embarked on the path of radical transformation of its political and economic system is discarding its fears of nuclear threats from the US and other nuclear countries of NATO. In view of Russia's constantly improving relations with China, it is also not a potential threat to Russia's security in the near future. All the CIS republics, to various degrees, depend on Russia and in no way represent a threat to its security. Some threats from the outside of the CIS area are possible (for instance from the south in Central Asia and in the Transcaucasus), but the Russian armed forces are adequate enough to repel such threats (especially in a situation when Russian forces patrol some of the CIS borders).

However, the problem of army reform is very acute for Russia, because poor financing of the armed forces over the past six years, widespread corruption in the military establishment, lack of discipline plus the shameful defeat of Russian troops by the Chechen irregulars, make a reorganization of the Army (including drastic curtailment of its size) a top priority for the Russian leadership.

In view of the deplorable state of the conventional forces, Russia relies on its nuclear weapons and the threat of their use in any armed conflict, as the main deterrent to potential aggressors or its allies. Its military doctrine does not preclude the use of nuclear weapons in a case of an attack against Russia.

However, the expressed political wish of Russia is to live in peace with all its neighbors and other countries, and to use its armed forces only for peace-making or peace-keeping operations on a mandate from the UN or other international bodies or at the request of a government of a CIS republic. The more concrete issues of Russian interests and actions vis-à-vis various regions of the world will be discussed in the following chapters.

Notes

[1] For instance, the majority of the non-rural population practically lived in barracks, but, with a gradual rise in the industrial level of Russia and the need to give some bonuses to those working "cogs" that were highly qualified, barracks underwent some upgrading: from one or two-storied wooden ones, they became five-story prefabricated cement buildings (without elevators) with tiny individual apartments, bathrooms and, occasionally, in big cities, even running hot water. But barracks in essence they remained! Even in Moscow - the capital city of Russia - such buildings comprise 85% of residential housing (*Segodnya*, 19 March 1997, p.2). However, great numbers of working class people continue to huddle together in dilapidated wooden barracks. Besides, at the peak of Stalin's repression there were, on a yearly average, about 12 million pure slaves, concentrated in the GULAG camps throughout Russia. Many of their inmates were simply expended within a few weeks.

[2] Soviet authors never called Sino-American rapprochement détente. They did not understand that it was Mao Zedong, not Kissinger, who first got the idea of restarting a balance of power politics in Eurasia in order to get rid of Moscow's overbearing patronage. Nixon and Kissinger just sniffed the wind, got the hint and acted accordingly.

[3] There is a version that Yuri Andropov - the then head of the KGB - allegedly acquainted the CPSU Politburo with documents purportedly showing that Afghanistan's President Hafizulla Amin was an old agent of the CIA, who wanted to summon Americans to help him (which was a total nonsense because Amin was a devoted Marxist and a left-wing radical, who resisted any outside interference into Afghanistan's affairs). The decision to intervene was a collective CPSU's Politburo decision, though the plan of action was devised in secret by the Soviet "big five": Brezhnev, Suslov, Andropov, Gromyko and Ustinov. Gorbachev and Shevardnadze undoubtedly knew about the preparation for invasion. But being candidate (non-voting) members of the Politburo they did not have to formally sign the decision. That allowed them to claim later on that they "knew nothing" about the plans for intervention (see *Journal of South Asian and Middle Eastern Studies*, Winter 1994. Special issue devoted to Soviet quagmire in Afghanistan, containing translations of top secret Politburo documents on the decision to intervene). After the intervention, the Soviet leadership secretly encouraged Iraq's Saddam Hussein to attack Iran, hoping that the latter would thus be distracted from openly interfering in Afghanistan on the side of the mujahedeen.

[4] Occupying 76% of Russia's territory (5,019,305 square miles out of 6,592,800), Siberia is a habitat for about 16% of Russia's total population. The poor transportation infrastructure in Siberia prevented the former Soviet government from building a radar station, necessary for early warning of ICBM attack across the Arctic ocean, at the northern edge of Siberia (which would be compatible with

the conditions of the US-USSR 1972 ABM Treaty) and literally compelled Russia to build such a station in southern Siberia, near Krasnoyarsk, close, at that time, to the sole railway line connecting European and Siberian parts of Russia, though the site chosen was in flagrant violation of the Treaty, as Moscow itself finally admitted at the end of the 1980s!

[5] In 1962 when Kazakhs in Xinjian experienced heightened repression from the state, some 60,000 sought and received asylum in the USSR (Ted Robert Gurr, *Minorities at Risk*, p.202).

[6] Membership of the collective security arrangements was later expanded to include Georgia and Azerbaijan.

[7] In accordance with the bilateral Agreement on the state border of 16 May 1991 between China and the USSR, which Russia recognized as binding, and the subsequent accord on the very short Western stretch of the Russian-Chinese border (between Mongolia and Kazakhstan), signed in September 1994. The agreements left open for further talks the delineation of the two small border stretches on the Ussury river opposite Khabarovsk and at the Bolshoi island on the Argun river in Chita province. The demarcation of the border was completed in November 1997. Russia gave China up to 37.5 square miles in the Maritime territory of the Far East. That concession gave the governor of the territory - Nazdratenko – grounds to make a world-wide fuss accusing Moscow of kowtowing to the Chinese, though, strictly speaking, the problem of state borders does not lie within his sphere of authority. The governor, however, was probably unaware of the fact that by accepting such a settlement China actually dropped its former claims to about 600 square miles of Russian territory!

[8] Gerald Robbins, 'The Post-Soviet Heartland: Reconsidering Mackinder'. *Global Affairs*, Fall, 1993, p.99.

[9] *Nezavisimaya Gazeta*, 19 August 1992, p.4.

[10] Alexander Lebed, 'Gde predel razumnogo sokrashcheniya armii?' [Where's the limit to a reasonable reduction of the army?] *Nezavisimoye Voennoye Obozreniye* ["Independent Military Review" - supplement to the *Nezavisimaya Gazeta*], No. 1 (5), January 1996, p.1. In another issue of the same review two retired Russian generals stressed as one of the functions of the Russian Navy "the task to defend the interests of Russia beyond its borders" (Vladimir Lozovoi and Viktor Solov'yev Arkhivazhnaya gosudarstvennaya problema [Super-important state problem] *Nezavisimoye Voennoye Obozreniye* No. 2 (6), January 1996, p.4).

[11] *The New York Times*, 15 January 1994, p.6.

[12] *The Washington Times*, 31 May 1994, p.A14; 1 June 1994, p.A3. There is also no mutual targeting between Russia and Britain, Russia and France, Russia and China. These countries concluded similar agreements with Russia later.

[13] "It is impossible to exclude sharp turns in the policy of certain countries, which might increase tension and create a real military threat for Russia, as well as for

other independent states. In this connection one cannot help being concerned about the American "Defense Guidance for 1994-98 fiscal years", which stipulates a number of measures aimed at establishing complete USA dominance in the world and to form the *superpower* image of itself in the world" (see Col.-General A. Danilevich (Ret.) and Colonel Yu.Tikhomirov (Ret.) 'National military doctrines of the CIS states: certain approaches and formulations' V*oennaya Mysl*, No 2, 1993, pp.19-20). And, to quote "straight from the horse's mouth", the US President's Decision Directive, issued in November 1997, "calls for US planners to retain long-standing options for nuclear strike against the military and civilian leadership and nuclear forces in Russia. Such planning reflects a widespread view among military officials in both nations that each side still poses a potential nuclear threat to the other" (R. Jeffrey Smith, 'Clinton Directive Changes Strategy on Nuclear Arms Centering on Deterrence. Officials Drop Terms for Long Atomic War', *Washington Post*, 7 December 1997, p.A01).

[14] Despite constant complaints from the Russian military about poor financing of the armed forces from the state budget, Russia continues to remain in the top category of countries - record makers in the realm of military expenditures. Its military expenditures in 1996 totalled 7.4% of GDP. Only seven countries of the world are ahead of Russia in this respect - North Korea, Oman, Iraq, Croatia, Kuwait, Saudi Arabia and Israel (*Izvestia*, 17 June 1997, p.1).

[15] *The Washington Times*, 26 October 1993, p.A14; *Rossiiskiye Vesti*, 20 January 1994, p.3; *The Moscow Tribune*, 12 December 1994, p.6; *Izvestia*, 2 September 1995, p.1; *Nezavisimaya Gazeta*, 25 December 1997, p.4; *Rossiiskaya Gaseta*, 14 August 1998, p.9, "Information regarding such 'gifts of labor' that surfaced recently", *Rossiiskiye Vesti* notes, "attests that some definite changes occurred in the realization of the program of development and production of advanced types of weaponry and military hardware with long-term potential, and that there is a marked shift in its financing" (Ibid.).

[16] See, for instance, Yaroslav Bilinsky, 'Germany as a Factor in U.S.-Russian Relations: An Essay on a Growing "Invisible" Challenge' in George Ginsburgs, Alvin Z. Rubinstein and Oles M. Smolansky (eds), *Russia and America. From Rivalry to Reconciliation*, Armonk, New York and London: M. E. Sharpe, Inc., 1993, p.236.

[17] During the January 1994 Russian-American summit meeting in Moscow, President Yeltsin and President Clinton signed a plan to quell nuclear proliferation by capping trade in the high-tech goods used to make the weapons.

[18] At their Helsinki summit in late March 1997 the Presidents of Russia and the United States agreed that there was considerable scope for cooperation in TMD. They said they would explore integrated cooperative defense efforts, such as the provision of early warning support for TMD activities, technology cooperation in areas related to TMD and the expansion of the ongoing program of cooperation in

TMD exercises (*USIS Wireless File. EUR 509.* March 21, 1997). On the surface everything seems to be O.K. But the fact is that the Pentagon is now working on six systems of TMD (plus continuing R&D of strategic defense), while Russia does not have the means to work even on a single system. Helsinki's understanding between the two presidents on the problem of missile defenses eroded the former agreements on what is permissible and what is not in anti-missile R&D (especially Yeltsin's consent to still consider "tactical" anti-missiles with the speed of 5.5 kilometers per second). Such a decision meant that the ABM Treaty of 1972 with its specific prohibition on testing anti-missiles "in the ABM mode" was *de facto* lifted. It became absolutely clear after the five countries (the US, Russia, Belarus, Kazakhstan and Ukraine) on 26 September 1997 signed in New York six agreements, ostensibly in elaboration and formal consolidation of the understandings reached at the Helsinki summit. There are three noteworthy points in these agreements. The first point (which emerged so to say by default) is that the area, encompassed by the 1972 ABM Treaty, shrank and now consists only of the territories of the five aforementioned countries, while the territories of 11 FSU republics (that, together with the territories of the four FSU republics that signed the agreements, constituted in 1972 the integral territory of the Soviet Union) are now excluded from this arrangement. Second, that there will be no limit on the velocity of the interceptor missiles of the higher-velocity TMD systems. And, finally, third - in a mockery of common sense - that determining the compliance of a Party's own higher-velocity TMD systems with the 1972 ABM Treaty will be the *national responsibility* of each Party. In other words, through the acquiescence of Russia the ABM Treaty was made absolutely vapid by these clauses (*Official Texts from the United States Arms Control and Disarmament Agency.* Washington, D.C.: Office of Public Affairs. 26 September, 1997).

[19] *Nezavisimaya Gazeta,* 26 December 1996, p.1.

[20] *Segodnya,* 15 April 1997, p.4.

[21] *Rossiiskaya Gazeta,* 25 April 1997, p.3; *Nezavisimaya Gazeta,* 25 April 1997, p.1. Reportedly the permitted combined numbers of armaments in the zone for all the four CIS republics are: tanks - 3900, armored vehicles - 5800, artillery - 4500 pieces, military planes - 290, military helicopters - 434 (*Izvestia,* 15 April 1997, p.3). This agreement represents a logical conclusion to the agreement on strengthening confidence in the military sphere, signed in Shanghai by the same parties on 26 April 1996.

[22] *Izvestia,* 18 November 1993, p.4.

[23] On 10 March 1997 Viktor Mikhailov, the then Minister of Atomic Energy of Russia, speaking at an international conference in Russia devoted to the problem of control over nuclear materials, declared that as of that day there was not a single Russian nuclear warhead outside of Russian territory proper - neither in

Ukraine, Belarus, or Kazakhstan. "Besides that", he said, "half of the Russian nuclear arsenal has already been dismantled" (*Segodnya*, 11 March 1997, p.1).

[24] "Russia's nuclear arsenal is the biggest in the world, with anything from 9,000 to 21,000 warheads" (*The Guardian*, 8 February 1997, p.8).

[25] *The New York Times*, 24 May 1992, p.A15.

[26] In January 1996 Russia agreed to compensate Kazakhstan for the bombers with the transfer to Kazakhstan's armed forces of a number of Russian-made fighters (SU-25, SU-27 and MIG-29).

[27] *The Washington Post*, 4 February 1994, p.A1.

[28] Those 32 SS-19s have the manufacturer's guarantee for use until the year 2009. Among the bombers were 10 TU-160 (BLACKJACK in NATO's designation) and 15 - TU-95M (BEAR-H) that were still operational. In partial payment Russia was going to supply Ukraine with spare parts for other Russian-made weaponry in the Ukrainian arsenal. At the time of writing the bargaining with respect to bombers is still going on. Russia, evidently, wants to beat the price down, knowing very well that, if Ukraine does not sell them to Russia, it will have to destroy them in accordance with the START I Treaty (*Segodnya*, 16 January 1996, p.10; 2 December 1996, p.1; *Izvestia*, 10 June 1997, p.2).

[29] They argue that Sevastopol was a city, directly subordinated to Moscow and not to the administration of the Crimea. Hence, the transfer of the peninsular to Ukrainian jurisdiction did not automatically change the status of Sevastopol as a city, controlled by Moscow. By the way, the Russian foreign office does not subscribe to such an interpretation and considers Sevastopol, as presently, a Ukrainian city.

[30] "Relations between Russia and Ukraine are stable", according to the Moscow political scientist Alexey Bogaturov. "This is a special kind of stability - it is a dynamic stability, which does not exclude the existence of quite a few arguments and differences of opinion. The main thing is that all of these are fully balanced by the understanding existing both in Moscow and Kiev of the unacceptability of break up for both countries. Russia and Ukraine are not following the established European patterns in their relations with one another. The eighth year of almost constant friction did not produce a single case of a rise in tension. Unnoticeably for any perfunctory observer both capitals in fact came to an agreement on an issue very important for bilateral relations: they 'agreed not to differ' without bringing matters to a head" (*Nezavisimaya Gazeta*, 24 April 1997, p.2).

[31] *Izvestia*, 18 November 1993, p.4.

[32] Ibid.

[33] Addressing a forum of the Russian Civic Union at the end of February 1993 President Yeltsin said: "The time has come when the appropriate international organizations ought to grant Russia special powers as a guarantor of peace and stability on the territory of the former Union" (*Izvestia*, 4 March 1993, p.4).

[34] *Izvestia*, 3 December 1993, p.3.

[35] Take, for instance, the conflict in Abkhazia between the Georgians and the Abkhaz, in which Russia was heavily criticized for allegedly acting on the side of the Abkhaz. "We said to the British, the French, 'Come and help, come and do something'", Yuli Vorontsov, the then Russian Ambassador to the United Nations, noted. Initially the Security Council voted to send 50 military observers to Abkhazia, but no peacekeeping troops. Finally fewer than two dozen eventually reached Abkhazia. "The international community does not have the will to act. We have tried everything possible to get the West to address this conflict. But there is no reply. We have to do something on our own" the Russian Foreign Minister told *Newsweek* magazine (*Newsweek*, 11 October 1993, p. 37).

[36] *Novoye Russkoye Slovo*, 22-23 January 1994, p.7.

[37] There are 11.3 million Russians in Ukraine that account for 22% of the total population of the republic. Russians compose more than 68% of the total population of the Crimea and, respectively, 43.2 of the Donetsk, 43.8 of the Lugansk, 31.1 of the Zaporozhie, 31.8 of the Kharkov and 22.9% of the Dnepropetrovsk provinces. There are also large numbers of other non-Ukrainian nationals living in these provinces (Samuil Gil, 'Ukraina na rubezhe 93-go and 94-go' [Ukraine between 1993 and 1994] *Novoye Russkoye Slovo*, 14 February 1994, p.5).

[38] The government of Georgia in 1996 ratified the treaty with Russia on Friendship, Cooperation and Mutual assistance on the understanding that Russia would help it successfully resolve the problem of separatist Abkhazia. However, the Georgian Parliament decided to tackle the ratification of another treaty - on the status of Russian troops in Georgia - only after its conflict with Abkhazia was resolved to the satisfaction of Tbilisi. Gradually the Georgian parliament became ever more impatient with Russia's procrastination in helping Tbilisi to restore its authority over Abkhazia. If real Russian help on this issue is not forthcoming soon, the parliament threatens to annul all the agreements with Russia, allowing it to have bases for Russian troops, including border guards, on the territory of Georgia.

[39] Colonel V. Cheban, 'Russia in the system of modern military-political relations', *Voennaya Mysl*, No. 4, 1993, p.5.

[40] *Izvestia*, 18 November 1993, p.1.

[41] *The Washington Times*, 5 November 1993, p. A14.

[42] *The Washington Post*, 5 November 1993, p.A34. Indeed, the new Russian pledge with regard to the use of nuclear weapons repeated almost word for word the pledge made by President Carter on 13 June 1978. As announced by the then Secretary of State Cyrus Vance the pledge states: "The United States will not use nuclear weapons against any non-nuclear weapons state party to the Non-Proliferation Treaty or any comparable internationally binding commitment not to acquire nuclear explosive devices, except in the case of an attack on the United

States, its territories, armed forces, or its allies, by such a state allied to a nuclear weapons state, or associated with a nuclear weapons state in carrying out or sustaining the attack" (*The Washington Post*, 13 June 1978, p. A2). *Inter alia*, the new formulation contravenes Article 2 of the 1991 Alma-Ata Agreement, signed by the erstwhile three nuclear republics of the CIS (Belarus, Kazakhstan, Ukraine) and the Russian Federation on joint measures with regard to nuclear weapons, which points out: "participant states of the present agreement confirm the obligation of no first use of nuclear weapons" (*Diplomaticheskiy Vestnik* No. 1, 15 January 1992, p.10).

[43] *The Times*, 8 February 1997, p.14.

[44] Russian (land-based) strategic missile forces are to solve not less than 50% of battle tasks of all the strategic nuclear forces in a retaliatory strike, and more than 90% of those if launched on warning (in Russian - *v otvetno-vstrechnom udare* - H.T.). "Such a deterrent is the most important condition for ensuring strategic stability", acccording to the Commander of the Strategic Missile Forces of Russia Colonel-General Vladimir Yakovlev, who was appointed to that post by President Yeltsin after a drastic reshuffle of the Russian High Command in the Summer of 1997 (*Nezavisimaya Gazeta*, 4 July 1997, p.1).

[45] Colonel V. Zakharov, 'Yadernoye sderzhivanie v sisteme voennykh mer predotvrascheniya voiny' [Nuclear deterrence in the array of military measures of war prevention], *Voennaya Mysl*, No. 2, February 1994, pp.8-11. "But if a country does not possess conventional weapons powerful enough to ensure deterrence, then it cannot liquidate nuclear weapons, even if all other countries do away with their nuclear weapons", adds Vasily Krivokhizha, Deputy Director of the Russian Institute for Strategic Studies (cited in *Rossiiskiye Vesti*, 5 May 1994, p.6). Many Russian analysts point out that after the inclusion of the East European countries into NATO, the bloc will have four times more conventional armaments than Russia.

[46] When announcing the new troop level ceiling, the Minister of Defense at the time, Pavel Grachev, simply ignored the first Russian Law "On Defense", then still operational, which clearly stated that the strength of the armed forces of the Russian Federation during peace time could not exceed 1% of the size of the Russian population (150 million). The 1992 Law was amended by the special decree of the president only two months later - on 24 December 1993 (Decree No. 2288). The article, requiring that the numerical strength of the Russian armed forces in peacetime must not exceed 1% of the total population of the country, was removed from the Law, alongside a number of other paragraphs establishing the scope of authority of the parliament with regard to Russian armed forces. Such authority was heavily curtailed. Paragraphs, defining the degree of Russian military aid to other countries on the basis of international laws, to which Russia is a party, and stipulating that its international treaties on defense are to be ratified by the

parliament, which was also authorized to control the disbursement of military aid, were cut. The fact that the Law, adopted by the duly elected parliament, was *ex post facto* unilaterally changed by President's fiat was again a demonstration of the total arbitrariness of "supreme power" in Russia, of its complete disregard of the due process of law.

[47] The 3 million figure was given by President Yeltsin at his press-conference in Moscow on 10 June 1994. "We cannot, society cannot today maintain a 3 million-strong army", Yeltsin said rejecting the demands of Russia's armed forces command for a substantial increase in Russia's military budget for 1994. "The whole of the Soviet Union had 3 million, and [now] Russia has 3 million servicemen" (quoted in *The Washington Post*, 11 June 1994, p.A15). This admission by the president showed once again that the Russian top brass, who consistently reported that the armed forces of Russia had been by mid-1993 cut to 2.3 million, were habitually lying. In fact in 1996 Russia had more than 4 million men under arms, a bigger number than the old USSR had, Yeltsin's statement notwithstanding. An additional 1 million or more consists of forces belonging to other ministries and committees, besides the Ministry of Defense: the Interior Ministry (the MVD), the Federal Security Service, Border guards etc. In 1995 various armed formations existed in 23 (!) ministries and departments of the Russian government, "including joint stock companies to where every second recruit is sent to 'defend the Motherland'" (*Argumenty i Facty*, No. 9, 1995, p.2). One of the obstacles to curtailing regular armed forces has been the stubborn resistance of the Generals' corps. Even some moderate reduction of 300 Russian army divisions (almost all of them - understaffed) would require the retirement of about 700 generals, which for a long time was unacceptable to the Ministry of Defense.

[48] *Segodnya*, 7 February 1996, p.5.

[49] In the beginning of April 1997 the newspaper *Nezavisimaya Gazeta* reported plans to further cut paratroop forces - from 48,500 to 35,000. "If the armed forces of the Russian Federation are totally cut by 11.8% then the paratroop forces are being curtailed almost by one third", commented the paper. "Thus today a slow death of one of the most efficient arms of the Russian military service is occurring" (*Nezavisimaya Gazeta*, 3 April 1997, p.2).

[50] *Izvestia*, 26 October 1996. The Russian Ministry of Interior in contrast to the US department of the same name commands police forces throughout Russia, including some special crack forces like OMON (the units of militia for special tasks) and some others. The Ministry officially does not release figures on its troops strength.

[51] Speaking about the navy, it is worth noticing that four out of the five air carriers that have been built for the Soviet navy are now decommissioned, some of them sold to foreign firms for scrap iron.

[52] *The Times*, 8 February 1997, p.14; *Nezavisimaya Gazeta*, 8 February 1997, pp.1-2., The chief editor of *Nezavisimaya Gazeta*, Vitaly Tret'yakov, asked Rodionov: "Do you not have a direct telephone line to the President?" "There is a line", answered the Minister, "but it is direct only in one way. When the President calls me up (though he has not done it for a long time) I pick up the receiver. But when I use the direct line, connecting the Minister of Defense of Russia to the President of Russia, the receiver is picked up by other people". Tret'yakov described this episode in an editorial entitled 'Igor Rodionov Staked His All' and commented that the President, who is simultaneously Commander-in-Chief of the Russian armed forces did not react at all to the desperate letter of his minister (Ibid.).

[53] "Lawful government is hanging by a thread, while the army is unable to defend it: some personnel are harvesting potatoes, others don't want to fight...", this is how Yeltsin himself described his attempt to summon the army to his support in his confrontation with the Russian parliament in October 1993 (Boris Yeltsin *Zapiski prezidenta* [President's Notes] (Moscow: "Ogonyok", 1994), p.385).

[54] A political analyst of the newspaper, *Nezavisimaya Gazeta*, writes: "Yeltsin can safely ignore the attempts of the Duma to kick him out of office. But if he is impeached by the army, then, instead of a bunch of blabbing deputies, the Russian political stage will be occupied by a new sailor Zheleznyak, who, under the tank guns aimed at the Kremlin, will announce to its inhabitants that the "guard got tired!" (allegedly with such words a sailor by this name dispersed in January 1918 on the orders of the Bolshevik leadership the lawfully elected Constituent Assembly of Russia that started its first session in the Tavrichesky Palace of Petrograd, thus opening the way to the establishment of communist dictatorship - H.T.) (Igor Korotchenko, 'S armiyei shutki plokhi', [The army is not the one to be trifled with], *Nezavisimoye Voennoye Obozreniye*, 1-6 March 1997, p.2).

[55] *Izvestia*, 22 May 1997, p.2. The author thinks that such a demand was not just a mere pretext to dismiss Rodionov. Somebody, evidently, finally enlightened the President that paratroopers on the loose, demobilized, uncontrolled, with their alleged loyalty to Lebed, who is dreaming of presidential office, would be much more dangerous to the powers-that-be than as soldiers of disciplined units under the control of a reliable commander.

[56] *Izvestia*, 24 May 1997, p.1.

[57] Rodionov was supposed to make a lengthy report on military reform but the President cut him short and ordered him to sit down. When going to his seat Rodionov reportedly said: "Let this whole business go to... (expletive deleted)!" (*Izvestia*, 24 May 1997, p.1). This whole story is just one example of a non-stop backroom struggle that Russian rulers devote 90% of their time to!

[58] *Nezavisimaya Gazeta*, 14 February 1997, p.1.

[59] The Chairman of the Duma Defense Committee, Lev Rokhlin, 'Obrashchenie k Verkhovnomu Glavnokomanduyushchemu vooruzhennymi silami Rossiiskoy Federatsii ot 23 iyunya 1997 goda' [An Appeal to the Commander-in-Chief of the Armed Forces of the Russian Federation and to servicemen of June 23, 1997], *Nezavisimoye Voennoye Obozreniye*, No. 24 (51), July 1997, p.2.

[60] It is common talk in Russia now that all the problems of payments to working people and servicemen are presently decided by so-called *trishkinization*: by taking money from everybody else and from all the government programs and giving them in a particular period to those, who happen to be the focus of the President's special attention at that moment in time. In this way, the huge accumulated debt to pensioners was finally reimbursed by the end of June of 1997, after which it again began to accumulate because the government's attention switched to the army. The term *trishkinization* takes its origin in the Russian folk tale about a certain tailor by the name of Trishka, who used to repair dresses by cutting a piece of cloth from one part of a dress and sewing it into another, say from a flap to a sleeve. As far as the author can judge, the very term *trishkinization* was coined by an American called Smith, who compiled the first open report on the atomic energy in 1945. He used it to describe the methods of building the Soviet atomic industry.

[61] *Nezavisimaya Gazeta*, 5 July 1997, p.1.

[62] Allegedly Rokhlin was shot in his sleep by his wife from his own personal handgun. Sycophantic Moscow media found the motives for such a shooting irreproachable. Come to think of it, they assert: the General was late for his son's birthday party and after the party the wife had to stay up alone to do the dish washing! However, the majority of honest Russian political analysts do not believe the official yarn and are convinced that it was a political assassination, executed very professionally.

[63] 'O deijstvennosti gosudarstvennoi vlasti v Rossii. Poslaniye Prezidenta Rossiiskoy Federatsii Federalnomu Sobraniyu' [On the effectiveness of the state power in Rossiya. The message of the President of the Russian Federation to the Federal Assembly] *Rossiiskiye Vesti*, 17 February 1995, p.4.

[64] On 14 December 1995 the presidents of Bosnia-Herzegovina, Croatia and Serbia signed the Bosnian Peace Treaty in a formal ceremony at the Elysee Palace in Paris. They pledged to honor the right of hundreds of thousands of refugees to return to their homes, respect human rights, and resolve their differences by peaceful means. The signing of the Treaty was witnessed by the leaders of the United States, France, Germany, England, Russia and Spain, whose nations had struggled for years to convince the warring parties to put aside their hatred and to step onto the road of reconciliation.

[65]"This is an historic development", said William Perry. "I have spent my entire carrier as a Cold Warrior, and I never dreamed there would be a Russian brigade

operating in an American division following commands of an American general to secure peace in Central Europe" (*USIA Wireless File*, 13 December 1995, p.74).

[66] 'Ob Ukreplenii Rossiiskogo Gosudarstva' [On the Strengthening of the State of Rossiya] The message of the President of the Russian Federation to the Federal Assembly, *Rossiiskaya Gazeta*, 25 February 1994, p.6.

[67] *The Washington Post*, 27 September 1994, p.A10.

Chapter Four

Russian Interests in Europe

Russia's European interests are multifarious. They include security, political, economic, and cultural interests as well as an interest in developing contacts between individual citizens and their associations.

Given the demise of the USSR, the mellowing of a regime at the core of the FSU, political and economic transformation and a heavily disrupted and crumbling economy, Russia ceased to be a bugbear for Western Europe, though, one has to admit, not everybody West of Russian borders is absolutely sure.

Nevertheless, it is clear that given the pitiful state of Russia's armed forces and their command structures (vividly demonstrated by the Chechen fiasco) and Russian troop withdrawals from the Eastern part of Germany and the territories of all other former Moscow's satellites in Europe and the Baltic republics, the prevailing opinion among the Western establishment is that Russia will not be able, at least for a while, to mount a successful military attack on Western Europe,[1] even if there is a drastic shift in Russian leadership towards the radical right or left.[2]

For its own part, the Russian leadership, which has stopped singing the tune of an "imperialist threat" from the West, is fairly sure that there is no military treat to Russia from Western Europe, though the continuing existence of NATO, which was created as an anti-Soviet bloc, is extremely worrying to some Russian strategists.

Russia's security situation assumes that at the present time there is no longer a direct counterbalance between Western European and Moscow military forces across the border. Russia is separated from Western Europe by the belt of presently neutral states, Ukraine, Belarus, Lithuania, Latvia and Estonia. However, what at one time was a second belt of neutrals, consisting of the former Soviet satellites of Bulgaria, Rumania, Hungary, Slovakia, and Poland, is gradually being transformed into NATO territory. In the North-West, Russia is still essentially separated from NATO by the double barrier of neutral bourgeois states of Finland and Sweden. Only two small stretches of Russia's border touch the territory of the NATO countries, namely Norway and Poland (a future member of the bloc) both of whom border on the Russian enclave along the south-eastern shore of the Baltic sea - the Kaliningrad region.

Of course, in Russia and in Western Europe, nuclear weapons exist that can shoot over these "neutral belts" and the geostrategic situation is not frozen, but in the process of change.

However, after Chernobyl, only those favoring suicide could think of nuclear war in Europe. Hence the only viable means any side or state can employ to influence the course of geopolitical change in its favor are, essentially, political (diplomatic) and economic strategies. And the struggle for influence goes full steam ahead in Europe.

The problem of NATO expansion

Despite the demise of the Soviet colossus and great transformations taking place in Russia, Cold war thinking and the idea of "sides" did not completely disappear. All the protracted international debate about the possible geographical delineation of the "NATO sphere" is rooted in and informed by the Cold war mentality and perceptions on both "sides".

The debate in the United States, Western and Eastern (minus Russia) Europe proceeds from the assumption that non-FSU Eastern Europe countries plus the Baltic states constitute a "vacuum" in post-Cold war Europe. This is the epitome of Cold war mentality. According to this approach, which has many proponents in the United States, if this or that country of Eastern Europe is not "ours" (that is American) and is no longer "theirs" (Russian) then it is no-man's land, which "creates a dangerous power vacuum in Europe's heart".[3] In other words, if we do not grab these countries quickly into "our camp" (*Amlag*? - from the Russian "lager" - camp), they will surely be speedily enticed or scared back into "theirs" (*Ruslag*?)!

One has to frankly admit, however, that Moscow's procrastination in withdrawing troops from Latvia and Estonia, Russian political and economic pressure on Ukraine and similar actions, against the backdrop of the rise to political prominence of the revanchist party of Vladimir Zhirinovsky in the early 1990s, and the extreme brutality of Moscow's military action in Chechnya, contribute a great deal to a continued Cold War mentality in the West. On the other hand, however, one can view the intention of the United States and some West European powers to expand NATO eastward as a natural geopolitical impulse in the balance of power game: the winners in the Cold war decided to formally collect the stakes by expanding their zone of control, all the sweet words about the "new world" and "strategic partnership" notwithstanding.

It is also clear that Russia has a hard time working out a consistent intelligible policy towards Europe, while all the previous serenades of Gorbachev regarding the "common European home" were nothing but political gobbledygook. Yeltsin's nonchalant approval of Poland's desire to join NATO (incredible from the point of view of Russia's national interests) during his visit to Poland in August 1993 vividly demonstrated the total lack of any well thought-out Russian strategy on Europe.[4]

I will not dwell on all the pros and cons of expanding NATO eastward because so much has already been said, and the expansion is already proceeding apace. To recapitulate all the intricate arguments advanced by the discussants will be a sheer waste of time. It is better to assess in *Realpolitik* terms how the matter looks from Moscow's centrist (that is - not extremist) point of view.

First, it is absolutely clear, that whatever arguments are advanced from Washington, Bonn or London, the desire to capitalize on Russia's present weakness in order to cement the positions of the respective countries for future encounters with Russia as a geopolitical, not ideological, rival is central to their policies towards Russia. Many Russian intellectuals (not connected with government policy) have been asking for almost 10 years: will American and NATO excess-pressure end some day? will the time finally come when the United States feels fully satisfied with the gains it got as a result of the collapse of the "evil empire"? and hence when will the West stop pressuring Russia "from positions of strength" for more and more political concessions, retreats and/or total capitulation? The honest answer to these questions (and not a polite public answer in the spirit of "diplomatic correctness") is that American pressure to yield more will never stop.[5] This is in the nature of the political struggle and any international politics is a struggle for power and influence. To stop the retreat of Russia is possible only by generating counter-pressure, if and when Russia is able to do it.

In an article in the journal *Foreign Affairs*, entitled 'Build a New NATO' (this author would rather call it 'Grab the Booty We Have So Far Neglected'), which was amazing in its raw and revealing cynicism, the three RAND corporation analysts argued that NATO should rejuvenate itself and move aggressively eastward to "project democracy". To achieve this goal, they advocated the creation of a "Force Projection Command responsible for developing the military plans and forces needed to conduct operations beyond NATO's traditional borders", in order, it appears, to "secure the gains of the Cold War". One of the great gains is Eastern Europe and, as the accompanying map in the journal demonstrated, NATO is supposed to incorporate into its ranks not only all the former Soviet satellites, but also Ukraine, Belarus and Finland. (However, Bosnia or Serbia are not included in the present NATO configuration, where the bloc dismally and infamously for four years did nothing to stop the wholesale slaughter of innocent civilians, while NATO is pictured by the present supporters of expansion as brave enough to become engaged even on a nuclear level in Eastern Europe!) Otherwise, the RAND analysts argued, NATO would go out of business. Posing the "NATO dilemma" in such a way, they confirmed perennial claims by former Kremlin rulers that NATO has always been an aggressive bloc.[6] Even allowing for the fact that an article even in the *Foreign Affairs* does not represent official thinking, this article actually foretold everything that followed, while official justification for the expansion was portrayed as extremely noble and honorable.

Second, while the CIS republics are inescapably developing under the spell of Russia, because the latter is not only powerful, but also a generous donor in the CIS context, the former Soviet Union's satellites in Eastern Europe, as well as newly independent Baltics, are very afraid of Russia and the possibilities of its new intrigues and pressure. Hence the Visegrad agreement on military cooperation between Poland, Hungary and Czechoslovakia,[7] and the desperate desire and frantic efforts on the part of all Eastern European states to obtain the protection of NATO should come as no surprise. This thrust westward was stimulated by the August 1991 "putsch" in Moscow, the shelling of the Russian parliament by Yeltsin's forces two years later, and by the wholesale slaughter in Chechnya between 1994-96. This East European drift to the cover of the West is not to be stopped, even if the West ceased encouraging it.

Third, the NATO "Partnership for Peace" (hereafter simply PfP) initiative, adopted by the NATO Council in January 1994 on American prompting and much criticized by certain impatient Western statesmen and journalists as an "unnecessary concession to Russian sensibilities", was in reality nothing of the kind. It was actually a new phase in the plot to move the NATO border eastward, which started with the creation of the North Atlantic Cooperation Council (NACC) in December 1991. The PfP scheme, like the NACC, has been a "holding operation", a new cover up for the same goal: a more or less expeditious inclusion of the core East European states (the Czech republic, Hungary, Poland) into the North Atlantic bloc. Such augmentation of NATO might be followed by the incorporation of the Baltic states, depending upon Russia's reaction to the first phase of the scheme. Moreover, it is continually stressed that it will be the NATO leadership who will decide which countries, and in what order, join NATO.

The most succinct explanation of the design underlying the PfP was given by the Deputy Secretary of State, Strobe Talbott at his confirmation hearings in the Foreign Relations Committee of the US Senate on 8 February 1994, when he stated:

Developments in Russia, of course, will profoundly influence what kind of security structures evolve in Europe - and indeed, across Eurasia. If Russia hews to a course of internal reform, respect for its neighbors independence, and cooperation with the West, NATO will continue to evolve in the direction of maximum inclusiveness. If, however, reform in Russia falters, if new threats arise, NATO will be able to work through the Partnership to protect regional stability through closer ties - including NATO membership - with the active participants. And we will have the deeply enhanced military and political relationship through the Partnership for Peace on which to build.[8]

The PfP scheme made armed forces, defense planning and the budget processes of the 26 countries that joined the PfP transparent to the United States authorities. By developing joint training exercises, NATO actually gained some measure of control over the national armed forces of these countries. It also created a pool of peacekeepers to ease the burden of the member countries of NATO in various policing operations in Europe, and maybe even beyond its borders. Meanwhile, the training and adaptation of the first batch of selected candidates is already in full swing.

Fourth, in order not to challenge Russia directly, the PfP has been covered with the veneer of a democratic arrangement. It is open to all the countries of Europe, including the CIS republics, all of which, with the exception of Tajikistan, have already joined the Partnership. The invitation to Russia to take part in the "Partnership for Peace" was a smoke screen invented to blunt Russian apprehensions and to disarm Russian diplomacy in obstructing the scheme to bring NATO closer to Russian borders. After some hesitation, Moscow finally swallowed the bait and joined the PfP. On 31 May 1995 at the session of the North Atlantic Council in Noordwijk, the Netherlands, the Russian Foreign Minister accepted the Russian Individual Partnership Program under the PfP, and the document on "Areas for Pursuance of a Broad, Enhanced NATO-Russia Dialogue and Cooperation".[9]   Thus the trap, prepared for Russia, closed. The new document, legalizing on the Russian part, the extension of NATO, that was signed in Paris in May 1997, essentially repeats the conditions of the Individual PfP program for Russia , worked out by the bloc's strategists.

Fifth, the expansion of NATO eastward is first and foremost needed to boost declining US influence in Europe, through the only effective leverage vis-à-vis Europe left in the American hands, the NATO mechanism, over which Washington dominates. This is why the American leadership would not be satisfied, if East European countries just joined the Western European Union, a purely European defense organization, without joining NATO. The latter's eastward expansion is also heavily pushed by American defense industries, as there will be a large new market for US armaments in the neophyte countries because of the required arms standardization.

Sixth, it has been one of the most vital national interests of Russia not to allow the present belt of East European states, gradually shedding the vestiges of communism (the states that served as a *cordon sanitaire* against the bacilli of Communism before World War Two and were turned into military bridgehead of Soviet communism to pressure Western Europe after the end of that war), to change their present neutral status and to become a bridgehead of the powerful Western military bloc close to Russia's borders. Now this interest has been betrayed by Yeltsin and his government.[10]

It is indicative of American duplicity that the very same people, who only recently recognized as "organic" the nature of the connection between Russia and the states of Eastern Europe, and were eager to settle for the latter's neutrality in exchange for the continuation of *perestroika* in the Soviet Union, are now itching to further undercut Russia's international positions, and isolate it, by going along with such a brazen challenge to Russia's security as the expansion of NATO to the East.[11]

Seventh, because such an incorporation has occurred in spite of all the previous efforts by Russia to prevent it,[12] it will become an obstacle to true partnership between Russia and the Western countries, despite the signing of a pacifying document. The forms and methods of inevitable confrontation will depend on the health of the economy and socio-political developments in Russia.

Eighth, moves to incorporate the aforementioned states into NATO against Russia's will, might generate, and are already generating, a tremendous upsurge of nationalistic, revanchist forces in Russia that will inevitably strongly influence the future course of Russian foreign policy.[13]

Ninth, while this policy towards Russia on the part of the United States and its allies, which can only be defined as perfidious, will be gradually implemented, Russian foreign policy (even under Yeltsin, who now acts as an American puppet!) will seek every opportunity to undercut the interests of Western states, wherever Russia can get away with it, without serious repercussions. One such arena of action might be the UN Security Council. The CFE and the INF treaties, and the START II treaty, might also become casualties of the process.

Tenth, if and when East European countries, including the Baltic republics, are finally sucked into the NATO bloc, and Russia, to remonstrate, will, say, make a military move against the Baltics, which were integral part of the Russian empire for 200 years, will the West be prepared to unleash a Third World War in order to defend them? This is the crucial question that ought to be answered before the NATO authorities put in high gear their "brilliant scheme" of "pacifying Russia", while grossly infringing its national interests.[14]

Finally, due to the total collapse of Russian reforms and the resulting ruin of Russian economy, the present Russian leadership can only hope to survive on donations from the West.[15] Because of this, the Kremlin did not have any alternative but to reluctantly agree to the expansion of NATO. The current leaders of Russia, who are still engaged in dividing the spoils among themselves (privatized property for example) decided not just to silently swallow this bitter pill, but to present to the Russian public the country's humiliation as their "victory". In order to receive additional support and subsidies from NATO countries and Western financial institutions, the Russian leaders gave their blessing to the "limited expansion by NATO", whilst duping their own people by stressing that Russia will proceed along its own lines and retain a say by being present at G7 meetings of industrial countries as an equal partner, having the opportunity to discuss Russia's security problems with representatives of NATO in the specially created NATO-Russian Council and by retaining US government and private investments for Russia's ailing economy.

This was the essence of the "compromise" (as the Russian capitulation is called in Moscow) at Yeltsin's meeting with President Clinton in Helsinki at the end of March 1997. Yeltsin actually okayed NATO's expansion, which he so vehemently opposed only a month before.

This extremely shameful deal, which actually undermines Russia's national interests, was signed for a few flimsy "privileges" for the Russian President and his ruling clique. It very much resembled the capitulation of the Lenin's government in Brest-Litovsk before Germany exactly 79 years earlier. As is well known, for the option to formally stay in power in a country on its knees, Lenin then gave Germany numerous chunks of Russian territory, made monetary contributions and as a result Lenin *de facto* established Berlin's *Diktatur* over Russia's policies. Yeltsin did the same thing by opening up Russian mineral wealth for unlimited exploitation by foreign firms and actually giving Washington the final say over Russian foreign and domestic policies. The only difference between Yeltsin and Lenin is that Lenin had some real hope of quickly ridding Russia of her humiliating conditions as a result either of the imminent revolution in Germany, or its defeat by the allies in the ongoing war (both hopes proved to be well grounded). Yeltsin and his cronies, while trading Russian vital interests for their private gains, have no such hopes, except perhaps that the United States might be merciful and give some small financial donations, because America will hardly find more complaisant bailiffs in the present Russia.

While Russian leaders and the pliant media described the Founding Act and Yeltsin's signing it as a new "historic achievement" of Russian diplomacy, the US Secretary of State, Madeleine Albright, quite cynically presented this Act as a sort of "pacifier" for Russia, which is what it really is. In an interview with Jim Lehrer on the PBS-TV News-hour on 14 May 1997 Secretary Albright emphasized that "As a result of this NATO-Russia Founding Act, we are able *to anchor* Russia within a European system" (that is to deprive Russia of the freedom of manoeuver by giving nothing in return). This is evident from the exchange between Lehrer and Albright:

LEHRER: The Russians wanted a voice in the new NATO decisions.   Does this agreement give it to them?
ALBRIGHT: Let me explain something.   There are really two parts to this.   NATO has a sacrosanct council, the North Atlantic Council, which makes the military decisions on behalf of NATO.   *Russia will have no voice in that at all.*
What this document does is create a new joint NATO-Russia Council where Russia will, indeed, have a voice, and where we will be talking about a whole host of issues that have to do with cooperation in Europe or outside of that area.   But *what's very important for people to understand is that Russia does not and will not have a veto over any action within NATO itself - the enlarged NATO or the current NATO....* Even now there is a 16 plus-one, NATO plus Russia and other countries, discussion about various issues and policies.   So what this document also does is in some way institutionalize something that's already going on...
LEHRER: On some specific things.   What does this agreement say about the placement of nuclear weapons and any new countries added to NATO?
ALBRIGHT: *What is important about this document, it has taken basic known NATO doctrine and embodied it within this document.*   It has been NATO doctrine that there (was), *under current circumstances*, no intention, plan or reason to use nuclear forces within the potential new members of NATO...
LEHRER: What about limits on troop deployments in the new countries?
ALBRIGHT: Again, what this did *was take a document that was issued NATO in March of this year* in which the NATO members agreed that they had no plans to station *substantial* combat military forces in the new countries, but that they needed to fulfill their missions by having interoperability; the ability to reinforce and to coordinate, to integrate...Subsumed within that, is the idea that those forces will need to use some existing infrastructure, and they will use the infrastructure that they need in order to fulfill that particular mission...
LEHRER: So when you say "infrastructure," you mean... military bases of some kind?
ALBRIGHT: Military bases.
LEHRER: *No special limits put on the number of potential NATO installations in this agreement?*
ALBRIGHT*: No. There are no limits on that.*   They are to be adequate for the mission as I described it.
LEHRER: As decided by NATO?   Not in consultation with Russia?
ALBRIGHT: *As decided by NATO* (emphasis mine - H.T.).[16]

One has to add that by signing the Founding Act, Russia voluntarily struck out the Helsinki Final Act of 1975 that fixed the post World War II order in Europe and opened up opportunities for building a new post-Cold war Europe by creating an institution for this purpose - the Conference for Security and Cooperation in Europe (CSCE) which was later turned into the Organization for Security and Cooperation in Europe (OSCE), with exactly that purpose in mind. This Act assigned to Russia equal status with other participants (all European countries plus the US and Canada) and an important role in building the new Europe. Most of the political changes that have taken place in Europe since that time have come under the auspices of the OSCE. Despite the fact that the Founding Act pays lip service to the OSCE, calling it "the only pan-European security organization" that "has a key role in European peace and stability",[17] the Act actually liquidated this aspect of the OSCE's role and transferred the appropriate functions to NATO, where Russia will play the role of a charwoman. A US State Department official who invented the heading for the agreement between Russia and NATO, fixing such a new Russian role, was smart enough to name it the Founding Act. As a result, the document creates the illusion of continuity of the Helsinki process, while in fact, through its very content, it makes a total break with it, and *de facto* annuls the Helsinki Act of 1975 as far as procedures for all-important European decisions are concerned.

Yeltsin definitely did not understand all the long-term negative implications of the Founding Act for Russia. When signing it in Paris on 27 May 1997, Yeltsin, in a fit of rapture for such a "historic achievement of Russian diplomacy", announced that he would take all the nuclear warheads aimed at the NATO countries off Russian nuclear missiles.[18] It took a week of non-stop clarifications by Russian military and diplomats to explain to the world that the President just meant zero targeting of the appropriate warheads, not really dismantling them!

Finally, one more negative repercussion for Russia, stemming from its approval of NATO's expansion and the resulting deal with the bloc, was that by acting in such a way, Moscow itself contributed to its isolation in the future. If Russia had stood firm on NATO enlargement, it, at least, might have retained a strong influence over the successor states on this issue. Now, when Russia is lounging around the bloc, it is much harder to stop them joining NATO. It would hardly have been feasible, for instance, for Ukraine to challenge Russia by signing a Charter with the bloc, with its essentially anti-Russian implications (as Ukraine did at the Madrid NATO summit), if Russia had adamantly opposed the bloc's expansion. And if

Ukraine went "the Russian way", and, probably, will go even farther, why not Moldova, not to speak about the Baltics?

The role of Germany

Germany played a prominent role in the scheme to drag East European countries into NATO as full members. The Secretary General of NATO, Herr Manfred Woerner (who died suddenly in August 1994), the German Defense Minister, Volker Ruehe, as well as many other representatives of the Bonn leadership, actively lobbied for the speedy incorporation of Poland, Hungary and the Czech republic into NATO and made appropriate arrangements with Poland and other countries of Eastern Europe for joint military exercises, training of their officers, standardizing equipment, etc.

Such an activity on the part of Germany cannot but puzzle, because any objective analysis of the geopolitical situation in greater Europe unambiguously shows that the better fortunes of Germany lie in a cooperation with Russia, not in alienating it. The fact remains that Germany has no great opportunities for further economic expansion within the confines of the European Union: it has already tapped most of them. The "historic" Franco-German Alliance is the product of fright, not sincerity, on the part of France, and anyone slightly familiar with the subject is well aware of this.[19] And, generally speaking, the European Union with its envisaged political consolidation will hold Germany too tightly for it to be comfortable.

At the same time, there are tremendous economic opportunities for German capital in the East, and of all the potentially most lucrative countries, Russia is number one. German entrepreneurs and politicians already have a significant foothold in Russia because of the special relationships that has developed in recent years between Bonn and Moscow, as a result of reunification and the influx of German money into the Russian economy. Current estimates show that Germany's share of international financial aid to the CIS countries has reached 60%, most of which goes to Russia. Of all the humanitarian aid granted to Russia and the NICs more than three quarters comes from Germany.

Hence, the current behavior of German politicians, trying to be more zealous than their NATO's allies regarding the expansion of the bloc's territory eastward, with the inevitability of such a move becoming a strong irritant for Russia, cannot but puzzle and begs explanation.

The only plausible explanation is that Germany, in the best traditions of *Genscherism,* is trying to conduct a dual-track Eastern policy: whilst indulging Russia, it simultaneously makes moves to safeguard itself in the event of some untoward developments in Russia. In a situation where Poland is an hour's drive from Berlin, Germany is undoubtedly interested in creating some sort of security belt in the East. German politicians fully understand that by moving the Western borders of Poland into former German territory, Stalin created an in-built security dependence of Poland on Russia and they want to change this situation, while the new Poland does not yet have enough time to make a thorough geopolitical evaluation of the evolving situation in Europe.

The Polish people well remember that only six years ago Helmut Kohl himself, along with other German politicians, was still questioning the validity of present-day western borders of Poland fixed by the Yalta agreements. So the possibility always exists that Poland might be frightened back into Russia's embrace whatever the current thinking in Warsaw might be. Without a friendly Poland, Germany will also have difficulties in continuing its efforts to establish an economic presence in the former German *länder* of East Prussia - now the Russian enclave on the coast of the Baltic sea named Kaliningrad province. For a very long time now, Germany has coveted an economic return to that territory.

Posing as the most eager advocates of NATO's eastward expansion, the present ruling politicians of Germany act as the most loyal, most devoted members of the NATO alliance, which was initially organized not only to thwart the potential aggressive designs of Stalin, but also to keep an eye on Germany. At the same time, this approach is also *de facto* blocking French attempts to transfer the weight of European military policy to the West European Union, where the French intend to *diriger*.

At the same time, Chancellor Kohl evidently has succeeded in establishing a special relationship with President Yeltsin. It was Kohl who energetically promoted close Russian association with the European Union (in the face of French opposition), who prodded Russia to enter NATO's Partnership for Peace and who lobbied with the Western leaders to make Russia a full-fledged participant in the G7 meetings of the industrialized countries. "The state of Russian-German relations at the present time is better than at any time during the two country's history", Chancellor Kohl stated in Berlin in July 1997.[20]

It seems that Bonn does not have any difficulty in explaining - in camera - all its manoeuvering to Russian leaders not of Zhirinovsky's type. And again, if the emergence of some Zhirinovsky-type boss in Russia becomes inevitable, all of Bonn's present safeguards will work in its favor.

However, all said and done, the grand strategy of Germany is a collusion with Russia. Of course, to achieve this Germany does not want to frighten Russia, where concern about a militaristic and expansionist Germany is still almost a gut feeling, though the generation brought up on anti-German passions is gradually passing away.

What are Russia's national interests in this situation? Moscow's experience so far convinces Russia that excessive Western pressure, as exemplified first of all by the policies of the United States, will not abate. The only Western country that in some way understands and empathizes with the plight of Russia, is Germany. Both countries, besides their clashes in the two world wars, have long-standing historic ties: less than two hundred years ago, 70-80% of the then Russian educated class was of German descent. Russian philosophy, literature and technology was strongly influenced by German sources. German settlers in Russia were model Russian farmers and, if not for the criminal paranoia of Stalin, Russian Germans would have now been the prime movers in rejuvenating Russian agriculture, instead of fleeing to Germany.

The mighty Bundesrepublik, still feeling to some extent restrained and constrained by its Western partners, and Russia - presently humiliated, internationally abused and very sensitive to attempts to isolate her - possess a sort of national affinity for each other.[21] And, while talk of a new Rapallo is surely an exaggeration, close cooperation between Russia and Germany might help both to improve their international standing and enable Russia to rejuvenate its ailing and totally disorganized economy. At one time Russian Foreign Minister Kozyrev talked about "the formation of a kind of axis of partnership between Russia and Germany".[22] A good understanding between the two countries will also help both handle the Poles, with their usual arrogant high-handedness towards everybody else, better.

"Unification", attests Fritz Stern, "has fulfilled the old national dream and attenuated - even on some level removed - Germany's dependency on its Western allies".[23]

So, from the point of view of Russian leaders of almost every persuasion, rapprochement with Germany is definitely in the national interests of the Russian Federation. Especially as there is no other country in Western

Europe that might be as helpful to and as understanding of Russia, as Germany is today.

Someone might talk of France, but the long experience of Russia (that is, probably, very similar to the experience of the United States in dealing with France) proves that France is too unreliable to hope for a serious long-term deal, Gorbachev views of France as a "natural ally" notwithstanding. This does not mean that Russia is not diplomatically involved with France. Russia is trying to work closely with France to strengthen the existing structures connected with European security. It energetically supported the French initiative for a Pact on Stability in Europe (in conditions when the CSCE structure already existed, this new pact was evidently proposed by Paris for the sole reason to put a French imprimatur on "the architecture of Europe").[24] France has been opening up diplomatic links with Russia because Paris felt that Russo-German ties were too strong. But, when in December 1993 President Yeltsin travelled to Brussels in the hope of signing an agreement with the European Union on cooperation and partnership, it was France that blocked such an agreement! This agreement did not materialize until June 1994 and came into force only on 1 December 1997.

It is also worth remembering that Russia in a way has one traditional obligation, stemming from the World War Two agreements among members of the anti-Nazi coalition: namely the obligation to watch over Germany so the latter will not misbehave, while it gradually increases its economic potential and international weight. This kind of "oversight" is - in the present dire state of Russia - more symbolic than real, and it acquires the feel of a real thing only because the other Western partner of Russia - the United States - retains the role (albeit not well advertised) of a second overseer of Germany and a *de facto* guarantor of its good international behavior.

The prospect of German-Russian collusion, beneficial for both sides, definitely undermines this potentially significant but realistically purely symbolic role of Russia. Nevertheless, this potential role represents a common ground in Russian-American relations. Too much Russian conniving with Germany will alert the United States, which will try, to put it crudely, to punish Russia for any such overtures. On the other hand, too strong an orientation by Moscow on Washington regarding its policy on Germany will undermine German trust in Russia, with the possibility that Russia might be deprived of assured technological help and investments that could not be easily replaced by some from the United States. This is the big dilemma for Russian policy.

The United States is not facing such a dilemma in mapping its strategy vis-à-vis Germany because it does not depend on Germany in the same way Russia does. However, how the United States behaves towards Russia will have a great influence on the formulation of Moscow's policy toward Germany.

At the time of writing, the Clinton administration's policy constitutes some sort of a special arrangement with Germany, as shown by the US promotion of a leadership role for Germany on the continent, as if she has stepped into America's shoes. But this is a sort of empty gesture because with the departure of American troops from Germany and a general weakening of America's position in Europe such a role for Germany within the confines of Western and Central Europe is guaranteed without any American blessing. And again a close partnership between Germany and Russia will only help Germany to assume such a role. This sums up the potentialities of further Russo-German rapprochement.

Wider European interests of Russia

Russia's flirtation with Germany is just one aspect of the balance of power politics in Europe, that started to be energetically played by every sovereign country of the continent and by some outside powers after the end of bipolar confrontation. With all its diminished political clout and economic disabilities, Russia might remain a strong player in the game due to its geopolitical weight, if she eases somewhat her American shackles. Russia has really no staunch allies in Europe now and that is why it strongly clings to the one country that might be considered a strategic ally - Serbia.

Moscow claims "natural affinity" with Serbia because Serbs are "fellow Slavs" and, like Russians, they are Orthodox Christians. Bosnians are also Slavs, though they are mostly Muslim in their religious affiliation, while Croats and Slovenes are Christians. However, out of all of them Russia sided with Serbs.

There is no logical explanation of such a mutual devotion, except for the fact that one can speak of a collusion of the two semi-outcasts of Europe, still faithful to some extent to communist internationalism. Russia, suffering wounding blows to its pride, still shunned by some respectable European institutions and Milosevic's Serbia - a bogeyman to the world, ostracized by the West.

It is not that Moscow totally approved of the methods the Serbs used to expand their territory. To a certain extent, Russia's stubborn support for Serbian "solutions" based on the ethnicity principle backfired against Yeltsin's policies at home, making it more difficult for him to deal with the national republics within the Russian Federation, some of whom are not averse to use ethnicity as the main principle of state-building. But, it seems, nobody in Moscow thinks that deep, while the struggle between Zhirinovsky and the leader of the Communist Party of Russia Gennady Zyuganov for the allegiance of masses, suddenly aroused by nationalistic slogans, forces the President to try and outdo them on their own turf.

Yugoslav Serbs – "Slav brothers" - with their particular stand in the Balkan conflict were chosen by the Russian government as a means for Russian self assertion, for the attempt (that failed in the final analysis) to break out in its foreign policy from the bondage of the US Department of State. Moscow suffered a colossal loss of power and influence, the loss of many of its "territories and possessions", to use an American term, but suddenly decided to take a firm uncompromising stand against NATO's ultimatum to Serbs in February 1994, the ultimatum that was actually prompted by the United Nations Secretary-General. This Russian stance demonstrated that Moscow was still a force to be reckoned on decisions relating to European security.

By supporting his "Serbian brothers", Yeltsin and his staff demonstrated (first and foremost to their own electorate) that ostensibly they were not running dogs of the West, as their opponents - the Russian nationalists - claim. Russia's room for manoeuver is heavily circumscribed by its past (including the Soviet period) losses, which made her weak, and by her real dependence on the West, at least in trying to avoid a resurgence of the Cold war. This is why Russia did not use its veto in the UN Security Council when it came to the brass tacks of Serbian behavior. But at other times, Russian politicians have been accentuating their solidarity with Serbia, and this solidarity and cooperation developed in direct proportion to the increase in NATO's pressure on Serbia and Russia.

However, there was more   pretense than substance in Moscow's stance on the Yugoslav crisis. A famous Russian philosopher, remarked at the beginning of this century:

Come to think of it, need Russia suffer and struggle for one thousand years, become Christian with St.Vladimir and European with Peter the Great, while constantly occupying during all that time a peculiar niche between the East and the West, and all this - in order to turn in the final count to be a tool of the Serbian "great idea"...![25]

Whatever leverage Russia can extract for herself from the Yugoslav crisis, responsible Russian politicians realize that Russia must seek some more effective leverages in Europe than threats of or moves towards a confrontation, because confrontation will backfire first and foremost against Russia.

In an extreme case, Russia theoretically might use leverages such as stopping oil and, especially, gas supplies to Europe, or tightening the screws on Western companies, banks or joint ventures operating in Russia. However, in the final analysis, such tactics will backfire on Russia and it will be extremely difficult to restore amicable relations if the quarrel goes too far.

The only non-offensive way for Russia to make Western Europe listen to her suggestions or pleas more attentively is to more skillfully practice the balance of power diplomacy in Europe or even on a global scale, by exploiting her geopolitical situation vis-à-vis different sub-coalitions with divergent interests in the Western grouping of states. However, this is also problematic: Russia has lost her independence in mapping out her policy.

Another venue is to energetically develop and use the mechanisms of the Organization on Security and Cooperation in Europe. Although the idea of a conference on European security emanated from Moscow way back in the 1950s, Moscow was wary of the organization during its evolution in the period 1975-1990. It wanted the CSCE to be devoid of any real decision-making and peacekeeping powers in case they were used to interfere into the internal affairs of the Soviet Union, namely on the grounds of monitoring observance of human rights etc. This is why the CSCE mechanisms that were created, initially proved inefficient in tackling conflicts, such as those in the Transcaucasus or Yugoslavia. This inefficiency also backfired on Russia which had to deal more and more with NATO instead of relying on the OSCE.

Nonetheless, the OSCE has gradually started to get more involved in peacekeeping operations in Europe and in overseeing European political events. More pragmatic mechanisms for reacting to the developments in Europe have been created and tested. At this very moment, the OSCE was practically killed off by Moscow's acceptance of NATO as the main organization for the European security. The Clinton-Yeltsin collusion in Helsinki and the resulting NATO-Russian agreement that puts all the decision making on larger problems of European security onto NATO means that the OSCE has lost much of its relevance. Nowadays, it will not be Russia, but the West European partners of the United States, who will try to reverse the impact of Russia's betrayal not only on its own vital interests, but on European identity, independence and freedom of manoeuver, as well as on the equilibrium of the global balance of power.

However, the main problem goes deeper than Russia's blessing of NATO and the demise of the OSCE. While concentrating all their attention on the problem of NATO expansion, Russian leaders have somehow lost the sense of their own European identity. All the alleged wonderful success in compiling a joint NATO-Russian document, 90% of which consists of borrowed or stolen pledges, declarations and promises contained in other, earlier documents defining East-West relations and NATO strategy, is not worth a single unrealized step in the direction of Russia's integration with Western Europe - economic, political, cultural, as well as in the spheres of transportation, communication, etc. The Founding Act did not solve a single Russian problem, because this document represents the outdated mentality of the past projected into the future.

War (including the Cold war) ended quite a while ago, but its former ringleaders on both sides of the Iron curtain, which were supposed to disappear, continue to blow up bridges, leading to the "enemy's camp" and hamper traffic of any sort between the two sides.

All the fuss about NATO membership or non-membership in a situation where there is no threat of large-scale military conflagration in Europe and, more importantly, no danger to European security from the new Russia - is just petty squabbling, provoked by non-European forces, who have prospered far too long on the divide and conquer strategy!

While the idea of a common European home, advanced by Gorbachev in 1990, was for him just a good slogan devoid of any real content or intent, it is basically a very viable, very fruitful idea for Russia and her Western neighbors to pursue, an idea with many positive implications. But did Russia make any real efforts to build a solid foundation for such a home, or at least to provide some cement for it? The answer is no. The attention of Russian leaders focuses on the United States - their guide and patron.

As to Washington itself, its government, while distracting Russia with the residues of Cold war activities, has been smart enough to energetically work on the expansion of non-military transatlantic cooperation and partnership, building bridges to Europe with Transatlantic Labor Dialogue, Transatlantic Business Dialogue, and dozens of other imaginative ventures, from transatlantic AIDSNET to a "telecity" and a digital library projects because American leaders fully appreciate that it will be common political, economic, scientific, cultural interests and endeavors, not arms or rusty chains of NATO, which will keep Europe a close partner, not adversary, of America. Russian strategic thinking, if any, in this respect is far behind her transatlantic model-country.

The common question regarding integration with Europe in the ruling quarters of Russia sounds like this: can we really learn anything from the European integration experience, when the integration - economic and other - in the FSU was much more advanced than is now the case in Western Europe? Those, who pose such a rhetorical question, do not understand the difference between the two methods of integration: one – "Soviet style" – involving brutal compliance, the other, a modern European one, characterized by cautious and patient efforts to find areas of common ground and to expand that ground by consensus. Thirty years of such strenuous work has produced palpable results in raising living standards, improving social services and in opening up the borders to the free movement of people and goods. In this way, a new European identity of members of the European Union is being developed, an identity that, at the same time, does not suppress or destroy the specific cultures and mores of a multiethnic EU. I doubt very much that there are members of the present Moscow establishment who realize that it is not the American experience in global expansion, but the experience of European integration that blazes the trail into a global society of tomorrow.

At the same time, present day Moscow-inspired reintegration within the CIS, done mostly by way of solemn declarations without real daily substantive efforts to expand practical industrial, commercial and cultural linkages among the "integrating" republics, accomplishes very little and undermines the very idea, as the non-stop integration between Russia and Belarus demonstrates. It remains in the realm of wishful thinking without practical efforts to create a new community without customs and other barriers to personal and business contacts. High officials solemnly abolish customs on the Russian - Belarus border, but local gangs with the connivance of regional officials (who get their share of the booty) practice virtual highway robbery on the roads connecting the two countries, by illegally stopping all passing commercial vehicles on the main highway connecting Minsk with Moscow.

There is absolutely no desire to study and import EU practices. One might add to this the systematic sabotage of all integration initiatives within the CIS by pro-American lobbies in all the CIS republics. The US is not interested in such developments and urges its agents of influence to put spanners into any works aimed at creating and improving close economic and political links between Russia and Belarus with the intended extension of such network to some other CIS republics, including Ukraine.

Russia's union with Belarus and consequent steps, already made, to expand business and other contacts on a grass roots level further West to Poland and Germany will really help build a pan-European, or, to be more exact, a Eurasian home from the Atlantic to the Urals and beyond in which the economies of Russia, Belarus, Ukraine could be organically complementary to those of Central and West European countries.

I sincerely believe that one of the hidden motivations behind the US scheme to speedily include the three countries of Eastern Europe into NATO has been, *inter alia*, to overburden them with new colossal military expenditures (to modernize and to standardize weaponry, to improve the infrastructure) in order to create additional barriers for them to becoming full-fledged members of the EU, and, because these countries now constitute a natural gasket between Russia and Western Europe, in such a way to slow down, if not to stop altogether, the process of the gradual liquidation of all barriers on free commercial traffic between these two parts of Europe. ("Gasket", by the way, is the term some Ukrainians use in describing the role Washington designated to their country in the context of Russian business ties with the rest of Europe.)

I fully understand that some people, especially Americans, might object to the invocation of the term "gasket" in the above context. American leaders assert that by incorporating new members into NATO they are unifying Europe, not dividing it. Such a point was made by many high-placed American officials briefing reporters on the eve and during NATO's Madrid summit on 8-9 July 1997.

This gives rise to a couple of questions: Why has the United States, which did so much in the past to prevent West European integration, tolerated the European Economic Community only because Washington was afraid to alienate its allies and clients in the Cold War confrontation, become so enthusiastic about the "unification of Europe"? Is this just because it is unification the American way (via NATO expansion), which might create for the US a "pocket Europe"? And do Americans really want the EU to rise as a global force to be reckoned with?

Many people in the ruling strata of the West European countries are quite positive about the necessity of further rapprochement with Russia on an institutional basis as a means of making Europe a real stronghold of international order in the 21st century. According to David J. Heilbron Price, the Vice-President of the Robert Schuman Institute for Europe in Brussels:

The EU's most important problem is stabilizing long-term relations with Russia. Unfortunately it is not considered the most urgent. This is probably the only time in history when we have had a chance to unify the whole continent for peace. The EU's efforts have been remarkable in one sense but are totally inadequate to achieve that goal...
The most important pan-European indicator is the human spirit. Are we giving Russians hope? Are they feeling more welcome and integrated in Europe after three-quarters of a century of Soviet Communism? On the basis of these questions our policy has dismally failed.[26]

Today's Europe faces great and potentially uplifting tasks. It can no longer afford past disunity, if it wants to become a real force in the new global geopolitical context and to compete on equal terms with the United States, Japan and the rising giant - China.

But why should the EU and West Europe as a whole want to integrate with Russia? Is not Russia a challenge to it, that is best isolated, not embraced? The answer is obvious: without Russia, Europe is not really Europe - only half of it. And not only geographically. It is no coincidence that even during the height of the Cold War and at a time of a very strict discipline in the opposing politico-military camps, it was prominent West European leaders, such as Winston Churchill, Konrad Adenauer and Charles de Gaulle, who initiated the first real détente with Russia after the initial drastic cooling of relationships. This was not out of charity or fear, instead they realized that globally Russia - whether strong or weak - remains important and in fact might be very useful on occasion, so that Europe "would not be taken for granted as a docile... vassal by the friendly superpower" to quote Luigi Barzini.[27]

Even if, during that tense period, West European leaders found it useful to do business with an unfriendly, menacing Russia, is there not more reason to believe that today's cooperative and sincerely friendly Russia is destined to become an active member of the new European community of nations, and has much to contribute to its prosperity by its resources, the industriousness of its people and by its whole history as an integral part of the European "concert of nations"? The only development that might change West European attitudes towards Russia might be the collapse of Russia as a single entity. But even in this case, though unlikely in the immediate future, it is better for West Europeans to gain a solid foothold in Russia and its economy, instead of being helpless observers of developments. A totally isolated, embittered and wild Russia, or a Russia which is just pure colony of the United States (or China?), are alternatives that are not very acceptable to West Europeans irrespective of their political beliefs.

Of course, Russia, despite its accession to the Council of Europe, is still far away from becoming an integral part of a wider politico-economic Europe. And the only realistic course for Russia, in order not to allow herself to be totally subjugated to the United States and its global schemes, is to:

- work more closely and consistently with the old and emerging pan-European institutions,
- try to really penetrate the new economic space of post -Maastricht and post-Amsterdam Europe,
- deepen cooperation with Germany, France, Italy and lesser countries of Western Europe, and to
- restore economic and invigorate political ties with the countries of Eastern Europe that are also suffering economically from a sudden "divorce" with Russia.

The first step in deepening political cooperation among Russia, Germany and France has been made with the creation of the so-called *Troika,* with the decision of the heads of the three countries to conduct regular meetings. The first such meeting took place in Russia in March 1998. However, one cannot entertain great hopes with regard to such a venue to enhance European identity as long as the Russian president remains an errand boy of Washington with Paris and Bonn also contending for Washington's favors.

A more flexible Moscow policy towards the Baltic republics would also be instrumental in building new bridges to Western Europe. Such a policy might persuade these republics to stay neutral as the best option for their security. At least, the Russian powers that be seem to be starting to understand that much.

Conclusion

Thus, we can see that for the past several years Europe has been the focus of attention for Russian politics and diplomacy. Not just all of Europe, mainly its NATO member- countries. Unfortunately, this dialogue on the future of Europe and Russia's role in it, has been conducted by Moscow not with EU countries, but with Washington.

Although Russian diplomats were active in deliberations with the capitals of the European countries, such as Germany, France, Britain, Italy, most of their efforts were concentrated on dealings with the United States, because the US was the main force pushing NATO's expansion eastward, and this was universally considered in Russia as a danger to its security. It was not just the expression of the residues of the "Cold war mentality", but a realistic appraisal of the situation: NATO was and is first of all a military bloc, organized essentially on the platform of preparations for a war with Russia, and there was no visible change in NATO's *raison d'être*.

On the one hand, one has to admit that it was natural for the United States to try to gain a new foothold in Europe through the use of the only effective mechanism that remains in the hands of Washington to deal with Europe, namely that of the Atlantic Alliance in which America predominates. The powers that be in Washington, when assessing the evolving European situation in *Realpolitik* terms, longed to get their due as winners in the Cold war. "What is ours is ours, so let's talk about yours" to use the immortal pronouncement of President Kennedy. However, on the other hand, by expediting ever more strongly the idea of NATO's expansion, America's leaders alienated large sectors of the Russian population who see this as confirmation of US arrogance and lust for power and its unwillingness to appreciate what Russia has done to liquidate tensions in Europe and world-wide and to strengthen peace. In their incessant promotion of this project, the White House and the US Congress assumed that Moscow leaders were in a lurch, that they would not last long without American financial and other help and support, and, as a result that they would finally swallow any US scheme, if the US helped them to stay in power. Such reasoning has proved to be correct.

This was the underlying justification, albeit not widely advertised, why President Yeltsin finally acquiesced in the Founding Act, absolutely worthless for Russia, and signed it, thus legalizing from the Russian side NATO's anti-Russian stratagem (after months of bombastic denunciations by the President himself of NATO's intentions). In this way, Yeltsin and his younger assistants and advisers, not only sold out one of the most vital national interests of Russia in the realm of its security, in fact they betrayed the expectations of many West European leaders, who, unable to directly oppose the ever more unbridled United States, were secretly hoping that firm opposition by Russia to the US plan would help them to be more assertive vis-à-vis Washington in defending their own national interests. I firmly believe that no well informed politicians in Europe expected so speedy and so slavish Russian capitulation.

Russia's sheepish succumbing to Washington on the problem of NATO's enlargement was not its only blunder. Another one was its lethargic policy towards European countries. Political relations with the East European republics (the former satellites of the USSR) are almost frozen. Exchanges with other European countries are more or less normal, especially in the economic sphere, but no bold initiatives were launched to strengthen the European base of Russian diplomacy. The only exceptions to this pattern are Moscow's relations with Germany and a deep Russian involvement into the developments in Bosnia-Herzegovina, where Russian diplomacy was heavily tilted in favor of the Serbs.

Though Germany seems to be a natural strategic partner of Russia, it did not do anything to stop NATO expansion, despite the fact that during the reunification of Germany its leaders, headed by Helmut Kohl, made solemn promises that NATO would never expand in an eastward direction. Despite such perfidy, Germany, objectively, still remains the most organic potential partner of Russia in the New Europe. And the most vital Russian interest in its European politics is further rapprochement with Europe and gradual integration into European institutions. To do this, Moscow must reassess and activate its policy vis-à-vis Europe and conduct a dialogue about the future of Europe, on the one hand, and the paths for it to finally become a formal member of a new pan-European community, on the other. This dialogue must be conducted directly with European governments and   ·

the public, and not via Washington, or via US controlled NATO-Russian council, as is the case at present.

Though Europe ought to become the focus of Russian diplomacy, Russia does have some promising alternative options for its diplomatic activity in the eastward direction - in Asia. Such options will be discussed in the next chapter.

Notes

[1] "The likelihood that Russia will reassemble its conventional military forces to threaten Europe again is not high. A new Russian dictator would spend most of his military resources trying to restore the old Russian empire. While this would spread fear and instability in Europe, it would not represent the kind of concentrated threat posed by the Soviet Union during the Cold War"(Kim Holmes (ed.), *A Safe and Prosperous America. A U.S. Foreign and Defense Policy Blueprint* (Washington, DC: The Heritage Foundation. May 1993), p.10).

[2] It is now difficult to use terms such as "left" and "right", when describing the alignment of political forces in Russia, because the terms have changed their meaning. The traditional left, associated with the Communist Party, is now actually right of the Russian political center, while some allegedly right of center movements, such as the Liberal Democratic Party of Zhirinovsky and some other patriotic organizations often attack the government from the "left". On this see Jim Guirard, 'Coming to Terms with a "Communoid"', *The Washington Times*, 13 February 1994, p.B4.

[3] *The Washington Times*, 28 February 1994, p.A13.

[4] Some prominent American "Kremlinologists" now assert - tongue in cheek -that it was actually Yeltsin, who gave the go ahead to the idea of NATO's expansion eastward by publicly encouraging Poland to join the bloc. Before that, they say, no statesman in the West would be reckless enough to think that NATO could get away with such a project.

[5] The United States, having started from an understandable insistence that, to demonstrate its good will and peaceful intentions, Moscow should withdraw from Afghanistan, and having gained numerous colossal foreign policy concessions made by Gorbachev, now demands that Russia should renounce the CIS as its sphere of influence. This will definitely not be the last US imposition. Max Singer argued in *The Washington Post* that since Russia (in contrast to the FSU) is now convinced that the United States is not challenging it, Russia (not together with the US but alone) should give up all its nuclear weapons and the United States should stop paying Russia for the upkeep of those weapons (i.e. it should discontinue aid) (*The Washington Post*, 13 July 1994, p. A16. It was printed on the editorial page

without comment.). One can recognize some logic in such a view, if the absence of an American challenge to Russia had been proven, but it had not! Singer and his sympathizers must realize that there is a limit to American teasing and, yes, challenging the "Russian bear".

[6] Ronald Asmus, Richard Kugler and Stephen Larraby, 'Building a New NATO', *Foreign Affairs*, September/October 1993, pp.27-40.

[7] On 15 February 1991, the leaders of Poland, Czechoslovakia, and Hungary at a summit in the Hungarian town of Visegrad signed a declaration, pledging cooperation on matters of common concern. After the break-up of Czechoslovakia on 1 January 1993, both the Czech Republic and Slovakia became members of the Visegrad group.

[8] Deputy Secretary-Designate's Confirmation Hearing. *US Department of State Dispatch, Bureau of Public Affairs* (further – *Dispatch*), 14 February 1994, pp.74-75. On the same day when Talbott spoke before the Senate Committee, Walter Lippman of *The Washington Post* wrote: "Offered originally as a way to link the NATO alliance with the new democracies of Eastern Europe, including Russia, the program is now being portrayed additionally as a protective grouping against Russia if things go wrong in Moscow" (W. Lippman, 'NATO Peace Partnership's New Look: A Protective Shield Against Moscow', *The Washington Post*, 8 February 1994, p.A11).

[9] The document envisages a dialogue and cooperation between Russia and the Atlantic alliance through the sharing of information on issues regarding politico-security related matters having a European dimension; political consultations, as appropriate, on issues of common concern; and cooperation in a range of security related areas, including peacekeeping. The document was essentially agreed upon during earlier consultations between the North Atlantic Council and Russian Foreign Minister, Kozyrev, in Brussels in June 1994. Kozyrev (presently - a deputy in the Duma) is one of the most prominent representatives of the American lobby in the higher echelons of the Russian government.

[10] It is noteworthy that during all the prolonged discussion of the problem of NATO's expansion, Russian diplomacy never worked closely with its former satellites. Speaking before Russian journalists in June 1997, the Foreign Minister of Poland said: "I am personally surprised and flabbergasted by the fact that Russia did not launch any initiative with respect to Poland and other countries of Central Europe. For example, it would have been good to hear: Well, all right - you long to be in NATO - join it, what do you think of our own relationships? It would have created quite a different basis for discussion and it would be possible to conduct such negotiations in quite a different way. As it was, we negotiated with Russia via the West" (*Izvestia*, 18 June 1997, p.3).

[11] I have in mind the famous London briefing of American ambassadors in Europe in December 1975 by Helmut Sonnenfeldt, the then Counsellor for the State

Department and chief assistant of the Secretary of State Henry Kissinger. In that briefing, Sonnenfeldt described the relationship of Russia with the countries of Eastern Europe as "organic". In the State Department summary of his remarks, released later, Sonnenfeldt unequivocally admitted that Eastern Europe "is within their (Russians - H.T.) scope and area of natural interest", even of "vital interest" to Russia (quoted in *The New York Times*, 6 April 1976, p.14). Later in 1990, Dr. Kissinger himself in a *Newsweek* article saw as "the most realistic security system" for Europe the one consisting of "a neutral belt [of states] composed of Poland, Czechoslovakia and Hungary on the Austrian model" (see Henry Kissinger, 'A Plan for Europe', *Newsweek*, 18 June 1990, pp. 32-37). Now Dr. Kissinger sees the only way to a peaceful Europe via members of the Atlantic Alliance: "The future of Eastern Europe and of the successor states of the Soviet Union are not the same problem... This is especially true of the Visegrad countries of Poland, the Czech Republic, Hungary and Slovakia. Without ties to the Western Europe and Atlantic institutions, these countries will become a no-man's land between Germany and Russia. And for these ties to be meaningful the Visegrad countries will have to belong to both the European Union and the Atlantic Alliance" (Henry Kissinger, *Diplomacy* (New York et al.: Simon & Schuster, 1994), p.823).

[12] During his visit to Brussels in December 1993 to meet with representatives of the European Union, President Yeltsin, evidently enlightened by his own government debates on European policy emphasized that if NATO is augmented "Russia will view such a step as detrimental to its interests". In his speech at the CSCE summit meeting in Budapest in December 1994, President Yeltsin, turning to the problem of NATO's eastward expansion, remarked that "Europe, before it had time to get rid of the legacy of the 'Cold war', runs the risk of immersing itself into the 'Cold peace'" (*Diplomaticheskii Vestnik*, No. 1, January 1995, p.5).

[13] According to General Lebed: "What could the President do for the future of Russia in the situation that has emerged? There is only one dignified way out - not to sign any agreement at all, if we cannot have a legally strong treaty. The question about our attitude towards the expansion of NATO ought to be suspended, with the expansion thus turned into a willful action... We should remember that the United States for half a century did not recognize the legality of Soviet "occupation" of the Baltic countries, and were keeping on their territory the embassies of the states that ceased to exist...Regretfully, it is impossible to prevent the signing of a document between Russia and NATO. It has been composed in the interests of the present ruling regime and contradicts the strategic goals of Russia. This is why, in case the "Founding Act" is signed, the posture of the national-patriotic forces should boil down to a total denial of the legitimacy of NATO's expansion" (Alexander Lebed, 'Rossii podbrosili dokhluyu koshku' [Russia has been planted with a Dead Cat] *Izvestia*, 27 May 1997, p.4).

[14] "The accession into the North Atlantic Treaty of East European states, including the Czech Republic and Poland, that have already announced their readiness to deploy on their territories tactical nuclear weapons from the NATO arsenal...will have extremely negative repercussions for their security", a highly placed officer of the Chief Operational Directorate of the General Staff of the armed forces of the Russian Federation, who asked to remain anonymous, stated in an interview with the newspaper *Nezavisimaya Gazeta*. According to this source, the reaction to such developments might be "some tough retaliatory measures, that will include a revision of the basic tenets of the Russian military doctrine and of Moscow's policy of nuclear deterrence" (Igor Korotchenko and Mikhail Karpov, 'Russia's nuclear missiles will be retargeted onto the Czech Republic and Poland', *Nezavisimaya Gazeta*, 7 October 1995, p.1). The newspaper accompanied the story with a map, showing the directions of the main strikes of Russian forces against the countries in question.

[15] While in Washington at the end of April 1997, Russian first Vice Premier Anatoly Chubais, when asked what the Russian government would do with the US$1 billion additionally promised to Russia by the World Bank, without hesitation replied: "We shall use it to pay wages to workers" (*Russian TV news*, 30 April 1997).

[16] *USIS Wireless File. EUR 405. 15. 5. 97.*

[17] 'The Founding Act on Mutual Relations, Cooperation and Security between the Russian Federation and the North Atlantic Treaty Organization', *NATO Press Release*, Paris, 27 May 1997.

[18] Literally the President said: "From everything that we have aimed at the countries represented at this table, we shall take off warheads" (*Nezavisimaya Gazeta*, 7 June 1997, p.2).

[19] It was President Mitterand of France who in 1974 signed this Alliance with Chancellor Kohl, but it was the same French President who simultaneously restored the celebration of the Victory over Germany day, previously repealed in France. It was none other than President Mitterand, who at the first signs of the possibility of reunification of Germany in 1990 rushed in panic to Kiev to meet with Mikhail Gorbachev to try to use him to block unification.

[20] *Nezavisimaya Gazeta*, 5 July 1997, p.1.

[21] In a poll conducted by the All-Russia Center for Public Opinion, only 4% of Russian policy-makers and experts named the United States as Russia's number one friend, whereas 22% put Germany in first place (cited in *The Washington Times*, 4 January 1994, p.A13).

[22] *Novoye Russkoye Slovo*, 20 July 1993, p.5.

[23] Fritz Stern, 'Freedom and Its Discontents', *Foreign Affairs*, September/October 1993, p.122.

[24] The Pact was signed in Paris on 20 March 1995 by the representatives of 52 countries. It consists of the Declaration, reiterating the well-known principles of peaceful cohabitation, and the roster of bilateral treaties between European states. It would be a miracle if the Pact contributes anything to the strengthening of stability in Europe.

[25] Vladimir Solov'yev, *Russkaya Ideya* [The Russian Idea] (Moscow: Tovarishchestvo tipografii A.I. Mamontova. 1911), p.15. Konstantin Eggert, a news analyst of the Moscow newspaper *Izvestia*, believes that the "one-sided pro-Serbian stand, adopted by Moscow solely to spite Washington, contributed to the protraction of the war. But what is more important, is that such a stand was not buttressed by the real influence in Belgrade" (see K. Eggert, '"Great Power" foreign policy costs too much', *Izvestia*, 16 December 1995, p.3).

[26] *How much popular support is there for the EU?* (Brussels: The Philip Morris Institute for Public Policy Research, April 1997), pp.11-12.

[27] Luigi Barzini, *The Europeans* (London: Penguin Books, 1984), p.21.

Chapter Five

Russian Interests in Asia

Russia is a Eurasian country which occupies 41% of the territory of Europe and 30% of the land mass of Asia. As mentioned earlier, the Asian part constitutes 76% of its territory and 70% of Russia's borders are in Asia, including a lengthy maritime border on the Arctic and Pacific oceans.

Such a geographical location, historically gave Russia an advantage in dealing with both Europe and Asia. It made her a land bridge between the West and East and it also gave her immense strategic depth in the event of an attack either from the West or East. However, such a position is also a handicap in a two-front war, which Russia through diplomatic skill and sheer luck, managed to avoid in modern times.

Which way, Russia?

There are two aspects to Russian policy vis-à-vis Asia that ought to be considered: First, there is the problem of the identity of the new Russia -- is Russia part of the West, East or Eurasian? and second, what are the real national interests of the present day Russia in the Asia-Pacific?

The problem of Russian identity, of the Russian idea, as Russian philosophers used to say, is important because the coloration, if not the determination, of the Asian policy of the Russian Federation depends upon it.

The theme of a split orientation, of dualism of the national psyche of Russians, was a perennial subject of intellectual debate in Russia before the October 1917 revolution. This debate was rekindled after the demise of the Soviet Union when a separated Russia got a more clear image of herself. There is no consensus on this problem because the old quarrel between the so-called Westernizers and the Slavophiles, that is adherents of the idea of Russian uniqueness, continues. And, as usual, the

Slavophiles are more nationalistic and more original than the Westernizers.

The paradox lies in the fact that Russian Slavophiles or their present day followers are more West European in their style of thought, logic and constructs, than true Westernizers, who lacked originality of thought and are slaves of fashion, imitationists.

As a well known Russian poet, Denis Davydov, a hussar general and a guerrilla fighter during Napoleon's invasion into Russia in 1812, wrote, as if about today's Russia:

> Every milksop, every crook,
> Who's in his affairs
> Slave of current fashions book,
> Puts on liberal airs.

"For a Russian Westernizer-Asian", the Russian philosopher Nikolay Berdyaev wrote, "the West is a promised land, an appealing image of perfect life". But Slavophiles "were the first Russian Europeans because they were trying to reason independently, European-style".[1]

One of the spokesmen for the earlier Russian Eurasian movement, N. Alekseyev wrote that:

The Eurasian movement wants to overcome the West not from the outside, but from the inside - from the very spirit of the West, that has become nowadays for a Eurasian person his own... Such an overcoming is seen by Eurasians in the "exodus to the East", consequently - in the adoption of those values which formed the basis of Eastern cultures but were ignored and rejected by the modern West. The gist of the matter is not to Asianize Russia and the whole world, but to build a new culture on the deliberate synthesis of the East and the West - a Eurasian culture... The West itself in its modern spiritual crisis starts to treat the East differently, begins attentively to listen to it and to understand it.[2]

One cannot help noticing that these lines, written half a century ago, sound very contemporary.

Nowadays the difference between Slavophiles and Westernizers in Russia has become blurred, though modern Russian Westernizers are still essentially "slaves of the West" in contrast to their more independent-minded opponents. However, the emerging consensus (shared by most Russian intellectuals) is that Russia in its further social development has to follow its own unique ways and traditions because Russia is neither a purely Western nor purely Eastern nation, but blends in its nature a combination of both cultures, psyches and even genes (due to 200 years of occupation by Mongols).

Such a Eurasian Russia can become a bridge between the West and the East not only in a purely physical sense as a venue for trade, transportation and communication, as it is now, but also as a moderator in a "global village" that is gradually evolving towards greater integration among various peoples, towards international multiculturalism.

At the same time, there are opinions that Russia is too late for such a role because "bridging" has already happened in a different way without Russia:

The vision of Russia as a bridge between Europe and Asia is an illusion. In the second part of the 20th century, the real merger of the European and Asian economies and cultures started without Russia - note the increasing number of Asian nations approaching and even entering the world economy "nucleus". Unlike the situation in the last century, Russia's mission is not in bridging Europe and Asia, but rather in joining the rapprochement.[3]

The role of Russians (both as people and authorities) in the old empire and in the FSU was unifying, not divisive, if one takes into account the daily life and cohesion of the country. Bearing in mind, the inhuman nature of Bolsheviks' totalitarianism and the oppressive character of Tsarist rule, it would be wrong to dismiss the beneficial impact of Russian influence on the cultures of many nationalities in the former USSR.[4]

It would be incorrect to view the considerable presence of ethnic Russians in all the republics of the FSU only through the prism of state-supported "russification" by colonists and exiles. Russians as more mobile, more active and initially better educated people in the Union (together with Armenians, Ukrainians, Balts) were migrating into the remotest corners of the Empire in search of better opportunities and living conditions and, sometimes, less constraining surroundings than the big townships of the European part of Russia could offer.

It was a natural way of mixing ethnic groups and cultures in a country that, due to the immobility and specific traditions of many of its national groupings, never became a true melting pot (something similar is nowadays happening in the United States as well, where purely white immigration is overwhelmed by a "rainbow" immigration, creating distinct ethnic enclaves in the USA). This is why the majority of the intellectuals in the FSU recognize such a role for Russia. The argument becomes more heated when the problem of a social set up is being discussed.

Quite a few people in Russia, including many prominent authors and politicians, reject a simplified notion that democracy is synonymous with a Western model of government. They assert that Russia developed its own tradition, whilst accepting globally established basics of democratic governance, and has to evolve in her own unique way, which was interrupted by the 1917 October revolution led by the Bolsheviks. In this way, she has to harmoniously combine in her societal development the best features of both worlds (Western and Oriental), preserving herself as an intercultural and inter-civilizational phenomenon. Especially as Russia is and will remain a multiethnic society even within its present borders, a society with strong ties with the East.

But, if the new society becomes Eurasian in a true sense, whether as Russia alone, or in a continued configuration of the reformed CIS, another problem will arise. As Vladimir Solov'yev noted exactly 100 years ago:

> O Rus', in all your agonizing
> What kind of future you've devised,
> What kind of East you're realizing:
> The East of Xerxes or of Christ?

Despite the fact that President Yeltsin and his government colleagues have often been seen in a church - with a candle in one's (wrong) right hand - during major Orthodox Christian festivities, Russia so far is to a great extent a pagan country - a land of Xerxes, a land of crude materialism, unrestrained greed, wholesale lawlessness and criminality, corruption in high quarters and of crass immorality.

The democratic development of Russia is impossible without a genuine spiritual revival and renewal, which is no mean feat in its present turmoil and in a situation when even peaceful God blessed America, with its notion of human rights stretched up to the skies, is skidding off the path of morality. However, such a revival, if and when it happens, will not necessarily mean that Russia will stick with West European or American institutions of government and will become totally Western-oriented.

As far back as 1927, a Committee of Eurasians in the Soviet Union, formulated a sort of a credo:

Who are Eurasians? What do they want to achieve? Eurasians are those, to whom Russia has opened itself as a unique cultural and historic world, they are those for whom Russia is not just a state, but one sixth of the planet, neither Europe, nor Asia, but a separate middle continent – Eurasia, with its own specific culture and historic fate. All the copying of western forms of life to be applied to Russia is contra-natural. It brought trouble in its wake and will continue to bring major catastrophes.[5]

Past problems and interests

The national interests of Russia vis-à-vis the East have been changing with the passage of time, with the industrial development of Russia itself and of the neighboring countries, and also due to the influence of other factors of "grand politics".

Initially, after the October 1917 revolution, the Soviet Union probed for "soft spots" in Asia to promote its brand of communism. Soon after the establishment of Soviet power in Russia, Lenin convened the First Congress of the Peoples of the East in Baku in 1920 which was attended by 2,000 delegates from 32 countries. He tried to stir up anti-Western movements in the region.

In striving to undermine the West's "colonial rear", Moscow's Bolsheviks were not averse to ally even with indigenous bourgeois forces struggling against Western influence and Western capital. A typical example was Moscow's alliance with the Kuomintang in China in the 1920s and 1930s and its support for the Indian masses in their struggle against British colonial rule. The victories of communists in China and in North Vietnam after the Second World War inspired the Kremlin to lend greater support to national-liberation movements, and to use communist and generally any anti-Western forces and movements, when unleashing attacks on Western positions in Asia.

At the end of the 1960s, the historic quarrel between Moscow and Beijing forced the Kremlin to abandon the idea of the global expansion of monolithic communism, evidently because the guidance and the leadership of Moscow in such a process could no longer be sustained. There ascended in the East - in full compliance with the predictions of leading Marxist theoreticians - a younger, more vigorous center of communist power, whose leader rightfully started to claim pre-eminence after the oldest surviving patriarch of communism - Stalin - passed away. Such a prospect did not suit the communist nuclear superpower and its then leader Khrushchev. This was one of the main reasons for the rupture between Moscow and Beijing. This historic break in the communist ranks, for the second time in recent history (the first instance was a split between Moscow and Belgrade in 1948 patched up somehow later), unambiguously demonstrated that nationalism was a far more superior social force than communism. But the lesson was not readily digested either by Western Kremlinologists, Sinologists and other demonologists, or by the Kremlin itself.

Because Moscow could not count on any significant pro-Moscow communist forces in Asia (except Vietnam), it virtually abandoned its strategy of subversion in Asia and started to play by the "classic" balance of power rules. Realizing this change, many smaller countries of Asia started to use their connections with Moscow in order to play Russia off against the United States, China and Japan. Despite all the incessant pumping up by Washington of the "Soviet menace" in Asia, most of the Asia-Pacific countries were more apprehensive of American, Chinese and Japanese moves and actions than of those by the USSR. This accounts for the lack of resistance to Moscow's low-key diplomacy in the region. It was really low-key, because Moscow largely concentrated its efforts on the US and European directions in its foreign policy. Even its American strategy was, so to say, oriented Westward and not across the Pacific. Actually Gorbachev was the first Soviet leader, who once returned from a visit to the United States via a Pacific, not an Atlantic, air route.

The only exception for Moscow in Asia was China. After the Kremlin rulers split with Beijing in the 1960s, China became, for the purpose of Moscow's strategic planning, an offensive country to be contained and intimidated. The main goal of Russia's policy in Asia became the strategic isolation of China through the creation of "collective security" in Asia via an anti-Chinese platform.

The USSR failed in its policy of encircling China, and the very term "containment", used by some Soviet analysts with regard to China, was evidently wrong, because China was not expanding in any direction. It was Soviet communism that earlier tried to expand in Asia through proxies such as, initially, North Korea and, hopefully, China and Vietnam, and subversive pro-Soviet communist forces in Indonesia, Malaysia, Laos and the Philippines. But after Moscow's break with Beijing, such a strategy was abandoned. Then in December 1979 when the Soviet Union invaded

Afghanistan, it was not so much for the sake of "spreading communism" or 'breaking through to the Indian ocean', rather, from Moscow's point of view, it was geared towards preventing the collapse of a communist regime, warding off a possible US invasion in Iran and, finally, Moscow sought to browbeat China.

Other important goals for Moscow in the Asian-Pacific region were the strategic deterrence of the United States (as part of a global superpowers mutual deterrence) and the strengthening of economic and diplomatic ties with the regimes in the region not openly hostile to the Soviet Union.

The conventional and nuclear arms build up in the Asian part of the Soviet Union naturally alarmed Japan. It viewed such a process as directly undermining its own security (which was the impression that the Soviet government wanted to generate in the minds of the "militaristic Japanese" who, after the defeat in the Second World War, still "had the audacity" to demand the return to Japanese jurisdiction of a few small islands around Hokkaido seized by the Soviet troops during the war with the explicit permission of Moscow's war-time allies).

While flexing its military muscles in the Far East for almost 50 years, Moscow actually failed to comprehensively develop Siberia on a par with the development of Russia's European part. Although quite a few military industries and power stations have sprang up in that part of Russia, Siberia remains an underdeveloped, albeit heavily polluted, land, populated essentially by prison inmates and legal deportees, or by temporary workers who came to the region to make a "quick rouble" before going back to Europe. (This does not include the sparse indigenous people, who have been dragging out a miserable existence under the constant drumbeat of official reports about unheard of achievements in socialist welfare in Siberia.)

Aware of the unsatisfactory economic situation in Siberia and the Soviet Far East, Moscow rulers adopted a number of comprehensive state plans concerning the accelerated development of these regions, but none of them were ever fulfilled, while the 1970s and the beginning of the 1980s saw a tremendous expansion of military infrastructure and military forces in Siberia as a component part of the intimidation tactics against the Chinese.

Orlando Figes writes that the transformation of nature

was central to the Marxist plan and Siberia had vast stretches of nature to transform. But the dream of harnessing nature to the needs of man, soon turned into the nightmare of destruction. Today, the air of Siberia is polluted with chemicals, its Arctic coasts contaminated by radioactive waste, and Lake Baikal, which once held a fifth of the earth's fresh water, is not so fresh anymore.[6]

Moscow's most fatal mistake was the total absence of a plan or procedure to increase the permanent population of the region, where only about 13% of the total population of Russia lives (It was only 7% compared to the total population of the USSR). Something similar to the US Homestead act, even if adopted after the Second World war, would have drastically changed the demographic picture of Siberia. But that was, of course, unthinkable in Soviet conditions when the generosity of authorities failed to go beyond giving a worker or a peasant a tiny plot of 0.15-0.20 acre for his "personal household needs".

The Asian initiatives of Gorbachev and problems of the new Russia

During his "peace offensive" of the 1980s, Gorbachev was trying to reassure public opinion and the governments of Asian countries (including Beijing) with an avalanche of proposals and projects of a confidence-building nature. But most of them were too artificial or too superficial to be practical. Their essence was more conferences, more highfalutin declarations and more "solemn pledges" instead of patient work for the solution of the existing "knots" of tension in Asia.

While talking grandiloquently, Gorbachev did not move his little finger to really open up Siberia and the Far East for economic integration with adjacent prospering economies or to create a real stimuli for the people of Russia to move East to settle in the region, which for the duration of Soviet power remained a sparsely populated country of around 20 million constantly migrating people.[7] Gorbachev continued to build up the Soviet Navy in the Far East, to extensively use Soviet military bases in Cam Ranh Bay and Danang in Vietnam, and he also transferred to Siberia from the European part of Russia, some 20,000 tanks plus significant numbers of artillery and other equipment, so that it would not be counted under the Treaty on the reduction of conventional forces in Europe (CFE Treaty).

To Gorbachev's credit, he re-established normal relations between Russia and China and ended Soviet military intervention in Afghanistan (which, however, continued senselessly under Gorbachev for three more years instead of being wound up in six months). Gorbachev also took some nuclear weapons out of the Asian part of the USSR in accordance with the INF Treaty.

After the Soviet Union's demise at the end of 1991, the situation for Russia as far as its Asian part is concerned, changed drastically. Though, as stated earlier, Russia continues to occupy the heartland of Eurasia, a territorially and demographically curtailed Russia, possesses a different geo-strategic "weight" and/or clout in Eurasian geopolitics, especially given modern means of warfare, communication and transportation. Even from the point of view of traditional communicational infrastructures, modern highways in Siberia are practically non-existent. During 70 years of Soviet power, the Russian authorities only recently managed to add only a second railway line (not yet completed) which crosses Southern Siberia from West to East, 200-300 miles to the North of the old Trans-Siberian line built by the Tsarist regime.

Handicapped by a deep economic crisis and great social turmoil, Russia, on top of a continuing US military presence in Asia-Pacific, has had to deal with the two rising economic giants of the modern world (Japan and China) and with a number of lesser rapidly developing countries, such as South Korea, Singapore, Malaysia and Taiwan. Russia has to deal with them at a time when Moscow's control over its distant regions, such as provinces of the Far East and Eastern Siberia, is becoming less and less efficient, while separatist tendencies in these provinces are on the increase.[8]

From the point of view of security, Russia is now no longer facing an "aggressive China" of Moscow's own distorted imagination, but quite peaceful so far, but a formidable China with a rapidly growing military potential (including a strategic nuclear one) which must not go unnoticed.[9] China's 1.2 billion people, essentially ethnically homogeneous, to the North face the sparsely populated plains of Southern Siberia.

For the first time since its skirmishes with Japanese troops in Mongolia in 1938, Russia has to plan for defensive, not offensive, operations in this part of its world. Worse yet, Russia has to tackle peaceful Chinese penetration into its territory after its borders with China became transparent due to some hair brained decisions by the Moscow central government and local authorities. Such an overpowering of Russia by China has been a concern of the Russian people since Mongolian times.[10]

Nowadays, according to some estimates, there are more than 2 million Chinese immigrants (mostly illegal) on the Russian side of the border in the Far East, among 7 million indigenous people. Experts of the Far Eastern branch of the Russian Academy of Science assert that it is already possible to speak of a new Chinese national minority in the Russian Far East.[11] This minority is closely linked to 100 million Chinese in the North Eastern provinces of China, namely Manchuria. Every Russian schoolboy now knows that China has been advancing claims to its former Chinese territory, which was ceded to Russia in the middle of 19th century.

Russia is also worried about its new "soft underbelly" consisting of five independent FSU republics of Central Asia. Not only Moscow (as a sort of the CIS boss), but many neighboring countries, including China, now practice assertive diplomacy and aggressive commerce in these republics.

"China is not the dark horse any more [in the region]. It has totally eclipsed Turkey and Iran. They are just also-runs compared with China", according to Ross Munro of the Foreign Policy Research Institute in Philadelphia, who has carried out a major study of the region. "The economies of China and Central Asia have become remarkably complementary. While Kazakhstan and Kyrgyzstan rely on China to supply consumer goods, China finds use for these republics' industrial commodities, such as chemicals, fertilizer and steel".[12]

Russian relations with another Asian giant - Japan - were soured. Throughout *perestroika* and post-*perestroika*, Moscow's leaders have been fooling Japan with their alleged desire "to solve" the problem of the so-called Northern territories. To the Japanese, this means returning these small islands, which never belonged to Russia in the first place, to Japan. They were occupied by Soviet troops on 8 August 1945 after Moscow unilaterally broke the Soviet-Japanese neutrality treaty of 1941 and entered the war against Japan, although the latter was already on the verge of capitulation after atomic bombing by the United States. For the Russian government, however, "the solution" means procrastination, because no Russian leader in the present atmosphere of rising nationalism would dare relinquish the possession of these islands, after Russia has "given away" Eastern Germany, Eastern Europe and "lost" half its population and almost a quarter of the territory of the original Soviet Empire.

The "comprehensive" plan for the "solution" of the problem on the basis of "law and justice", as proposed by Boris Yeltsin, envisages a gradual settlement over the next 20 years. This process involves five stages:

- an acknowledgment of the existence of the territorial issue by the Russians (first stage),[13]
- conversion of the disputed islands into a free enterprise zone (second stage),
- demilitarization (third stage),
- the conclusion of the formal peace treaty with Japan, but no transfer to Japan of the title to the territories (fourth stage), and, finally,
- the fifth, and final, stage is as yet unclear and, according to Lev Sukhanov, Yeltsin's assistant, "would have to be realized by the new generation of politicians".[14]

When Yeltsin finally visited Japan in October 1993 (after twice postponing the official visit) no progress toward resolution of a long-standing territorial dispute was made.

However, if in the 1960s and 1970s, Tokyo was inclined to accept a partial solution (with Japanese scholars offering more than a dozen options for solving the problem, only one of which actually required an unconditional return of the islands to Japan), nowadays Japan demands that the islands be returned![15] In the present situation, when Russia desperately needs foreign aid for its crippled Far Eastern economy, especially in the form of private investments, a wealthy Japan can easily last longer than Russia, and does not need to do anything.[16] Furthermore, it appears that Russia, despite Yeltsin's promises in Tokyo, has not yet moved to his "third stage" because the demilitarization of the disputed islands has been blocked by the Russian military.

In November 1996, the new Russian Foreign Minister, Yevgeny Primakov, proposed to his Japanese counterpart, Yukikhiko Ikeda, a "new approach" to the problem of South Kurils. This "great idea" boils down to a joint exploitation of mineral wealth of the islands and the joint development of fisheries and fishing in the region. Primakov said that negotiations on that score could skip discussions of the sovereignty problem. The Japanese politely promised to look into the proposal. Clearly Primakov's offer was geared towards making progress on Yeltsin's plan, whilst also addressing the desperate economic position of the islands.[17]

After the establishment of diplomatic relations between Moscow and Seoul in 1990, Russia placed great hopes on its economic relations with South Korea. The theory was that, while Japan procrastinated, South Korea in its role as a Japan substitute "would provide Russia with an entry into Asia while jump-starting the economy of Russia's Far East".[18] Regretfully, these hopes have not materialized so far. As of the end of 1995, South Korea invested a mere US$50 million in Russian projects. Its investment in China, by comparison, has grown from US$6 million in 1987 to US$598 million in 1993. Even the far smaller economies of the former Soviet republics of Central Asia have attracted more Korean investment than Russia so far.

The only "trump card" of Russian diplomacy in the region was the Democratic People's Republic of Korea (the DPRK or North Korea). Although Moscow's relations with North Korea worsened after Russia established relations with Seoul and curtailed military supplies to North Korea, the Russian leadership felt that in the confrontation between North Korea and the United States, fuelled by Pyongyang's refusal to play by the rules of the Non-Proliferation Treaty, of which it is a member, Moscow could act as a mediator, just as it had done during the Bosnian conflict, and reap some diplomatic victories. This petty Russian scheming around Pyongyang's non-compliance with the treaty was probably the only "leverage", albeit a flimsy one, Russia had regarding its contemporary diplomacy in the Asian-Pacific. However, the complex political and economic problems facing Russia in the region are not being tackled via a solid strategic approach, but are characterized by muddling through as the Russian authorities think that the situation will change for the better by itself, if Russia waits patiently. But will it change in the desired direction?

Russian national interests in Asia

The demise of the USSR pushed in a geopolitical sense the epicenter of Russia towards the East. The fact is that in its European west and south, Russia lost her independent manoeuvering space.

On the western fringes of Russia two belts of newly independent states (the former Warsaw Pact countries plus the European republics of the ex-USSR that have Western Europe as a natural center of gravitation) presently separate Russia from Europe, while in the European south, Russia is separated from the countries of the Middle East by the former Soviet Transcaucasus republics. It is only in the east that Russia immediately borders on the three great powers of the modern world - the United States, Japan and China, and only in the north and in the east, does Russia have unhindered direct access to the ocean. At the same time, the center of economic life of the world has been shifting towards the Asia-Pacific.[19]

Objectively such a situation would have given Russia an additional incentive to energetically practice its diplomacy and to expand commercial relations in that part of the world, if it were not for the miserable state of Russia itself. Realistically speaking, Russia in its present state is lacking almost all tangible levers of diplomacy and politics in Asia. Of course, Russia can still manoeuver among other players in an attempt to stay afloat diplomatically, and dangle its immense untapped natural riches in Siberia and the Far East as an incentive for foreign entrepreneurs. However, the manoeuvering, not supported by the visible accoutrements of power, and the offerings of natural riches for development, not ensured by a stable and propitious business climate, do not constitute much of a persuasion. Up until the beginning of 1998, Russia was the only one of the big countries of the region that was not a member of the Asia-Pacific Economic Cooperation (APEC) forum founded in 1989 under the sponsorship of the United States and Japan to discuss and solve key economic issues.[20]

Russian military power in the Far East is pathetic. The land forces, though numerically still strong, are actually in a chaotic state; many units are heavily engaged in illegal commercial practices which enrich commanding officers but ruin discipline and morale. In a telegram to the President and the Prime Minister of Russia sent in the winter of 1996/97 by Viktor Kopylov, the Commander of the Siberian military district, on instructions from the Military Council of the district and officers' meetings, the Commander stated:

I report that due to the shortage of finance a catastrophic situation is emerging in the armed forces of the Siberian military district... Such a situation is the beginning of the open phase of the liquidation of the armed forces. This is the main topic at many officers meetings that are currently taking place. The failure by the country's leadership to adopt decisive measures will make the process irreversible. As citizens and patriots we draw your attention to our common responsibility for the defense of the country.[21]

The Pacific Navy is in a very bad shape (except for the SSBNs - strategic missile-carrying submarines): many combat ships just rust at mooring stations, with radiation leaking from the old submarines. Two comparatively new aircraft carriers in the fleet - the Novorossiysk and the Minsk, together with 44 other navy ships were sold for scrap metal to South Korea.[22] Discipline among recruits is at its lowest level. Scandals connected with savage hazing practices in the Naval forces, the under-nourishment of sailors and the recurrent accidents with military equipment, have all undermined the morale of personnel.[23]

The plan to cordon off the Sea of Okhotsk as a sanctuary for SSBNs (which attracted international attention during the Soviet period) has stalled, with the cessation of new construction or deployment of these submarines. As long as this situation persists, the existing SSBN force in the Far East will age, and there is a chance that this deployment will completely fade away sometime after the year 2000.[24]

In such a situation, all the appeals of Russian military theoreticians for Russia to be actively engaged in the formation of a new structure of security in the North Pacific remain nothing but high-sounding projects devoid of substance. These projects include:

- the revival of Gorbachev's idea of multilateral negotiations with the goal of providing a new structure of security in the Asia-Pacific,
- the creation of a system of crisis management with the establishment of a supporting center for strategic studies,
- limiting conventional and nuclear armaments in order to achieve "minimal deterrence", and
- tripartite arrangements (Russia, USA, Japan) with the aim of alleviating existing tensions in the Kuril and South Sakhalin maritime zones etc.[25]

It seems that the only viable security project so far is the ASEAN Regional Forum (ARF), established by the ASEAN post-ministerial meeting in 1993.

The idea of the ARF is to get the United States, China, Japan, Russia, Canada, South Korea, Vietnam, Laos, Australia, New Zealand, Papua New Guinea along with the ASEAN group of states and the European Union involved in security discussions via a form of "preventive diplomacy". The Forum acts as an annual high-level conference on security issues.

The five annual meetings of the Forum took place in Bangkok at the end of July 1994, in Brunei in 1995, in Indonesia in July 1996, in Malaysia in July 1997 and in Manila at the end of July 1998.[26] In 1996, Russia achieved the status of a full-scale partner of ASEAN in annual dialogues, a privilege also enjoyed by the US, Japan, India, China and the European Union. In June 1997, Russia and ASEAN established a Joint Committee on Russian-ASEAN Cooperation at a conference in Moscow.

Some of the aforementioned ideas, proposed by Russia, if implemented, could enhance peace in the Asia-Pacific region. But the effectiveness of a Russian contribution to all such confidence and security-building measures will to a large extent depend, first, on whether Russia could think past its immediate problems of survival and, second, on an improved image of Russia as a power in the North Pacific on a par with other key players.

However, while "Russia's role (in the North Pacific - H.T.) as a potential threat has faded",

Russia's regional interests and policies are still in flux, despite the positive changes of the last several years. Russia remains a significant regional military power without explicit cooperative relations with the leading regional actors - the United States and Japan. Often in the current discussions about Asia, Russia has been omitted, as if it has dropped out of the Asian scene and is therefore not a factor to be considered. As a result, one of the major centers of power in the evolving regional situation does not have a clear role or position. Russia's foreign policy in the East Asia - North Pacific region is clearly in need of further positive engagement and adjustment in order to create normal conditions for itself and to establish genuinely constructive relations with Japan and the United States.[27]

To boost Russia's Eurasian role, Defense Minister Grachev in the spring of 1994 tried to sell to NATO members Moscow's own idea of Pragmatic Partnership for Peace, as he named it. He proposed creating a collective security system in Europe based on the Conference for Security and Cooperation in Europe, while additionally creating a system of collective security in Asia with Russia acting as a connecting link between the two systems. However, none of Russia's partners was enthusiastic about this proposal.

In the immediate future, Russian national interests in Asia seem to boil down to the realization (to the extent possible) of the following tasks:

- Prevention of a secession of the Far East and Siberia (or some provinces) from RF and the attraction of foreign investments in the region.
- Active involvement of Siberia and Russia's Far East regions in the international economic cooperation in the Asia-Pacific region.
- Maintenance of the balance of power in the North Pacific with whatever means of manoeuver available to Russia nowadays.
- Development of regional cooperation with the United States and Canada, including some steps in the military sphere.
- Maintenance and development of friendly cooperative relationships with the People's Republic of China.
- Improving relations with Japan and development of extensive Russo-Japanese economic cooperation.
- Extensive development of economic ties with the South Korea, while maintaining cooperation with the North Korea.
- Improving in every way possible (through economic cooperation, trade, sales of arms etc.) friendly relations with the countries of South-East Asia; and
- Continuing the development of diplomatic, political and economic relations with Australia and other South Pacific nations.

The above list is a recapitulation of the tasks that the current Moscow government is trying haphazardly to carry out in Asia. To what extent will Moscow succeed in realizing these goals?

In the current atmosphere of limited stabilization in Russia, with the pronounced centripetal trends on the CIS scale, separatist tendencies in Russian provinces seem to have dwindled and been replaced by a growth in economic regionalism. This does not mean that in any future political and economic crisis such tendencies will not re-emerge. But for the time being, local governments in Russia's Asian provinces seem to be satisfied with their scope of authority and with a less strained relationship with Moscow. At the same time, it is clear that given the tremendous influx of Chinese into Russia's Far Eastern territories, local leaders have developed a more enlightened long-term view of the potential consequences of their urge for independence.

Foreign businessmen, including American, Japanese and South Korean, are now becoming more active in the Russian Far East, though most of them are still avoiding long-term investment in the Russian economy in view of the many uncertainties in the politico-economic situation and the lack of a proper legal base. As a result a Free Economic Zone created around the port of Nakhodka is not yet considered attractive enough for tangible investments. Furthermore, many other joint ventures of substance discussed between Russia and Asian businessmen are still suspended in thin air.[28]

The main potential investor - Japan - until mid-1997 has been essentially marking time waiting for developments on the territorial issue.[29] So the prospects for a substantial infusion of foreign capital into the economy of the Russian Far East and Siberia (with the exception of offshore oil production, precious stone mining, lumber and fishing) remain unlikely for the immediate future. If and when the investment climate improves, investment will probably mostly go into raw materials production. At the same time, joint ventures of another type, based solely on barter and speculation, are proliferating, especially Russian-Chinese ones. Under priced Russian machinery, trucks and equipment are being bartered for shoddy Chinese consumer goods, foodstuffs and drinks which are often dangerous to consumers health.[30]

Maintaining the balance of power

Maintaining the balance of power in the Asia-Pacific region depends on the policies pursued by every major player in the area, which in the current situation is not an easy task to define.

Despite its important geostrategic location, Russia is presently the least influential of the four main participants of the East Asian "concert": the United States, Russia, China and Japan. It is clear that the main mediator in the region continues to be the United States, though in not too distant future, it will be replaced by China (the future number one superpower, if not in the world at large, then for sure in the Asia-Pacific).

The use of military might and presence notwithstanding, a foreign policy influence will be propagated more and more through non-military channels, including personal and organizational ethnic connections, indigenous financial institutions, the mass media, geared towards particular audiences, cultural affinities, religious affiliations, regional economic agreements and some other conduits. The United States with a handicap, its arrogant Americanism, has to compete with the indigenous Asian structures and connections in the region.

In this evolving situation, the main focus of attention for the United States (as for other participants in the game of nations in Asia) is China and fluctuations in its politics. And, as before, the basic factors that will determine American relations with China are the hard geopolitical realities, not the lure of some universal blissfulness "beyond peace".[31] Since the threat of Soviet aggression has disappeared, the United States does not need a close relationship with China, and the Chinese, for their part, 'no longer need the United States to protect them against possible Soviet aggression" (however hypothetical that protection might have been). But the United States still needs China "to reign in North Korea's ominous nuclear weapons program", to blunt "China's ability to disrupt our (US-H.T.) interests around the world", to have a huge Chinese market etc.[32]

In a situation when "China and Russia exist in an uneasy 'Asian détente'"[33] as Richard Nixon astutely observed, the United States needs China to continue its not so delicate balancing act in the new Russia-United States-China-Japan quadrangle. At the same time, "[t]he United States as a geopolitical counterweight to Japan and Russia has a unique attraction for Beijing".[34]

In Moscow, it appears that Washington would very much like to use China to put additional pressure on Russia in order to finish it off as an influential entity in Asia and elsewhere, and finally consolidate, so to say, an American victory in the Cold war. Of course, such an aim is not well advertised, but sometimes it surfaces in the recommendations of influential American politicians.

Henry Kissinger, for example, in a veiled way called for the creation of geopolitical "counterweights" to Russia, while "supporting Russian free markets and Russian democracy".[35] Zbigniew Brzezinski in a less diplomatic way called for "some quiet American-Chinese political consultations" regarding the Central Asian area of the ex-USSR, "given China's growing economic impact on the region".[36]

In a subsequent elaboration of his obsessive idea, Dr. Brzezinski calls not only for some tactical collusion with China, but for an alliance with "Greater China" (as it follows from the map, accompanying the article, China is to become greater at the expense of the adjacent territories of Mongolia, parts of the FSU's Central Asia, Pakistan and Afghanistan, as a reward for its services to Washington!). Such a China, ever grateful to the United States, could be "co-opted into a wider framework of international cooperation, [and] become an important strategic asset - equal to Europe, more weighty than Japan - in assuring Eurasia's stability".[37] "Stability" of this kind assumes Russia becoming a "loosely confederated" state "composed of a European Russia, a Siberian Republic and a Far Eastern Republic". Such a "decentralized Russia would be less susceptible to imperial mobilization",[38] which, evidently, will be very propitious for the imperial designs of the United States (and, may be, even Poland?).

The "good geopolitical reason", underlying Brzezinski's advice, was the desire to somehow cut Russia off from this part of Asia.

Russia's leadership definitely cannot help noticing such ideas, which are confirmed by concrete US actions vis-à-vis China. President Clinton, who boosted his popularity during the 1992 election campaign by criticizing human rights abuses in China, was rather quick to learn the basics of geopolitics. He restored military cooperation with China, cancelled by President Bush after the 1989 Tiananmen Square massacre, allowed the sale of high-tech computers and other modern technology, including rocket engines to China and created a joint US-China commission on defense conversion that critics say would assist Beijing's efforts to obtain US weapons technology. Clinton also extended the most favored nation trade status (MFN) to China. He not only reconfirmed such a status for China in May 1994, but no longer made it conditional on China's human rights record, changing the pattern that had previously existed.

While the United States actually continues its policy of Chinese containment (this is why the U.S. keeps 300,000 strong military forces in the region), the official language of Washington in conversations with China over the last few years, has become milder. According to American leaders and officials, the Clinton administration's approach to China is one of "comprehensive engagement, seeking areas of cooperation and dealing directly and frankly with areas of difference".[39] Washington cautiously balances its relations with Moscow and Beijing, treating both evenly at high level meetings.

While Moscow watches these US moves with some apprehension, it is on the way to developing new post-Cold war relations with its great Asian neighbor.

President Yeltsin and Prime Ministers Chernomyrdin and Kiriyenko have visited Beijing. During Chernomyrdin's visit to China in May 1994, the two countries signed six agreements on trade cooperation and other fields of mutual interaction.

In September 1994, during a Russian-Chinese summit in Moscow, Presidents Jiang Zemin and Boris Yeltsin, signed a joint statement on the non-targeting of strategic missiles on each other (similar to the agreements that Moscow has with the United States and Britain) and they also agreed to slash the number of troops stationed on both sides of the Russian-Chinese border.

As mentioned earlier, in the spring of 1996, during Yeltsin's visit to China, a five power agreement between Russia, Kazakhstan, Kirghizia, Tajikistan and China was signed as a confidence-building measure in the military sphere.

In addition to the new five-power agreement on the mutual reduction of armed forces in the border zone, President Yeltsin and Chairman Jiang Zemin signed a joint Declaration on the Multipolar World and the Formation of New International Order in 1997. The Declaration stresses the multipolarity of the present international system, considering it a positive achievement. In a direct allusion to US policy, the Declaration emphasizes that "no country should strive for hegemony... and to monopolize international affairs".[40] In the Declaration, the two leaders defined relations between Russia and China as those of "equally trustful partnership, directed at strategic interaction in the 21st century".[41]

The continuing rapprochement with China is undoubtedly the only reasonable course of action open to Russia at the moment. For the past few years, Moscow is actively developing its cooperation with China in the military and technical-military fields. For example, Russia has sold China SU-27 jet fighters, S-300 surface to air missile systems, and modern T-80 tanks, and also transferred new military technology via computer hook-ups. Some reports suggest that more than 1,000 Russian defense specialists are either working in or visiting China.[42] The Kremlin now sells more than a billion dollars' worth of weapons to Beijing annually.[43] China and Russia signed a five-year military cooperation agreement as well as one strengthening cooperation between the defense industries of the two countries, allegedly for the purpose of conversion.[44]

In July 1994, General Pavel Grachev and his Chinese colleague, General Chi Haotian, signed an intergovernmental agreement "On Preventing Dangerous Military Activities" in Moscow. The agreement set forth the possible circumstances under which military personnel of the two countries could inadvertently find themselves on the other side's territory and procedures for smoothly resolving such incidents.

One might argue that by strengthening cooperation with China in the military field, Russia has increased the dependence of China on the Russian military hardware, on the one hand, and lessened the appeal to China of any such offer from the United States. One might also add that seeing the writing on the wall, Russia consciously opted to be a junior partner of China for a while.

There is also a theory circulating among some Russian foreign policy analysts in Moscow that it is worthwhile resuscitating a bipolar system, albeit not on an ideological basis as before, but on pure considerations of *Realpolitik*, in order to create a tangible counterweight to the overbearing United States:

To address an alternative idea of a "second pole" is made necessary by the shortcomings and dangers of a "monopolar system": the monopolism of the United States as a sole global leader can tragically destabilize international relations. The bipolar system by its very nature is a more stable basis for the cooperation between the centers of world politics.

Such a system can give the countries of the Third world, China and Russia the ability to defend their common and individual interests in a more or less organized form and thus guarantee greater effectiveness of their efforts.[45]

This call for the restoration of the bipolar system may be far fetched, but it is definitely in Russia's interests to continue strengthening its ties with China given NATO's increased pressure from the West. The signing of the Founding Act with NATO was a great blunder not only because of the damage it caused to Russian national interests in Europe, but also because this action limited Russia's freedom of manoeuver in the international arena by tying it to NATO and its policies, without any real strategic benefits for Russia. China, which has been willing and ready to enhance its cooperation and partnership with Russia, because such an alliance would give both countries much broader possibilities in the Asia-Pacific, for example by not allowing the United States to gain a dominating position in the region, was tremendously upset by Moscow's behavior. Chinese leaders have started to suspect Moscow and view its rapprochement with China as simply a ploy to make the US agree to a NATO-Russia Treaty.[46] It also shows once again that Russia's long term "strategy" is synonymous with the phrase "the left hand does not know what the right hand is doing". Incomprehensible for a normal analyst, Russia's attachment to NATO, despite the fact that all the cream will go to the North Atlantic bloc, while

Russia is left even without skimmed milk (if one talks of Russia as a country, not about its particular leaders who are highly satisfied by what they got from the deal), heavily undermined the possibilities for Russian diplomacy. In this situation, the much talked about potential triangle of closely cooperating states -- Russia, China and India -- which might have created a strong geopolitical (not ideological) counterweight to American hegemonic aspirations in Asia, does not seem viable at present, as long as NATO keeps "non-aligned Russia" in its harness.

Some Russian strategic analysts, whatever they now say publicly, believe that a stable long-term Russian-Chinese alliance is not really on the cards. They suspect China of manoeuvering between the two powers - Russia and United States, considering the latter to be its main enemy and an obstacle to Beijing's designs in the South East Asia. Proceeding from the fact that "Russia in the next 10 years will not be able to concentrate its attention eastward",[47] the present Beijing leadership is inclined to further improve relations with Russia in order to have more freedom of manoeuver southward. Beijing has also taken into consideration the fact that close military relations between Russia and Vietnam have been severed[48] and it realizes that an independent Mongolia and Kazakhstan, bordering on ethnically non-Chinese regions of China, are not exactly sympathetic to Chinese ambitions and so would be potential allies of Russia in any future confrontation. This is why, whatever its grievances against Russia, China will not be ready in the observable future to try to settle scores in the North via the use of military power.

However, despite these considerations and cooperation with Moscow, the Chinese occasionally like to show their teeth to their erstwhile "big brother" by detaining Russian merchant ships in the East China sea or asserting their rights of way on the Ussury river on the still non-delimited stretch of the river at Khabarovsk.

It seems that a thorough analysis of the international situation, made by the Chinese leadership in preparation to the XV Congress of the Communist Party of China that met in September 1997, convinced them that the best strategy for China in the international arena would be a return to a posture of equidistance between Moscow and Washington. At the US-PRC summit in Washington in October 1997 Chairman Jiang Zemin and President Clinton declared their determination "to build toward a constructive strategic partnership between the United States and China through increasing cooperation to meet international challenges and promote peace and development in the world". That is a formula similar to the one contained in the Russian-Chinese communiqué of 24 April 1997.[49]

In the face of all the current, and hypothetical developments discussed above, Russia cannot but be wary of both China and the United States in Asia. Its only real potential ally is Japan and many people in the ruling circles of Moscow understand this. However, through its political line on the South Kuril islands, Russia has painted itself into a corner in its relations with Japan, from which Yeltsin (or anyone else in his place) cannot extricate Moscow, without being accused by the powerful nationalist opposition of "betraying Russia's national interests". Frequent shelling by the Russian coast guard ships of Japanese boats, fishing near the South Kurils, does little to contribute to an improvement in Russo-Japanese relations. At the same time, the main real national interest of Russia in Asia lie in a politico-military alignment with Japan.

Japan is desperate to liberate itself from the shackles of an American "friendly embrace". The straight jacket of Japanese-American security treaty of 1960 becomes ever more tight for Japan bulging from its wealth and clout.

The actual disappearance of the Soviet/Russian military threat to Japan, which is fully understood by Japan, has undermined the foundations of the security treaty with the US. Mass protests in the autumn of 1995 against an American military presence in Okinawa (where 70% of U.S. military installations in Japan are based) vividly showed the whole world that a permanent American military presence on Japanese territory is coming to an end. The Japanese ruling elite longs to freely engage in a sophisticated play of balance of power politics and not simply follow the leader, especially when the leader itself is vacillating. For this purpose, Tokyo seems prepared to forgo the "consolation dowry" (in the form of $50-70 billion deficit in its trade with Japan which the United States pays Japan yearly for its allegiance). Moreover, no amount of small American concessions to the Japanese (such as the closure of some U.S. military bases on Okinawa), will change that.[50]

Despite massive investments in the Chinese economy, Japan is unwilling to go for an alliance with China firstly, because it will always remain a junior partner of China (as is the case of Japan's alliance with the United States) and, second, because such an alliance will greatly irritate both the United States and Russia and might produce a strong impetus for Russian-American collusion in Asia. At the same time, a gradual alliance with a politically and economically weak Russia (especially in its Asian part) will boost Japan's independence and give it even greater room for manoeuver vis-à-vis China and the United States. All the preconditions for a really organic interaction between Russia's Siberia (rich in timber, coal, oil and other raw materials and having a qualified, but currently underemployed work force), and a financially and technologically superior Japan, exist. This is well understood in Japan.[51]

Although Japanese leaders, because of their stubborn insistence on the primacy of a territorial settlement with Russia, have themselves created a barrier for deeper understanding and cooperation with Russia, they are not as dumb as Moscow's politicians. They have been giving Russia enough economic and diplomatic bait to prompt it to reconsider its dawdling Asian policy. The US$1 billion that Japan pledged to help Russia (and is gradually disbursing) is not a large sum for Japan. Nonetheless, it is quite a sizable credit to come from a country bitterly angry with Russia.

The first side to make a decisive breakthrough in the long-stalemated relationships was Japan, not Russia. Speaking on 24 July 1997 at the Japanese Society of persons having identical economic ideas, Ryutaro Hashimoto, the then Prime Minister of Japan, presented the concept of "Eurasian diplomacy from the Pacific angle", underscoring the importance for Japan to develop constructive relationships both with China and Russia.

The man, who as recently as the Spring of 1997 vehemently objected to the acceptance of Russia into the G7 exclusive club of leading industrial nations,   declared that it was necessary to make relations between Japan and Russia as dynamic, as relations between other major powers of the Asia-Pacific. He stated the three principles on which new relations between the two countries ought to be based: trust, mutual interests, and long-term vision. He advanced the idea of a speedy conclusion of the peace treaty between the two counties through the solution of the Northern territories problem on the basis of a Tokyo declaration, adopted at the Russian-Japanese summit in October 1993.[52] Evidently, one of the main considerations, underlying the sudden move by Hashimoto, was the desire to do something to prevent drastic changes in the geopolitical balance in Asia. It was not the result of some advice from Washington, as some people might think. On the contrary it was an implicitly anti-American move: a decision not to give up Russia, so to say by default, to an exclusively American domain. Such a move was in a way Japan's "constructive engagement" of Russia.

As is known at the end of 1996 a very influential American policy-making public institution - the New York Council on Foreign Relations - produced its Asia Project Policy Report, entitled "Redressing the Balance". The report advised the US government to begin conducting a more assertive policy in Asia in order to redress the balance that had ostensibly started to tilt unfavorably for the United States.[53] So the Japanese move concerning Russia might be called redressing the balance Japanese style - to compensate Japan's chief ally's overbearance by involving a disappearing Russia more   closely in   Asian affairs. One other consideration was the desire to acquire Russian support for Japan's claim to become a permanent member of the UN Security council.

Hashimoto revealed to his audience that the basic points of his speech were coordinated with President Yeltsin at the G7 meeting in Denver in June 1997.

At the beginning of November 1997 the two leaders met in the Siberian city of Krasnoyarsk. During this so-called meeting without neckties the two leaders made a pledge to conclude a formal peace treaty by the year 2000 and discussed a number of large-scale economic projects for mutual development. As is known, there was a change of government in Japan after the parliamentary elections in the Summer of 1998. The new Japanese Prime-Minister Obuchi publicly confirmed that he will continue the course of his predecessor towards Russia.

With the demise of the Soviet Union, Japan acquired one more effective leverage to pressure Moscow, namely its dealings with all other ex-USSR republics that are very interested in developing extensive economic and other connections with Japan and legally now have nothing to do with the Kuril islands problem. In order to emphasize that the problem of Northern territories is a Russian and Japanese problem, Japan might even possibly conclude separate peace treaties with the non-Russian republics.

So the balance of the quadrangle is now in a state of flux because a move by any participant might drastically change the equation.

Untying the Korean "knot": a negative lesson for Russian diplomacy

If official Russian policy regarding the "Korean question" over the past few years has demonstrated anything, it is the absence in the policy-making circles in Moscow of a clear comprehension or a definition of what Russia's national interests are or ought to be. Instead of pursuing some clearly defined goal or goals, which might have improved Russia's position vis-à-vis other participants in the game of nations, on the one hand, and enhanced Russia's influence and standing in the North Pacific, on the other, Russian diplomacy has groped in the dark, rudderless, so to say, without any clearly defined objective. As a result, Russia did not improve its position or gain in influence, but instead came out of the so-called Korean crisis with a diminished status and much less ability to influence the course of events.

While being driven by the sole pragmatic consideration of staying abreast of events, Russian diplomacy demonstrated *how not to do* things. Unfortunately, this type of outcome - a flop - is a characteristic of the policies of the "reformist" government of Russia, both in foreign and domestic policies. As the Russian Prime-Minister Chernomyrdin put it: "we wanted to do it in the best possible way, but it came out as usual!". This phrase is applicable to almost everything the Russian government does nowadays.

During the events in question, a new ball, in the permanent post-World War Two Korean game of "chicken", started rolling when the North Korean dictator Kim Il Sung announced on 12 March 1993 that the DPRK will be withdrawing from the Non-Proliferation Treaty. In such a rude way, he answered the insistent demands of the International Atomic Energy Agency for a special inspection of two suspected nuclear storage sites at the North Korea's Yongbyon nuclear complex.

It is difficult to read the mind of a dictator, but surely Kim was very upset by Russia's betrayal and abandonment of its staunch ally - the DPRK - in favor of his hated enemy -- South Korea. It appeared, as early as 1990, that Article 1 of the 1961 Treaty of Friendship and Mutual Assistance between the USSR and the DPRK, (the Treaty that Russia inherited from the USSR), which obliged Moscow to come to the assistance to Pyongyang in the event of armed conflict, had been amended (presumably relieving Moscow of such an obligation).[54] In October 1992, the Russian Security Ministry made a well-publicized case of taking off the plane, bound for Pyongyang from a Moscow airport, a group of more than 60 Russian scientists, mostly nuclear missile specialists, who were contracted to work in the DPRK.

In general, relations between Moscow and Pyongyang considerably cooled in 1992-93 on the initiative of Moscow, enchanted by its new South Korean friends, as Russia was eager to demonstrate its loyalty to the United States and its other Western sponsors.[55]

So in a way, Kim Il Sung's démarche can be construed as an answer to the increasing international pressure on North Korea. It demonstrated his intention to go on building atomic weapons without any meddling from outside. When the international community increased its pressure on Pyongyang to open up[56] it removed the seals placed (by the IAEA - H.T.) on the Yongbyon five-megawatt reactor, and began to withdraw fuel rods that could be reprocessed to yield enough plutonium for four to five nuclear weapons.[57]

Fearful of such developments, Washington started unofficial talks with Pyongyang, promising various "carrots" if the latter behaved better. This was exactly what Kim Il Sung was looking for in his non-stop cat-and-mouse game with Washington.

At the beginning of June 1994, President Yeltsin was welcoming President Kim Young Sum of South Korea on his first official visit to Russia, during which the two leaders signed a declaration in the Kremlin affirming that relations between the two countries "are being transformed into a creative, mutually complementary partnership, based on the common values of freedom, democracy, rule of law, respect for human rights and market economy".[58] Later the same month, Jimmy Carter, the ex-President of the United States, came beaming from his "private" visit to Pyongyang with the good news that North Korea was prepared to enter into "good-faith talks" on nuclear inspections. Thus the American leadership had filled the niche left open by the withdrawal of Russia from a close and active relationship with North Korea (while not losing its tremendous influence with its ally - South Korea). Moscow's leaders, dazzled by their new friendship with South Korea, did not immediately realize that they were actually squeezed out of any mediating role in the "Korean nuclear crisis".

The problem of North Korea turning itself into a nuclear power by clandestinely making a few nuclear bombs is, realistically speaking, not a big deal for Russia. Russia, of course, was not helping the DPRK to obtain nuclear weapons, though it was Russia that helped it to build its atomic center at Yongbyon.[59] At the same time, Moscow is sure that, if the DPRK ever acquires nuclear weapons or has already manufactured a couple of usable ones, it would never be crazy enough to use them against Russia or

China.[60] However, the nuclear armament of North Korea might trigger Japan to make its own nuclear weapons. But this too would not worry Russia. Someone has yet to prove that it is safer for Russia to face only a nuclear China, than to plot its strategic policies when both - Japan and China - are nuclear-armed. Leaders in Moscow know that the nuclear armament of Japan (if this has not happened already) will be more of a worry to the United States and China, than to Russia.[61]

The only irritating consideration for Russia in relation to the problem of Korean nuclear armament was Pyongyang's withdrawal from the Non-Proliferation Treaty and its break with the UN's IAEA. This created a nasty precedent beneficial for all would-be nuclear rogue states and for all the countries that are not yet parties to the Non-Proliferation Treaty. Such a precedent might undermine the non-proliferation regime and this is definitely not in Russia's interests. Only with great difficulty and with American support, did Russia persuade two ex-USSR republics to renounce their nuclear status. Moscow then agreed to all the non-military punishments that the UN Security Council might have devised for North Korea. However, Russia (like China) would hardly sanction any military action against North Korea or quietly swallow some such unauthorized action, such as unilateral American bombardment of North Korea's nuclear weapons production facilities. (The case offered is purely hypothetical because, despite all the hearsay, no American government will have the guts to do this!)

It was presumed that playing around the issue as a "highly involved party" provided Moscow with some importance in its Far Eastern diplomacy. Thus, as matters heated up in March 1994, the deputy foreign minister of Russia, Alexander Panov (the current Russian Ambassador to Japan), who was supervising Ministry policy in the Far East, declared that Moscow was intent on observing the 1961 Treaty between the USSR and the DPRK and would "provide assistance to North Korea in the event of unprovoked aggression".[62] Though the next day, after the shocked world media exploded in amazement, Panov declared that "there was no change in the Russian policy with regard to the Korean crisis".[63]

Commenting on this episode, the Russian newspaper, *Izvestia* wrote that Russia is not eager to quarrel with Washington and Seoul because of the nuclear ambitions of Pyongyang. However, the newspaper recognized that Russia tried "to utilize the situation on the Korean peninsular to strengthen its position in Asia".[64] Foreign Minister Kozyrev's proposal to convene an international conference to discuss the problem of de-nuclearization of the Korean peninsular, later repeated by President Yeltsin, was a similar attempt to keep abreast of events.

But while aiming for this, Moscow, by deliberately distancing North Korea, actually lost all its influence with Kim Il Sung, and did not gain any greater influence on this issue with the United States, South Korea and Japan because all three countries, that rightfully considered Russia to be the main patron of Pyongyang and the chief spokesman for North Korea in the "councils of the mighty", quickly realized the impotence of Russia in dealing with Pyongyang. She could talk, but could not deliver anything. So Russian offers of "good services" and mediation became spurious and Russia was, not delicately, put aside from further negotiations on the issue between Washington and Pyongyang.

At the moment, it is hard to predict how the problem of "nuclear North Korea" will evolve. One thing is absolutely clear - the "nuclear crisis" connected with North Korea's improper behavior with regard to the IAEA safeguards, was blown out of all proportion by the U.S. administration and the media. Instead of playing down a threatening bravado coming from Pyongyang, which was upping the ante in order to get the maximum out of its negotiations with Washington, the U.S. media turned it into a real and immediate threat of war in Asia. This gave President Clinton the opportunity to get closely involved in the resolution of the crisis, while pushing Russia, its so-called strategic partner, on the sidelines.

The Clinton administration in its zeal to get the upper hand in the region's politics actually acquiesced in the summer of 1994 to Pyongyang's probable possession of a couple of nuclear weapons and it bought off the North Korean government with various sops (including the promise to provide to North Korea two modern light water nuclear reactors, of proliferation-resistant design, free of charge in exchange for the DPRK's agreement to terminate its existing nuclear program, freeze its existing nuclear facilities and to continue to remain party to the Non-Proliferation Treaty). The sole area of the debate in official circles in Washington concerned the amount of the bribe necessary for Kim Il Sung to change his mind. The death of North Korean dictator in July 1994 gave the White House additional stimuli and opportunity to buy out the new North Korean leadership. The US agreement with the DPRK along such lines, stipulating the establishment of diplomatic ties between Washington and Pyongyang in exchange for DPRK's promise to freeze its plutonium production and extraction program, was concluded in October 1994. Though the agreement contains a basic flaw, in that it postpones for at least 5 years inspection by independent experts of the suspect nuclear waste dumps in the North Korea (which would have allowed the IAEA to know the extent of diversion of plutonium for weapons building), such an outcome understandably further devalued Russia's North Korean trump card.

Frantic attempts by Russia to become a participant in the deal by offering itself as the supplier of light water reactors failed because of opposition by South Korea and Japan. To compensate, Russia tried to enliven its diplomacy towards Pyongyang. Some sources asserted that Russia was trying to restore its military ties with the DPRK[65] but after a thorough review of the situation, Moscow finally decided to strengthen its ties with the Republic of Korea (hereafter simply ROK).

The visit of Prime Minister Chernomyrdin to Seoul in September 1995 broke new ground in Russian-South Korean relations. Seoul agreed to cooperate with Russia in the sphere of military technology, and once again confirmed that it would accept shipments of Russian armaments (to the tune of US$209 million) in partial repayment of Russia's half a million debt to the ROK. The rest will be furnished in commodities. There are also some projects for building car assembly factories in Russia to sell Korean-made cars throughout Europe and for the construction of the two pipelines to supply the ROK with Russian natural gas.

Such a turnaround in Russian loyalties has been prompted by Moscow's realization that, for the time being at least, the United States and Japan have effectively prevented Russian economic deals with North Korea. On the other hand, Seoul has apparently decided to have another go at large-scale economic cooperation with Russia after Moscow officially notified Pyongyang that it would not prolong its 1961 treaty with the DPRK (that expired in the autumn of 1996) and offered to conclude a new treaty on friendship and cooperation which would not contain a mutual military assistance clause.

During four years since Jimmy Carter's visit to Pyongyang, the US and South Korea are desperately feeding the hungry population of North Korea, while Seoul from time to time catches the former's terrorists, but the nuclear project is hardly moving. Such a situation inspired Moscow to advance just another "Manilov's project". Arguing that, because of the financial crisis in Asia and constant antics of Pyongyang, it will be difficult for the Korean Energy Development Organization (KEDO - a body, specially created by the US, Japan and the ROK to finance and build light-water reactors in the DPRK), to bring its project in the near future to a successful conclusion, Moscow offered to quickly build with the KEDO's funds an atomic power station in the Maritime province of Russia to channel electric energy produced to North Korea. But the parties concerned declined the offer.

Moscow, meanwhile, has been gradually restoring its ties with Pyongyang, and has enough leverages left with both Koreas not to allow the US to completely squeeze Russia out of the peace process on the peninsular.

Russia and the United States divided Korea in 1945 and only both of them, working in harmony, could turn the 1953 Armistice agreement into a real and lasting peace, whether or not the two Koreas become united or remain separate.

Conclusion

This overview of Russian interests in Asia shows that Russia, as a Eurasian country (three quarters of its territory lies in Asia), has quite extensive interests in this part of the world. Having lost in the process of the USSR's transformation, its former Oriental compatriots (the people of Central Asian and Transcaucasus parts of the Union), the new Russia is now seeking to benefit from its place in the heartland of the Eurasian landmass on the crossroads between Asia and Europe. Such a location gives Russia certain advantages as a sort of a bridge between the two continents. Some advantages are, however, just imagined because new methods of transportation, communication etc. make the centrality of a certain position not that important. But the fact is that Russia continues to exist in-between the two great civilizations, two cultures - European and Oriental, whilst remaining an original civilization of its own. Russia has absorbed the best (and often the worst) features from both civilizations and digested them into its own unique culture, which is respected throughout the world.

As we saw earlier, Russia now finds itself in a very difficult situation, given its ruined economy, heavily damaged ecology, and its tired and hungry population, which is disillusioned with the "reforms" that have brought only suffering and pain. The Asian part of Russia is in an even worse situation - many have fled to European Russia because living conditions in Siberia and the Far East are appalling. For instance, the Russian Pacific Navy, once a very formidable force, is presently in a very pitiful state having lost many of its ships due to neglect and aging without replacement. The leverages of Russian diplomacy in Asia-Pacific are negligible in comparison to the tasks facing Russia. It is no wonder therefore that Russia is unable to ensure its national interests in Asia.

The balance of forces in Asia is heavily influenced by the level of cooperation/competition between the four great powers: the United States (which borders on Asia in the Pacific), Russia, China and Japan. Russia tries to be equal to its three big partners, seeking to cooperate with them in creating a durable peace in the Pacific.

However Russian relations with the United States across the Pacific are insignificant: there is very little trade and exchange of personnel. All this is probably due to the fact that for 45 years, it was just a matter of confrontation between Navies and missiles, and so both countries have yet to find appropriate areas of constructive cooperation across the Pacific, besides the fishing trade, timber and ore exports from Russia.

Russian relations with Japan are marred by the unresolved dispute over the four South Kuril islands that Russia occupied in 1945, but which are considered by the Japanese to be their territory, illegally seized.

After a big rift with China in the 1960s, Russian-Chinese relations drastically improved in the 1980s and '90s and are evolving towards strategic partnership. However Russia's close relations with NATO, have increased Chinese suspicion about Russian real intentions. For its part, Russia is very wary about Chinese peaceful penetration into the Russian Far East by way of migration through semi-open borders. Despite all these suspicions and worries, Russian-Chinese relations are rapidly proceeding on the development of a mutual border and other confidence-building measures, including a reduction of troops.

Russia is trying to enlarge its circle of partners in Asia by restoring its partnership with India (including cooperation in the armaments sphere), improving its understanding with Pakistan and by making efforts to secure long-term economic cooperation with the ASEAN countries, whilst continuing a political dialogue with them. Russia has established very good relations and fruitful economic cooperation with the Republic of Korea, but in the process it lost North Korea as its closest ally. Washington used this mistake on Russia's part to make itself (with the support of

China) the sole mediator between the two Koreas. The United States also launched an initiative to dissuade North Korea from any attempts to make nuclear weapons but at a price. Since 1993, it has negotiated with the authorities in the Democratic People's Republic of Korea about making it a certified non-nuclear country. Russia could help the US on this, but so far the United States is keeping Russia out of the negotiations, thus impeding the peace process on the Korean peninsula, not easing it.

Notes

[1] Nikolay Berdyaev, Sud'ba Rossii [The Fate of Russia] (Moscow: Izdaniye G. A. Lemana i S.I. Sakharova, 1918), p.60.

[2] N. Alexeyev, Dukhovnye predposylki evraziyskoy kultury [Spiritual prerequisites of Eurasian culture] *Evraziyskaya Khronika*, XIth Issue (Berlin: Speer & Schmidt, 1935), p.16.

[3] Andrei Zagorsky, 'New Russia in a new world' (a summary of the report prepared by the Center for International Studies at the Moscow State Institute of International Relations) *Moscow News*, No. 9, 1992, p. 12.

[4] Even a vehement critic of Soviet colonialism, an émigré from Russia, the Chechen Abdurakhman Avtorkhanov, concedes that it is ironic that the Bolsheviks themselves were the ones who created "national culture, national intelligentsia and national cadres" in the non-Russian republics (A. Avtorkhanov, *Imperiya Kremlya. Sovetskiy typ kolonialisma* [Kremlin's Empire. The Soviet type of colonialism] (Vilnius: Shareholders society of Moscow's association of electors and INPA firm, 1990), p.208).

[5] Quoted in Gennady Zyuganov, *Drama vlasti. Stranitsi politicheskoi avtobiografii* [Drama of Power. Pages of political autobiography] (Moscow: Paleya, 1993), p.174. Zyuganov is the leader of the Communist party of Russia.

[6] *The New York Times Book Review*, 16 January 1994, p.13.

[7] Nowadays there is a sheer outflow of people from these regions due to the impact of the reforms. For example, according to the head of the administration of the Khabarovsk territory, half a million people left the Far East in the period 1990-96 (*Segodnya*, 25 July 1996, p.5). In addition, every third resident has departed from the Magadan region, whilst the Chukotka peninsula has lost about 40% of its population (*Izvestia*, 2 August 1995, p.5). Tens of thousands more people cannot depart simply because they do not have the money to pay for the trip.

[8] In no small measure such trends are enhanced by the silly policies of the Moscow central authorities, who do not provide substantial preferential terms for hard pressed businesses in Siberia and the Far East, and who allowed air and rail cargo fares to skyrocket to such levels, that it became unprofitable to do business

between enterprises located in the European and the Eastern part of Russia. Only in 1998 the fares were lowered.

[9] Presently China has more than 200 nuclear tipped ICBMs and IRBMs, quite a few of which can reach targets in the European part of Russia. The new Chinese nuclear missiles include the DF-31 with a range of 4,600 miles, and the DF-41 ICBM, which has a range of 7440 miles. China also plans to design and produce advanced jet fighters by the year 2000. Chinese military spending, which according to Western estimates amounted to US$100 billion in 1994, is constantly rising. In 1994 alone, the official military budget of China increased by 22% over 1993. "It is now becoming clear that China has ambitions to create a strategic force of modern, highly accurate, mobile, solid-fuel ICBMs" (*The Washington Post*, 8 May 1994, p.C3. See also *SIPRI Yearbook 1992. World Armaments and Disarmament* (London: Oxford University Press, 1992), pp.81-82; *The Washington Times*, 5 May 1994, p.A12).

[10] Mocking the notion of Russia as the "Third Rome", Vladimir Solov'yev who thought that Russia would be punished for her arrogance and deviations from the true ways of Christ, wrote at the end of last century:

> O Rus', forget your former glory,
> Your double headed eagle - overrun
> And yellow children, as their quarry,
> Play with your banners' rugs for fun!

Emphasizing a "Chinese menace", Vladimir Zhirinovsky said: "If *demorossy* (that is representatives of the Democratic Russia movement - H.T.) stay in power, then 50 years hence your children that live in the territory from the Far East to the Urals will only be speaking Chinese" (V.V. Zhirinovsky, *O sud'bakh Rossii*. Chast III. *S moei tochki zreniya* [On the fate of Russia. Part III. From my point of view] (Moscow: "RAIT", 1993), p.16).

[11] *Novoye Russkoye Slovo*, 25 November 1993, p.6. Moscow responded to these concerns in January 1994 by removing twenty Russian border checkpoints from the control of local governments and putting them under central control. It also terminated the liberal visa system and restricted the issuing of visas to Chinese businessmen (see Tsuneo Akaha, 'Russia in Asia in 1994', *Asian Survey*, January 1995, p.103). In August 1995, a border policing agreement was signed between Moscow and Beijing.

[12] *The Washington Times*, 24 November 1993, p.A10.

[13] Certain Soviet scholars have been presenting such an "official acknowledgment" of the existence of the dispute by Mikhail Gorbachev during his visit to Japan in April 1991 almost as an heroic act of monumental proportions, as

if there was no decision by the Supreme Soviet of the USSR in 1956 to return at least two of the disputed islands to Japan, after the conclusion of the peace treaty.

[14] Lev Sukhanov, *Tri goda s Eltsinym. Zapiski pervogo pomoshchnika* [Three years with Yeltsin. Notes of the Chief Assistant] (Riga: "Vata", 1993), p.193.

[15] On the eve of his planned visit to Japan, Yeltsin wrote, "I began to calculate, how many options we have, including all the nuances and proposals. It appeared there were fourteen. The piquancy of the situation was that the Japanese themselves had only one option: the islands always belonged to them and ought to be transferred to them" (Boris Yeltsin, *Zapiski presidenta*, p.185).

[16] This is why it is depressing to read in Russian newspapers, some commentaries about Japan being "too late for the train"!

[17] The special "Kuril program", adopted by the Russian government in 1994, actually remains but without finance. By the end of the summer of 1996, the administration of the Sakhalin island that manages the program had only received 24 billion roubles (less than US$5 million) from the Federal budget, some of the debt of 1995. Not a single rouble was received out of 124 billion roubles, earmarked for 1996 (*Izvestia*, 23 August 1996, p.2). Describing his visit to the South Kurils to deliver humanitarian aid, Eduard Topol, the well-known Russian author, now living in the United States, wrote in *Izvestia*: "A taiga warped by army vehicles, where not a single decent road was built during the 50 years of Soviet power. Some deserted quarries, and rotting parapets of military shelters. The skeletons of amphibious vehicles, tanks, missile launchers rusting in a fog. Dumps of fittings, reinforcing steel and houses destroyed by nature's earthquakes and by the human devil-may-care attitude. As if somewhere in the brains of the supreme rulers there was always concealed a notion that this is not their land, but an alien one, that would have to be returned sooner or later...". That's how the Kurils look like, Topol concluded (*Izvestia*, 24 September 1996, p.5).

[18] *The Washington Post*, 4 June 1994, p.A13.

[19] "Asia is by far the most dynamic economic region of the world. In the coming decades, this is where the major action will be. The average growth rate in Asia in 1992 was 6.6%, compared to 1% in Western Europe and 2.1% in the United States. It has been estimated that by the end of the decade, East Asia will account for 30% of the world's GNP and that a billion Asians, virtually equal to the entire population of North America and Europe, will be living in middle-class households" (Richard Nixon, *Beyond Peace* (New York: Random House, 1994), p. 105).

[20] At the Vancouver meeting of the APEC leaders at the end of November 1997 Russia was admitted into the APEC together with Peru and Vietnam. The aim of APEC, now comprising 21 countries, is to create a zone of free movement of goods and capital in the region inhabited by one half of the global population by the year 2020.

[21] *Trud*, 15 February 1997, p.2.

[22] For US$80 per ton of metal (*Izvestia*, 18 August 1995, p.1). Altogether about 200 ships and submarines will be cut and sold as scrap iron (*Segodnya*, 3 August 1995, p.3). "A junior Russian naval officer, writing in 1992, told of the deplorable condition of the carrier Minsk (commissioned in 1978 - H.T.): piles of trash, rust, paddles of stagnant water. 'The heads...are blocked off. The officers heat water in kettles for washing up in the mornings, keeping the water in whatever receptacles they can find. They receive [fresh] water very rarely'....'the ship is dying'. I heard that statement from everyone with whom I spoke" (*The Washington Post*, 10 March 1994, p.A20). In June 1997, the prosecutor's office of the Russian Pacific Navy officially incriminated Admiral Igor Khmelnov, the Chief of Staff of the Russian Navy, who at one time was the Commander of the Pacific Navy. One of the charges related to the selling the Navy's ships abroad (*Nezavisimaya Gazeta*, 18 June 1997, p.6). Later investigation by the local procurator's office showed that initially both aircraft carriers were prepared to be towed to South Korea without the dismantlement of some of their arms and systems that are still considered super-secret by the Russian Ministry of Defense. It was customs at the Far Eastern Russian port of Vanino that finally managed to prevent this from happening. The investigation also discovered that while each carrier was sold for, roughly, US$4.5 million, both ships contained about US$12-14 million worth of non-ferrous metals that South Korean dealers received gratis (*Izvestia*, 20 August 1997, p.5). At the trial Khmelnov received a suspended sentence on an unrelated small charge. Evidently, his top brass buddies in Moscow, who got their "fair share" of the deal, managed to push the right buttons.

[23] For instance, as a result of an explosion in mid-May 1994 of 1,600 tons of ammunition in the biggest ammunition depot in the Far East (30 miles Northeast of Vladivostok), the Pacific Fleet air wing lost a quarter of its ordnance. The explosion was caused by two guards who tried to dismantle an air missile to steal some sellable parts. In 1995-97, several other large explosions occurred at ammunition depots in the Far East.

[24] *East Asian Strategic Review 1996-1997*, The National Institute for Defense Studies, Japan, 1997, p.169.

[25] See, for instance, Major-General A.V. Bolyatko (Ret.), 'Voenno-politicheskaya situatsiya i problemy formirovaniya novoy struktury bezopasnosti v Severo-Vostocnoy Azii' [Military-political situation and the problems of formation of a new structure of security in the North Pacific Asia] *Voennaya Mysl*, No. 2, February 1994, pp.2-6.

[26] "The forum was originally conceived in part as a way for Southeast Asia, economically booming but militarily weak countries, to bring China into a web of political and security contacts that would make it more difficult for the huge Communist state to throw its weight around in the region militarily.... However,

while China 'endorsed' the forum, it appeared to give it a lukewarm welcome" (*The Washington Post*, 26 July 1994, p.A14). At the Brunei meeting, the Russian Foreign Minister proposed to adopt a "Code of interstate intercourse in the Asia-Pacific".

[27] Vladimir Ivanov, Principal Editor, *Japan, Russia and the United States. Prospects for Cooperative Relations in the   New Era.* A Conference Report (Washington, D.C.: United States Institute of Peace, July 1933), p.4.

[28] One such joint venture is the Tumen river (in Russian - the Tumannaya (Foggy) river) project supported by the United Nations Development Program. At a cost of US$30 billion invested over the next 20 years, this project envisages developing the Tumen river as a major free port zone serving Russia, China, North Korea and Mongolia - a sort of North Asian Rotterdam. However, the project is proceeding very slowly. Some Russian bosses in the Far East, jumping mad at the fact that the last 10 mile long stretch of the river before its estuary constitutes the border between Russia and North Korea, assert that China, by gaining (through alleged "Russian negligence") direct access to the Sea of Japan, will be able to intercept most Russian foreign commerce and transportation services in the region. So they deliberately put obstacles in the way of implementing the project.

[29] The share of Russia in the Japanese overseas investments is less than one tenth of one percent: US$299 million out of US$422 billion (*Izvestia*, 25 August 1995, p.5). In all, at the end of 1993, Russian enterprises with foreign capital accounted for only 1% of the total production of goods and services (*Nezavisimaya Gazeta*, 2 October 1993, p.2). At the same time every week up to 20 private firms or joint ventures with the participation of Chinese businessmen are registered in Russia. China is actually leading all other investors in Russia on the number of opened businesses. However, as a rule, Russian-Chinese joint ventures do not produce anything and only act as middlemen.

[30] "Over the past few years, Chinese-Russian non-central government controlled local trade...was worth US$5 billion in 1992, US$7.68 billion in 1994 and around US$10 billion in 1994. More than 6,000 Chinese companies have established trade offices in China's neighboring Heilongjiang province" (Eric Hyer, 'Dreams and Nightmares: Chinese trade and immigration in the Russian Far East', *The Journal of East Asian Studies*, Summer/Fall 1996, p.300).

[31] "Like the nations of 19th century Europe, the Asian states eye each other up as potential strategic competitors and conduct their relationships at least in part on the basis of geopolitics. Fostering an Asian equilibrium is therefore central to world peace and must be a key objective of American diplomacy" (H. Kissinger, 'China: The Deadlock Can Be Broken', *The Washington Post*, 28 March 1994, p.A21).

[32] Richard Nixon, *Beyond Peace* (New York: Random House, 1994), pp.122-131.

[33] Ibid., p.125.

[34] *U.S. News & World Report*, 6 December 1993: 'The Wealth of Nations'. Editorial by the Editor-in-Chief Mortimer Zuckerman. "We should capitalize on that leverage...", added Mr. Zuckerman.

[35] Henry Kissinger, *Diplomacy*, p.817.

[36] Zbigniew Brzezinski, 'The Premature Partnership', *Foreign Affairs*, March/April 1994, p.81.

[37] Zbigniew Brzezinski, 'Geostrategy for Eurasia', *Foreign Affairs*, September/October 1997, p.61. "To recognize this fact", adds Dr. Brzezinski, "China could be invited to the G7 annual summit" - evidently a regal honor by his assessment.

[38] Ibid., p.56.

[39] This statement was made by Jeffrey Bader, Deputy Assistant Secretary of State for East Asia and Pacific Affairs (cited in *The USIS Wireless File. Eur 213.* 18.3.97).

[40] It's interesting to recollect that in the 1970s the septuagenarians that sat on the Soviet Politburo went nuts over a similar phrase in the Sino-Japanese communiqué about the normalization of relations between the two countries. In a worldwide outcry, they branded the proposed clause in the treaty of peace and friendship between China and Japan as rabidly anti-Soviet (thus themselves confirming that Moscow did nurture hegemonic aspirations!). For several years after that, Moscow managed to browbeat Japan not to sign the treaty with China that would contain such a clause. When the Moscow leaders failed, and Tokyo and Beijing finally signed the treaty in 1978 with the anti-hegemony clause, Russia started to militarize the South Kurils by deploying a large number of troops and military hardware there. Nowadays the potential hegemon is unable even to provide these troops with regular meals, not to speak about anything else (see M.G. Nosov, *Yapono-Kitajskiye Otnosheniya* [Relations between Japan and China] (Moscow: "Nauka", 1978), pp.165-174; Herbert J. Ellison (ed.), *Japan and the Pacific Quadrille. The Major Powers in East Asia* (Boulder and London: Westview Press, 1987), pp.116-120).

[41] *Rossiiskaya Gazeta*, 25 April 1997, p.3.

[42] *The Washington Post*, 8 May 1994, p.C3, referring to a report in *The Far Eastern Economic Review* the previous summer.

[43] *The Washington Post*, 4 September 1994, p.A39.

[44] In February 1996, Russia agreed to help China build its own plant to produce SU-27 fighters under Russian license.

[45] 'Natsional'naya Bezopasnost: Rossiya v 1994 godu' [National Security: Russia in 1994]. Moscow: *Obozrevatel* [Observer], special issue, 1993, p.123. This report was commissioned by a number of Russian financial, managerial and public organizations and prepared by experts working under the auspices of Moscow's *Obozrevatel* journal and the international non-government research corporation,

RAU. It is interesting that Vladimir Zhirinovsky heartily supports Moscow's rapprochement with Beijing. Speaking at a huge rally in Moscow on 1 May 1993 he said: "It is in our and your interest to go for an alliance with Germany and let Poles agonize and Czechs think over what will happen to them. Also - for an alliance with China. This is a continental model: Berlin-Moscow-Beijing. We shall have a united territory and tremendous space. Nobody will be able to threaten us because it will be the mightiest economic complex: Germany - Russia - China. And the most powerful army" (*O sud'bakh Rossii*. Chast III. *S moei tochki zreniya* [On the fate of Russia. Part III. From my point of view] (Moscow: "RAIT", 1993), p.38).

[46] According to *Izvestia's* Beijing correspondent "Among leaders in Beijing, a suspicion grows that Moscow's readiness to swear eternal friendship with its Asian neighbor is dictated by considerations of the moment in its play with NATO" (*Izvestia*, 29 May 1997, p.3).

[47] 'Glavny protivnik - SSHA, real'naya opasnost - Rossiya' [Main adversary - the USA, Real danger - Russia]. (A reprint of a pamphlet "Will the Chinese army win in the next war?", published by the Pedagogical University of Chongqunig, PRC.) *Novoye Russkoye Slovo*, 24 June 1994, p.47.

[48] However, Russia will keep its air-naval base in Cam Ranh Bay at least until 2004 (*The Moscow Tribune*, 28 July 1995, p.3).

[49] *USIS Wireless File. EUR 313*, 29.10.97.

[50] Noting that the Japanese make adjustments to changing circumstances "by the accumulation of apparently imperceptible nuances", Dr. Kissinger also believes that the foreign policy of Japan will change. He argues: "A determined economic competitor, it paid for freedom of manoeuver in the economic field by subordinating its foreign and security policies to Washington's. So long as the Soviet Union could be perceived as the principal security threat by both countries, it made sense to treat American and Japanese national interests as identical. That pattern is not likely to continue" (Henry Kissinger, *Diplomacy*, p. 827).

[51] "Delicate Moscow-Beijing ties will complicate Japan's relations with China. If we have to choose between the two giants, we will probably lean toward the Soviet Union, which will have cast off rigid Marxist-Leninist ideology", the well-known Japanese politician, Shintaro Ishihara, wrote in a much-talked-of book about American-Japanese relations (Shintaro Ishihara, *The Japan That Can Say No* (New York et al.: Simon & Schuster, 1991), p.109).

[52] Hashimoto Ryutaro, 'Evraziyskaya Diplomatiya' [Eurasian diplomacy] *Nezavisimaya Gazeta*, 12 August 1997, p.5 (translated from the Japanese).

[53] See *Redressing the Balance. American Engagement with Asia*. Asia Project Policy Report. Sponsored by the Council on Foreign Relations, New York, 1996.

[54] This statement was made by President Yeltsin to journalists at a press-conference on 2 June 1994 (*Segodnya*, 3 June 1994, p.1).

[55] At the 1994 G7 meeting in Naples, President Yeltsin informed his colleagues that Russia had even stopped delivering spare parts for arms to North Korea (*The Washington Times*, 12 July 1994, p.A10).

[56] On 11 May 1993, the UN Security Council adopted a resolution urging North Korea to accept international inspections and to reconsider its decision to withdraw from the NPT.

[57] R. Jeffrey Smith, 'North Korea Defies Atomic Energy Agency', *The Washington Post*, 15 May 1994, p.A29.

[58] *Novoye Russkoye Slovo*, 3 June 1994, p.4.

[59] In 1991, on US prompting, Moscow put pressure on North Korea to sign a nuclear safeguards agreement with the International Atomic Energy Agency (IAEA), which it finally did in January 1992.

[60] Actually the Russian KGB, as early as 1990, discovered that North Korea manufactured an atomic explosive device. In June 1994, the newspaper *Izvestia* published a complete text of the secret memo of the then Chairman of the KGB, Vladimir Kryuchkov, to the Soviet leadership dated 22 February 1990 detailing such information. "According to the information received", the memorandum noted, "the development of the first atomic explosive device has been completed at the DPRK's nuclear research center, located in the city of Yongbyon... At present, no tests of the device are planned, in the interests of concealing from the world public and international monitoring organizations the very fact that the DPRK has produced an atomic weapon" (*Izvestia*, 24 June 1994, p.4).

[61] "If", Henry Kissinger wrote in *The Washington Post*, "after much American huffing and puffing, North Korea emerges with a nuclear weapons capability - or a capability it can rapidly activate - stability in Asia, America's role in Asia and nonproliferation will all be gravely jeopardized" (*The Washington Post*, 6 July 1994, p. A19). The same can be said about Japan, with even more emphasis.

[62] *Izvestia*, 31 March 1994, p.3.

[63] *Izvestia*, 1 April 1994, p.3.

[64] Ibidem.

[65] See *Izvestia*, 23 December 1994, p.1.

Chapter Six

Russian Interests in the Middle East

Greater Middle East

After the demise of the USSR, the definition of the Middle East in geopolitical terms changed. For the purposes of *Realpolitik*, a greater Middle East is composed of the five groups of states:

1. The countries of the traditional Middle East region incorporating the Arab countries of North Africa and the Arabian peninsular as well as the fledgling state of Palestine;

2. The Turkish language countries: Turkey, Azerbaijan and the four ex-USSR Central Asian republics: Kazakhstan, Kyrghizstan, Uzbekistan and Turkmenistan;

3. The Persian language grouping of Iran, Tajikistan and northern Afghanistan;[1]

4. Armenia and Georgia, which are situated in the Transcaucasus together with Azerbaijan, but stand apart from the Muslim world as Christian countries, both of which have ancient cultures and their own languages. However, via their specific location and historic connections with the surrounding countries, they are part of the region by default; and finally

5. The state of Israel.[2]

This Greater Middle East (the new "arc of crisis" or according to Zbigniew Brzezinski's definition - the Islamic crescent[3]) is characterized, like the more narrow, traditional one, by high levels of tension and turmoil

227

despite the fact that the historic conflict between Israel and the Arab states is gradually being alleviated. It is the region that (with the exception of Israel, Armenia and Georgia) shares a common religion - Islam - though religion as a unifying force is questionable, except for certain cases of confronting "infidels". An important feature of the region is that the conceivable unity of Islamic states in a conflict with outside (foreign) enemies is superseded by internal wars between clans, religious and ethnic factions in many of its countries. In many cases these continuing internal wars are rather severe, as is the case in: Afghanistan, Tajikistan, Turkey, Azerbaijan, Iraq, Algeria, Lebanon, Somalia, Sudan, Yemen.

The novelty of the situation consists in the fact that several ex-USSR republics with unstable regimes and rather pronounced clan structures, are now actively engaged in the politics of the region. As members of the Commonwealth of Independent States, de facto presided over by Moscow, they lean heavily down South, seeking some additional support for their independence. The fact that the states of the traditional Middle East, such as Saudi Arabia, Kuwait, Israel, Turkey and Iran, are now actively engaged in the politics and economics of the former Soviet Central Asia is an additional reason to treat the greater Middle East as a specific new region of conflicts. Actually one might say that the situation in the region is only beginning to unravel into a new geostrategic environment.

From Moscow's point of view, this region is extremely important not only because it directly borders on Russia proper, but also because in the Transcaucasus, it borders on the most volatile region in the Russian Federation itself - the North Caucasus region with several dozen tiny nations, actually mountain warrior ethnic groups, which Russia has tried to pacify for more than 100 years and not totally succeeded. Stalin even deported several of these nations into the inner reaches of Russia, but their rehabilitation and return to their original territories over the last 20 years, has only added fuel to the fire, as various groups fought each other in a quest for territory. In all probability the struggle for the turf in a literal sense, which is exacerbated by a high density of population and by the legacy of Stalin's attempts at the annihilation of certain ethnic groups, is likely to remain the main cause of armed conflicts in the region. One more problem is the growing mass of unemployed people, both local and refugees from other regions. This is a "boiling pot" which is automatically breeding strife.

The small nations and ethnicities, constituting a quarter of the North

Caucasus population and now loosely united in the Confederation of the Peoples of the Caucasus, are generating a great deal of trouble for the central authorities in Moscow for several reasons:

- through their militant separatism (Chechnya),
- fighting between armed bands of irregular ethnic militias (e.g. between the once exiled Ingushi and Ossetians in South Russia, in which Ingushi have been trying to win back some territory where they once co-existed with Ossetians), or
- through meddling in the conflicts in the Transcaucasus (such as the help militant sects of North Caucasus gave to Abkhaz fighters in their struggle for independence from Georgia).

The whole Caucasian region is a powder keg for Russia and not only for it alone, because small ethnic wars on the Northern slopes of the Caucasian mountain range and to south of it, might detonate a large bomb in that part of the world.

Russia's vital national interests

The most vital national interests of Russia in this zone can be defined as follows:

- To quell flames of fighting in the North Caucasus and to assert Moscow's authority.
- To preserve the ex-USSR's Transcaucasus and Central Asia at least as an undisputed Russian sphere of influence, if a complete return of these republics into the Russian fold proves impossible.
- To prevent discrimination against more than 10 million Russians living in the region, to guard their human rights.
- Not to allow the ousting of Russia and its companies from lucrative economic, transportation and communication projects in the region.
- To develop normal friendly relations with all the countries of the region, including Israel as an important economic partner and as a source of modern technology; and
- To restore, as far as possible, Russia's position and influence in the Arab world without a return to outright confrontation in the region with the

United States and Western Europe.

The fulfillment of all these tasks is necessary primarily for the stabilization of the situation in the Caucasus region and in Central Asia, where Moscow in turn needs to restore a single economic and, to a certain extent, unified political space under its control. This is also needed in order to give Russian foreign policy some muscle and/or teeth in its competition with the Western powers for supremacy in the region - not on an ideological basis as before, but on *Realpolitik* grounds of satisfying national commercial, security and other interests.

The well-known fact is that up until 1991 the Soviet Union, due to the Cold war, was a powerful factor in Middle Eastern politics. Not only because of its multifarious political, economic and military connections with the Arab countries and Iran, but first and foremost because the Soviet Union played the role of a counterweight to the United States in the region (in the global arena in general). But while in the global geopolitical context that role was to a large extent symbolic, in the Middle East, with its sharp and distinct division into the two hostile camps, regularly colliding on a battlefield (the Arab countries and Palestinians versus Israel), the Soviet Union's active support of radical Arab nationalism was indispensable in view of the latter. Arabs considered the Soviet Union to be the only real counterweight to the excess pressure from America in favor of Israel. The feeling in the capitals of the radical and even not so radical Arab countries was that their countries will be politically and militarily incapacitated, if not for the countervailing presence of the Soviet Union in the region.

This assumption explains why political and economic efforts by Washington, the   grand stratagems of Henry Kissinger, Zbigniew Brzezinski and others failed to "expel Soviet influence from the Middle East", as America had hoped.[4] Even the most sophisticated plans dismally failed. Despite the constant defeats of Arab countries in wars with Israel, or, more to the point, exactly because of that, the Soviet Union's presence, balancing that of the pro-Israeli United States, remained undiminished not because of Moscow's imperial persistence, but because of the wishes of many Arab states. This fact is so elementary, it hardly requires further elaboration.

Moscow excluded itself from the Middle East by its own volition in August 1990, when it aligned itself with Washington in the condemnation of Iraq's aggression against Kuwait (agreeing later to join the coalition against Iraq - an official Moscow ally - in operation "Desert Shield"). On 16 January 1991 that operation was transformed into operation "Desert Storm" - the coalition's armed forces attack on Iraq.[5]

However, the momentous historic significance of such a change in the Kremlin's posture with all its long-term implications for the Soviet Union's positions in the Middle East was definitely lost on the narcissistic Gorbachev when on 9 September 1990 in Helsinki he signed a Soviet-American Joint Statement on the Persian Gulf Crisis with President Bush.[6]

The unsuccessful attempts by Gorbachev to play the role of mediator or peacemaker during the UN forces stand-off with Iraq, and his later efforts to stop the land offensive against Iraq under conditions more favorable to Iraq's Saddam Hussein than the latter finally got from the coalition, vividly illustrate Gorbachev's delusion regarding Moscow's new role (to be exact, the loss of it) in the Middle East.

But if Gorbachev did not grasp the fact that Moscow's traditional role in the Middle East had just ended, the Soviet Union's Middle Eastern allies and clients immediately sensed what was in store for them. This is why it was not difficult for Washington after the defeat of Iraq to organize a new Middle East peace conference with the full-scale participation of Arab states and with some preconditions actually favoring Israel. The Soviet leader for his support of the coalition was given a carrot by President Bush - a position of a figurehead co-chairman of the Madrid conference, which set in motion the process of negotiations, that in the final analysis, produced a historic reconciliation between the PLO and the state of Israel, with the PLO getting Gaza and some territory on the West Bank to start its own state.

In all subsequent developments Moscow (representing since the end of December 1991 just one of the 15 ex-USSR republics - Russia) was largely irrelevant. A leading expert on the Middle East, Israel's Galia Golan, confirms this, when she says:

Indistinguishable from the United States in its policies, weakened and preoccupied with internal strife, Moscow, even before the break-up of the Union, had virtually ceased to be a player in the Middle East arena in any but a purely symbolic way. The United States has continued to grant Russia a certain status, acknowledging it as a successor to the Union and relating to it *as if it still constituted a world power* (emphasis mine - H.T.).[7]

Though during the past six years Moscow made some noises to prove its relevance to politics in the traditional Middle East region, it succeeded in persuading only itself.

But in the larger context of a new greater Middle East Moscow's role remains relevant and important. First of all, because the borders between the FSU southern republics and the adjacent countries became new trouble spots for Russia.

In the FSU European south it is a troublesome border of Armenia with Turkey and of Azerbaijan with Iran, while in Central Asia the main trouble spot is the border between Tajikistan and Afghanistan.[8] As is known, it is essentially Russian troops that are now guarding most of these borders.

The problems in the Transcaucasus

At the time of the collapse of the Soviet Union, the Transcaucasian region was the most militarized in the FSU. On a small territory 200 miles wide and 440 miles long, an infrastructure and stock of military hardware and supplies for two military districts (one army, the other, border guards) existed, together with supplies stored for the Caspian sea Navy and a brigade of the Black sea fleet. Furthermore, the territory was the base for the 19th anti-aircraft defense Army, the 34th air Army and quite a few special military units under Moscow's direct command.

The collapse of the Union led to practical wholesale plundering of the existing stocks of military equipment and weapons (including tanks, armored personnel carriers and military aircraft) by local nationalist forces and gangsters. By some expert evaluation Russia left in the Transcaucasus about 20,000 railway cars with various sorts of ammunition that was later used in military battles in Ossetia, Abkhazia, Georgia, Azerbaijan and Nagorno-Karabakh. Such saturation of the region with weapons and ammunition, left without control, was to a great extent responsible for the wholesale carnage there in the 1990s.

Both Turkey and Iran are now actively involved in the situation in the Transcaucasian republics. They are not only involved but energetically compete with each other for influence.

Jan Cienski of the *Deutsche Presse* writes:

For centuries the Caucasus was a battlefield between Iran and Turkey. The struggle for control ended only when Russia conquered the entire region in the 19th century. Now the collapse of Soviet power has reintroduced the possibility of Turkey and Iran regaining influence in the area.[9]

Iran has been actively engaged in commercial relations with Azerbaijan. It was also providing some help to Azerbaijanis (or Azeri Turks, as they are also called) that fought losing battles with Armenian forces over the Armenian enclave of Nagorno-Karabakh in their republic that in 1992 proclaimed its independence after several years of futile attempts to see justice coming from Moscow. Iranian instructors train Azeri troops and several times Iran permitted Azeri troops to move through its own territory to get to the rear of Armenian forces. Iran is also providing shelter to some of the 2 million Azeri refugees in the region that moved down south. While helping Baku, the Iranians are cautious not to infuriate Russia, because Russia presently is the only supplier of heavy weaponry to Iran; the former is also very wary regarding the intrusion of outsiders into CIS space. Simultaneously Iran's leadership is also worried about the possible involvement of its own Azeri population (15 million versus 7.5 million in Azerbaijan) in the Azeri-Armenian conflict in the Transcaucasus and the prospect of that conflict turning into a war for the creation of a greater Azerbaijan.[10]

Turkey, tremendously aroused by the fact of Turkish speaking FSU republics becoming independent, is enthralled by Pan-Turkic dreams of the restoration of the erstwhile greatness of the Ottoman empire. Turkey has a traditional historic quarrel with Armenia and helps Azeris in various ways, including the supply of arms. It also has been trying to intimidate Armenia by concentrating its shock military units on the Armenian border and periodically making statements threatening Armenia for its support of Karabakh's struggle.[11] At the same time the leadership in Ankara is well aware of the danger of miscalculation when a seemingly local conflict might turn into Turkey's military clash with Russia - a historic patron of Armenia. That is why in meeting with Russian authorities Turkish leaders endorse negotiations as a method to untie the Caucasian politico-economic knot.

More than 1,000 mujahedeen from Afghanistan were also fighting on the Azeri side, not to mention Russian and other nationality "soldiers of fortune" fighting for hard currency on all sides in the region.

This disorder was exacerbated by the war between Georgia and its erstwhile ethnic province of Abkhazia, which managed to separate from Georgia in 1993 with the semi-clandestine Russian help.[12] Now, when the Abkhaz government is negotiationing with the government of Georgia with the help of Moscow's mediation, the former demands that the problem of its association with Georgia be decided on the basis of *international* law. Russia herself created such a precedent in its preliminary settlement with Chechnya. There is also a smoldering conflict between Georgia and South Ossetia (which is formally a part of Georgia but wants to join its sister republic of North Ossetia across the border in the Russian Federation). The conflict was dampened but not extinguished by the agreement that brought in Russian-Georgian peacekeeping troops under United Nations auspices. They were deployed in July 1992 on the border between South Ossetia and Georgia. On top of that a clan war in Georgia, triggered by the *de facto* collapse of central Georgian authority, has been destroying the last vestiges of cohesion of the republic. (The situation somehow stabilized in 1995 under the leadership of Eduard Shevardnadze, who in November 1995 was elected as President of Georgia.) And again it is the Russian army which is now securing peace on the Abkhazia-Georgia border. The solution of all these problems became more difficult because, as was predicted, the so-called settlement in Chechnya opened a Pandora's box of problems for Russia and the other republics of the CIS. And not only within the Commonwealth, according to the Russian historian Nataliya Narochnitskaya:

The failure (of Russia) to liquidate a criminal hot-bed has led to its utilization by interested parties, surrounding Russia, in order to return the Caucasus into the orbit of Islamic politics in the most complex global combinations that resist state control. Two hundred years of work in the South by Russia, holding supreme power, its presence in the Black sea, the military-strategic balance in the Mediterranean, the fate of the Crimea, of the Transcaucasus (first of all of Armenia and Georgia), the future of all the eastern Christian world and of all those who are driven towards Russia in the Caucasus and over its range was put at stake in Chechnya.[13]

Trying to capitalize on the existing turmoil, an independent Chechnya in the summer of 1997 made a move with very long term subversive implications for stability in Southern Russia: it proposed to create the Organization for Security and Cooperation in the Caucasus, thus attempting to transfer the decision-making authority from Moscow to a new regional body. The Security Council of the Russian Federation, which under its secretary at the time - the former speaker of the Russian Duma, Ivan Rybkin - surrendered in negotiations with Chechnya one position after another, seems to be ready to discuss this project with the Chechen leaders.

As is well known the Russian army presently guards the external borders of Armenia and Georgia. While Russia continues to be the sole patron and defender of Armenia (a small mountainous republic of 3.5 million people squeezed between a 7.5 million Azerbaijani and 57 million Turks), the two other FSU Transcaucasus republics evidently feel that Moscow is the only reliable power-broker in the region and guarantor of stability. That is why both Georgia and Azerbaijan, who abstained from joining the Commonwealth of Independent States, finally joined the CIS in the fall of 1993, considering closer association with Moscow the only way out of their predicament. In 1994-95 Armenia and Georgia legalized through separate agreements with Russia the establishment of Russian military bases on their territories. Azerbaijan, however, continues to resist the deployment of Russian troops on its territory, though some Russian troops have been sent to Nagorno-Karabakh to separate the warring sides.[14]

Referring to the importance of its peace-keeping and peace-making duties and to general Russian military weakness on the flanks, the Russian government for more than two years has been seeking changes in the 1990 Treaty on Conventional Forces in Europe (the CFE Treaty), rightfully asserting that some treaty limits fail to take into account new borders and circumstances resulting from the collapse of the Soviet Union in 1991. Moscow's main request was to be permitted to increase the quota for the Russian treaty-limited weaponry in the so-called flank areas - the Leningrad area and the northern Caucasus - that were established by the Conventional Forces Treaty, including its subsequent emendations.[15] Finally a compromise solution was found. The new arrangement does not change the number of conventional forces that Russia can deploy along its southern and northern flanks, but certain regions of Russia have been excluded from the official map of the flank areas of Russia.[16]

Russia is mediating in the negotiations between Azerbaijan, on the one hand, and Armenia and Nagorno-Karabakh (which has been finally recognized as an equal party in the negotiations and not just a proxy of Armenia), on the other.[17] It also mediated among warring clans of Georgia helping to quell rebellious forces opposed to the central government of Eduard Shevardnadze in Tbilisi.

One should also not underestimate other leverages in the Russian hands such as the fact that all the southern region is still connected to the Russian power grid and its telecommunications network.[18] Russia also controls all the waterways that connect the Caspian basin to the Black Sea, and all the gas and oil pipelines, leading out of Kazakhstan and Azerbaijan, for the time being pass through the Russian territory.

Such a Russian role helps Moscow to preserve Transcaucasia as its sphere of influence, whatever criticism this role meets in the West. Evidently the success of Moscow's role in the region to a great extent depends on the prospects of situations in all the three republics being stabilized, on the final arrangement of the status of Chechnya, and on the restoration of economic cooperation between the three republics and Russia to a much wider - pre-CIS - scope than is the case now. For this purpose it is very important for Moscow to have some measure of control over the most sought regional commodity - oil. However, in this field there happened some real disappointments for Russia.

The fact is that recently discovered colossal deposits of oil and natural gas in the Caspian Sea area – inshore and on the shelf – make the region the third largest source of oil and gas in the world (after the territories of the traditional Middle East and Russia). The demise of the USSR led to the intense struggle among international oil and gas monopolies for control over these deposits. The on- and off-shore fields on both sides of the Caspian Sea – Western (Azerbaijan) and Eastern (Kazaksyan's, Uzbekistan's and Turkmenistan's) – attract foreign investors some of whom have already reached agreements with the governments of the appropriate republics for the exploitation of oil and gas fields (American Chevron Corp. with the government of Kazakhstan; an international consortium, headed by British Petroleum, that signed a US$8 billion contract with the government of Azerbaijan to develop Caspian oil fields; governmental agreements of Kazakhstan with China and Iran, similar agreements between Turkmenistan and Iran etc.).

However, the main struggle for the overall control of the oil and gas riches of the whole area goes between Russia and the United States (plus Turkey, which acts as the US proxy). The essence of it is not so much about the national affiliation of the firms that are involved in the oil and gas business in the area, as about the overall control over pipelines. Speaking in February 1998 at the US Senate Foreign Relations subcommittee on international economic policy, Jan Kalicki, the

Administration ombudsman for energy and commercial cooperation with the NIS, said:

On the energy front, we are leaving behind the post-Soviet pioneering phase of development when companies and governments worked together to establish the framework for oil and gas development. The central challenge now is to build the diversified transport network needed to bring large quantities of oil and gas to outside markets. Decisions are being shaped now on where oil and gas pipelines will be built and who will build them. These decisions will affect the competitiveness of US firms and products and our trade with these countries for decades to come...
Stable and assured energy supplies from the Caspian will reduce our vulnerability to disruptions in world energy supplies.[19]

That is why the most sticking point has been the choice of the main route for the transportation of extracted oil.

The Azerbaijan-Armenian conflict presently prevents the pipeline from being built across Armenia to Turkey, though the latter together with Western oil companies has been desperately struggling in favor of the project, arguing that building such a pipeline would make peace between Azerbaijan and Armenia, a vested interest for both countries. The ostracism of Iran by the United States makes it, for the time being, almost impossible to use Iran's territory for the purpose, though Teheran managed to persuade the government of Turkmenistan to jointly build a gas pipeline through Iran. At the same time there are some other projects in the phase of realization: to build a gas pipeline across Turkmenistan-Afghanistan to Pakistan (the chief contractor in the appropriate consortium is the US company Unocal Central Asia),[20] to build two oil pipelines from Kazakhstan to China and Iran (this is done on the basis of intergovernmental agreements between the PRC and Turkmenistan).

Nevertheless until very recently it appeared that Russia was winning in the struggle for the main oil export route.

In 1995 all the interested parties agreed that the so-called early Azerbaijani oil from the new oilfields will be transported through the territory of Russian Federation to the terminal in the Russian port of Novorossiisk on the Black Sea. In order to quickly start the oil deliveries by route to Novorossiisk, Russia swallowed its pride and agreed to let the deliveries of early Azeri oil go through a pipeline existing in Chechnya. The deal that Moscow negotiated with Grozny – the capital of Chechnya –

once again confirmed the independence of Chechnya. It is getting higher rates of payment for the transit of oil than the Russian regions crossed by the pipeline. (The first Baku oil started to flow through this pipeline in the Spring of 1998.) Reciprocating, Russia had agreed that another pipeline for the early Azerbaijani oil would be built through the territory of Georgia to the terminal of Supsa on the Georgian coast of the Black Sea, near the Port of Poti (this pipeline is to be finished in the Spring of 1999).

But the main pipeline for the new oil of Central Asian republics was, as Moscow hoped, to be the one built by the Caspian Pipeline Consortium (CPC) under the auspices of the governments of Russia, Kazakhstan and Oman with the participation of several international oil firms, including the US Chevron, Arco, Mobil, British Gas and Shell, Russian LUKoil and some others. This pipeline about 950 miles long is to be built from the Tengiz oil fields in Western Kazakhstan and pass through Russian territory to the modernized terminal in Novorossiisk. The US$2.6 billion project is scheduled to pump initially 29 million tons of oil a year.

This rather secure route through the territory of Russia to a deep-water terminal on the Black Sea gave Russia some debatable ground to demand a share in all joint oil ventures negotiated by the CIS republics with foreign companies and additional blackmailing power with regard to the respective CIS republics.[21] However, though the debates concerning the CPC pipeline have been going on for several years, its actual construction at the moment of this writing has not yet started, while the composition of the consortium and the quotas of its participants has undergone several changes during the past years.

Meanwhile, by mid 1998 it became perfectly clear that the main export oil pipeline will not be the one that is going to be built by the CPC, but the one to be built by the new building consortium, organized by the US, Azerbaijan, Georgia and Turkey across the territories of the three last countries thus connecting Baku with the Turkish terminal of Ceyhan on the Mediterranean Sea. It will transport not only the Azerbaijani oil, but also oil from the east coast of the Caspian Sea, because the governments of the Central Asian republics together with the government of Azerbaijan decided to build an oil pipeline to Baku across the Caspian Sea. The harebrain (from the point of view of Russian interests) agreement between Russia and Kazakhstan of 6 July 1998, on the sectoral division of the Caspian seabed between them (along North-South median line, which was welcomed by all other, but Iran, coastal countries, which are going to follow suit) makes it impossible for Russia to prevent such a development.

Such a decision was adopted by the interested parties in the Summer of 1998 under the tremendous pressure of the United States which officially promised to spare no expense for the building of the pipeline. The decision also demonstrated the real policy aspirations of the NIS republics in question, despite all the lip-service of their leaders regarding their "friendship" with Russia. Thus Moscow was effectively pushed aside not only from a lucrative business, but to some extent from the grand politics of the regional states as well.

The problems of Central Asia

Former Soviet Central Asia (with Kazakhstan included into greater Middle East for the purpose of this chapter, though it is not exactly a Central Asian country) is, from the point of view of Moscow's foreign policy, another part of the troublesome expanded Middle East. Absolutely artificial borders between the republics make a hodgepodge out of regional ethnicities. The borders, that six years ago nobody even knew existed, are now becoming bones of contention. For instance, Tajikistan has already put territorial demands to neighboring Kirghizstan. The 600,000 strong Uzbek community in Kirghizstan, that well remembers the 1990 massacre, is gravitating towards Uzbekistan. Tajiks of Uzbekistan dream of reuniting with their own nation. And so on and so forth.

On top of ethnic conflicts there is an incessant struggle between various clans often overflowing into violent clashes: for example, between southern and northern Kirghiz and southern and northern Tajiks. And there is a universal hatred towards Russians as people who, so to say, personify erstwhile oppression by Moscow, though many of indigenous Russians have had roots in Central Asia for several generations. When Moscow's "divide and rule" policy lost its second element the local populations were left only with great and seemingly irreconcilable divisions among and within themselves.

Moscow still does not treat that part of the FSU as a foreign territory, partially because Russia considers it has the responsibility to alleviate and adjudicate ethnic and other quarrels in the region. With the sole exception of Belarus, the FSU Central Asian republics are still closest to Moscow and all of them are heavily dependent on Russia economically and in providing for their security.

Of the five republics, three - Uzbekistan, Turkmenistan, Tajikistan - are still purely authoritarian regimes ruled by former Communist party bosses, each of whom also happens to be the head of a dominant national clan at the moment. The two others are "partially democratic" according to the U.S. Freedom House definition. Both Kazakhstan and Kirghizstan are building some foundations of democracy, but the growth of nationalism, the continuing grip of the old party elite on power structures, and rising unrest on the part of the groups that consider themselves deprived of their fair share of power, tend to enhance a strong-arm rule on the part of the presidents of all five republics. All of them had a high percentage Russian population,[22] though Russian minorities in most of them have diminished during the past six years as a result of the massive exodus of terrorized Russians fleeing to the Russian republic.

It is mainly due to the authoritarian rule in the republics that ethnic tensions (often turning into ghastly clashes between clans and pogroms of minorities), as well as the unrest generated by the appalling conditions of existence of the impoverished masses, have not so far turned into large-scale civil wars, with the sole exception of Tajikistan.

The civil war in Tajikistan resulted in 1992 in the entrenchment in the capital of the republic - Dushanbe - of an old-style stalwart communist regime (headed by President Imomali Rakhmonov) with its power base in the south of the republic and with a totally alienated population in the north-east. Rigged elections to the national parliament conducted in February 1995, in which the opposition refused to participate, did not in any way change the character of the regime. An oppositional coalition of strange bedfellows - Tajik democrats and strong Muslim nationalists - found shelter in neighboring Afghanistan (among about 100,000 refugees from the civil war in Tajikistan) and started to fight the regime in Dushanbe with the help of the Afghan mujahedeen.

The shaky nature of the Tajik regime prompted Moscow to organize a military coalition for the defense of Tajik border with Afghanistan with the participation of all other Central Asian CIS republics. The core of the military force of the coalition is the 10,000 strong 201st motorized infantry division of the Russian army, deployed in Tajikistan. Together with Russian frontier guards and some smaller units, they represent a 25,000 strong Russian military contingent in the republic, that helps secure internal order and patrols a volatile Tajikistan border with Afghanistan. There are also three battalions of peacekeepers from Uzbekistan, Kazakhstan and Kirghizstan. Russian economic aid and officers also help sustain small national armies in the rest of the Central Asian republics.

The problem for the Central Asian republics is that they, at one and the same time, want to stick close with Russia and simultaneously keep separate from it.

On the one hand, the Central Asian republics want to preserve the single economic, communication, transportation space, because their economies are very heavily integrated with the economy of Russia and would require a very long time to adapt to an international and/or purely Central Asian, if not just home, market. Their hopes for big foreign investments in their extracting industries are not materializing so far, and their dominating agricultural sectors need restructuring to become efficient. They need the expertise of highly qualified Russian workers that are now emigrating *en masse*. And they also feel they need Russian military protection (at least for a while) from obvious and hidden dangers from abroad. The proverbial pull of these republics to their southern "Muslim brethren", extensively discussed in all the articles about Central Asia, is evidently not that strong since the old Communist elite that governs the republics, though its members are nowadays fond of putting on Muslim garb in public appearances, is actually afraid of Muslim fundamentalism and its potential destructive influence on their societies.

Hence, there are various proposals to strengthen the CIS. However, the latter is strong on adopting at its summits various solemn joint resolutions and projects, but has no real mechanism to see that these decisions are implemented. The most notable idea for the reorganization of the CIS was Kazakhstan President Nursultan Nazarbayev's proposal for a Eurasian Union, an entity that is supposed to be much more cohesive than the present CIS with some really joint operations and supranational institutions. But this idea was not supported by Moscow.

On the other hand, all these republics want to develop their national identity, to create purely national institutions, to de-Russify their societies and to start conducting their affairs with Russia on an absolutely equal footing. The growing pressure of mainstream nationalists in these republics makes even more broad-minded of Central Asian leaders, like Kazakhstan's Nazarbayev or Kirghizstan's Akayev, cater to their demands, infringe the rights of Russian national minorities and actually try to squeeze Russians out of their republics. The resettlement of immigrant Kazakhs from abroad in the north of Kazakhstan, populated by Russians, and Nazarbayev's decision to transfer the Kazakh capital from Alma-Ata to the predominantly Russian city of Aqmola (a.k.a. Akmolinsk, later renamed Tselinograd, the city that originated around a Russian fortress built in 1830) are vivid examples of such a policy.[23]

The Russian government for its part definitely wants to preserve the CIS area of Central Asia as its sphere of influence. It also wants to protect the Russian minorities in these republics despite their diminishing numbers. Russia surely needs a military presence on the outer borders of these states until and unless its more than 3,000 miles steppe border with Kazakhstan becomes clearly defined and well protected. And, whatever might be Washington's point of view, Russia will do all it can not to allow penetration by military or para-military forces from the outside into the CIS territory as that will further destabilize the shaky peace or the semblance of peace in some republics.

Russia also wants to preserve a single economic space, but not to pay too exorbitant a price for this.

In 1992 Russia provided US$17 billion, or 21.4% of her gross domestic product (GDP) in aid to the CIS countries in the form of free of charge cash transfers, credits and excessively low prices.[24] Today Russia continues its aid to the CIS countries on a similar scale. Turkmenistan, Kazakhstan and Uzbekistan are the indisputable favorites of Russia. The sum total of Russia's free aid to these states in the first half of the 1990s came to an amount that is unprecedented in world economics - from 45% to 70% of their national GDPs, or almost the total amount spent on wages and salaries in these republics![25]

That is why in concluding various bilateral treaties and agreements with these republics Russia is unwilling to go for more binding long-term economic arrangements with them. This in turn explains why Nazarbayev's idea of the Eurasian Union had a cool reception on the part of the Russian president.

Russia's government has also been incapable of sufficiently improving the precariously dangerous situation on the Tajik-Afghan border.

To Moscow's timid nagging of Rakhmonov to a dialogue with the forces of the opposition, the latter answered with absolutely pro-forma moves. It was clear to any observer that the low-intensity military conflict in Tajikistan could not continue for a long time in such a subdued form. The communist government in Dushanbe had only some limited time to negotiate with Tajik opposition forces on the other side of the border (and with headquarters in Iran). Especially in a situation where a lot of people in Tajikistan itself supported the opposition.[26] That support periodically flared up in different regions of the republic in the form of local uprisings or mutinies organized by local military commanders. But Moscow, while admonishing Dushanbe's government to continue talks with the opposition (under UN auspices), actually did very little to promote a negotiated peace, which would have required some drastic changes in the composition of that government in the first place. Acting like this (and actually totally disregarding the tragic results for Russia of a similar Russian policy stalling in Afghanistan), Russia was gradually creeping into a new version of the Afghan war (which had all the chances at being fought on former Soviet territory). The accumulated bitterness of mujahedeen leaders and of the Tajik opposition, whose rather reasonable proposals for a settlement have been constantly rejected by Dushanbe, finally exploded into a large-scale guerrilla-type war against the government's forces. In conditions of the high Pamir mountains and present Russian logistic and other weaknesses such a war was threatening to become a loosing game for Dushanbe, as well as for Moscow, even if the latter decided to double or triple its troop strength in the country with a territory equal to that of France.[27]

In talks with Moscow's officials and Dushanbe's representatives the leaders of the united Tajik opposition invariably stressed that they did not demand the departure of Russian troops from Tajikistan. One of the leaders of the Tajik opposition, Hodgi Akbar Turajonzodah, the spiritual father of Tajik Muslims, who was actively participating in the negotiations, said:

We offer Russia and other CIS countries to become the guarantors of composing a Constitution that would exclude the possibility of the creation of a theocratic state. We are aspiring towards a secular, democratic regime, in which religion would be separated from the state. And the Constitution should contain a clause that would prohibit changing it for 30-50 years.[28]

In 1996-97, the opposition, frustrated by the unwillingness of Dushanbe's bosses to make some reasonable deal with it at the negotiating table, increased its military activities inside the republic and across the border from Afghanistan. As a result, some armed units of the opposition appeared in the vicinity of the Tajik capital. Such developments, alongside increased pressure by Moscow, finally forced Dushanbe to make a real effort in concluding a comprehensive agreement with the opposition. There was also one more factor that sharpened the apprehensions of both capitals regarding the possibility of dangerous developments and boosted their willingness to speed up the process of national reconciliation in Tajikistan; namely the quick advancement of Talib forces (mujahedeen warriors, supported by Pakistan, who in September 1996 seized Afghanistan's capital) towards the southern borders of the CIS. Having occupied about 80% of Afghanistan's territory, these Islamic warriors, representing the Pushtun tribes that traditionally predominated in the country, moved the fighting to Afghanistan's northern provinces populated by Uzbeks and Tajiks. The fact that the CIS started to clandestinely help the "old" Afghani government's troops to fight Talibs[29] made the prospect of war spilling over the border into CIS territory very real (as was the quite probable influx of tens of thousands of refugees into the territory of the three Central Asian CIS republics). All this made Moscow and Dushanbe conclude a deal with the opposition.

In negotiations in Moscow, Tehran and Dushanbe, all sides by the summer of 1997 had worked out a far-reaching general agreement for restoring peace and national reconciliation in Tajikistan. This agreement, that incorporates many more limited agreements and understandings between the two sides, envisages an indefinite cease-fire, the creation of a joint Commission for national reconciliation, establishes a period of one and a half years for the full implementation of the agreement and provides for the inclusion of the opposition representatives into the government of Tajikistan and the opposition's basic military units into the regular armed forces of the republic.

On 27 June 1997 in the Kremlin, the head of the Tajikistan government, Imomali Rakhmonov, and the head of the opposition, Sayid Abdullo Nuri, officially signed an agreement in the presence of President Yeltsin and many VIP witnesses, including UN representatives and foreign ministers of the adjoining countries. The widely empowered Commission for national reconciliation started its work. But it seems that there are powerful forces in Dushanbe that want to sabotage the process of reconciliation.[30]

The vacillation of Moscow in its Central Asian policy prompted the leaders of the Central Asian republics to come closer together in order to deal with Moscow collectively.

The first such step was the meeting of the four Central Asian leaders

(Tajikistan was not represented) in Bishkek, Kirghizstan's capital, on 23 April 1992. The goal of that meeting was the creation of a *de-facto* association with a view to seek greater economic cooperation and coordination among the five republics. However, the meeting took place with the presence of the Russian Foreign Minister.[31]

The next meeting of the five Central Asian states took place in Tashkent on 4 January 1993 and this time it was really separate. The heads of the five states made the first real step towards closer interaction by creating a Central Asian Regional Union. An accord was reached on the creation of a concrete mechanism for regularly monitoring the implementation of interstate and intergovernmental treaties and agreements. Many observers saw in the decisions of the conference a serious step towards a new Turkestan (as the region was called in the old days because of the prevalence of the Turkic language and peoples), as a protection against Moscow's dictate.[32] The convening presidents expressed their indignation at the fact that Russia operates in the CIS like a "big brother" often ignoring the opinions of junior partners and failing to consult with them on procedural and substantive issues.

But the fact is that Russia cannot operate in any different way. If Kazakhstan's Nazarbayev behaves among the Central Asian Five almost like a big brother, why then should Russia behave differently? It might even not be deliberate. Put simply Russia's strategic and economic weight makes such a type of interaction unavoidable.

However, neither Moscow's patronizing attitude, nor its financial infusions into the economies of Central Asian countries are enough of a leverage to prevent the closer association of these countries with some potentially anti-Moscow implications, or to ward off all the attempts by the external states to gain positions of influence, and not just economic ones, within the Central Asian republics.

In February 1994, the three republics - Kazakhstan, Kirghizstan and Uzbekistan - created a customs union and in July 1994 they agreed to create a close economic and military union of 40 million people. In March 1998 Tajikistan joined the Central Asian Union as it is officially called now. Foreign observers see the new bloc as an attempt to strengthen the bargaining power of these republics with Russia and as a move to pool economic resources at a time of deepening crisis.

There are some other steps the Central Asian newly independent countries are taking to loosen their dependence on Russia. One such step -

the efforts to create a Euro-Asian railway and modern highway links, essentially bypassing Russian territory. In December 1995 the presidents of Georgia, Azerbaijan, Turkmenistan and Uzbekistan signed an agreement on the creation of a transport corridor throughout the Caspian - Transcaucasus region for shipping goods from Central Asia to Europe. This agreement is aimed at restoring the famous Great Silk Route that used to connect Europe with Asia in the Middle ages. In 1997-98 several conferences were held, devoted to the discussion of practical ways to implement this project. For instance, in April 1997 there was a meeting of representatives of 18 countries in Tashkent (continued later in the Kirghiz town of Osh), which reviewed concrete plans to build a railway Andijan-Osh-Kashgar line (Kashgar is the city in the Chinese north-western Xinjiang province) that ought to become the main link between China's railway system and that of Western Europe. These systems will be connected either by the railway ferry across the Caspian Sea, or by circling Caspian Sea down south through Iran. (The recently built railroad line already connects Iran with Turkmenistan.) The project is actively supported and financed by China, Japan and the European Union. Of the West European countries, the most active is Germany which made a strategic stake in developing close economic and military ties with Uzbekistan.[33]

Such developments encourage outlying countries, such as China, India, Pakistan, Iran, Turkey, as well as the US and the countries of Western Europe, to launch bolder actions in the region, which Russia is unable to stop.

Moscow can verbally remonstrate with Washington, Tehran or Ankara, but it has little practical power to stop outsiders in turning an historical Russian sphere of influence into, first, a "no-man's land", a "power vacuum", in American terms, and then into a "legitimate sphere of state interests" of the United States or another country, like Turkey or Iran.

Is there some deterrent to such a brazen dismissal of the vital state interests of Russia? It is exactly in the agonizing moments of such a search for a deterrent that Vladimir Zhirinovsky stepped onto the international stage in all his arrogant brilliance.

The Zhirinovsky factor

Instead of pleading for empathy and understanding, this devoted student of geopolitics indulges the public in some discourse on the subject. You have again started to press Russia from the flanks - he sort of snaps back to the West. And you are going out of your way to eliminate our presence in the South. But I'll show you that we have also learnt something from Admiral Mahan and Halford Mackinder!

"It is necessary", reasons Zhirinovsky, "to do away forever with the dangerous situation on the southern borders of the Fatherland and to help peoples, neighboring on Russia, to regain a quiet life, to liquidate all hotbeds of war and tensions, which lead to confrontations, conflicts".

How to do it? It's very simple, he says, just follow my own geopolitical concept:

I do not want to give it my own name, say "the Zhirinovsky formula", but it is necessary to clearly realize, that the last "dash to the South", the arrival of Russia to the shores of the Indian ocean and the Mediterranean Sea, is in fact a realistic solution of the task of saving the Russian nation. For, when other parties are talking about cutting off Kazakhstan, Kirghizstan and the Middle Asia, they do not understand, that Russia is thus being pushed into a tundra, where there are only mineral resources, but where a man cannot live and develop.

Will anyone object to such a move? Very few - says Zhirinovsky. Only Kabul, Teheran and Ankara. But there are no such people - Afghans, there are Pushtuns, Tajiks, Uzbeks that inhabit Afghanistan. Iran is actually a Southern Azerbaijan, that is ready to unite with Northern Azerbaijan. And what is Turkey? It is Kurds - up to 15 million of them in the Eastern Anatolia province of Turkey. It is also partially Armenian territory. As to Western Turkey it actually gravitates towards Bulgaria and Greece. One should remember that the Turks captured Constantinople - the capital of the Byzantine empire - and renamed it Istanbul. Cyprus also wants to get rid of Turkish occupation. So practically everybody will be happy. Japan, China, India and Germany because all these countries will improve their geopolitical positions as a result of the re-carving of the South and corresponding yielding or leasing of some northern territories to those respective states. Zhirinovsky continues:

America - the only country that could confront us, will yield in this case. It values its own destiny. She will not deprive herself of the opportunity to live as she does today just because of three countries: Afghanistan, Iran, Turkey. While Russia has nothing to lose. It is her last line. Russia has either to cross it or perish... We shall march south as liberators, in order to do away with violence, which is rampant over there now. Hundreds of nations. In blood. They wake up and fall asleep accompanied by bullets. Explosions. They live under coercion and looting. But a Russian soldier will put an end to all this; the Russian army will put an end to the violence, to an outrage over human culture. And Russian soldiers themselves will stop at the shores of warm Indian ocean, establishing new outposts, villages, settlements, places of recreation there.[34]

How does this formula looks to Russian democrats?

"The absolutely crazy goals of war", commented Yegor Gaidar, the former Prime Minister of Russia.[35]

"[T]he crazy ideas of 'driving to warm seas'", according to Andrei Kozyrev.[36] But saying this Kozyrev just happened to be speaking to the public, the Western media. Because in reality he did not consider Zhirinovsky's posturing that crazy (however unrealistic it might seem).

Zhirinovsky's bravado allowed Russian foreign policy, which was absolutely sheepish in the beginning of the 1990s, to regain some assertiveness, to gate-crash enfeebled Russia into a respectable place in the councils of the mighty. In point of fact, all Moscow's foreign policy after the December 1993 elections in Russia evolved for a while in the shadow of Zhirinovsky.

At that Zhirinovsky (with his tough and knowledgeable advisers in the back rooms) does not just spin his examples out of a thin air. When talking about the volatile situation in the appropriate regions, he exaggerates and twists the facts, but does not invent them.

Today, the old border between Tajikistan and Afghanistan hardly exists, as Afghan General Dostum's Uzbek militia routinely crossed into Tajikistan to protect fellow Uzbeks there. Actually the family of the General resides in Tashkent. According to informed sources the reunification of Tajikistan - one Afghan, the other formerly Soviet - has progressed considerably since 1988, even though it did not make the same headlines as the unification of Germany did.[37]

Almost half of the Iranian population is of non-Persian stock: Azeris, Kurds, Baluchis, Arabs, Turkomans (Turkmen), Bakthiaris and Baha'is. Nationalist appeals coming from Baku resonate in Iran. They win rapturous reception and stir up irredentist feelings there. The Iranian authorities are worried that independent Azerbaijan might eventually wrestle away Iranian Azerbaijan. Then Iranian Kurds and Turkmen will also move to unite with their kin.[38]

As for Turkey it has a large Kurdish population fighting for independence and a quarter of Turks have their roots either in Azerbaijan or in the Balkans.

The West fully understands the role Zhirinovsky plays in Russian foreign policy. Thus George Melloan comments:

For a country that still subtly practices military blackmail, Vladimir Zhirinovsky has been a godsend. His ranting since he won heavy voter backing in last year's [1993] Russian parliamentary elections has convinced a lot of Europeans and Americans that Russia is still dangerous. Mr. Yeltsin and his colleagues are not above exploiting such fears. Foreign Minister Andrei Kozyrev was dropping dark hints about the risk of "World War III" while he was smoothly taking over the discussions that produced yet another Bosnian 'peace plan'.[39]

According to *The Washington Times* analyst, Martin Sieff, "Vladimir Zhirinovsky is not talking meaningless nonsense in his wild nuclear threats. He has a coherent, well-thought-out theory of how to use Russia's nuclear clout".[40]

As for the Turks and Iranians they comprehend quite well that, if they start to overdo things as far as the CIS space is concerned, they might run into some really unpleasant encounters.

"Digging through his personal archives, Mr. Elekdag (a former Turkish ambassador to the United States - H.T.), echoing views held widely among senior Turkish government officials, produces piles of recent Russian statements as evidence that President Boris Yeltsin's policies toward Central Asia and the Caucasus differ only in nuance from those of nationalist politician Vladimir Zhirinovsky", and he argues that "Zhirinovsky's views reflect Russian thinking".[41]

To sum up it is proper to quote an anonymous Western diplomat, who observed: "If a person of Zhirinovsky's kind were heading Russia today, there would hardly be a talk in the West about NATO's eastward expansion"!

However Zhirinovsky's star faded in the last couple of years. His antics do not amuse people any more. The fact is that in the local elections, held throughout Russia in 1997, not a single candidate of Zhirinovsky's Liberal

Democratic Party won. The crashing of the Russian army by the Chechen irregulars and Moscow's capitulation to the US on the problem of NATO's expansion vividly demonstrated to the whole world that all the militant threats from some Moscow extremists are nothing but bluff.

The traditional Middle East

While disappearing from the Middle East as a policy making influential, Russia did gain some new connections in the region as a result of joining the anti-Iraq coalition. Moscow (still under Gorbachev) established diplomatic relations with Riyadh and the United Arab Emirates. It got US$4 billion credit from the government of Kuwait and also signed a defense agreement.[42] And Russia also developed strong economic and cultural ties with Israel. However, all these ties are not a big deal in comparison to Moscow's former role in the Middle East. The expected investments of Arab sheiks into Russian oil industry did not materialize. No big new arms market appeared.[43]

Close ties with Israel, as it soon transpired, became a constraining factor for Moscow's policy in the region. As it happens Tel-Aviv now has more leverage with Moscow than vice-versa. Moscow tries to rectify this by somewhat cooling its relations with Israel.[44] Occasional Russian distancing from totally pro-American policy bothers Israel. During the meeting with President Clinton in Washington, the then Israeli Prime-Minister Rabin reportedly was quite direct in telling the US President: "Russian meddling into the Middle Eastern peace process is a danger for our region".[45]

At the same time, the UN embargoes against Iraq and Libya became devastating for the second largest currency earner for Russia - its arms exports.[46] The idea (which, incongruously, was for some time entertained even by the Russian Foreign office) that the United States might be willing to share some of its arms markets with Russia as a way of appreciation for Moscow's support in the Gulf crisis proved to be one of the most bizarre notions ever entertained by Moscow.

The frustration over the losses was very skillfully utilized by the Russian nationalist opposition, which actually first consolidated itself in 1990 around the issue of resistance to the idea that Russian military forces should take part in the coalition's military operations in the Gulf. The thought of the possibility of such participation, hinted at by the then Soviet Foreign Minister, Shevardnadze, was totally abhorrent to the majority of

Russian people, while Russian democrats energetically called for such an involvement as a gesture of "solidarity with the democratic West in a just cause". The struggle by Russian nationalists against democrats on this issue at the end of 1990 tremendously improved nationalist standing among the masses, who thought that Gorbachev and his government were just insane to think about sending Russian boys into a new battle on foreign land right after the tragedy of the Afghan war.

After the demise of the Soviet Union, the Russian government is continuing its competition with Russian nationalists over its policy in the Middle East, which helps explain some of the moves of Russian diplomacy in the region during the past seven years.

This diplomacy boils down to Moscow's attempts (sometimes rather awkward ones) to restore some of its former positions in the Middle East, regain the lost markets and, generally, - to infuse a semblance of independence into Russian policy in the Middle East. The modest achievements of this diplomacy so far are a substantial improvement of relations with Iran, the resumption of an arms trade with Syria and Kuwait, and the opening up of an arms market in the United Arab Emirates. However, the present pitiful state of Russian influence in the Middle East is not so much determined by the end of the bipolar confrontation or the slump in Russian arms sales in the region, instead it is due to the fact that Russia does not have at the moment adequate instruments of influence that are really relevant in the present world: financial, commercial, educational, communication, informational and technological. It cannot utilize any of these. It can only provide some poorly manufactured military hardware.

In November 1994 the Russian Prime Minister Viktor Chernomyrdin made official visits to the Arab countries of the Persian Gulf. His priorities were oil, money and arms. He managed to initiate some arms deals, but did not succeed in getting credits or investments for the Russian oil industry.

Russia for many reasons - economic and political - cannot go very far in its relations with the rich conservative regimes in the area. It is also afraid of the possibility that these Muslim countries plus China might penetrate too deeply into Russia's "soft underbelly" of Central Asia and Transcaucasus. At the same time Moscow has lost a lot of clout with the radical Middle Eastern regimes, such as Iraq, Libya, Syria. These regimes face a lot of difficulties and uncertainties and grope for a reorientation of their policies. Russia itself evidently does not have a coherent strategy for dealing with the changing Middle East. It just offers arms to anyone for hard currency and it makes diplomatic motions (like summits with Yitzhak Rabin and Yasser Arafat) purporting to prove its relevancy to the ongoing peace negotiations.

To remind the world of her importance, Russia occasionally threatens to use its veto power in the UN Security Council when appropriate Middle East subjects are being decided. It also keeps its naval presence in the Persian Gulf. However, for the time being it is not a serious player in the region. Russian carpetbaggers in Abu Dhabi (many of them - in its prisons) symbolize as much the state of modern Russian economy as the operational level of its diplomacy in the region.

At the same time it is clear to Washington that to completely exclude Russia from the politics of the Middle East (which is much closer to Russia than to the United States) is impossible, if only for the present confluence of Transcaucasus, Central Asia and the Middle East proper, and inadvisable at that. If Russia were totally shoved out of the region, she could turn to a really oppositional policy, albeit on non-ideological grounds, that will complicate matters for the United States.

It does not mean that the considerations of partnership with the United States and of general good relations with the West will no longer be relevant for Russia, provided that its present moderate regime continues. It only means that on certain directions in its policy (say, in relations with Iran or Iraq, when the embargo against the latter is lifted) Russia will be choosing options with less attention to the interests of the West.

In the summer of 1994 Russia was making a great deal of effort to stop a civil war in Yemen, or, to be more exact, to prevent the routing of South Yemen by North Yemen. There were reports that Russian warplanes and pilots, financed by Saudi Arabia, conducted secret bombing missions against the North Yemen's forces.[47]

Rumors were also circulating of a secret meeting early in 1994 of some Russian politicians, representing the interests of the Russian military-industrial complex, with a group of Iraqi officials headed by the chief of Iraq's security service, who is a relative of Saddam Hussein. Commenting on those rumors *Moscow News* wrote that

irrespective of whether there was or there was not a clandestine meeting of Russian politicians with Iraqi secret servicemen, a rapport between the positions of Russia and Iraq in the near future is hardly questionable. The course on the restoration of the alliance between Moscow and Baghdad is caused first of all by the concurrence of the strategic interests of both countries along many parameters.[48]

Russia was the first to urge the UN Security Council members to consider establishing a mechanism for gradually lifting sanctions against Iraq in response to the alleged positive steps by the latter to accommodate the UN.

During a mini-crisis in the Persian Gulf, which developed in October 1994 as a result of Iraq moving about 60,000 of its troops closer to the border with Kuwait, the Russian Foreign Minister, Andrei Kozyrev, hastily flew to Baghdad to make a deal with Hussein. The latter promised to recognize the existing Iraq-Kuwait border as permanent in exchange for the lifting of sanctions against Iraq imposed by the UN Security Council. The deal fell through because Washington reacted very negatively to the Russian initiative. Under pressure from President Clinton Yeltsin gave the OK to the Russian representative in the UN security council to vote for a new resolution censoring Iraq and warning it of "serious consequences" of continuing a power play. However, the developments around that crisis fractured the anti-Iraqi coalition.[49]

During another crisis in the Persian Gulf in September 1996, brought about again by the actions of Saddam Hussein, the United States did not dare ask the UN Security Council to sanction its new bombing of Iraq with cruise missiles (because Washington was well aware that it would not have got the authorization for the bombing). The crisis resulted from the use by Iraq's leader of his troops to help one of the warring Kurdish factions in Northern Iraq that was turned by the United States into a special exclusion zone for Hussein's army. Evidently, on the eve of a presidential elections in the US, President Clinton decided to demonstrate to the world that he was the main conductor of Middle Eastern affairs. Using the threat of a veto in the Security Council, Russia (together with China and France) blocked a resolution, sponsored by the US and UK, that in a backhanded way put all the blame for the rising of tensions in the Gulf onto Baghdad's leadership. The United States finally had to agree to the implementation of the earlier Security Council's decision permitting Iraq to sell US$2 billion worth of its oil to pay for medicines and food for Iraq's population every six months.

The very critical reaction of Moscow to the US military action helped Russia to continue the dialogue with Iraq and to make arrangements for new business deals with it, which would be realized after the Security Council lifts its anti-Iraq sanctions. That is probably one of the reasons why the United States is dead set against any further easing of those sanctions or repealing them altogether.

Sensing that, Saddam Hussein in November 1997 challenged the United States again. He accused American inspectors - members of the United Nations Special Commission (UNSCOM) in Iraq, that supervises the liquidation of Iraq's weapons of mass destruction, of a special bias against Iraq and demanded that they leave the country. Finally, the Iraqi government ejected American experts from the country and all other members of the UNSCOM followed them in protest. Such developments started a new crisis with instant US threats to undertake a new bombing of Iraq.

The crisis was resolved without the use of arms through active mediation by President Yeltsin and Russian Foreign Minister, Primakov. They managed to find a formula that led to the withdrawal of the ultimatum by the Iraqi government, which allowed the UNSCOM inspectors (including American members of the team) to resume their work in Iraq. At the same time it allowed Baghdad "to see some light at the end of the tunnel", giving it the hope that the intrusive work of inspectors will come to an end within a reasonable period of time and the sovereignty of the country will be fully restored.

The arrangement along these lines was approved by representatives of the five permanent members of the UN Security Council at a predawn meeting in Geneva on 20 November 1997. (By the four foreign ministers and a high level diplomat from China). The world media started to talk about Primakov's "sparkling triumph".

Though US Secretary of State, Madeleine Albright, was among the ministers, who okayed Primakov's proposal, she and other members of the American government immediately after that started to downgrade the achieved result. "The United States has not agreed to anything" declared Albright, as yet unsure of her boss's reaction, at her first meeting with reporters in Geneva.[50] And the reaction was predictable: anything, not negotiated by the United States, is suspicious. A rather vicious campaign was whipped up in the US media against the arrangement. Though UNSCOM team resumed its work in Iraq, the American press was claiming that Moscow's mediation did not achieve anything. Washington started brandishing weapons again, threatening to bomb Iraq. President Clinton asserted that for such an action he did not need any authorization from the UN.

But with all its hue and cry Washington did not dare resort to military action and had to swallow the fact that it was Moscow which was instrumental in avoiding a new conflagration in the Middle East. The authority of Russia among the Arab states, that this time were unanimously criticizing American belligerence, was thus boosted. From many capitals of the Arab countries came an explicit appeal to Moscow to invigorate its activities as a peace maker in the region.

While Russia is desperately looking for new arms markets in the Middle East, its leadership undoubtedly underestimates the fact that the region (the whole greater Middle East) is literally saturated with modern high technology weapons, as was so clearly demonstrated to Moscow in Chechnya. After the Gulf war of 1991, the United States sold to Israel, Egypt, Saudi Arabia and some other countries in the region colossal amounts of the most sophisticated weaponry. These weapons are to be used, not displayed in museums. Any small conflict in the region might ignite tremendous fighting, involving several nations, with which bigger powers would be unable or unwilling to cope. This ever present danger in the Middle East, which ought to be tackled in a well thought out, sophisticated way by means of preventive diplomacy of the cooperating great powers, is in fact not only neglected but deliberately sustained, to say the least. The reality of the competition between the "guardians of global morality and human rights" for a "big buck" in arms sales means that any constructive efforts or intentions are doomed.

Evidently, the game that is developing in the Middle East will include some limited cooperation between the United States and Russia with regard to regional affairs of secondary importance, with the United States trying to keep such interactions limited and with Russia trying to generate some initiatives of its own to demonstrate the success of Russian diplomacy.

A new balance of forces and interests in the Arab Middle East, stemming from the reconciliation of Israel with the PLO, Jordan and, conceivably, Syria will give Moscow the possibility to search for a new niche of its own in the intrigues in that part of the world. Moscow might also advance suggestions for broader cooperation with the United States (and thus - for an expansion of its own role) in working out an accord on the limitation of transfers of certain types of weapons into the region, as well as press for creating a broad regional security pact with the United States, the European Union and Russia acting as its guarantors.

Some limited competition will develop between Russia and other CIS republics in expanding commercial and other ties in the Middle East. It is absolutely clear, for instance, that Nursultan Nazarbayev would like for Kazakhstan to become the bridge, joining East and West, Muslim and Christian countries, a role that Russia is aspiring towards. Some such ideas are not alien to Uzbekistan's Karimov as well. Both Karimov and Yeltsin are worried by too active and speedy a rapprochement between Turkmenistan and Iran. It is certain that four of the five Central Asian republics plus Russia will be strongly resisting the spread of Islamic fundamentalism. President Karimov warns: "We were late in Tajikistan, and if we do nothing we might become late in Turkmenistan as well...".[51]

At the same time Moscow is developing and cultivating its own close ties with Iran. Russia and Iran are united in their opposition to the US policy in the region based on the "divide and rule" principle - the policy that is trying to pit Azerbaijan against Russia, Russia against Georgia, to present Iran as a sort of global monster and to isolate it etc.

Iran also plays a very constructive role in the settlement of the civil war in Tajikistan, while the leaders of certain FSU Central Asian republics would not mind if the conflict drags on. NATO expansion endangers not only the national interests of Russia but also those of Iran as well because of expanding NATO activities in Central Asia. (Using the PfP mechanisms NATO is organizing joint training exercises with Uzbekistan and Kazakhstan actually in the rear of Russia and Iran.)

In a situation when Turkey ever more actively intrudes in the political and economic space of the Transcaucasus and Central Asian CIS republics, Iran serves as a useful counterweight to Turkey, striving to establish itself as the number one influence in the region.

Finally, trade relations between Russia and Iran are very advantageous to Russia because of the large proportion of Iran's imports from Russia. One field of economic interaction is the Russian help in building Iran's nuclear power station in Bushehr. The building of this station was begun with the help of Germany and France, but the United States, displeased with the anti-Israeli stand of Iran, managed to press the two countries to quit the construction. Russia agreed to step into a deal on the request of the Iranian authorities. In January 1995 Moscow signed the contract with Iran to be implemented over the next seven years. It will bring Russia about US$2.7 billion.

The United States is making quite a strenuous effort to undermine that contract, speculating on the alleged possibility of Iran using these power reactors to produce weapons-grade plutonium for the Iranian atomic bomb project. However, Iran - in contrast to Israel - is a member of the NPT Treaty and allows IAEA inspectors unhindered access to its atomic power facilities. But in actual fact, the US vehement stand against the Russian-Iranian deal is generated not so much by non-proliferation considerations, but by the desire to push a competitor out of a very lucrative international market. The fact is that the United States and Russia together control more than 70% of the global market on equipment for nuclear power stations. By 2005 the size of this market will probably double and the American government is ready to go the whole hog to curtail the Russian share in that market. For this reason the US authorities make a lot of noise about the alleged defects of Russian-produced equipment, though it works quite well in many countries and the Chernobyl disaster was the result not of the equipment's malfunction, but of human error. (The engineers, that in April 1986 conducted a "safety experiment" on the fourth power bloc of the Chernobyl station that was destroyed, deliberately switched off all the in-built safety systems to preserve the "purity" of the test!)[52]

Another sphere of Russian-Iranian interaction is military-technical cooperation. Though Russia is circumscribed in this business by its adherence to the Vassenaar arrangements that replaced the COCOM regime of control over the export of advanced technologies, it continues to sell military hardware to Iran. At the end of 1996 Tehran received from Russia the last - third - submarine of "Kilo" class that was delivered on a contract signed at the time of the Soviet Union's existence.

At the end of 1996 it was reported that in the next 10 years Russia will increase its deliveries of military hardware to Iran at a cost of US$4 billion.[53] In a sort of a retaliation the US Congress in the Spring of 1998 put several Russian enterprises and a research center on a black list of businesses the US firms and banks are forbidden to deal with.

At the time of writing the CIS republics of the greater Middle East are members of NATO's Partnership for Peace. What influence, one might ask, will such membership have on relations between Russia and these countries? Probably the immediate practical influence of such membership will be insignificant. Russia will continue to deal with these countries not via Brussels, but directly. It is hardly feasible that the NATO command will attempt to substitute itself for Russia as an advisor on military matters in these countries, or will succeed in moving them towards standardized NATO weaponry and procedures. However, the participation of the Central Asian republics in the Partnership allows Western nations greater access to them in order to observe and learn about Russian weapons and procedures. To put it bluntly, the West is obtaining a somewhat greater presence in the Russian "underbelly", which is no mean feat.

Conclusion

So for the purpose of analyzing the interests of Russia in the Middle East, this chapter introduced the notion of the Greater Middle East. In this concept the Transcaucasus and the Central Asian republics of the FSU are also included in the Middle East, because nowadays they constitute a single entity with the traditional Middle East through very close connections with the latter's Islamic countries - Iran, Turkey, Saudi Arabia and other Arab countries. Most of these FSU republics (with the exception of Armenia and Georgia that are Christian countries) practice the same religion - Islam - and are also rich in the prime marketable commodity of the Middle East - oil.

The greater Middle East is as volatile as its traditional core, because most of the NICs of this region are still in the process of a painful transition from being powerless parts of a single mighty entity - the Soviet Union - to a fully-fledged members of the global community of nations, masters of their own destinies. Such a transition is complicated by the rise of virulent nationalism in these states, all of which are multinational, and by the clan struggles within the title nations. (The logic of a multitude of separatists all over the world is simple: if Quebec struggles to separate from Canada, or if, say, the FSU Central Asian republics managed to separate from Russia, why can we not do it on the same grounds?)

To gain some capital for the necessary reforms, many of these republics first of all sold to foreign companies some of their mineral deposits - primarily oil and gas, as well as some other raw materials. The accompanying struggle for the possession of such resources, involving internal groupings and foreign businesses, could hardly contribute to stabilization.

If one generalizes, the basic national interest of these republics, *as practiced by their present ruling clans*, is the speedy sale of natural riches of those countries. This constitutes the prime "national interest" of most of them.

The prime national interests of Russia in these NICs are connected with security (through a common defense of the outer borders) and with the need to preserve this area as her sphere of influence. Russia also strives not to let out of her control the oil and gas transportation systems of the CIS, as well as general transportation systems. Understanding the importance of such systems for a country's genuine independence, the NICs try to somehow outwit Russia in the struggle for their control. Russia, together with Iran, held for a while to a principle that the Caspian Sea should have a regime of an open sea, but under the pressure of the other coastal CIS republics agreed to divide the seabed into national sectors while keeping waters undivided (after that Turkmenistan and Iran went one step further and divided waters in their sectors of the sea as well!).

Due to the rise of separatism among small ethnicities in the region, there are many conflicts there, sometimes exploding into local wars of "national liberation" (the Nagorno-Karabakh clash with Azerbaijan, wars in Abkhazia and South Ossetia in Georgia, ethnic strife in Kabardino-Balkaria, skirmishes on religious grounds in Dagestan, North Ossetians fighting Ingushi - all in the South of Russia etc.). There are also acute tensions with occasional clashes between national minorities and majorities in the FSU Central Asian republics, not to speak about a cracking down on ethnic Russians in these republics.

Russia is interested in quelling the flames of fighting in the NICs, especially in the Transcaucasus, in order to prevent the transformation of local conflicts into a bigger Caucasian war. However, the fiasco of Russia's war with Chechnya, which *de facto* and to a great extent *de jure* wrestled independence from Russia, created a precedent, welcome to all separatists in the region, because it gives them the legal grounds to also claim complete independence. Russia's role as a moderator in many such conflicts has been heavily damaged by such a precedent.

It was also very much in the national interests of Russia to stop the fratricidal fighting between the government of Tajikistan and the forces of the opposition, that were initially forced to flee to Afghanistan. The extreme subservience of Tajik President Rakhmonov to Moscow, very convenient for the latter, made Moscow unwilling to nudge him into a settlement with the opposition. Only when the Moscow leaders finally realized the imminent danger of a total conflagration in Central Asia, due to the advance of Afghan Talib warriors into regions of Afghanistan populated by Tajiks and Uzbeks, did Moscow push for a general agreement on reconciliation between the conflicting parties of Tajikistan.

In the traditional Middle East, Russia hopes to restore some of its positions of influence, which it voluntarily yielded to the United States before and after the Gulf war of 1991. The main leverage, still held by Russia with respect to the Arab countries of the region, is the old Soviet one - the sale of arms (now - only for hard currency - not almost for nothing as before). Due to its cheap labor and a reputation as a good armaments manufacturer Russia has already gained anew the second place in the international weapons market.

Russia has some grounds for thinking she will return some day into the Middle East in her former role as a counterweight to the United States, this time, as its geopolitical, not ideological, competitor. Because of the increasingly heavy tilt in US policy in the Middle East towards Israel (as confirmed by the Republican-dominated US Senate vote for making Jerusalem the capital of Israel, which was too much even for President Clinton), Russia can play the role of moderator in the Middle East politics. Of course, for such a role to materialize Russia has first to put its own house in order. Russia objectively could play such a role, while keeping good relations with Israel, where former Soviet citizens constitute a sizable majority of the population.

The Middle East - greater or traditional - is not the only place in the world where the interests and policies of the two nuclear superpowers - Russia and the United States - collide even when Russia is more or less a docile partner of the United States. This problem is examined in the next chapter.

Notes

[1] The Tajik language closely resembles Dari, the Persian language of Afghanistan, which is similar to Iranian Farsi.

[2] There is also a big Kurdish population split essentially between Turkey, Iraq and Iran, that is continuing to struggle for national independence, but so far does not have any influence on the formulation of the foreign policies of any of the above states.

[3] See Zbignew Brzezinski, *Out Of Control. Global Turmoil on the Eve of the Twenty-First Century* (New York et al.: Charles Scribner's Sons, 1993), p. 214.

[4] "I felt confident enough" says Kissinger about his days in the Nixon's administration, "to tell a journalist that the new administration would seek to expel Soviet influence from the Middle East" (Henry Kissinger, *Diplomacy*, p.738).

[5] The author will not dwell here on some of the most compelling reasons for such a change of heart by Moscow, because they have been discussed thoroughly elsewhere during the past six years. The bare fact is that facing the dilemma: either sincerely with the West and the majority of world community against Iraq, or against the world community with Iraq, Moscow chose the first option.

[6] "We are united in the belief that Iraq's aggression must not be tolerated," said the Statement. "Nothing short of a return to the pre-August 2 status of Kuwait can end Iraq's isolation" (*Public Papers of the Presidents of the United States. George Bush. 1990.* Book II - *July 1 to December 30, 1990* (Washington: U.S. G.P.O. 1991), pp. 1203-4.). The implications of this action for Soviet positions in the Middle East were additionally obscured for Gorbachev by the decisions of the Arab heads of state to join the coalition force in the Gulf.

[7] Galia Golan, *Moscow and the Middle East. New Thinking on Regional Conflict* (New York: Council on Foreign Relations Press 1992), p.81.

[8] According to reliable estimates, as of July 1993, there were 189,000 servicemen of various national armies, 97,000 Russian servicemen, and 34,000 troops under joint Russian-Turkmenian command in Central Asia. In Transcaucasia, there were 55,000 national army troops and 15,000 Russian servicemen (Robert D. Blackwill and Sergei A. Karaganov (eds.), *Damage Limitation or Crisis? Russia and the Outside World* (Washington-London: Brassey's Inc., 1994), p.212, note 13).

[9] *The Washington Times*, 18 September, 1993, p.A8.

[10] The nationalistic Popular Front of Azerbaijan, that was formed in November 1989, and in 1992-93 ruled the republic, hinted in its platform at the idea of greater Azerbaijan and proposed opening of the borders of Azerbaijan with Iran to allow for social and cultural exchanges between the two sides. The borders became actually open for some time during the period when the leader of the Front Elbulfez Ali Elçibey was the president of Azerbaijan. He often referred to his country as "northern Azerbaijan" and even called for the overthrow of the Islamic Republic of Iran (see Daniel Pipes in Michael Mandelbaum (ed.), *Central Asia and the World. Kazakhstan, Uzbekistan, Tajikistan, Kyrgyzstan, and Turkmenistan* (New York: Council on Foreign Relations Press, 1994), p.61). The authorities in Iran remember well that for a short while in 1945-46 Moscow managed to set up an allegedly independent Azerbaijani state on Iranian territory.

[11] Flying to a meeting in Tashkent at the beginning of April 1993 the Turkish president Turgut Ozal quite explicitly spoke in favor of the use of force to stop the Armenian offensive in Azerbaijan. "One shouldn't be afraid of military intervention", he said to a group of accompanying journalists. "We have to show

our teeth" (*Novoye Russkoye Slovo*, 6 April 1993, quoting the Turkish newspaper *Hürriyet*).

[12] While fighting against Georgian troops with the help of Russian units and Chechen volunteers, the leaders of Abkhazia asserted that they would be quite satisfied if they were allowed to join Russia as an autonomous republic. Evidently, Russia's top brass was very worried about the drastic curtailment of their access to the Black Sea shores (due to independence of Ukraine and Georgia) and made a stake on helping Abkhazia to separate, without thinking about the long term political repercussions of such a precedent.

[13] N. Narochnitskaya, 'Politika Rossii na poroge tret'yego tysyacheletiya' [The Policy of Russia on the Threshold of the Third Millennium], *Mezhdunarodnaya Zhizn*, No. 9, 1996, p.34.

[14] Populated mostly by Armenians the Nagorno-Karabakh autonomous region was put under Azerbaijan's jurisdiction in 1921, after Stalin negotiated a treaty in the Transcaucasus between Communist Russia and Turkey. The strife between Armenians and Azeris in the region escalated in 1988 and, after Moscow proved incapable of solving the conflict, a full-scale war broke out in 1992. As a result Armenians seized almost one quarter of the territory of Azerbaijan, including a big stretch of land that separated Karabakh from the Armenian republic. Today Karabakh is a self-proclaimed republic and a cease-fire with battle-weary Azerbaijan has been holding since 1994.

[15] Negotiated in the final days of the Cold war, the Treaty, signed in Paris in November 1990 by the heads of the 22 countries, sets the limits not only on the number of heavy weapons that can be deployed in the countries-parties to it, but also on the number of weapons that can be deployed in specific border areas. After the FSU's CFE limits had been divided by the Tashkent agreement among the European republics that emerged from the ruins of the USSR, Russia had to reduce its military equipment levels in its northern and southern regions from about 11,500 pieces in each region to no more than 4,360 (1,300 tanks plus 1,380 armored vehicles, plus 1,680 artillery pieces).

[16] On the day when the CFE Treaty reduction period came to an end - 16 November 1995. The CFE participants in 40 months achieved the verified elimination of almost 50,000 pieces of the Treaty limited equipment (TLE), including 11,000 pieces of Russian military equipment (*USIA Wireless File*, Moscow, 20 November 1995, pp. 23-27). On the same day the Joint Consultative Group of the CFE Treaty (now embracing 30 nations) agreed to the proposed solution. The new Flank Agreement (which ought to be ratified by the participating countries) excludes the Pskov region in northern Russia, Volgograd, Astrakhan, parts of Rostov region and a small section of Krasnodar territory in southern Russia, as well as Odessa region in southern Ukraine, from specific original CFE limitations on the TLE in the flank zones. In other words, it makes flank zones

geographically smaller, though all the original limits in the diminished zones remain in force. These changes were worked out in consultations with the two NATO members - Norway and Turkey - most concerned with the Russian armaments in those zones. Lynn Davis, the US Under Secretary of State for arms control and international security policy noted that "the CFE Flank Agreement is critical to ensuring the CFE treaty's long-term viability and preserving security and stability in Europe... The Flank Agreement does not authorize an increase in any state's overall permitted holdings of the TLE, nor does it change the equipment limits for flank zones" (*USIS Wireless File. Eur 208.* 29.4. 97). At the beginning of December 1997, during his official visit to Sweden, President Yeltsin announced that Moscow will cut its land and naval forces in the Northwest Russia by 40%.

[17] This mediation goes in parallel with the efforts of the international "Minsk group" of the OSCE that in 1994 reached an agreement with the warring sides to establish an international peace-keeping force for the region. The latest suggestion of the Minsk group of mediators for a settlement in Karabakh, made under the influence of the oil pipelines route problem and, probably, with some prompting from the US, envisages the recognition by Armenia of the status of Karabakh as an autonomous region of Azerbaijan. If Armenia agrees to this, the negotiators promise, Yerevan will obtain from Baku a very broad autonomy for Karabakh.

[18] By the way, the total debt of the CIS countries to Moscow for the energy resources supplied to them stood, at the beginning of 1996, at US$4 billion (*Finansoviye Izvestia*, 24 January 1996, p.1).

[19] *USIS Wireless File. EUR 307.* 25.2.98.

[20] It seems that the victory of the Taliban movement in Afghanistan makes the project realizable, because Talibs, supported by Pakistan, welcomed the project.

[21] At the end of June 1994 the Russian government in a letter to the British Embassy in Moscow officially announced the introduction of a Russian veto over all the deals relating to Caspian oil that are being negotiated between the CIS republics and foreign companies. The Russian government, purporting to be very much concerned with the ecological consequences of the Caspian basin oil development, stated that all projects that are not explicitly sanctioned by Russia "could not be recognized". In a retaliation against Moscow, the Turkish government announced new regulations for navigation through the Black Sea straits, limiting the passage of supertankers. The Turkish decision evoked a strong protest from Moscow and the initiation of the project to transport oil to Europe through a pipeline laid across Bulgaria and Greece.

[22] The totals are as follows: Kazakhstan - 38%, Kirghizstan - 21.5%, Turkmenistan - 9.5%, Uzbekistan - 8%, Tajikistan - 7.6%. Altogether around 9.5 million people (T.R.Gurr, *Minorities*, pp.211-212).

[23] "The creation of Kazakh-dominated Kazakhstan", writes Graham Fuller of the RAND Corporation, "implies a delicate process of gradual Kazakh takeover

throughout the country, including the north, but done so imperceptibly as not to spark /Russian/ secession there" (*Central Asia and the World*, p. 129, note 1). By the way, in 1998 the new capital of Kazakhstan was again renamed, because some wise guy discovered that "Aqmola" in old Kazakh language means "white grave". Now the capital is called Astana, which in Kazakh literally means "capital". Officially the Kazakh government moved to its new residence on 10 June 1998. Official translation.

[24] *Izvestia*, 14 July 1993, p.2.

[25] *Izvestia*, 16 September 1993, p.4.

[26] The support has been so widespread that any Russian commander is actually afraid to fight alongside Tajik government military units, because while pretending to be fighting "aggressors" in the daytime, the same soldiers at night hunt Russian soldiers and officers to kill them. In 1995-97, hardly a week passed in Dushanbe when a Russian soldier or officer was not killed.

[27] In accordance with the new law on military service men called up on conscription can be dispatched to serve outside Russia only with their consent.

[28] *Novoye Russkoye Slovo*, 20 May 1994, p.40.

[29] A colonel of the Afghan government forces - the pilot of a MI-17 helicopter - who went over to the Talibs in June 1997, told journalists in Kabul that he was transporting armaments from Kulyab in Tajikistan to the Panjshir valley in Afghanistan. He said that at the base in Kulyab there were six Russian A-24 transport planes, that regularly carried arms and ammunition from Iran (to Afghan government forces -H.T.) (*Nezavisimaya Gazeta*, 10 June 1997, p.1).

[30] "The opposition found itself brazenly deceived. Tens of thousands of people, who believed in promises, put down their arms and returned to the homeland. But their houses were occupied by other people. They cannot find work. They have no hope for the future. President Rakhmonov carried out a brilliant operation. Having put on the toga of a peacemaker he received from international organizations millions of dollars 'to promote a peace process'. Having lured the refugees to return with his promises, he practically wiped out the external opposition, turning it into an internal one, which he did not reckon with" (*Novaya Gazeta*, No. 3 /475/, 1998, p.3).

[31] "This underscored the continuing truth of the evolution of post-Soviet states, that Russia remained the dominant determinant in inter-republic relations", commented Martha Brill Olcott, a well-known American "hand" on Central Asia (*Central Asia and the World*, p.30).

[32] "The specter of a new Turkestan - some kind of confederation of Central Asian states - has become a real prospect looming on the horizon, a prospect that could become a reality if the CIS does not succeed in overcoming its inability to function. Furthermore, such a turn of events threatens Russia with the loss of strategic allies in Central Asia, and the Central Asian states could reorient

themselves toward the Asian world once and for all", *Nezavisimaya Gazeta* declared at the time (*Nezavisimaya Gazeta*, 6 January 1993, p.1).

[33] According to the vice-speaker of the German parliament Uzbekistan "is the main partner of Germany in Central Asia" (*Zavtra*, No. 18, May 1997, p.2). Presently Germany ranks third in the volume of Uzbekistan's exports. The German Bundeswehr launched a long-term program of teaching and training Uzbek's servicemen. Among Uzbek students in German military academies there are even persons of the deputy defense minister's rank. Germany intends to establish a German military advisers service attached to the units of the armed forces of Uzbekistan (*Nezavisimaya Gazeta*, 24 April 1997, p.3).

[34] Vladimir Zhirinovsky, *O sud'bakh Rossii. Chast II. Poslednij brosok na yug* [On Russia's fate. Part II. Last dash to the south] (Moscow: RAIT, 1993), pp.27-42.

[35] Yegor Gaidar, *Postroit Rossiyu* [To build Russia] (Moscow: Evrasiya, 1994), p.26.

[36] *Rossiiskaya Gazeta*, 2 February 1994, p.1.

[37] The report on the prospects of the CIS integration, published in September 1994 by the Russian Federation Foreign Intelligence Service, confirmed the trend by noting that "there are forces in Afghanistan that seek to detach the north and create from it a Farsi-speaking state that would include Tajikistan" (*Rossiiskaya Gazeta*, 22 September 1994, p.6).

[38] See *Central Asia and the World*, pp. 61-69.

[39] George Melloan, 'Russia's "Great power" Claims Are No Joke'. *The Wall Street Journal*, 11 July 1994, p. A13.

[40] Martin Sieff, 'Zhirinovsky nuclear threats seen as reign-of-terror plan'. *The Washington Times*, 17 December 1993, p.A19.

[41] *The Washington Times*, 12 February 1994, p.A8.

[42] These are identical to the agreements Kuwait previously concluded with the United States, Britain and France.

[43] Though Russia is presently involved in arms deals with 6 Arab states of the Persian Gulf the general prospects are depressing: "One cannot see any merchants from the Orient at the defense plants /of Russia - H.T./ that have to stop one after another their conveyor belts", laments Russian politician Vasily Lapitsky, adding that "Arabs also keep silent regarding the investments into Russia's oil and gas industries" (*Nezavisimaya Gazeta*, 30 March 1994, p.4).

[44] Such an occasional distancing is mostly put on in order not to endanger Moscow's close relations with Palestine and the radical Arab countries. In reality good business relations between the two countries are expanding. The latest example is the decision by Moscow and Tel-Aviv, adopted in the Summer 1997, to jointly produce an AWACS-type (Airborne Warning and Control System) plane A-50, designed mostly for export into Third world countries. However, at the end of

1997 Tel-Aviv suspended this agreement, allegedly because of close Russian relations with Iran.

[45] *Novoye Russkoye Slovo*, 1 August 1994, p.8 (Rabin's quote is a translation from Russian).

[46] According to Sergei Glazyev, the Russian Minister for foreign economic relations, who later became the only member of the Yeltsin government to resign in protest over the shelling of the Russian parliament - as a result of the introduction of international embargoes on trade with Iran, Libya and Yugoslavia, Russia lost US$16 billion (*Izvestia*, 22 January 1993, p.1).

[47] *The Washington Post*, 4 August 1994, p. A31.

[48] Quoted in *Novoye Russkoye Slovo*, 27 July 1994, p.6.

[49] Russia and France with great reluctance voted for the said resolution which was much diluted in comparison to the initial American draft to accommodate the positions of the two countries. The zeal of the Russian government for a speedy lifting of sanctions against Iraq is quite understandable. In the Summer of 1994 Moscow signed a protocol with Iraq on trade and economic cooperation. The protocol essentially said that immediately after the lifting of sanctions Iraq would repay its US$7 billion debt to Russia. Besides, the Iraqis expressed the readiness, once the sanctions were lifted, to conclude contracts with Russian firms for construction works and deliveries of equipment and goods to the tune of US$8-10 billion (*Izvestia*, 15 September 1994, p.1). As to "Saddam's Pyongyang Gambit", as Charles Krauthammer aptly called it in reference to the North Korean blackmailing tactics vis-à-vis Washington, it vividly demonstrated to the whole world the extent of erosion of the US international clout under the Clinton administration. One would think that against the background of Iraq's experience during the "Desert Storm" campaign just a stern warning from Washington to Saddam Hussein, the type of "You strike across the border and you are out for good", would suffice. Instead, Washington started to counter Saddam's sheer bluff by playing the game on the latter's terms and deployed 40,000 American troops in Kuwait. Later on the political wise guys around the administration, like Charles Krauthammer, started to invent some new "no trespass line" within south Iraq, the crossing of which by the Iraqi   armored vehicles would invoke "serious consequences", as if the Iraq-Kuwait border itself does not represent such a clear-cut international no-trespass line.

[50] *USIS Wireless File. EUR 404.* 20.11.97.

[51] *Novoye Russkoye Slovo*, 27 July 1994, p.6.

[52] "The trade war against Russia on the nuclear power stations market, launched by the United States, has no equals, because the winner will gain potential access to a great deal of money that cannot be earned even in present highly profitable arms trade business", according to Radjab Safarov, vice-president of the Center for

coordination of Russo-Iranian programs (cited in *Nezavisimaya Gazeta*, 20 March 1997, p.5).

[53] *Segodnya*, 30 November 1996, p.3.

Chapter Seven

Russian versus American National Interests

It is banal to state that not all the national interests of Russia coincide with those of the United States. Today, as during the Cold War, there is and will be in the future some coinciding interests between the two countries, as well as parallel, divergent and antagonistic interests. At the same time, in the new times, when Russia and the United States ceased to be irreconcilable ideological opponents, gripping each other in a deadly clinch, the scope of coinciding and parallel interests of the two countries on the global arena is much wider than before. In order to discuss this issue, it is necessary to provide a paradigm of the United States national interests and of its corresponding behavior.

American national interests and Russia

In brief outline, American national interests boil down to the following:

- To stay a Number One power in the world arena.
- To have sufficient military forces prepared to fight to guarantee its security and defend its vital interests without recourse to anyone else's help.
- To contribute to the maintenance of peace and stability in the world in concert with the other members of international community and with the help of the United Nations mechanisms and procedures.
- To advance human rights everywhere and to promote American style democracy abroad.
- To protect the lives and well-being of American citizens world-wide.
- To stop the proliferation of nuclear, chemical and biological weapons.
- To help observe international treaties and agreements to which the

United States is a party and to actively participate in the workings of the United Nations and other international organizations which the United States belongs to.

- To maintain close relations with the European allies of the United States, with the European Union and to help preserve and enlarge NATO as the organization of Western security and as the chief instrument of the US influence in Europe.
- To maintain relations with Japan as a close ally and economic partner of the United States and further improve relations with China and India.
- To do everything possible to prevent the domination of a single power over the Eurasian continent.
- To treat Latin America as a de facto sphere of influence of the United States.
- To defend Israel and to promote the peaceful settlement of Middle Eastern problems.
- To ensure access to vital raw materials outside the US, especially oil; and, finally,
- To develop mutually beneficial friendly relations with all the countries of the world, including Russia and the other newly independent states, and to aid economically the underdeveloped countries that are of special interest to the United States.

Of course, this is just a brief, not exclusive, list of the multifarious national interests of the United States, but it is sufficient for the purposes of this study.[1]

As for the broad interests of the United States vis-à-vis the new Russia, they are to a great extent influenced by the legacy of an almost 50-year long active struggle of the United States against the evil empire of the Soviet Union.

First of all, the ruling elite of the United States considers the collapse of the Soviet Union its greatest victory following the end of World War II. This collapse removed from the world arena the main enemy of the United States, a superpower that international and American public opinion considered to be an equal to the United States. The elimination of the most formidable ideological and military American opponent, without a real fight, completely and absolutely satisfies one of the most vital national interests of the United States. This is why a restoration of the Soviet/ Russian empire in any form, even in the looser shape of a consolidated and newly integrated Commonwealth of 12 independent states (the CIS), goes directly against vital American interests. Washington will do everything within its capabilities and power firstly, to prevent the progressive consolidation of the CIS around Russia and secondly, to hamper the strengthening of Moscow's fiat in the CIS.

To achieve this goal, American political strategists rely heavily on the attitudes and behavior of the individual leaders of the CIS republics. In this context, the United States is interested in encouraging and nourishing separatist and nationalistic feelings in other CIS republics, especially Ukraine.

The American leadership and specialists on Russia agree that the changes that took place in the   USSR/Russia are irreversible in a sense that it is already impossible to restore the Stalin-Brezhnev regime with its ideology of global communist advancement.

According to one White House report:

The end of the Cold War fundamentally changed America's security imperatives. The central security challenge of the past half century - the threat of communist expansion - is gone.[2]

However, American leaders and experts are not sure whether Russia is moving towards a full-fledged democratic system of American or West European type or stopping at the present model of a *de facto* authoritarian regime with mixed economy, namely, if the state still reigns supreme. This is why the American leadership (Democratic and Republicans alike) continue to promote the further de-statization of Russia and the creation of a solid economic and legal base for the free enterprise system.

Pro-American and pro-Western businessmen and educated young people of Russia who believe in Western moral, social, economic values, and consider them their own, have great hopes for economic growth in Russia and other CIS republics. To cultivate and encourage such attitudes, America seeks to create a substantial group of "agents of influence" of America in the CIS republics. So far the United States has been very successful in this endeavor. Young people in the present ruling strata of Russia hold a very pro-American outlook and mentality.

As far as the more specific interests with regard to Russia are concerned, there are six overriding goals against which all other interests and actions of the United States vis-à-vis the FSU republics will evolve:

1. To preserve and expand American control over Russian foreign and domestic policies via placing pro-American agents in the top Russian leadership and making Russia ever more financially dependent on the United States and the world financial institutions under its influence.

2. To take out as many of Russia's "nuclear teeth" as possible, and render blunt those remaining.

3. To prevent the resumption of the arms race by Russia and see to it that Russia completely eliminates its chemical and bacteriological weapons in accordance with the international treaties to which Russia is a party. For the time being, minimizing, if not eliminating, the possibility of fissionable materials, biological and chemical warfare substances, nuclear, missile and related technologies spreading (illegally or legally) from Russia is a major American goal.

4. Not to allow Russia to incorporate the three Baltic republics, Finland and the East European countries into its sphere of influence and to block similar attempts by Russia in the Middle East or anywhere in the world. America will do everything possible to prevent the restoration of the Russian empire.

5. To entrench Russia as a raw material adjunct of the West, a reliable supplier of gas, oil, precious stones and metals, timber, furs and some semi-finished industrial products. To this end, America wants to keep Russia dependent on agricultural imports from the United States and other foreign countries; and

6. To prevent Russia's union with Germany, China or Japan or any of these countries.

While starting work on this study, I had in mind one more important American goal towards Russia, namely to prevent the disintegration of the Russian Federation into a multitude of small fiefdoms (whatever forms of government are introduced). This goal, in my opinion, was just a reaffirmation of American policy towards Russia dating back to the times of President Woodrow Wilson. I had in mind point 6 of his famous 14 points speech made after the Russian revolution of 1917 in which he called for the "evacuation of all Russian territory and such a settlement of all questions affecting Russia as will... [obtain] for her the independent determination of her own political development and national policy".[3] Wilson then assumed that, if such a disintegration did occur, the United States would have lost Russia to its competitors -- Japan, China, Germany,

Turkey, Iran -- who happen to be geographically closer to Russia. However, after observing US behavior towards Russia over the past six years, I reached the conclusion that the preservation of the integrity of Russia no longer constitutes an important goal for Washington. In the new world of borderless economics, trans-national banks and corporations, the presence or the absence of a central authority in the territory, which US corporations are interested in, is no longer that important for the US. America's present successful dealings with the 15 separate republics that previously constituted the USSR convinced American leaders that the smaller an entity, the easier and cheaper it is to deal with. The main thing is to be economically entrenched in key areas, such as mineral deposits, or to have a control over the relevant industries or their main enterprises. This is the new global Yankee philosophy, which is just being tested in various regions, such as the former Soviet Union.

All other interests of the United States with regard to Russia and the other newly independent states derive from the goals described above, namely:

- To fight, together with Russian authorities, international terrorism, drag trafficking and international organized crime.

- To ensure that Russia implements bilateral and multilateral arms reduction and other treaties and agreements to which it is a party.

- To gain as much as possible information relating to Russian armaments, nuclear and military technologies, the military-industrial complex etc. in order to be in better position to (a) steer Russia away from the idea of re-militarization and (b) improve and modernize on the basis of acquired knowledge America's own armaments.

- To help convert the Russian military sector over to peaceful uses. With this goal in mind, the aim is to involve Russia in cooperative ventures in space and other non-military spheres of business activity.

- To promote U.S. private business ventures in Russia, especially in the production of energy resources and raw materials.

- To tear away former Warsaw Pact countries and the three Baltic republics from the Russian sphere of influence and to irreversibly include them in the system of Western alliances and institutions.

- To work with Ukraine, Georgia, Azerbaijan and Central Asian CIS republics to diminish their dependence on Russia and to turn them, as far as possible, into a sphere of influence of the United States.

- To engage Russia in partnership relations without compromising in the process American interests.
- To gradually involve Russia in the network of financial, economic and political terms in the Pan-European and global Western-oriented institutions.
- To prevent Russia from resuming its imperial designs on Asia, Africa or Latin America, while not obstructing the development of economic and other non-political ties between Russia and the countries of the Third world.
- To ensure that Russia does not re-emerge as a counter-balance to the United States in the Middle East; and, finally,
- To strengthen and modernize US military forces which would be used in case of untoward developments in Russia and to keep US nuclear forces in a combat-ready state.[4]

These goals will determine the United States behavior towards Russia, other CIS states and the countries of Eastern-Central Europe for the next 10-15 years. No doubt the methods of implementation of these goals will change, as will the priorities, in conjunction with the transformations of the international environment, fluctuations in the moods of American public, rotation of personalities in the White House and majorities in the U.S. Congress and so forth. There will be constant debates among various interest groups of the American elite regarding a proper course towards Russia and the CIS republics, but essentially the policy of the United States lies within the aforementioned framework, with the particulars modified along the way. Because the evolution of Russia cannot be fully predicted at this stage, it is impossible to sketch in an exact picture of the nature of cooperation/competition between Russia and the United States.

As for the CIS republics, which are mostly dominated by old-style communist and semi-feudal elites, several unexpected developments and social transformations might occur, which will greatly influence Washington's policies vis-à-vis these states.

Does Russia have its own foreign policy?

It is clear that, at least for a decade, Russia is likely to remain weak, immersed mainly in the problems of its internal economic and political stabilization, ethnic strife and regional insubordination, while its political elite will be consolidating its grip on society, after emerging from a dozen years of the so-called *perestroika*, "reforms" and other experiments.

Ethnic Russian nationalism is also likely to grow putting its imprimatur on the conduct of foreign policy. Under the spell of nationalist and conservative forces, Russian foreign policy goals will be adjusted to a greater or lesser extent, depending on the balance of internal forces. However, due to the total poverty of Russia and the collapse of all "plans" to invigorate Russian industry and agriculture, Russian foreign policy will remain totally subservient to Washington, as was the case during the last six years since the demise of the Soviet Union. Actually, the terms of the Founding Act, which Russia finally got by pleading with the United States over NATO's expansion eastward, are highly humiliating for Russia. This was partly the outcome of negotiations carried out by Andrei Kozyrev, who up until 5 January 1996 was Russian Foreign Minister and universally considered as a sycophant of the United States. While he was dismissed by the President, allegedly as a concession to Russian public opinion, hardly anything has changed under the new Minister, Primakov, except, perhaps, for the words used. No Russian leadership can presently switch to a confrontation with the United States, or even to a policy of mild resistance against its undesirable actions.

Even the craziest Russian leaders cannot afford any real confrontation with the United States, though they can act in an unfriendly, uncompromising way verbally, symbolically, in order to gain some concessions from America, or to make it more difficult for Washington to continue to conduct Russian foreign policy. (Russia might elect this kind of president some time in the future, but the chances of such an outcome are not very great.)

As everybody knows, a policy of bluff from a position of weakness worked well with respect to the United States in the time of Khrushchev. However nowadays, after the ignominy of the Chechen military campaign and the open admission by the Russian authorities of the pitiful state of the Russian armed forces, such a course of action (bluff) does not seem open to the Kremlin.[5]

In view of the tectonic character of social transformation that accompanied the breakdown of the Soviet Union and the emergence of 15 independent states, it would be naive to think that American aid allocated to Russia over the past six years to the tune of US$7.5 billion (plus US$1.2

billion authorized by the U.S. Congress in accordance with the Nunn-Lugar Cooperative Threat Reduction program to help Russia, Belarus, Kazakhstan and Ukraine to dismantle nuclear missiles) can be considered an effective leverage to steer Russia onto the path to democracy. Even if one adds about US$40 billions formally designated to Russia by other countries of the world and international financial institutions (with the substantial participation of Washington in obtaining this aid), such sums are minuscule in comparison to the Herculean chores of social, economic, infrastructural, psychological transformation and the ecological clean-up facing the people of a huge country, such as Russia, which is groping for a new road of development. One has also to proceed from the fact that quite a substantial part of the money allocated has been embezzled in Russia and/or returned to the donor countries through purchases of their services or commodities.

Thus the evolution of Russia so far, purportedly towards a freer and happier society, has not been the result of some pressure or "oiling" from the outside, as the cases of post Second World War Japan or Germany might be viewed, but instead is the consequence of the efforts of *Rossiyans*. The people of Russia are stumbling and groping in a political semi-darkness of a fractured society, incapacitated by the collapse of industry and agriculture, for what they think might be a better future for their grandchildren (as the great majority of Russian adults do not expect to live to see that radiant future themselves).[6]

So, following the break-up of the Soviet Union, Russia has continued to meekly follow the United States in the international arena. It was not because Russia was, so to say, bribed or lured into cooperating, but because there was no other way for her to behave.

The positions of Russian government became virtually identical to those of the United States on the United Nations, on the Middle East, South-East Asia (Cambodia) and North-East Asia (North Korea) and on arms control, arms reduction and non-proliferation.

Such a course was predetermined by a number of factors.

As a result of Mikhail Gorbachev's desire, when the Soviet Union was still alive but already hardly kicking, to obtain a *peredyshka* (respite) from the intolerable burden of the Cold war, which the Soviet Union started but did not have the guts to win. The only difference between the Gorbachev "era" and Yeltsin's rule is that during the latter, Russian foreign policy became slightly more honest in openly admitting US guidance in comparison to the cunning, scheming, manoeuvering of "smart Alec" Gorbachev. "Slightly more", but not entirely, because, as it is clear to anybody following Russian politics, Yeltsin's pledge before the audience of the U.S. Congress in June 1992: "There will be no more lies – ever" has still not been fulfilled.

The break-up of the Soviet Union and the emergence of an independent Russia, added a number of other factors to the "de-nationalized" foreign policy. These include:

- the Russian leadership's tendency to focus upon internal problems (mainly on the division among themselves of the former "all people's" property) and on a political struggle at the top;
- the realization by the powers that be of their impotence on the world stage; and
- the assumption that, since a new Russia is striving to create democracy, it is a good idea to follow the United States' lead, because a "democratic Russia" that renounced a class struggle and a quest for an overseas empire and released from its grip not only its reluctant allies, but even its own "Union brothers", cannot, by definition, pursue any goals that would substantially differ from those of the great American democracy that supports Russian democrats in their confrontation with the forces of the old regime. As Russia has been weakened by internal turmoil and economic troubles, it will be satisfied with the de facto role of a junior partner of the United States in the international arena, while still formally remaining a nuclear superpower.

The euphoria, festival of brotherly love, friendship and universal blissfulness was undercut by a growing sense of self-awareness and uneasiness on the part of the masses concerning the totally submissive foreign policy behavior of Russia. Another factor was the temporary weakening of influence in the Russian politics of the democrats/liberal intellectuals, who represent a distinctively pro-American school of thought and who initially played an important role in government affairs in Russia. (Since 1997 they have been back on top again.) The undermining of their positions was mainly the result of their total corruption, when in power, and their failure to deliver on constant solemn promises of forthcoming economic improvement. It was also the result of a popular sentiment against their pliant behavior on the international stage.

Next is the general disillusionment in the United States, because of its unwillingness to do something really substantive to help Russia and to somehow reward her for innumerable actions that the majority of Russians considered one-sided concessions to the West. American economic aid was hardly felt by average Russians who firmly believe (not without grounds) that the bulk of the aid has simply been plundered by the high officials of the Russian government acting in conjunction with American advisers and consultants. At the same time, many in Russia have begun to feel that Washington is manipulating Russian democratic leaders in the pursuit of its own selfish interests.[7]

One more reason for the disappointment with US behavior vis-à-vis Russia was formulated by a group of essentially pro-American Russian intellectuals on the eve of Helsinki summit between Clinton and Yeltsin. They stated:

The United States, while encouraging in every possible way reforms, the reduction of the military might of Russia and arms control agreements, demonstrates by each step, with amazing shamelessness, that the weak are not respected and can safely be ignored.[8]

One can add to these reasons the rather intemperate, loose personal behavior of Western visitors (businessmen, consultants, etc., invariably classed by a man in the street as "Americans") in Moscow and other Russian cities, and their political brazenness, when any petty clerk arriving to Moscow would only be satisfied with meeting at least the Premier.

A sobering phenomenon was also the realization that, despite unprecedented Russian new openness, the United States was not going to lower its guards against Russia or to stop snooping (symbolized by American subs prowling in Russian territorial waters and the intensified activities of the CIA and DIA in Russia). Then there was the incessant pressure of various groups of American officials coming to Russia to obtain more and more information of a confidential nature, and seeking access to facilities that in any other country are usually closed to visitors, even from the friendliest of foreign nations.

The majority of Russian intellectuals together with certain politicians and businessmen have reached the conclusion that the immediate goal of the United States business circles is to turn Russia into a Third world country - a supplier of raw materials. This position is confirmed by the pattern of American investments in Russia.

Every Russian adult knows from his schoolbook texts that "the Great October Socialist Revolution" was performed in Russia under the leadership of Bolsheviks in order to prevent Russia sliding into a role of an agricultural as well as raw-materials adjunct of the "imperialist countries". It became absolutely clear, after 70 years plus of Bolshevik rule, that Russia was incapable of performing the first of these two functions - that of a supplier of agricultural goods to the world market - a role it successfully played under the Tsars. So it is infuriating to many Russians that the "American saviors" are intent on perpetuating for Russia the only demeaning function the Bolsheviks left for it, that of a supplier of raw materials.

But the real eye openers for Moscow were the realization that the government of the United States does not share Moscow's attitude to the "near abroad", namely as a legitimate sphere of Russian concern and interest, as well as Washington's rude interference in the FSU's deal with India to sell it cryogenic rocket engines. When Kozyrev tried to explain the importance of that deal to US Secretary of State Christopher, he treated Kozyrev like an errand boy, remarking: "Andrei, you've got to do better".[9] Other instances include the Clinton administration's attempts to prevent the sale of three Russian military submarines to Iran, to disrupt a very profitable Russian deal to build light water atomic power reactors in Iran[10] and the refusal by the United States to concede some part of its huge international arms market to Russia.

Violent and growing right and left wing opposition converged in the Russian Front for National Salvation which branded the Yeltsin government "an occupation regime", a puppet of the United States and Western financial sharks.

Initially Yeltsin and his lieutenants dismissed all such insinuations as a delusions of the "lunatic fringe". But after the shock of the December 1993 parliamentary election results, the President had to reassess the situation. This was the time when Russian foreign policy started to come out from under the American spell (under the cover of Russia's populist nationalists).

In the spring of 1994, a major debate began in Moscow regarding the essence and direction of Russian foreign policy. The consensus that emerged was that Russia in no way should be a junior partner of the United States, only an equal partner. It appeared that serene relationships between the two countries over the previous two years were a kind of a childish delusion on both sides, which was dubbed in the Russian media as the "foreign policy romanticism", "honeymooning", "infantile pro-Americanism" of Russia, etc.

It also dawned on Russia's policy-makers that *Rossiya* has a set of national interests quite different from those of the United States and it has to pursue these interests independently and to advance them "in an assertive and, where necessary, tough manner".[11]

In seeking to shift towards a more independent foreign policy, Russia over-emphasized the need for a world condominium of "the two equal partners". For instance, Kozyrev claimed that the strategic partnership between Russia and the United States was not premature, as Brzezinski and several other American politicians and scholars asserted, but late in coming! He stated:

Russia and the United States together with other countries have to tackle two inter-related problems. First, the mutual formation of a strategic partnership, reinforced by the corresponding institutions and resources and, second, the need to immediately fine tune a mechanism for the coordination of approaches towards the most important international problems.[12]

At the end of 1995 and during the first half of 1996 the impression was that a new Russian foreign policy - more independent, more assertive, more nationalistic - was emerging. But this was an illusion fostered by some militant, uncompromising nationalistic pronouncements on foreign policy issues in the new Russian Duma, elected at the end of 1995 as well as by President Yeltsin himself during his re-election campaign of 1996. Soon after the elections, it became clear that all these forceful, angry speeches were simply a means of attracting votes. No real change had occurred. After President Yeltsin finally started to function (after several months of post-operation rest) it transpired that, despite his occasional "tough talk" against NATO and the criticism of American policy, Moscow's foreign policy line has remained fairly constant: obedience to the American line. The Duma, elected in December 1995, where the forces of official opposition predominate, did not really possess the power to influence the course of Presidential foreign policy, apart from blocking the ratification of particular international treaties. The Russian Constitution, adopted in 1993, gives absolute power to the President in this regard.

As for the Russian masses, their economic problems and the constant decline in their living conditions make the majority of people totally indifferent to foreign policy problems, as Russians are primarily concerned with the daily struggle for survival.

So foreign policy, as in Soviet times, is formed by a very narrow circle of members of the ruling establishment, a group that essentially follows Washington's line.

For Russia, evidently, now and for the immediate future "there is simply no alternative to genuine partnership" with the United States.[13] Whatever Russian diplomatic bravura might be, Russia is too weak and too dependent on friendly and essentially tranquil international environment for its social progress and its very survival, to be able to confront the United States, on whose good will external support largely depends.

Russia, definitely, will not follow in the American footsteps on every international issue. However, in the final analysis, if pressed hard by Washington, it will yield on most issues, with almost no exception.

On certain issues, Russia will cooperate with the United States grudgingly, making a lot of noise and remonstration, but it will not quarrel with America, because there is really no alternative. All benefits for Russia, such as postponing debt re-payments, receiving foreign credits from partners and international financial institutions, obtaining other forms of aid and business counsel in a multitude of ways, insignificant as each act of assistance might be, taken individually, form a network of relationships that it would be suicidal for Russia to break. So Russia for the time being will have to go strategically alongside the United States and the West in general, though tactically it might sometimes wish to demonstrate its independence.

As far as the United States is concerned, its general tactical line seems to be to keep Russia peaceful, non-belligerent, in order to help Russia de-militarize and continue to play by the established international rules.

The best summing up of America's current public "task" vis-à-vis Russia was made by the late US President Nixon, who said:

No single factor will have a greater impact on the world in this century than whether political and economic freedom takes root and thrives in Russia and the other former Communist nations. Today's generation of American leaders will be judged primarily on whether they did everything possible to bring about this outcome. If they fail, the cost to their successors will be unimaginably high.[14]

It is a correct assumption on the US part that if solid democratic institutions, decentralization and private property are put in place in

Russia, the better the chances are for Russia's non-belligerent behavior and her constructive cooperation with the United States and the rest of the world. However, it is absolutely wrong for the United States to equate the rise and fall of political personalities in the Russian establishment with either the increase or decrease in the prospects of democracy in Russia. She is still ruled by communists - reformed and unreformed, but the US media arbitrarily and very often wrongly divide these communists into "true democrats" and "liberals", on the one hand, and "authoritarians" and "imperialists", on the other, using for such a division criteria that work in a US context but which are unsuitable in the present Russian situation.[15] Thus myths are created, which are then taken as "facts" by American politicians and the general public.

For example, Yeltsin, a dyed in the wool communist and *apparatchik*, a man bent on the use of authoritarian methods in politics, was made by the US media to appear as an exemplary democrat, while a hundred unscrupulous persons in the Russian establishment of the Gaidar-Chubais brand, that are totally rejected by the overwhelming majority of *Rossiyans* of every persuasion (because of their absolute contempt for the common man), are presented as genuine exponents of Russian public opinion and almost as "saviors of Russian democracy". The American tendency to equate democracy with the specific US way of life is also not very helpful for a real understanding of the processes that are now going on in Russia.

At the same time, it is perfectly clear that, despite all the present disabilities of Russia, Washington considers it as still too strong to be 100% sure about Moscow's "proper" conduct and the impossibility of Russia's reversion to some old ways of behavior in the international arena. Therefore, as a precaution against such an eventuality, Washington, while helping Russia to develop along a democratic path, is not averse to utilizing any opportunities, as they arise, to undercut Russia strategically and militarily. As far as one can judge, the American establishment considers the best option for such tactics, the use of the FSU republics in some ingenious ways as counterweights to Russia.

It is also quite obvious that the behavior of Russia in the post-Soviet space to a significant extent influences decisions by Washington, concerning its policies towards Russia, while the general precepts of the US grand strategy towards Russia are developed on the basis of an assessment of the overall socio-economic situation in Russia and the progress of its reforms.

Converging interests

Despite the end of the horrifying Soviet Union, the liquidation of the ideological underpinnings of the Russian-American conflict and all the lip service on both sides to "strategic partnership" as the essence of new American-Russian interaction, there are surprisingly few issues or spheres of global politics on which Russian and American national interests coincide or come close.

The main explanation for this is that both countries are great powers, occupying important places in the global geopolitical space. This is why competition between them continues, even though it is no longer of an ideological nature; instead it represents pure great power rivalry. However, one side competes with a huge handicap. The United States also competes with China, on the one hand, and Japan, on the other. Despite the fact that the Cold War has supposedly been "successfully overcome", Russian-American relations are still largely determined by the images, superstitions, fears and emotions of the Cold War, which are deeply ingrained in the psyche of the ruling elites and among the general population of both countries.[16] As a result, every case of friction between Russia and the United States and every slight misunderstanding and differences of opinion are blown out of all proportion by the sensation-hungry media or politicians on both sides who immediately cry "the Cold War has started up again". This is perpetuating the Cold War game.

The interests of the American and the Russian governments converge in the area of conversion of the military industries of Russia to peaceful production. The readiness of the US government and the US Congress to involve Russian industries in space projects and the building of a new International Space Station (thereby saving Russian facilities and their personnel) is a good example of genuine American help in the reconstruction of Russia. The cooperation of the United States and Russia in the building of a space station has encouraged active cooperation in other areas, such as the field of aeronautical sciences. With US help, Russia, as is well known, also received access to the international launch services market.

The Russian government has been entertaining the hope that the new more cordial relations between Russia and the United States might facilitate joint Russian-American research and the development of anti-missile defense. But this was a naive dream.

As early as the beginning of 1992, America's anti-missile "Star Wars" program worked out a plan to take advantage of the old Soviet Union by acquiring some of its most advanced technologies and hiring about a thousand of its scientists and engineers.

There have also been some tentative moves to explore joint efforts in ABM defense, such as setting up a joint center to provide early warning of a ballistic missile attack as well as high-level consultations on a system of Global Protection Against Limited Strikes (GPALS) and theater missile defenses (TMD).

But all of a sudden on 29 January 1992, President Yeltsin put forward a concrete proposal on cooperation and the use of GPALS.[17] This was too bold a move to be accepted by the American defense community. Nevertheless, three joint working groups were set up to evaluate

- the concept and functions of a global system of ABM defense,
- R&D and testing possibilities and other aspects of technological cooperation, and
- the ways and means to strengthen non-proliferation.

A senior joint group to review and guide their work was also established.

The Russian leaders in offering to join the GPALS project hoped to save an important sector of its military-industrial complex by receiving American financial support for its R&D and even for some of its production facilities. They reckoned that participation in such a grand project would diminish the inevitable growth of unemployment in Russia and thus also help to generate support for the Russian leadership.

There were also some Military-Industrial Complex (MIC) managers, arms designers, Generals and even arms controllers (!) in Russia who considered Russian-American cooperation in the field of military technology a temporary sham which was needed simply to help Russia to revamp and strengthen its MIC on a new scientific and technological base.

However, America entertained different hopes in relation to Yeltsin's proposal. For Washington, Moscow's initiative signaled, first of all, Russia's readiness to revise the 1972 ABM Treaty, which was a welcome turn to the Bush administration, although Moscow's experts did not realize this at the time. However, while both sides were manoeuvering around the idea of space defense cooperation, the US administration changed and President Clinton rejected GPALS and curtailed work on the SDI. As a consequence, the brilliant idea that both countries could develop a joint space defense system died a natural death.[18]

At the Russian-US summit in Moscow in May 1995, President Clinton received the okay from President Yeltsin to deploy theater missile defenses, despite the fact that given modern technology such a system might have some strategic defense capability. However, in the spirit of partnership, "the presidents undertook to promote reciprocal openness in each other's activities in the TMD systems and in the exchange of corresponding information".[19]

It is too early to predict how the TMD project will evolve. There are a number of American senators urging the US President to avoid agreements with Russia that might constrain the TMD development in any way. As Professor Jack Ruina, a world-renowned American expert on the subject, states, all these senators "would like to have the ABM Treaty ignored completely".[20] At the same time, whereas the United States faces no theater ballistic missile threat to its territory, the Russians do. So the Washington initiative, opening the way for the TMD deployment by both countries, might, in the final analysis, be more beneficial to Russia than the United States, especially as TMD will be able to cope with the missile threat from the American nuclear-capable Allies, such as Britain and France, because their missiles are actually theater missiles in the context of appropriate Russian-American definitions.

Nevertheless, the Russian military are very suspicious that R&D in TMD is actually used by the United States for the development of strategic defense. The increased pressure of influential Republican senators favoring US withdrawal from the 1972 ABM Treaty and the Joint US-Russian Statement on the ABM Treaty adopted at the summit meeting in Helsinki in March 1997 confirms the apprehensions of many Russians.[21] While formally "recognizing the fundamental significance of the ABM Treaty"[22] the statement actually blurred the distinction between strategic and non-strategic ballistic missile defenses.[23]

Both countries have suspended nuclear weapons tests and together with other members of the official five-nation "nuclear club" joined the comprehensive ("zero yield") Test ban treaty which was overwhelmingly endorsed at the United Nations in New York on 10 September 1996.[24] America and Russia also intend to make a very serious effort to ban the production of fissile materials for nuclear weapons purposes.

Russian and American efforts were instrumental in persuading the Non-

Proliferation Treaty (NPT) review conference in the spring of 1995 to extend the NPT unconditionally and indefinitely.[25] The interests of both countries are undoubtedly converging on the issues of non-proliferation of nuclear, chemical and biological weapons. On these problems, representatives of both countries work hand in glove in drawing up bilateral contacts and in international fora. In the Spring of 1994, for instance, Russia and the United States agreed to permit each other to inspect the facilities where plutonium triggers from dismantled nuclear warheads are stored. The agreement removed one of the thorniest issues that had divided the two countries, namely how to reduce their nuclear arsenals. President Yeltsin also gave his okay for Russia to join the Missile Technology Control Regime (MTCR).[26]

The converging interests of both countries in nuclear non-proliferation helped persuade Ukraine to agree to become a non-nuclear nation. There are no disagreements in principle between the US and Russia regarding the necessity to make North Korea abide by the norms of Non-Proliferation Treaty which it signed, although there are differences regarding tactics in this case, as we saw above.

The national interests of the United States and Russia coincide on the issue of reducing nuclear arms to the ceilings established by the START I Treaty. Both countries began to implement the requirements of the START I Treaty and the parallel unilateral initiatives (outside the framework of the treaties) by dismantling their nuclear warheads. The United States has been very helpful in providing Russia with the equipment necessary for the safe and secure dismantling (SSD) of nuclear weapons in accordance with its Cooperative Threat Reduction (CTR) program. This program provides technical and expert assistance regarding the dismantling and destruction of nuclear, chemical and other weapons of mass destruction in the ex-USSR. Since its initiation in 1991, this program has concentrated on Ukraine, Belarus and Kazakhstan. Lately, the CTR program has been pursued in Russia as well. The U.S. Department of Energy in conjunction with the personnel of American nuclear laboratories is increasing the level of cooperation with the relevant agencies of Russia regarding safe storage, transportation and the stock-taking of weapons-grade nuclear materials.[27] At the end of 1995, practical projects were carried out at 26 storage facilities in the ex-USSR. By his directive of 28 September 1995, the US President authorized the accelerated implementation of the plan aimed at drastically increasing the safety of nuclear materials stored in the territory of Russia and the three other republics of the former USSR.

In a good-will gesture, the United States agreed to buy 500 tons of highly enriched uranium which would be obtained as a result of the destruction of nuclear warheads in the FSU over the next twenty years.[28]

At the May 1995 summit in Moscow both leaders reconfirmed their commitment to work together to ensure that the nuclear materials coming out of the dismantled nuclear weapons are properly secured and accounted for.

In January 1996, the US Senate ratified the START II Treaty.[29] There is a general feeling in the Russian Duma that the conditions of START II put Russia in an inferior position vis-à-vis the United States, which makes the ratification of the Treaty by the Russian parliament not an assured outcome, especially given NATO's enlargement.

In order to edge the Russian parliament towards ratification of START II, President Clinton offered and President Yeltsin agreed in Helsinki to start negotiations on START III immediately after START II comes into force. The joint statement on the parameters of future reductions in nuclear forces envisages the establishment by 31 December 2007 of lower levels of 2,000-2,500 strategic warheads for each of the parties. To coax the Duma, President Clinton agreed to extend the deadline for the elimination of strategic nuclear delivery vehicles under the START II Treaty until 31 December 2007. Nevertheless, in accordance with the Helsinki agreement, Russia by 31 December 2003 has to deactivate all strategic nuclear delivery vehicles, which will be eliminated under the Treaty, by removing their nuclear re-entry vehicles or taking other steps. At the same time, at later negotiations the deadline for the reduction in the number of nuclear warheads, carried by the US Minuteman III ICBMs with multiple warheads, was moved to 31 December 2007. Such flagrant inequality in the procedures will assuredly add in the Russian Duma many more "nays" to those voting against the ratification of START II. While demonstrating his "good will", President Clinton, *inter alia*, annulled the consent given by the US Senate to ratify the START II Treaty. Instead, it ought to be submitted again to the US Senate in a new form *after* the Russian Duma approves it, if it ever does.

Given the actual collapse of the Russian regular army, when nuclear weapons became the sole effective Russian deterrent, President Yeltsin's agreement to cut strategic nuclear arsenal of Russia by a further 30-45% (in comparison to the levels, envisaged by the START II) is incomprehensible. It is also very difficult to evaluate whether the US proposal about such deep cuts is a sincere one or represents instead just a new trick to make Russia execute her START II Treaty obligations. For this reason the proposed negotiations for further cuts might drag on indefinitely.

There is a strong suspicion among Russian experts that the new American proposal on still bigger cuts in strategic weaponry on a pure *bilateral basis* is simply an attempt to remove as many nuclear teeth of the "Russian bear" as possible, or, at least, to bring them down to such a level that any of the six systems of the so-called tactical (theater) missile defense, which are currently being developed in the US, could easily cope with such a "potential threat", especially if deployed in a country or countries bordering Russia. Such suspicion involuntarily creeps into the minds of Russian specialists when they assess the American proposals against the background of frantic Washington activity to enlarge NATO.[30]

Media reports about the US Joint Chiefs of Staff allegedly discussing an option of *unilateral* cuts in American strategic nuclear weapons by an even bigger percentage, than the one suggested by President Clinton in his proposal to Yeltsin in Helsinki, look very fishy especially when they are accompanied by reports that, if Russia does not ratify START II, the US will have to spend an additional US$10 billion to meet its strategic defense needs.[31]

The 1993 Convention on the Prohibition of Chemical Weapons, signed by more than 120 countries, requires the total destruction of such weapons within 10 years; whilst the 1990 bilateral Soviet-US Agreement on Destruction and Non-Production of Chemical Weapons stipulates the destruction of 95% of chemical arsenals on both sides by the year 2004. However, Russia does not seem to have the money and facilities to implement these agreements (i.e. the destruction of 40,000 tons of chemical weapons). Numerous reports have appeared in both the Russian and Western press regarding Moscow's attempt to continue manufacturing certain types of chemical weapons (i.e. binary weapons)[32] and its desire to hide its stockpiles, and these reports reveal that the best traditions of Soviet behavior have yet to disappear.[33]

A leading expert in the field, Lev Fyodorov, a doctor of chemical science and a member of the New York Academy of Sciences, declared in his book *Undeclared Chemical Warfare in Russia* that despite at least 120,000 tons of poisonous substances being destroyed between the 1930s-80s, the problem of chemical weapons destruction is far from solved. Summing up his conclusions, Fyodorov notes:

1. The Russian Military chemical complex refuses to provide information to society about its past activities in the military chemical field and tries to sustain the potential for chemical attack in a state of mobilized readiness.
2. In defiance of existing laws, ecological and medical problems of chemical weapons continue to remain classified.
3. The absence of trust between the authorities and the population of Russia is a major obstacle to chemical disarmament.
4. Occurrences of chemical terrorism in everyday life are the direct and inevitable consequence of widespread chemical terrorism by the state, the existence of chemical weapons in abeyance and the continuation of secrecy surrounding this problem.
5. No guarantees exist that the state has renounced its preparations for chemical warfare; and
6. Neither the legislative, nor executive powers are psychologically prepared for chemical disarmament.[34]

While the Chemical weapons convention came into force in the Spring of 1997, the Russian parliament (Duma) ratified it only on 31 October 1997. However, on 15 April 1997, the Duma adopted a special Federal Law "On the Destruction of Chemical Weapons" which was signed by the President and came into effect on 2 May 1997. A special Federal program for the liquidation of chemical weapons has been worked out, detailing the concrete steps to be taken. According to this decree, all chemical weapons in Russia will be destroyed in the period 1998-2005.[35]

The West is highly suspicious about Russia's fulfillment of the clauses of the 1972 Convention on the Prohibition of the Development, Production and Stockpiling of Bacteriological (Biological) and Toxin Weapons and on Their Destruction, which requires not only the liquidation of such weapons but also the cessation of all research with offensive biological agents.[36] Russian official explanations were found wanting by the West and its experts. Such suspicions, as is well known, led to the adoption by the U.S. Senate of the Helms amendment to the foreign aid authorization act prohibiting financial aid to Russia (other than humanitarian assistance) "unless the President has certified annually to the Congress in advance of the obligation or expenditure of such funds that Russia has demonstrated a commitment to comply with the Convention on the Prohibition of the Development, Production and Stockpiling of Bacteriological (Biological) and Toxin Weapons...". The same rule will apply to the Convention on the prohibition of Chemical Weapons.[37] Such behavior on Moscow's part has failed to promote "openness and mutual trust" as claimed by American and Russian summit communiqués. Evidently, strategic partners are not the ones who hide daggers behind their backs.

Taking into account the Russian military's apprehension and suspicion of the United States, a notion deeply ingrained in the psyche of military and civilian leaders, who believe that it is no crime to outwit "the imperialists", Russia's switch from deceit at any price to a really open house, is unlikely to occur quickly. This situation, regretfully, justifies the precautions Americans take when dealing with Russia on such matters.

On top of that, there is an increasing fear on the US side that Russian control over Russian nuclear, chemical, as well as biological warfare stockpiles, if any, is crumbling, and so this might eventually lead to the transfer of such materials to the rogue states of the world, despite the Kremlin's best intentions. Thus weapons grade uranium and plutonium allegedly coming from Russia, found in Germany in the Summer of 1994, increased Western anxiety and convinced some that the situation is getting out of hand, especially given the strong positions of the ruthless Russian Mafia in the administrative structure of Russia.[38]

On 30 June 1997, the US Department of Commerce in accordance with its Enhanced Proliferation Control Initiative added to its list of "entities of concern", several Russian nuclear research laboratories (Arzamas-16, Chelyabinsk-70 and several others), ostensibly identified with weapons proliferation. Since that date, any export shipment to these centers requires a special US license because "there is an unacceptable risk of diversion to activities related to nuclear, chemical or biological weapons or missile proliferation".[39] The Russian Foreign Ministry stated that this was evidence of the "recurrence of old thinking of the Cold war period and of a deceased COCOM", and added that a "policy of double standards operated, which Russia categorically rejects".[40]

Theoretically, fighting growing international crime syndicates (including illegal drug and weapons trade) is also one of the biggest areas of coinciding interests between Russia and the United States. However, the fact is that global partnership between the main crime clans of the world (the Sicilian and US Mafias, Colombian drug cartels, Japanese Yakuza, the Chinese Triads and Russian *Vorami v zakone* (thieves in law) develops at a much faster pace and more efficiently than the "pragmatic partnership" between the West and the East in the sphere of fighting criminals.

Hence, while the interests of the United States and Russia concerning various matters, described above, formally coincide, in reality Russia either deliberately equivocates on the implementation of its international obligations, or does not have financial and physical possibilities to carry them out. Such a situation, naturally does not facilitate a true partnership on such matters between the two countries.

Diverging interests

In most other spheres of US - Russian interaction, the national interests of the two countries tend to diverge, not converge. By this, I do not mean that there are no instances of convergence or that there is no conflict between the interests of the United States and those of the Russian Federation, not to speak about some head-on collision. Instead, both countries as great powers have their particular interests that do not coincide. Situations exist and will arise, when one of the sides, in trying to fulfill its national interest, might actually infringe the lawful interest of the other, either consciously or inadvertently. Since such interests are not confrontational, any friction might be resolved through compromise.

If one takes the region of Europe as an example, Russia, as well as the United States, would like to see it open, stable, democratic, economically integrating and collectively guarding its security through the existing and developing mechanisms. Furthermore, the United States would not like to be "squeezed" out of Europe just because the latter's need for American military protection against the "Russian bear" disappeared with the end of the Cold War. Russia, on the other hand, would like to be included in integrating Europe to a much greater degree than is currently the case.

Nevertheless, the United States (together with its allies) still considers NATO an instrument of essentially Western security, despite all the recent addenda to the original NATO structure, such as the NACC and the PfP, which were geared towards bridging the gap between the West and East of Europe and beyond it. After some hesitation, Russia joined the NACC (together with the majority of other FSU republics and Central and East Europe) and on 15 May 1995, she also joined the PfP by accepting the Russian Individual Partnership Program under the PfP and the document "Areas for Pursuance of a Broad Enhanced NATO-Russia Dialogue and

Cooperation". It is difficult to assess whether Russia's participation in these NATO structures improved or worsened its position in dealing with countries of the East. In Japan, such a Russian step was welcome, because Japan itself closely cooperates with NATO, but China, probably, became suspicious. However, Russia's signing of the Founding Act and the creation of Russia-NATO Permanent Council undoubtedly limited the possibility of Russian-Chinese joint actions to counter US intrigues in Asia.

Having gained nothing in the West through the signing of the Founding Act, Russia also lost its freedom of diplomatic manoeuver in the East. Creating such a situation for Russia was definitely one of the goals of American diplomacy.

Russia would prefer to see the basis for European security built around the Organization on Security and Cooperation in Europe. To this effect, Moscow proposed far-reaching reforms. These included, first of all, the creation of an executive body, a Security Council of sorts within the framework of the OSCE. Such a body had to be made up of representatives of these countries, including Russia, which have an active interest in solving the most urgent problems facing Europe. Such a body would have made it possible to expeditiously fashion appropriate responses to daunting political challenges that so frequently arise at present.

The United States and its Allies prefer to rely on NATO and to make it the main bulwark of European security order. With the evident intention of Washington to build European security around NATO, the OSCE from 1997 onwards will evidently play a secondary role in pan-European security matters.

The disagreements between Russia and the United States on this score were not merely casual and tactical, but essential and strategic. All said and done, the United States is still hedging its bets against a possible re-emergence of "Russian imperialism".[41] It also considers NATO, the last most effective leverage of American foreign policy in Europe and hence America is eager to increase such a leverage, not to diminish it.

Even among the core NATO group, there are growing contradictions generated, *inter alia*, by the gradual military withdrawal of the United States from Europe, which, in turn, increases national rivalry among the leading European members of NATO and produces different perspectives regarding politico-military-economic trends in Europe and beyond. Washington vehemently opposes the movement to "Europeanize" NATO, led by France, though in the long-term it will be forced to forgo some of its present positions in Europe and in NATO Command. Such a perspective explains the US desire to expand NATO, by incorporating into the bloc the states that *ipso facto* are very dependent on America. A much more "Europeanized" NATO is definitely in the national interests of Russia (so far as the bloc exists). But such niceties are beyond the comprehension of the present rulers of Russia.

The Balkans do represent an area of contention, not only between the United States and Russia. However, Russian "affinity" with the Serbs has been greatly exaggerated in the U.S. media. The Bosnian situation was a godsend for Russia and it gave her a role on Western councils trying to resolve the problem. Generally speaking, it is impossible for anyone to fence Russia off from the situation in the Balkans. The problems throughout the region are directly relevant to Russia's vital interests, especially its security.

Within this general context, Russian-American interaction will ensue, but this cannot be referred to as competition, because, as we stressed earlier, all the trump cards in the present situation are not in Russia's hands. The only advantage Russia has is that it is partially a European country, historically immersed in European culture, though for a time it was alienated from Europe by the Bolshevik regime. With social and economic stabilization in Russia and greater interaction between Russia and the European Union, Russia's influence in Europe is likely to grow, while America's role will diminish. But this is a long-term perspective, and it is dependent on the way Russia's transformation evolves. In the short-term, despite possible greater Russian involvement in established European institutions, Russia will still be on the sidelines of European political life, while its nuclear arsenal will continue to loom menacingly over Europe.

In Asia, there might be greater interaction between Russia and the United States, first and foremost via the Siberian-Alaskan link. But for this connection to develop, one has to wait for more favorable conditions for investment in Russia and for the creation of a more amplified infrastructure in Siberia and the Far East. The possibilities for mutually beneficial business and commerce across the Pacific between Russia and the United States are theoretically very great, but in reality everything is still in an embryonic state.

The main problem facing the region will be a balance of power politics in the quadrangle Russia-Japan-China-the United States. The interests of

Russia and the United States vis-à-vis the two other players diverge considerably. The United States is extremely sensitive about Japan's ties with Russia. Improved understanding, to put it mildly, of Russia by Japan (and vice versa) will worry the United States, whatever its leaders might say right now. It might bring about the liquidation of American bases in Japan (an outcome probably unthinkable now for the American strategists, in the same way an American military presence in the Philippines was "unthinkable" earlier) and lead to some other radical changes in the geopolitical situation in the region.

"The China card", to use a familiar expression, will be played vigorously by the other three powers, though in fact in the very short-term, it will be China that becomes a keeper of the bank in the Pacific. As was shown above, a weak Russia is extremely interested in maintaining an excellent rapport with China on all issues, except a peaceful Chinese advance into Russian Siberia and the Central Asia states.

The United States will try to pull China closer to itself and away from Russia using the tremendous leverage of American-Chinese trade, growing US investments in China and other "carrots", as well as Moscow's stupidity in formally attaching itself to NATO. This is a very complex and murky strategic problem which we will explore in greater depth later.

However, Russian-American competition for Chinese allegiance has not impeded joint ventures with American, Chinese and Japanese capital in the Russian Far East and Siberia, as at the moment, the conditions there are very favorable for foreign business.

The Latin American continent is a natural American sphere and Russia is unlikely to resume political-military penetration into America's "underbelly", as was the case with Chile, Nicaragua, Salvador and, of course, Cuba, during the Soviet era, though Russia will definitely expand its commercial ties with Latin American nations. While the Monroe Doctrine of 1823 was heavily influenced by Washington's concerns over the very bold moves of Russian merchants in colonizing the American West coast, one can hardly expect the re-emergence of such worries on the part of the United States in the present situation.

As for the "traditional" Middle East, Russia for the time being will play a very modest role, often going hand in hand with US diplomacy. But the US is well aware that it ought to be very vigilant regarding a Russian presence in the region, because Russia per force, due to geopolitical factors, is likely to increase its influence there. As one source puts it:

The Middle Eastern states, in which apprehensions with regard to the monopolar nature of the new world order are strong, view Russia as an indispensable factor of global and regional balance. This refers not only to the Arab states, but to Israel as well.[42]

Russian connections with states and regimes, that are "rogue" by the US definition, will continue to bother the United States, though the very grouping of these nations is changing. For instance, the PLO now gets financial help from the United States; Syria, as soon as it makes peace with Israel, might be re-qualified by Washington into some other, less obnoxious, category, followed by Iraq, after it ceases to be ostracized by the United Nations. This will give Russia, a better chance to play its own game, luring Arab investors and offering cheap arms and technical help. The Iranian regime, it seems, will hardly change its colors, though its rulers are evidently not averse to improving relations with the "great Satan". Nevertheless, Russian-Iranian relations will continue to be a sore point in Russian-American relations.[43]

The perennial volatility, endemic to the Middle East, will continue alongside a peace process and that will give Russia an opportunity to re-emerge as a player in the region, an American competitor of sorts, having connections with both radical and conservative Arab regimes, although, of course, in no way as an opponent of the United States, ideological or otherwise.

For the trend of greater Russian involvement to continue, the politico-economic situation in Russia itself has to stabilize considerably, otherwise Russia will not be able to do anything beyond mischief. With tact and skill, American diplomacy can involve Russia in really constructive engagements in the region which will not contradict the interests of the United States but go in parallel with them. However, this would require wisdom and foresight, but this is not characteristic of current US diplomacy.

It is another story when the problem of Russian-American interaction in the greater Middle East is tackled.

Conflicting interests

Theoretically, it seems that the United States government understands Russia's special interests in the "near abroad", namely the ex-Soviet

Republics. President Clinton, while on a visit to Russia not only described the Russian military as having been "instrumental in stabilizing" the political situation in Georgia, but added "that there are times when you will be involved, and are likely to get involved in areas near you, just as the United States was involved for several years in Panama and Grenada, an area near us".[44] At the end of July 1994, the United States finally supported a UN resolution giving Russia peace-keeping authority in Georgia and Abkhazia.

Nonetheless, the United States and Russia seem to be at loggerheads regarding Russia's activities in the "near abroad".

Russia, to put it quite bluntly, considers all former Soviet Republics its legitimate sphere of influence. Moscow's interests regarding the "near abroad" were very well summed up in an article in *The Economist*, which stated:

> Russia's strategy to reassert its status as a great power rests on three pillars. It wants to ensure that the former Soviet Union, and to some extent Eastern Europe, are recognized as Russia's sphere of influence; to prevent the use of these areas as platforms for threats to Russia; and to ensure that these areas serve as a bridge outward, not as firebreaks isolating Russia from the world.[45]

Of course, Moscow's policies vary according to the specificity of the region. In relation to the Baltic republics, Ukraine and Belarus, Russia is more circumspect than is the case with regard to the Transcaucasian or Central Asian republics. This does not mean that Moscow considers the latter less important than the former - nothing of the kind; rather the political situation in the western part of the FSU is less bothersome than that in the southern and eastern republics, where several civil wars are going on.

Both sides somehow accept that the liquidation of the Soviet Union created "power vacuums" in all the republics surrounding Russia. This is the case because most of these republics do not have sufficient troops to secure their own independence without some outside help. The very term "power vacuum", which, incidentally, dismisses local populations and authorities as absolutely irrelevant, was, as far as I can determine, made fashionable by John Foster Dulles, who used the term to refer to the rapid decolonization of the Third world nations after World War II. Dulles repeatedly warned Americans that, unless the United States filled this vacuum, it would be filled from the other dynamic source - Soviet communism. The Russian foreign minister warned that "there is a risk that the vacuum which has emerged will be filled with unfriendly troops".[46]

Some American political scientists are now eager to put Russia itself onto the list of "vacuums". For instance, Brzezinski, calls the "heartland" of Eurasia (i.e. the central part of Russia) a "geopolitical vacuum" or "contemporary history's black hole"[47] which is presumably a space free for anyone to fill on a first come first served basis. However, there are few foreign policy theoreticians abroad and no practitioners willing to plunge headlong into a "hole" stuffed with 20,000 nuclear weapons. At the same time, there are more than enough voices with threatening overtones, emanating from the United States, constantly warning Russia not to intrude into "power vacuums" left in the former Soviet Republics.

One can understand the concerns of the West, the United States in particular, regarding the danger of the restoration of the Russian empire, especially taking into consideration that some such historic urge, consciously or unconsciously, endures in the Kremlin. However, one would have to be blind not to see the real urge in non-Russian republics of the FSU for closer cooperation within the framework of the CIS, as the 1994 presidential elections in Ukraine and Belarus vividly demonstrated. One more recent confirmation of such a trend is the new union between Russia and Belarus approved by the majority of the population and the parliaments of both Republics. Nevertheless, there is some spacious middle ground between a "restoration of the empire" and the total rapture of connections among the former members of what used to be an essentially unitarian state. The role of Russia in enhancing the security of many of the newly independent states and/or preserving the remains of a common market for the common good cannot be and is not questioned by majority of its neighbors.

For the United States or any other Western nation to deny Russia influence in the adjacent smaller republics is abject hypocrisy in the face of a reality established by the global political tradition several thousand years ago. Nonetheless, and in defiance of President Clinton's acknowledgment of the normalcy, if not legitimacy, of the United States' involvement in its own "backyard" of Central America, many in the American political establishment are questioning a similar posture on Russia's part with regard to its smaller neighbors.

There can be, logically, no other posture, especially if we remember that many of the 25 million Russians residing in the "near abroad" are endangered by rampant nationalism, compared to the lives of a dozen or one hundred citizens that the United States' government usually feels is a sufficient enough reason to undertake military intervention.

Quite a few American politicians not only try to dismiss such concerns on Moscow's part but claim the right of the United States to fill the "vacuums" in the FSU. The new Russian leadership, according to Dr. Kissinger, "is not entitled to be handed (sic! H.T.) the sphere of influence that tsars and commissars have coveted all around Russia's vast borders for 300 years".[48]

So it appears that it is not geopolitical factors, historic liaisons and *Realpolitik* considerations (notions so dear to Dr. Kissinger) that determine in this world the character of relations between a great power and smaller surrounding states, instead the outcome is exclusively defined by the fiat of the United States![49]

It is impossible to adequately describe the intensity of the wild rage, albeit concealed, which such pronouncements generate in Moscow's policy-making circles, especially when such admonitions to Russia are coming from a country, that can, without so to say a wink, attack a small neighboring country situated within its "legitimate sphere of interest", capture its lawful head of state, and then incarcerate him for life through "due process" of *American* law, applied in the US provincial court.

Zbigniew Brzezinski writes:

With the Soviet Union's defeat in the Cold War and its subsequent disintegration, the United States is now able for the first time to inject its political presence in the new post-Soviet republics of Eurasia, all the way to the frontiers of China, as well as to dominate the Persian Gulf region on the southern fringes of Eurasia.[50]

This is true and Moscow cannot object. However, if the United States, guided, evidently, by its national interests, is expanding its political, as well as economic, cultural, and potentially even military presence in the Russian "near abroad", it is even more compelling for an adjacent Russia to keep its presence in the CIS republics.

Brzezinski, as mentioned earlier, calls for a replay of 1972 American-Chinese rapprochement in order to consolidate, as he delicately puts it, "geopolitical pluralism within the former Soviet Union", otherwise Russia, "eventually revitalized under the umbrella of the American-Russian partnership" will "again become the strongest power in Eurasia".[51]

Such suggestions are irresponsible and provocative. They are typical products of the Cold war mentality and err in a habitual overestimation of America's ability to police the whole world.

The formation of "geopolitical pluralism" in the space of the FSU, according to the Russian scholar, Nikolai Kosolapov, means the

absolute rejection of any special, even just political, role for the Kremlin within this space. It is clear that such a goal is unattainable without repeated curtailments of Russia's military arsenal, without radically weakening its economic potential and without the strongest pressure upon it from the West. But the combination of all these conditions would result in the establishment in Russia of a military-bureaucratic dictatorship sooner than Brzezinski's goals could be realized.[52]

In any case, American designs regarding Russia's near abroad, as they take shape in the internal debates in the U.S. establishment, are hardly compatible with the legitimate interests of Russia. The alleged "alternative" for Russia, as described by many American conceptualists: "either democratic or imperial Russia" is very misleading, though theoretically it is correct. The old Russian empire, either of the Tsars or of Soviet commissars, cannot be restored, whatever unconscious urge in this direction is entertained by the Kremlin. But no one will be able to deny Russia its legitimate sphere of interests in the near abroad, unless Russia itself disintegrates. This is why the more or less unanimously negative attitude of the American establishment to Moscow's involvement in the CIS space generates a permanent conflict of interests between Russia and the United States on this issue. Of course, Washington will try to play the "non-Russian republics card" and so the likelihood is that the misunderstanding and rift between Moscow and Washington will deepen and Russian ultra-nationalists will exert a stronger influence on Russian politics.

However, because the US Administration's policy vis-à-vis Russia is considered by the American public as a foreign policy success, the White House is not inclined to aggravate its relations with Russia, especially in a situation when America needs Russia's support in the UN Security Council for a number of its foreign policy moves. This explains the mollifying talk of President Clinton in Moscow in January 1994 regarding Moscow's and Washington's respective spheres of influence and it also explains a State Department document which was circulated in Washington on the eve of American military intervention in Haiti. As a consequence, a paper drafted by the State Department policy planning staff on the eve of the US-Russian summit in Washington in 1994 stated that the United States was prepared to accept a Russian role in various parts of the FSU as long as Washington's interests "are not adversely affected".[53]

Of course, it is difficult for the present elite of the United States and Russia, raised on the ideology of the Cold war, which stressed the irreconcilable clash of interests of the two powers, to switch to viewing Russian-American competition in the international arena in a more benign light and approach it in a more relaxed mood. These attitudes need to be changed because there are a number of challenges to the very existence of humanity which require full-scale and close cooperation between America and Russia, despite the fact that there are and will always be some irritating problems in their relationship, including the problem of each being "bossy" toward its smaller neighbors.

Conclusion

Russian-American relations remain the focus of attention of the political leaderships of both countries. Although there is no more ideological conflict and both governments approve of partnership, perhaps even strategic partnership, their relationships are not in actual fact a partnership, which can exist only between two more or less equal powers. Russia, first of all is now only a part of what used to be a mighty Soviet superpower, though it inherited all of the latter's nuclear weaponry. This inheritance allows Moscow leaders to claim that Russia is still a superpower. The reality is different, however. Russia was brought to a deplorable state by the experiments of *perestroika* and reform and so it is presently a middle-sized country by many economic indicators, trailing behind many prospering countries of the Third World. Since Americans respect only power, they now treat Russia as a third rate power and one that is not worth bothering with.

"The arrogance of power is the gist of the present policy of the West towards Russia. It dooms the West's relations with Moscow to growing misunderstandings, frustrations and even conflicts", as one report on Russian-American relations recently concluded.[54]

Such a conclusion is understandable, because Washington's policy is geared towards restraining and constraining Russia, while ostensibly helping it in various ways: firstly, to drastically diminish its nuclear arsenal; secondly, to prevent the consolidation of the CIS under Moscow's tutelage and, thirdly, to turn Russia into a raw material adjunct of the West.

The Russian government in fact contributes to the realization of such goals, which are negative for Russia, by meekly following Washington's footsteps in its foreign policy and adapting the essence and pace of its economic reforms to the directives of the US based international financial institutions.

Despite all this, Russia and the US have a few interests in common, namely strengthening peace and stability in the world, non-proliferation of the weapons of mass destruction, a reduction of nuclear armaments and fighting terrorism and drug trafficking. Russian-American cooperation in these matters needs to be further enhanced and developed.

There also exist some diverging interests between the two countries, which is a normal phenomenon, even between close friends. These differences consist of various evaluations of the situation in different parts of the world and the existence of different solutions to particular regional problems. The most sharp disagreements between Russia and the United States arise with regard to the policy of NATO's expansion eastward, which was energetically promoted by Washington, and the role of NATO and the OSCE in strengthening pan-European security.

Despite its strong disapproval of NATO's move eastward, the Russian government okayed the expansion by signing the Founding Act with the 16 present members of NATO.

Conflict between Russian and American interests arises because of the forceful intrusion of Washington into what Russia considers its lawful sphere of influence, namely the Commonwealth of Independent States. Prominent American politicians and political scientists insist that the US ought to have a free hand in the CIS to the detriment of Russia's vital interests, including that of security. Such demands spoil the atmosphere of bilateral relations and impede wider cooperation and understanding between Russia and America. But there are some different voices in the United States who understand the complex nature of the US - Russia interaction. Testifying at the hearings on the World threat assessment in the US Senate Intelligence Committee, George Tenet, Director of the CIA, commented:

It's clear to me that the Russians have a sense of their own national interest and they're going to pursue it, and it's going to conflict with ours in some way, shape or form. And we have to be enormously mindful of it.

We went through a number of different periods in our relations with the Russians immediately after the wall fell. I think they were falling all over themselves to do whatever we asked them to do. We're now at a period where this pragmatic nationalism has set in.

They have national interests that they are going to pursue because they think they still remain a great power. And they're going to do things that benefit their own national interest, and we have to just have our eyes wide open and understand what that's all about, because it will be a relationship that's both collaborative and competitive. And they will do things that we don't like and we're going to do things that they don't like, and we just have to accept that fact.

And that's simply where we are with the Russians at this point in time. But we have our interests and we are pursuing them, and I don't think anybody's backing down from doing that. But we have a Russian entity that is evolving, that is working itself through who they think they are and what their interests are and what they stand for. And managing that relationship will become more difficult than it has been in the past.[55]

Nevertheless, Russia and the United States are doomed to cooperate in many international spheres in view of the great challenges that humanity is facing because of the uncontrolled growth of the earth's population, rapidly worsening ecology, the increase in regional conflicts on ethnic and religious grounds, the spread of narcotics and the emergence of worldwide criminal Mafia chains.

Though Russia nowadays is not a match for the United States economically, the future of the world in the 21st century will largely depend on whether Russia and America, occupying huge spaces in the Eastern and Western hemispheres, can work together and with other countries in tackling all of the new problems that challenge humankind's existence.

Notes

[1] In a recent message to the US Congress on "A National Security Strategy for a New Century", President Clinton underlined the US   "three core strategy objectives" which were:

a. To enhance our security with effective diplomacy and with military forces that are ready to fight and win.

    b. To bolster America's economic prosperity; and

    c. To promote democracy abroad.

(*A National Security Strategy for America.* May 1997, p.1, Internet File:///D%7/C/INT/US-Besop/Strategy. htm#//).

[2] *A National Security Strategy of Engagement and Enlargement*, The White House, February 1995, p.1.

[3] R. Baker and W. Dodd (eds.) *The Public Papers of Woodrow Wilson.* Authorized Edition, Vol. III (New York and London, 1927), p.159.

[4] Explaining to his readers why the United States still spends US$250 billion a year on defense, the American political analyst, Jim Hoagland, writes: "If you could hog tie the Joint Chiefs of Staff and inject the four commanders of the nation's military services with truth serum, at least two of them would tell you that the real reason for keeping 1.5 million American men and women in uniform is to guard against a reconstitution of a global threat from Moscow" (Jim Hoagland, 'Americans Ought to Be Debating Military Ends and Means', *International Herald Tribune*, 28 March 1996, p.3).

[5] On 10 June 1997 all the commanders of Russia's armed forces military services were summoned to the new Russian Minister of Defense, General Igor Sergeyev. At the Central command headquarters of the General Staff, they reported to the Minister on the situation in their respective structures. "Generally reports have been not very comforting", Igor Korotchenko, a military analyst for *Nezavisimaya Gazeta*, wrote, "Today military units and formations of the Russian army, with the exception of the Strategic Missile Forces, a nuclear component of the Navy and the Paratroop forces, are not combat-ready and incapable of elementary fighting even in defense, not to speak of carrying out offensive operations" (*Nezavisimaya Gazeta*, 11 June 1997, p.2).

[6] The famous Russian poet, Nikolai Nekrasov in the middle of the 19th century, prophesied in a poem, well-known to every Russian, that the Russian people will finally rise and with their chests blaze a wide and clear path for themselves. "It's a pity, though, that neither myself, nor you will have an occasion to live in those wonderful times", added the poet.

[7] Yuri Vlasov, an author, former People's Deputy of the USSR parliament, and a holder of 28 top world records in weight lifting wrote: "We are not a free Russia, we are a Russian colony of the United States; our politicians are buffoons and mountebanks, because they decide nothing, having been put onto a stage to play roles that are not connected with real politics. Our press is obediently following the orders of the West. We are 'aborigines', not citizens of the state of *Rossiya*. The state is deliberately weakened, obliterated by the entire policy of 'our friend America'" (Yuri Vlasov, *Kto pravit bal* [Who manages the ball] (Moscow: Kedr,

1993), p.174). This is one of the mildest diatribes among many emanating from prominent Russian public figures who are totally disillusioned by Yeltsin's policy.

[8] Towards a Positive Agenda in Russian-American Relations. The Statement of the Working group of the Council on Foreign and Defense Policy of Russia (published in *Nezavisimaya Gazeta*, 14 March 1997, p.5).

[9] Alexei Pushkov, the then deputy editor-in-chief of the popular weekly *Moscow News* commented: "The Kremlin's cancellation of the transaction under evident American pressure was a watershed in Russian attitudes toward the United States, going far beyond the importance for Russia of the deal itself" (Alexei Pushkov, 'Letter from Eurasia: Russia and America: The Honeymoon's Over', *Foreign Policy*, No. 93, Winter 1993/94, pp.86-87).

[10] The reactors are of the same safe type that the US, Japan and South Korea intend to supply to the "rogue regime" of North Korea in order to minimize the latter's chances of using spent reactor fuel for extracting plutonium to make nuclear weapons.

[11] Andrei Kozyrev, 'Russia plans leading role in the world arena', *The Washington Times*, 15 March 1994, p.A14. "But, of course", added Kozyrev, "in so doing we must remain within the bounds of international law and seek to find a reasonable balance of interests" (*ibid.*).

[12] Andrei Kozyrev, 'Rossiya i SSHA: Partnerstvo ne prezhdevremenno, a zapazdyvaet' [Rossiya and the USA: Partnership is not premature, but late], *Izvestia*, 11 March 1994, p.3.

At approximately the same time, some Russian "theorists" began to argue that the real interest of "all humanity" consists in the increased activation of the policy of "imperial hegemony" by the leading industrial powers. They stated: "Humanity will only be able to survive today at the cost of mobilizing the resources of the most powerful states. Of all the possible dissections of the world into component parts, that have real socio-political significance, there is only one division left: the distinction between 'poor' and 'rich' nations. The most sensible thing to do is to couple the Russian railway carriage to the imperial train departing into the next millennium, before some desperado appears, who will couple it to the armored train that is still waiting on a shunting-track. Some say that Russia's imperial temptation might deal a blow to its good-neighborly, equal, mutually beneficial relations with independent states and former 'brotherly republics'. Those who reason in this way seem to forget that by having severed erstwhile 'brotherly' union ties, Russia needs to assert herself in a new way in accordance with her potential capabilities and the level of responsibility that objectively falls onto her shoulders" (Victor Gushchin, 'I vsyo-taki Rossii byt' [And still Rossiya will be], *Nezavisimaya Gazeta*, 17 September 1993, p.5). But this was empty talk: the US is hurrying into the new millennium but does not need heavy antiquated Russian carriage that will slow its speed.

[13] Andrei Kozyrev, 'Don't Threaten Us', *The New York Times*, 18 March 1994, p.A11.

[14] Quoted in the *Congressional Record*, 25 May 1994, H4054.

[15] A Christian journalist, Vladimir Semenko, comments: "Liberal neo-Bolshevism (irrespective of its superficial ideological masks) in its spiritual metaphysical depth is hardly distinguishable from totalitarian Bolshevism, though the political bustle on the surface may not make this clear" (*Nezavisimaya Gazeta*, 26 June 1997, p.6).

[16] In the case of Chinese-American relations, more than 20 years of increasingly cooperative interaction between the United States and Communist China, plus past American attachment to China as a victim of Japanese aggression, in many ways smoothed the rough spots in their relationship. As for Russian-American relations, one has only to open any major American or Russian newspaper and look through a couple of analytical articles on the subject to see many prejudices and fears of the Cold war emerging again and again. The best illustration of the residue of the Cold War mentality in the West was the exclusion by the West of Russian representatives from the celebrations of the 50th anniversary of the D-Day on the beaches of Normandy in June 1994. According to a *Washington Times* editorial, the representatives of the former Soviet Union, that lost 20 million in the Second Worl War, sapping the strength of the Third Reich, were not invited for "some pretty good reasons" that "are worth remembering", namely "the small matter of Molotov-Ribbentrop pact signed on 23 August 1939", which "for the price of half of Poland and all the territory East of there gave Hitler free reign to pursue his military designs in *Western* Europe" (*The Washington Times*, 7 June 1994, p. A16) (emphasis mine - H.T.). But then, objectively speaking, perhaps Britain and France should also have been excluded from these celebrations on the same grounds because a year earlier, on 29 September 1938, through "a small matter of the Munich agreement", they in fact allowed Hitler to pursue his military designs in *Eastern* Europe, giving him the *prize* of Czechoslovakia? On the Russian side, a good example of the vitality of the Cold war mentality was the procrastination with the small-scale joint exercise of Russian and American peace-keeping forces (250 men from each side) near Totsk in the Orenburg province (scheduled for Summer 1994). The Russian military high command (who received around US$2 million from the Americans for spending a week at the former nuclear testing ground) viewed this exercise positively. But nationalists in the Russian Duma whipped up a frenzy against "fraternizing with a potential enemy" and managed to persuade people that the scheme was not worthwhile. Only after several months of equivocation, did the Russian government finally give the go-ahead for the exercise which took place in September 1994.

[17] Initially the idea of cooperation between the two countries in the field of strategic defense and early warning systems was aired in a general form by

Gorbachev, when he was still the President of the USSR. After several unsuccessful attempts to persuade the US leadership to cancel work on the SDI (the Strategic Defense Initiative, President Reagan's pet space defense project), Moscow came to a sensible conclusion: "If you cannot beat them - join them!"

[18] "Hopes of creating a certain defensive protective shield of the global scope, which will set the developed countries against the countries of the Third world, look illusory. The possibility of such a confrontation will make Russia take a grave view of the matter and keep it from becoming a partner in the global system of anti-missile defense, in which the Americans would dominate. The majority of regional missile threats are not directed straight against the territory of Russia or its armed forces abroad..." (Vladimir Frolov, 'Protivoraketnaya oborona: problemy sokhranyayutsya' [Anti-missile defense: problems remain], *SSHA: ekonomika, politika, ideologiya*, No. 2, 1995, p.75).

[19] Russia-United States Joint Statement on Missile Systems, 10 May 1995 cited in *Weekly Compilation of Presidential Documents*, Monday, 15 May 1995, p.799.

[20] Jack Ruina, 'Threats to the ABM Treaty', *Security Dialogue*, September 1995, p.274.

[21] After meeting in Helsinki in February 1996, the Russian Foreign Minister, Yevgeny Primakov, and the US Secretary of State, Warren Christopher, agreed to organize a joint group of experts to work out a common approach to the ABM Treaty (*Nezavisimaya Gazeta*, 13 February 1996, p.2).

[22] *USIS Wireless File. Eur. 509. 21. 3. 97.*

[23] For quite a long time, Pentagon specialists were basing the distinction between the strategic and tactical BMD on the formula developed by John Foster, Head of research and development in the Pentagon in the 1970s. Foster stated that if you shoot an anti-missile at a target that goes faster than 2 kilometers per second then such a system comes under the ABM Treaty prohibition to give missiles, launchers or radars, other than ABM interceptor missiles, ABM launchers or ABM radars, the capability to counter strategic ballistic missiles or their elements in flight trajectory or test them in an ABM mode. In Helsinki, Yeltsin agreed to consider the target flying at 5 kilometers per second as a tactical one! In fact the new arrangement permits both sides unhindered development of all types of BMD defenses, eliminating prohibitions set by the ABM Treaty. "It's okay as a TMD as long as you don't shoot at a target that goes faster than 5 kilometers per second. In other words, there is an elasticity in this treaty that we've been able to adapt", Robert Bell, the US National Security Council staff's Senior Director for Defense policy and Arms control, explained to American journalists. "There are no speed limits established in the Helsinki agreement and there's no moratorium established with respect to flight testing of systems." The determination of the US compliance with the treaty, emphasized Bell, "will be our national responsibility; we can discuss it with the Russians in Geneva, but it is our national responsibility to determine

compliance" (*USIS Wireless File Eur 108*. 24. 3. 97). See also footnote 18 to Chapter 3.

[24] The fact is that a country like the United States or Russia with a highly developed technology can continue testing nuclear ammunition without big underground explosions, using so-called sub-critical physics experiments ostensibly consistent with the CTB Treaty. The experiments use chemical high explosives to generate high pressure so that this technique can be applied to nuclear material. No self-sustaining nuclear fission chain reaction is involved. It appears that a Russian scientist, Zakharov, who in June 1997 received a deadly doze of radiation at the Russian nuclear center Arzamas-16, was engaged in the preparation for such an experiment.

[25] "We have worked very closely with the Russians to conclude that indefinite extension" remarked Dr. Lynn Davis, Under Secretary of State for arms control and international security affairs (*USIS Wireless File*, 2 June 1995, p.15).

[26] Already in September 1993, Russia *de facto* accepted the conditions of the MTCR by signing a Memorandum of understanding on the issue of the export of missile equipment and technology with the United States. The important concession on the part of the United States was its recognition that cooperation in the space and missile industries among the CIS republics fell outside the restrictions of the MTCR. Russia became a full member of the MTCR in October 1995.

[27] In a Joint Statement on the Transparency and Irreversibility of the Process of Reducing Nuclear Weapons, the Russian and American Presidents agreed to "exchange on a regular basis, detailed information on aggregate stockpiles of nuclear warheads, stocks of fissile materials and information on their safety and security" (*Weekly Compilation of Presidential Documents*, 15 May 1995, p.803).

[28] In accordance with the Russian-US agreement on this issue, 500 tons of highly enriched uranium removed from nuclear weapons of the FSU, will be converted by Russia to low-enriched uranium, which will be bought by the US Enrichment Corporation, a US government company. Russia will earn approximately US$12 billion. Conversion would considerably lower the chances of the uranium being re-used for building nuclear weapons (*Dispatch*, January 1994. Supplement No. 1, pp.25-26).

[29] This Treaty means that each side must reduce its stockpiles of strategic warheads to between 3,000-3,500 by the year 2003. In 1994, both sides agreed to speed up the destruction of nuclear warheads under the START I Treaty. Rather than phasing in the required reduction over seven years, each side agreed to at once start removing the warheads from missiles and to begin the process of destroying them. "Both we and Russia are at the point of reductions now that we did not have to get to until 1999. We are both two years ahead of schedule in building down real nuclear dangers", remarked Dr. Robert Bell, speaking at the US Arms control association luncheon on 18 February 1998 (*USIS Wireless File. Eur 419*. 19.2.98).

[30] By the way, this is well understood by some American politicians. Speaking at a hearing in the Senate Intelligence Committee on World threat assessment Senator Roberts said: "[I] understand, in regards to NATO expansion, that we planted the flag. I understand it's probably going to happen. I understand we want the historical rewrite of Europe. I understand, in terms of Hungary and Poland and the Czech Republic, that they want their self- determination and they want entree to the European Common Market. I understand the president wants to make a speech on the 50-year anniversary of NATO. And I understand that we want to cage and tame the Russian bear.

But the Russians don't see it that way. And in all of my discussions with the members of the Russian Duma -- staff members, others -- Mr. Primakov is off the reservation. They're going to play the nuclear card to keep on the world stage. I don't think we have any chance for START II. I think it is fodder for the hard-liners. And I think it's in our vital national security interests to take a hard look at this. What's the tradeoff?" (*USIS Wireless File. Eur 314.* 28.1.98).

[31] *Izvestia*, 25 June 1997, p.1.

[32] Such weapons are composed of two non-lethal chemical agents that become lethal only when they are mixed at the time of an explosion of such a weapon.

[33] See, for instance, Villi Mirzayanov, Lev Fyodorov, 'A Poisoned policy'. *Moscow News*, No. 39, 1992, p.9; Michael Gordon, 'Russia Hides Effort to Develop Deadly Poison Gas, US Says'. *The New York Times*, 23 June 1994, p.A3; Martin Seiff, 'US Says Russia isn't coming clean with poison-gas data'. *The Washington Times*, 24 June 24 1994, p.A16. Speaking in the US Senate, Senator Helms said: "[I]t is believed that Russia has already produced 15,000 tons of... binary agent known as 'substance 33'. But Russia hasn't disclosed any binary chemical weapons, as they were required to do. They have disclosed only 40,000 tons in stockpiles of more common types of weapons" (*Congressional Record*, 15 July 1994, p. S9079).

One of the creators of the Russian binary weapons, Vladimir Uglev, disclosed that Russia now has chemical binary weapons that are about 5 to 8 times more deadly than the most powerful gas OV synthesized by Swedish scientists in 1956. "The substance I have synthesized can be easily disguised as a product of peaceful chemistry in case of international inspection" (Georgy **Vachnadze**, *Voenniye Mafii Kremlya* [Military Mafias of the Kremlin], Moscow: "Kniga, Ltd", 1994, p.120).

Alexei Yablokov, the Chairman of the Interdepartmental Commission on Ecological Security of the Security Council of the Russian Federation, adds: "Russia officially declared that it has about 40 thousand tons of chemical weapons. I believe that figure. However, we produced those weapons in much bigger quantities. Where are the remaining 150,000 or, maybe, 200,000 tons? Buried, burned, sunk. It is not known. This submerged part of the iceberg of chemical weapons problem represents a greater ecological danger than the civilized destruction of those weapons" (quoted in *Nezavisimaya Gazeta*, 24 March 1995, p.3).

[34] Lev Fyodorov, *Neobyavlennaya khimicheskaya voyna v Rossii: politika protiv ekologii* [Undeclared chemical warfare in Russia: politics versus ecology] (Moscow: The Center of ecological policy of Russia, Union for chemical security, 1995), pp.146, 273.

[35] While the Russian Duma, in contrast to the US Senate, failed to ratify the Chemical weapons convention in time for Russia to be eligible for participation in the governing and executive bodies of the Organization, that was created for the purpose of the Convention's implementation, from the start of the latter's work, the Duma, nevertheless, appealed to the first conference of states -- parties to the CWC -- asking the CWC to permit Russia to extend the designated time for the complete elimination of its chemical weapons stockpile and also soliciting additional international financial aid for this purpose (for the text of the appeal see *Rossiiskaya Gazeta*, 13 May 1997, p.6).

[36] See, for instance, John Barry, 'Planning a Plague? A secret Soviet network spent decades trying to develop biological weapons', *Newsweek*, 1 February 1993, pp.40-41 (reprinted in *Moskovskie Novosti*, No. 16, 7 March 1993, p.11A); 'US Officials Allege That Russians Are Working on Biological Arms', *The Washington Post*, 8 April 1994, p.A28; 'O chem rasskazal perebezhchik. Yest li u Rossii biologicheskoe oruzhie?' [What a defector told about. Does Russia have biological weapons?], *Novoye Russkoye Slovo*, 4-5 June 1994, p.14; Statement by Sen. Jesse Helms in *Congressional Record*, 15 July 1994, S9078-79; Mark Shteinberg, 'Bomba zaryazhennaya superchumoy' [A bomb loaded with super-plague], *Novoye Russkoye Slovo*, 15 July 1994, pp.13-14; Mariya Bronzova '"Umnoye" biologicheskoye oruzhiye' ['Clever' biological weapons], *Nezavisimaya Gazeta*, 19 February 1998, p.2, "Presently, she says, on the territory of Russia several plants are situated that at any time can start producing biological weapons, but whether we are ready to defend ourselves against the attack with such weapons is so far unclear". She also reports that a well-known accident in the biological weapons plant in Sverdlovsk (now - Ekaterinburg) in the beginning of the 1970s released into the atmosphere a new kind of biological agent which was gender and age selective. As a result, about 2000 Siberian middle-aged men died (*Ibid*).

[37] *Congressional Record*, 15 July 1994, S9078. Emphasizing that the problem of concealment of banned substances lies with the Russian military, Sen. Helms added: "I would not be surprised if President Yeltsin would secretly welcome this amendment" (*Ibid*. S9079).

[38] "The situation in the nuclear industry in the successor states of the Soviet Union is completely out of control", according to German security sources (see *The Washington Times*, 14 August 1994, p.A13). According to the Bavarian Interior Minister, Gunter Beckstein, there have been 123 cases of smuggling of radioactive

materials since the collapse of the Soviet Union in 1991, whilst Erwin Marschewski, the parliamentary internal affairs spokesman of Kohl's Christian Democratic party, put the total at 267 (cited in *The Washington Times*, 16 August 1994, p.A11). One source describes how Russian mafia dealers smuggled out of Russia 4.4 tons of beryllium - one of 16 nuclear-related materials that are supposed to be tightly controlled by the 31-member Nuclear Suppliers Group, which includes both the US and Russia ('The Russian Connection - Special investigative Report', *U.S. News & World Report*, 29 October 1995, pp.56-67).

[39] *USIS Wireless File. Eur 116. 30. 6. 97.*

[40] *Nezavisimaya Gazeta*, 9 July 1997, p.1. COCOM - the Coordinating Committee - was the organization of Western exporters, controlling exports of high technology into the USSR and other communist countries. It was dissolved after the end of the Cold war and replaced by the Wassenaar Arrangement on Export Controls for Conventional Arms and Dual-Use Goods and Technologies to which Russia is a party. But the US and some of its Allies still retain some additional secret controls over exports into a number of countries, including Russia and China.

[41] "The old Cold War tools of deterrence - strength, balance and arms control - can still help the United States respond to the threat that the nuclear weapons (remaining in Russia - H.T.) would pose in the hands of, for instance, a government in Russia that revived an adversarial relationship. This requires the United States to maintain a nuclear posture that clearly demonstrates how no nation would succeed in achieving its military or political objectives, if it initiated a conflict with the United States and its allies" (*Report of the Secretary of Defense to the President and the Congress*, January 1994, Washington, D.C.: U.S. GPO, p.59). Speaking at the hearing in the US Senate Special Committee on Intelligence on 5 February 1997, George Tenet (who was later confirmed as the Director of the CIA) stressed that a "continuing transformation of Russia" is first among the main "critical challenges" facing the United States (*USIS Wireless File. Eur. 424. 6. 2. 97*).

[42] The message of the President of the Russian Federation to the Federal Assembly in *Rossiiskiye Vesti*, 17 February 1995, p.5.

[43] During the Russian-American summit in Washington in September 1994, President Clinton wrestled from President Yeltsin a half-hearted pledge not to enter into any new arms sales deals with Iran after the existing contract, negotiated at the time of the Soviet Union's existence, expires. But it is doubtful that Yeltsin briefed the US president about the exact terms of that contract and its expiration date. In the Spring of 1995, the White House began to put pressure upon Russia to break its deal with Iran to build a light water reactor to produce electricity. It was alleged that Iranians could use such a reactor to produce weapons grade plutonium. This pressure outraged Russian public opinion because, while trying to undo the Russian

deal with Tehran, the United States offered to build two similar light water reactors in North Korea as a way of impeding its nuclear weapons program!

[44] *Weekly Compilation of Presidential Documents*, Vol. 30, No. 3 (24 January 1994), p.73.

[45] *The Economist*, 26 February 1994, p.49.

[46] Foreign Minister, Kozyrev, at the meeting with Russian ambassadors to the FSU republics (cited in *Novoye Russkoye Slovo*, 22-23 January 1994, p.3).

[47] Zbigniew Brzezinski, *Out of Control. Global Turmoil on the Eve of the Twenty First Century* (New York: Charles Scribner & Sons 1993), p.155.

[48] Henry Kissinger, *Diplomacy*, p.818.

[49] This idea of the United States as the Almighty becomes obsessive in the latest writings of Dr. Kissinger. "George Bush", he wrote, "presided skillfully over the final disintegration of the Soviet empire and the immediate consequences of that break-up. But he did not have to face the question of *what to put in its place*" (emphasis mine - H.T.) (Henry Kissinger, 'At Sea in a New World', *Newsweek*, 6 June 1994, p.36).

[50] Zbigniew Brzezinski, *Out of Control*, pp.156-157.

[51] Zbigniew Brzezinski, 'The Premature Partnership', *Foreign Affairs*, March/April 1994, pp. 77, 81.

[52] Nikolai Kosolapov, 'Novaya Rossiya i strategiya Zapada' [New Russia and the Strategy of the West] (Second article), *Mirovaya Ekonomika i Mezhdunarodniye Otnosheniya*, No. 2, 1994, pp.12-13.

[53] *The Washington Times*, 27 September 1994, p. A15.

[54] 'Towards a Positive Agenda in Ru ssian-American Relations', *Nezavisimaya Gazeta*, 14 March 1997, p.5.

[55] *USIS Wireless File. Eur 314. 28.1.98.*

Postscript

Throughout this book, I have reviewed the national interests of Russia - a new political entity in this world, though with a 1,000 year old history. The description and summary of these interests stemmed from my analysis of the relevant official documents of the Russian government (including its legislative branch), the annual messages of the president of the Russian Federation to the Russian parliament - the Federal Assembly - and the study of Russian public opinion, as presented in the media debate on Russian national interests. My aim was to penetrate, as far as possible, the thinking of the ruling class of the contemporary Russia on the problem of national interests, while appreciating that the latter's attention and thinking are essentially concentrated on matters that stand far away from the national interests issue.

There is one feature common to all of the aforementioned sources for a construction or just a presentation of the ramified "tree" of national interests: they all represent the mentality, the way of thinking of the present generation, namely the mentality of a people, who received their education and life experience essentially under Communism. Even the younger section of the present Russian leadership consists of people, who received their upbringing and higher education in the Soviet Union's institutions. This means that even the most unorthodox still have embedded in their minds a number of postulates and prejudices of the former communist society.

Despite the inhuman brutality of its first leaders, Soviet society in the 1970s and 1980s was not as inhuman or amoral as in earlier decades. Perhaps President Reagan was right in describing the Soviet system as an "evil empire", but he was definitely absolutely wrong when he asserted that the Soviet people did not share the same values as Western societies, because they did not believe in God. First of all, many Russians did believe in God even under Communism, and, secondly, even though quite a few people in the Union were atheists, the overwhelming majority of people (including non-believers) were devoted to the same Christian humane values, as their counterparts in Europe or America. (*Inter alia*, many of the values, officially recognized by Marxian socialists, were initially borrowed from the teachings of the Christian apostles.) The Russian people were compassionate, responsive, sincerely empathizing with those who were in trouble or in need, kind-hearted and peaceful. These characteristics are reflected in Russian literature, as well as in people's everyday behavior and habits.

However, the moment Liberty descended upon Russia as a result of *perestroika* and the introduction of democratic reforms, something really terrible and absolutely unexpected happened: almost overnight people changed. En masse they suddenly became amoral, greedy, envious, inhumanly cruel, bitter and angry. All moral principles were put aside in a search for money. Somebody has yet to explain such a sudden transformation. Not to mention ordinary people, archbishops of the Russian Orthodox church, who have achieved an unheard of before freedom to teach their countrymen the Gospel, are instead devoting much of their time to fighting like mad to obtain from the state privileged tobacco and alcohol licenses to allow them to import such commodities duty free!

It seems like all scum, dirt and froth has floated to the surface of Russian society and filled all the senior echelons of government. What kind of morality can one talk of when one-time First Vice-Premier Anatoly Chubais in the income tax declaration for 1996 put his earnings as 1.7 billion (pre-denomination) roubles,[1] while literally tens of millions of teachers, scholars, doctors, sailors, pensioners, miners and other workers in the country he manages, have a yearly income of only 3-10 million roubles, though for many of them, their monthly wages are paid 5-9 months in arrears!

In such a situation, the problem of Russia's national interests simply does not interest the majority of people. Their main interest boils down to getting daily bread for a hungry family for which they often wait in queues for hours, especially in the small towns and villages of Russia, while daily watching on television advertisements for wonderful hair conditioners or Revlon's cosmetics.

So it is a very narrow group of intellectuals -- journalists, scholars, writers, some government analysts -- who really think and talk about national interests and the future of Russia. Most of them agree that in the present situation, Russia has to renounce the thought of any ventures beyond its borders, except the expansion of its export trade, and to concentrate on the stabilization of the internal situation.

Security-wise, the most reasonable behavior for Russia in the foreign policy field would be to adopt a position of non-entanglement, or non-involvement in blocs of states. At present, Russia has borrowed a great deal from the United States - ranging from chewing gum to the method of organizing health insurance (the latter being the most absurd).[2] But it can profitably borrow the kind of foreign posture that the United States has practiced for more than a hundred years, when it was a weak and divided country. Russia's non-involvement in blocs - whether in the West, East or South - would enable her to introduce a more flexible foreign policy, alienate none of her potential partners, and at the same time, give Russia an opportunity to utilize her unique geopolitical position between the two civilizations for the maximum benefit of her security and well being. (Of course, continued integration within the CIS is an altogether different matter.) Regretfully, not very many Russian experts approve of such an idea, though, probably, most of them have never really thought it through. They are convinced that Russia as an heir to the imperial USSR, ought to be always engaged somewhere abroad, its present zero authority in international business notwithstanding.

For top Russian officials, realizing national interests is very often equated with being admitted to one or more exclusive Western clubs, such as G7, or the London club of money lenders, or onto the porch of NATO to be able to brag before the Russian public about some new "historic achievement", "proving" global recognition of Russia's grandeur. Such an attitude reveals that their thinking is parochial, perhaps even more moronic than of the old-type representatives of the Soviet *nomenklatura* who, while realistically measuring grandeur by the number of combat-ready divisions they had, understood in their heart of hearts that to reach true greatness Russia must demonstrate excellent economic performance and lead the world in innovation - technical, social and cultural.[3] It will be a long, long time before the mentality of the ruling strata of Russia will even reach past levels of mediocrity. And it will be an even longer period before Russia is able to repeat some of the technical achievements of the Soviet era, provide a better standard of living for her people and not to annihilate others. Such thoughts came to my mind as I wrote this postscript in a village less than 400 miles from Moscow. A standard television antenna on the roof of my house is able to receive a decent picture of only one (!) channel of Central Russian TV. This seems to be the only palpable achievement of almost half a century of the Soviet space program.

But humanity goes on. What will be the real measurements of a nation's grandeur, the criteria of a state's success in the middle of the 21st century? What will the very notion of *national* interests mean in the new conglomerate of ethnicities, races and populations in the new global village or - more to the point - global megalopolis? What will be the meaning and the role of a state in the new economy without borders, in a global market without customs, in a world of global communications web without censorship? These questions are extremely difficult to answer because the environment and the tools of modern men change so rapidly, but the habits and mores remain almost the same. These questions are even more difficult to answer when we consider Russia, because of the unpredictability of her development. The majority of Russians from the example of their own country are more and more convinced that what communist leaders of the FSU told them about the evils of capitalism was true! The greedy nouveaux riches riding in armored Mercedes deceive and rob them in dishonest banking schemes, whilst the "capitalist" government does not care one jot about their well being and more than that - it tries to solve budgetary problems exclusively at their expense. The judicial system in the main is in the hands of various mafias or corrupt top government officials. There are daily shoot-outs on the streets of large and small cities. Young girls dream of getting a "prestigious" job, that of a call-girl. Young men vie to get the lucrative job of a bodyguard for some small-fry city official, or to join the OMON (special militia) forces, which use the same brutal methods as a gangster brotherhood, except their actions are legal.

Wisely envisaging the possibility of such a turn of events in Eastern Europe, Pope John Paul II in his encyclical "Centesimus Annus", published in May 1991, warned that capitalism might be established after the fall of communism, but he added that it might also be full of injustices:

[C]an it perhaps be said that, after the failure of Communism, capitalism is the victorious social system, and that capitalism should be the goal of the countries now making efforts to rebuild their economy and society?...
The answer is obviously complex. If by "capitalism" is meant an economic system which recognizes the fundamental and positive role of business, the market, private property and the resulting responsibility for the means of production, as well as free human creativity in the economic sector the answer is certainly in the affirmative... But if by "capitalism" is meant a system in which freedom in the economic sector is not circumscribed within a strong juridical framework which places it at the service of human freedom in its totality, and which sees it as a particular aspect of that freedom, the core of which is ethical and religious, then the reply is certainly negative.[4]

Undoubtedly "capitalism" in modern Russia so far belongs to the second option outlined by the Pope.[5]

All the theoretical debates in Russia between the Slavophiles and Westernizers, conservatives and liberals, and patriots and cosmopolitans wither in comparison to the present gloomy economic and social background of Russia. At the same time, today's "partners" of Russia, both in the West and the East, are trying to drag her onto their own particular orbit and make Russia forget her thousand year old spiritual tradition and all in all, to lead Russia astray from her own destiny in order to use her as a leverage in their struggle on the international arena. "A ring of geopolitical interests, striving for historic revenge, is tightening around Russia", according to Natalia Narochnitskaya, and she adds that "Surrendering positions on one issue, creates a legal base for pressing Russia on another, thus creating a domino effect".[6]

The most sophisticated political scientists and physicists, who usually practice abstract social thinking as a hobby, are trying to imagine and describe the world of a distant tomorrow by generalizing bits and pieces of today's happenings, such as the Internet, world-wide communication and informational web, an avalanche computerization of everything - design, commerce, business, education, information, transportation, as well as the widening of global industrial cooperation when a metal is made, say, in Africa, a bolt in Latin America, an engine in Europe, the body of an appliance in Asia and a complete machine is assembled in the United States. Will it be important in such an environment whether Russia stays under a single government, or, instead a unified republic, where several dozens of communities exist, each of which is very proficient in its business pursuits, happy in its recreational activities, and satisfied with its social service provision? Hardly so. But what will be of real importance is which country's capital or capitals will run this whole process of global-wide economic, industrial and informational activities.

Whatever capital this might be, it is unlikely to be Moscow, although, paradoxically enough, the methods of managing this universal, planetarian economy will be similar to those used by Gosplan - the old Soviet State Planning Committee, if not outright borrowed from it. According to the Russian scholar Viktor Kuvaldin, such will be the retribution for a speedy degradation of (Russian) society in the 1990s. The set up will not be changed either by cunning foreign policy manoeuvers, or by a stake on the intellectual potential (as if the latter is not being destroyed together with Russia). A state strategy of national resurrection, aimed at the preservation and development of human capital – that's what is required. Otherwise we are destined to remain at the backyard of a global community in the 21st century.[7]

For many years, the communist propaganda machine was scaring the Soviet people with the "heinous designs" of "international imperialism" (in Lenin's sense of the unity, almost conspiracy, of capitalist nations), which actually never existed. Now the Russian mass media is simply dying of envy of the inimitable, magnificent and irreproachable West - again quite a transitory phenomenon, if it exists in reality. At the same time, not very many people fully appreciate that Lenin's "imperialism" finally did emerge in the form of a truly international capital and a market, in the forms of truly trans-national corporations and banks: an "imperialism"/capitalism that does not give one jot about a color of your skin, your religion, or political outlook, as long as you are an effective worker or ingenious manager, designer, creator. The people, who wield power in this new global realm, do not need gory wars to achieve their goals, sometimes the aim is simply personal enrichment. In the process, they enrich all those who are taking part in this process. Wars and clashes of a global nature are likely to continue because of a conflict of interest. But in the 21st century, conflicts will consist of capitalist cold wars: trade and financial conflicts fought via global financial/communication networks. One positive result of the invention of nuclear weapons is that they rendered a global military war impossible and in this way these weapons cancel themselves out, though they are still being stored in nuclear arms depots by several nations.

What will become of the notion of national interests, what transformations will occur worldwide and in particular countries is difficult to predict at this stage of development. However one thing is clear, the grandeur of countries, regions and cities will be based not on how much oil, iron or some other ore is being produced, but on the sophistication of their production and services, the intellectual level of their designers, the skill of their managers and on the well-being of their working people.

The worsening ecological threat, and the problem of how to combine rapid economic and industrial growth with the containment of this environmental threat, hangs over both rich and poor countries. This provides food for thought not only for Russians but for Americans as well, who presently think, to use an old Russian folk saying, that they have finally took God by the beard.

What are the possible scenarios of Russia's socio-political and economic development over the next 10-20 years?

The most probable outcome is that Russia will continue to muddle through trying to achieve a gradual transition to a free-enterprise system with significant government control over the economy. Politically and economically, its dependence on the United States and foreign capital donations will increase. Russia's economic growth, if any, will be to a large extent financed by foreign companies investing in the production of energy resources (such as oil and gas) and in industries producing primary materials. Russia's economic function as a raw material adjunct of the developed industrial powers will persist. Russia's agricultural sector will gradually emerge out of its deep crisis, though Russia's dependence on food imports is likely to remain substantial.

The only sector of industry, functioning more or less effectively, will be the military-industrial complex (MIC), producing weaponry and ammunition mainly for exports. The Russian government will try to persuade people that via this strategy it will reduce unemployment and obtain the hard currency necessary to buy consumer goods from abroad (which was done on a limited basis in the FSU as well). The problem here will be that such a MIC will only remain production-competitive on the world market for a limited period. To really develop and innovate the MIC has to be based on a broad base of the whole economy, mainly geared to the demands of an individual consumer, as is the case in the West. Keeping military technology and production on the cutting edge of modern science and technology with the rest of scientific and industrial base anchored in mid-20th century would mean that Russian military production industries are doomed, as the USSR discovered. So Russia will have only two options (if it wants to keep its military production prospering): either to join some foreign MIC (American or European), or to invest heavily in the fundamental scientific research, and in technological and industrial innovation in a private sector geared to the demands of a private consumer.

Because of the deep economic crisis and actual chaos in the industrial sphere of Russia, the second possibility will not be available to Russia for some time to come. Realizing this, the present Russian leaders, under the strong pressure of chief designers and managers of large-scale military enterprises, are trying, as a matter of priority, to save the space-gadgets sector of the MIC (including rocket engine and satellite production) as well as its aviation plants and supporting enterprises through greater cooperation with Western companies and other CIS republics. If such tactics are successful, then in the long-term this strategy will help the Russian government to accumulate enough capital to enable it to refocus its attention on the civilian economy (if the latter is not in total paralysis by this time) and to assist her ailing agriculture. But such a development will take a long time to achieve.

Standards of living for the time being will remain very low for the majority of the population, and will only improve at a snail's pace.

Such a scenario holds even if in the year 2000 or 2001, the (reformed) Communist Party comes to power (including holding the office of the President of Russia). Because whoever comes to power after Yeltsin (with a sole exception described below) will out of necessity (including the pressure of a tremendous foreign debt) cooperate with the US, Western Europe and global financial institutions, although the new leadership of Russia will undoubtedly attempt to loosen the coupling attaching Russia to the US locomotive.

Regarding national goals, the emphasis will be on greater independence in making political and economic decisions and moves on the international arena, on a more sophisticated manoeuvering among the various groupings and blocs of states. Connections with NATO will continue on a pro-forma basis without any real cooperation. (All this is based on the assumption that the Baltic states and Ukraine will formally stay out of NATO. If they are incorporated into it, a communist or a left-wing government will have to radically revise its relations with the US and the whole of its foreign policy strategy, even if such a revision adversely affects Russia itself.)

Because I dislike Herman Kahn type prognostication (when all imaginable future situations are sucked out of one's thumb), and feel that the probabilities of many imaginable situations are low, only two other likely situations need to be mentioned.

The first one is the collapse of Russia and its break up into different independent regions. Such regions will inevitably drift towards sizeable neighboring countries. (China and Japan will be the first to utilize such an occurrence for their own benefits.) This possibility will not make much difference for international capital as it will quickly adapt to such an eventuality and continue to use all the resources of Russia under its control, including the property it owns. But Russia, as a viable entity, will disappear from the Eurasian map, probably for good.

The other scenario, that cannot be altogether ruled out at this time, is connected with the coming to power in Russia, with the help of its armed forces, of a genuine strongman, a charismatic person who will try to rule with an iron hand. Though the leaders of several national republics within Russia might balk at this, their protests will be easily suppressed, because the broad masses of Russian population will totally support their new "savior". The only tactics of a potential dictator that might really succeed will be a speedy, almost immediate, improvement in living standards. This might be achieved by the confiscation of all the capital created through speculative operations and the use of Russian currency reserves to fill its market with cheap consumer goods, coupled with a parallel increase in the wages of the working population. The person, assuming such dictatorial powers (which are actually available to a Russian president through the norms of the existing Constitution), will be creating his power base among the masses of Russia, including small business people, to whom new benefits may be given. With the help of the Army and a loyal police force, he will destroy the networks of gangs of bandits and thieves using draconian measures, disregarding all the hue and cry from foreign organizations about the "violations of human rights in Russia" and the alleged illegality of his actions. The drastic reform of Russia's socio-economic sphere in the interests of the average person will be his only chance to survive and consolidate his power. He will also drastically cut the bureaucracy and imprison well-known crooks and embezzlers in high government circles. He may even publicly shoot some of the most notorious corrupt officials and embezzlers in Red square, because such an act will only increase his popularity among the Russian masses.

He will clean the Aegean stables of Russian politics and use the comprador bourgeoisie's wealth to improve the social provisions for the population. While acting like this, the new leader will collude with foreign banks and firms, operating in Russia. He will be smart enough to try to win them over to his side by giving all sorts of guarantees that the capital and income of foreign businesses in Russia will remain untouched, with all legal profits able to be transferred abroad without difficulty. He might even extend to foreign businessmen, willing to cooperate with his government, additional benefits and privileges. And he will first of all assure the leadership of the great powers that Russia will be bound by all its international treaties and obligations and will not infringe upon their interests. In other words, this new leader will act like a typical General Pinochet, whose successful reforms in Chile were the subject of much talk in Russia a while ago, but whose approach to reform has not been fully understood by the so-called Russian elite.

In order to preclude some forceful intervention into the politics of Russia from the patron of its former ruling clique, the new leader might publicly announce that he will not hesitate to use nuclear weapons to thwart attempts to introduce NATO's or some other forces into Russia.

Such a scenario is quite probable in Russia and the first candidate for such a job is General Lebed. There are other candidates besides him. The only two snags in this scenario are that, first, it will be tremendously difficult to pick up in advance a team of a few dozen like-minded co-workers: honest, honorable, knowledgeable, patriotic persons from all walks of life. This is a task bordering on the impossible in the present totally corrupted Russia. The same Lebed disappointed many of his former followers by his weather-vane behavior. The second obstacle refers to the amount of control the US will have by that time over Russian nuclear forces. It might appear that the rulers of Russia had already supplied Washington with some device blocking the launch of Russian strategic missiles, or that Moscow and Washington agreed to use some other trick with the same effect.

Everybody knows, of course, that the revolutions throughout human history started with the revolutionary leaders promising the masses a new, much better life. Although some of these promises were fulfilled, this was not immediately after the revolution, instead it was after the revolutionary leaders had passed away and the reform of society happened under the counter-revolutionary government that finished the revolution. The initial revolutionary push gave a volcanic impetus to the rulers that followed who introduced changes into that society.

Gorbachev's and Yeltsin's "revolutions from the above" were also built on tempting promises to the masses. But, as is usual in Russia, these "revolutions" ended in plundering rank and file people and leading to the tremendous enrichment of a privileged few, including the ringleaders. The reversal of such a "usual outcome" might really become an historic turning point in the fate of Russia. However, because of the Russian tradition, the last scenario does not seem feasible. Russia may be doomed to exist as a country that will continue to teach the rest of the humankind how not to do things, as one of her great intellectual rebels, Peter Chaadayev, pointed out a long time ago.

Notes

[1] *Izvestia*, 11 June 1997, p.1. On 1 January 1998 the Russian rouble was officially denominated. One new rouble was made equal to 1,000 old roubles.

[2] Russia after the revolution of 1917 was a pioneer in organizing free medical care for all its citizens. Gradually all the countries of Europe built their health insurance systems along the lines of the Russian model. The present rulers of Russia found nothing better than to abandon the well tested and quite successful Soviet system of medical care and to borrow for a totally pauperized country an extremely expensive consumer system of health insurance, although every intelligent person knows that the American medical-pharmaceutical-health insurance mafia is comparable with any other well established gangster mafia in the world.

[3] In a conversation on 9 September 1927 with the first official delegation of American workers to visit the USSR, Stalin said: "In the course of *the further* development of international revolution, two centers of world significance will emerge: a socialist center, drawing to itself the countries which lean towards socialism, and a capitalist center, drawing to itself the countries that incline toward capitalism. The battle between these two centers *for command of world economy* will decide the fate of capitalism and communism in the entire world" (J. Stalin, *Voprosy Leninizma* [Questions of Leninism] (10th Edition. Moscow: Partizdat TsK VKP(b), 1934), p. 194. Emphasis mine - H.T.).

[4] Excerpts From the Pope's Encyclical: 'On Giving Capitalism a Human Face', *The New York Times*, 3 May 1991, p.A10.

[5] In an introduction to the report on the state of Russian economy, prepared by the Security Council of Russia in the Autumn of 1996, and entitled 'Below the critical line' the newspaper *Nezavisimaya Gazeta* wrote: "According to the estimates of the economic group of the Security Council, headed by Sergei Glazyev, the state of (Russian) economic security is below critical by a number of key indicators. This means that in such a condition, it is not possible to ensure the necessary conditions for sustained socio-economic development, nor is it possible to uphold the required level of defense potential and to provide minimum social guarantees. Even maintaining the economic independence of Russia will be problematical" ('Za kriticheskoi chertoi' [Below the critical line] *NG-Stsenarii* /A supplement to *Nezavisimaya Gazeta*/, 19 December 1996, p.3).

[6] N. Narochnitskaya, *Politika Rossii*, p.28.

⁷ Viktor Kuvaldin, 'Rossiya v global'nom mire' [Russia in the global world], *Nezavisimaya Gazeta*, 7 June 1997, p.6.